LITTLE BIG HORN

ROBERT NIGHTENGALE

About the Cover:

The Cover is a composite of a painting originally created by the 19th Century artist, Cassidy Adams, and then modified by Otto Becker. It was published and distributed by the Anheuser-Busch Company in 1896, and since that date it has been estimated that over 150,000 copies have been printed.

While the painting has been criticized for certain historical inaccuracies (Custer, for example, did not carry a sword), it nevertheless captures the spirit of a mythical drama that no soldier lived to tell about.

Preface

Wherever possible, actual participants or primary sources have been used to tell this story.

Occasionally, minor spelling, grammatical, or stylistic changes have been made in quoted sources without changing essential meaning (Chicago Manual of Style, 14th Edition, 2.174-175).

ISBN: 0-9652889-1-9 (Soft Cover)
0-9652889-0-0 (Hard Cover)

First printing 1996

Printed in the United States of America

TABLE OF CONTENTS

Chapter Five

Chapter Six

Chapter Seven

Chapter Eight

Maps note: the battlefield map was drawn from an 1877 battlefield survey by Captain Philo Clark. The location of the Indian Village has been changed to correspond with Lt. Maguire's map of 1876.

Color Plates

SPECIAL ACKNOWLEDGEMENTS

Any project involving historical research must necessarily include many sources. The following individuals and organizations provided exceptional assistance in this project:

Donald H. Westfall from the Minnesota Historical Society; Edward A. Zimmerman, Lawyer; Terrence F. Flower, Professor, College of St. Catherine, St. Paul, Minnesota; Larry Millet of the St. Paul Pioneer Press; Tom O'Neil, Editor Little Big Horn Newsletter; Sister Jon Christine Wolkerstorfer, History Department, College of St. Catherine; Terrance J. Gough, U.S. Army Historian; Michael E. Pilgrim, Archivist; Kitty Deernose, Archivist; Howard Boggess, Director Big Horn County Historical Museum; Major George B. Eaton, U.S. Army Historian; Sam Fadala, Black Powder editor for Guns Magazine; Frontier Flags; John Swanson, legal investigator; Shawn and Charles Real Bird; Clayton Brown; Douglas McChristian, Chief Historian Little Big Horn Battlefield National Monument.

The following organizations also provided assistance:

Anheuser Busch Co.; Buffalo Bill Historic Center; Colorado Historical Society; Denver Public Library; Idaho State Historical Society; Kansas Historical Society; Library of Congress; Lilly Library; Monroe Library; Montana Historical Society; Mt. Vernon Public Library; National Archives; Nebraska Historical Society; New York Public Library; North Dakota Historical Society; Rock County Historical Society; Smithsonian Inst.; South Dakota Historical Society; U.S. Army Signal Corps.; Wyoming State Arch. & Historical Dept.; City of St. Paul Public Library; U.S. Army Historical Services.

Special thanks to:

Joe Nightengale, Gene and Ginny Oliver, Julie Maring, James and Bonnie Maring, John Kraig, Lisa Winkles, Charles Flower, Bill Wells, Thomas Lenway, Greg Horan, Conrad Bergman, David Lucey, Fred Neff, Jim Court, Dick Mekaa, Ron Nichols (Editor: The Reno Court of Inquiry), Mr. and Mrs. Brice Custer, John Allen, Don Woodside, Richard Johnson, Tony Nathe, Mary Beth Fletcher, Brian Priebe.

Clarinda Color: Jonathan Zats, Jeff Atkinson, Cindy Miller, Trish Finley, Geoff Brown, Gene Melander, Robert Jacobson, and all others who had a part in the production of this book.

The design and all portrait illustrations were done by artist, George Ostroushko

The cartography of this book was designed and produced by Mul D. Le, Mark T. Reineke, and Alan J. Willis at CartoGraphics Incorporated, Minneapolis, MN.

Printed in the United States of America by
DocuPro Services, Inc.
5616 Lincoln Drive
Edina, MN 55436
612-906-0000

INTRODUCTION

To paraphrase an old adage, the easiest way to start an argument is to bring up religion, politics, or Custer's Last Stand. Quite possibly, no military engagement in American History has been so studied as that of the Little Big Horn battle of June 25, 1876. Literally, tens of thousands of articles, hundreds of books, motion pictures, and documentaries have been produced on the subject. Amazingly, with all that, the battle remains as much of an enigma today as it was over a century ago.

A prominent historian once wrote that every nation needs a mystery. If that is so, then what really happened that hot June Sunday above the banks of the Little Big Horn River in Montana is certainly ours.

There was and still remains something in this engagement that is pivotal to the American character, and this is caused in no small measure by the central figure of that day - George Armstrong Custer. Certainly, no one individual in all of history has been judged by so many people as Custer, with that appraisal based *entirely upon just one day of his life!*

Much of the puzzle of that battle and man is the direct result of what was taken as "fact" almost from the moment news of the disaster hit the American press as the nation was celebrating its Centennial. Questions came fast and furious, and with these uncertainties came controversy. Simply, how could such a good leader of cavalry come to such a tragedy. It was a very political year. President Grant's administration was in shambles, Custer's testimony that previous spring regarding corruption in government and horrid treatment of the Indians had in no small measure brought on the controversies. Yet, another squabble was something neither the government or the army wanted.

If an impartial and totally truthful investigation were to be done, the lives and careers of many politicians and army officers were going to be ruined. A scapegoat was needed, and it was easy to kick the dead lion, for George A. Custer not only could not defend himself, but those close friends who could had perished with him in trying to serve those who now wanted him to take the responsibility for what had occurred.

So began a trail of cover-up, half-truths and outright lies to fix the blame and end the matter once and for all. "Experts" testified and wrote, surviving officers gave their opinions colored to do no harm to the "glory of the Regiment." Testimony was changed and documents mysteriously appeared and disappeared. And so the confusion began.

Author Robert Nightengale, to his credit, does not pretend to give a solution to the battle in this book. What he does do is present all the available facts on the matter, and present it in a cohesive and comprehensive fashion for the reader to make up his own mind. Based on his own studies and those of independently contracted research firms, the result is a work certain to generate as much controversy as the battle itself. Scholars and battle students may not agree with all that is presented here, but they will not be able to ignore it. Nightengale has gone a long way in seeking out the truth, and history will benefit from it.

— Thomas E. O'Neil

Thomas E. O'Neil of Brooklyn, New York, has been a student of Custerania for over thirty years and has written over two hundred articles on the subject as well as four books. (Articles have been published in the *L.B.H.A. Research Review and Newsletter, Blackpowder Annual.* Books include *Custer to the Little Big Horn: A Study in Command, Passing Into Legend: The Death of Custer, Custer to the Little Big Horn: A Retrospective, Home at Rest: The Story of the West Point Cemetery.*)

Mr. O'Neil received a Master's degree in history from University of California in 1967, taught advanced placement U.S. History in high school, and had to retire from teaching due to a hip injury.

He now owns his own publishing business, Arrow and Trooper, which specializes in Custerania and the western frontier. He is also currently the editor of the Little Big Horn Associates "Newsletter."

He served in elected office for nearly twenty years as an alderman and city councilman in McKeesport, PA. He has worked with a number of western scholars including John M. Carroll in editing books and articles of Custer interest. He does extensive research at Custer Battlefield, National archives, Library of Congress, and North Dakota Archives.

CHAPTER 1

Major Reno's Report —— Major Reno and Captain Benteen Deny Knowledge of Custer's Fate —— News Reporter Finerty's Statement —— Seventh Cavalrymen See Custer Uniforms —— Indians Speak of Captured Uniforms —— Field Glasses —— Lieutenant DeRudio and Private O'Neill's Narrow Escape —— The Weapons Used by The Indians —— Major Reno and Captain Benteen Knew of Custer's Fate

General George Armstrong Custer

In the early morning of June 27, 1876, Brigadier General Alfred H. Terry and a small army of infantry and cavalry soldiers, numbering about 450 men, reached the remains of a huge Indian encampment in the valley of the Little Big Horn River, Montana Territory. Upon entering the abandoned camp the soldiers discovered the site where almost 2,000 Indian lodges had been shortly before, along with numerous wicki-ups, small temporary shelters used by single warriors. The camp had numbered up to 15,000 people with the number of warriors estimated from 1,800 to 6,000. It was the largest gathering of Indians ever seen on the great plains of America.

As the soldiers examined the camp, they discovered huge quantities of Indian possessions scattered about, indicating that the inhabitants had left in great haste. An officer in General Terry's command, 1st Lieutenant Edward H. McClernand, later told of what the soldiers found:

Ascending the low sandstone bluff at the extreme sweep of the Little Big Horn River, we saw in our immediate front a large bottom where an immense Indian village had stood but a few hours before. A few tepees were still standing in which several dead Indians were found. The enemy had evidently left in haste. Numerous buffalo robes, blankets, tepee poles and camp utensils were scattered over the ground together with great quantities of dried meat.

The soldiers made other, more ominous, discoveries at the campsite, suggestive of a fearful fate concerning a second force of soldiers, also a part of Terry's command; a force that had been ordered to seek out and fight hostile Indians five days before. This was the regiment of the 7th Cavalry, which had separated from Terry's command on June 22, 1876, to search for and attack this same Indian camp.

From the evidence inside the village site it was apparent that the 7th Cavalry had succeeded in finding the Indians. In his account Lieutenant McClernand later commented upon a gruesome discovery he found in the Indian camp:

A buckskin shirt, a garment much affected on the plains in those days by some officers was found with the name Sturgis on it. It was discovered with blood stains and had been pierced in two places by a bullet It was assumed to have been the property of Lieutenant Sturgis of the 7th Cavalry.

General Terry's men found other articles belonging to soldiers including cavalry saddles, clothing, and camp equipment. While the soldiers examined the Indian camp a small scouting party under the command of 1st Lieutenant James H. Bradley returned from the bluffs east of the camp, across the Little Big Horn River, with news of a shocking discovery. The bodies of 197 soldiers had been discovered. They were stripped, mutilated, and in a morbid state

of decay. Lieutenant Colonel George A. Custer, commander of the 7th Cavalry, had been recognized among the dead.

Later that summer a newspaper reporter interviewed three soldiers who were with General Terry's command and they told of what they saw on the Custer battlefield:

We found General Custer lying partly on his right side, hatless and bootless; his uniform was stripped of its gaudy trimmings, his pockets turned inside out and their contents missing; his face was uninjured, but upon his body were several bullet wounds, any one sufficient to cause instant death. These wounds must have been inflicted at close quarters, and after he fell.

Across Custer's breast lay, face downward, the semi-nude corpse of the Sergeant of the 7th Cavalry, whose name I can not recall just now. This poor fellow was robbed of everything but his undershirt; the crown of his skull was knocked away, his ears cut off, his left leg chopped asunder and the rest of his frame perforated with rifle balls.

"These atrocities were general?," interrupted the reporter.

Yes, sir, and even worse in many instances. Tom Custer's [General Custer's brother] *heart was literally dug out. The red devils appeared to have vented their savagery upon his remains. Tom used to be very open in his prejudice against the Sioux. Because of this fact his body was, perhaps, the most mutilated.*

"How was it that his brother, the General, escaped similar treatment? The Indians may never have a more implacable foe," the reporter observed.

Oh, they were afraid of him dead as well as alive. His body was the only one that met with a soldier's end, and his uniform the only one that was, with the exception stated, left undisturbed!

"Was there much scalping practiced?"

Very few of the slain had hair long enough to scalp. We noticed that those who had hair long enough were scalped, while those whose hair was too short were either beheaded or brained The savages must have been exasperated where scalping was an impossibility. They varied the monotony by cutting off noses, ears, limbs and perpetrating other indignities, and conducted the butchery with method at times, for we would come across a pile of heads here, or stacks of arms and legs there, and so on.

As a rule, however, noses, ears, heads and limbs were scattered all over the battleground. Some of the heads were impaled on poles stuck into the ground for that purpose. In three or four cases the amputations were performed with surgical neatness: in all others, mere chopping was the manner.

"Were all of Custer's dead accounted for?"

All but 2nd Lieutenant Harrington of Company C. It is believed that he was taken prisoner and borne away for torture. We identified every officer but him. The beheaded privates we had difficulty identifying, their heads being mixed up and scattered around; only privates were beheaded.

"Did they evacuate in a hurry?"

Somewhat in a hurry, as in several of the tepees or lodges I picked up damaging circumstantial evidences of their complicity in the Black Hills outrages, for which we are endeavoring to punish them. In one lodge, I found a Methodist hymn book with the name of "Moseman" or "Mossman" inscribed on the flyleaf; in another lodge I came across a dilapidated Banjo, minus strings, with D.W. '73" whittled on the barrel. Mining tools, manuscript letters and prospecting outfits attested further to their guilt. Swallow-tail coats and other fashionable attire of the finest material and make were included in my mental noting.

The 7th Cavalry, however, had numbered nearly 675 soldiers and scouts. Where was the remainder of the 7th Cavalry, and were there any survivors? Had the entire Regiment been wiped out? 2nd Lieutenant Charles F. Roe, also of General Terry's command, described what happened after they had discovered the bodies:

We moved on up the valley and in about two miles found Major Reno [second in command of the 7th Cavalry], *with the remaining seven companies*

entrenched on top of a high hill, and at the foot of the hill in the plain were dead bodies of soldiers and horses. General Terry and his staff went up to Reno and found that they had been surrounded and fighting constantly for two days. They had been 30 hours without water and could have held out only a little while longer as ammunition was running out. They had a great many killed and about 50 wounded.

Lieutenant Roe also added the following:

They knew nothing of Custer.

As the survivors of the 7th Cavalry were questioned it became clear that Custer and the entire regiment had found and attacked a huge Indian encampment two days before, on June 25, 1876, after Custer had divided the regiment into five battalions.

One battalion under Major Marcus A. Reno, who was the second in command of the regiment, had attacked the camp and retreated. A second battalion under Captain Frederick W. Benteen, the third ranking officer of the 7th Cavalry, had advanced and reinforced Reno after a retreat to the bluff, which the soldiers were now on. A third battalion escorting the pack train had joined Reno shortly after Benteen and there the Indian warriors had besieged the combined force for two days until the arrival of General Terry and reinforcements.

Of Custer and the five companies with him, which had made up a fourth and fifth battalion, Major Reno and Captain Benteen said they knew nothing except that Custer and the force with him had been last seen advancing across the bluffs to the north of Reno's position. The Battle of the Little Big Horn had been fought and the 7th Cavalry had suffered a terrible defeat.

Major Reno's Report

Major Reno's report of the battle, dated July 5, 1876, described in detail his version of the Little Big Horn fight. As the only detailed official report by a participant, Reno's report is perhaps the single most important document relating to the Battle of the Little Big Horn:

Headquarters 7th Regiment Cavalry
Camp on Yellowstone River
July 5, 1876
Captain E. W. Smith
A.D.C. and A.A.A.G.:

The command of the Regiment having devolved upon me, as the senior surviving officer from the battle of June 25 and 26, between the 7th Cavalry and Sitting Bull's band of hostile Sioux on the Little Big Horn River, I have the honor to submit the following report of its operations from the time of leaving the main column until the column was united in the vicinity of the Indian village.

The Regiment left the camp at the mouth of the Rosebud River, after passing in review before the Department Commander, under the command of Brevet Major General G.A. Custer, on the afternoon of the twenty-third of June, and marched up the Rosebud 12 miles and encamped. 23rd – Marched up the Rosebud, passing many old Indian camps, and following a very large lodge-pole trail, but not fresh, making 33 miles. 24th – The march was continued up the Rosebud, the trail and signs freshening with every mile, until we had made 28 miles, and we then encamped and waited for information from the scouts.

At 9:25 p.m., Custer called the officers together and informed us that beyond a doubt the village was in the valley of the Little Big Horn, and that to reach it, it was necessary to cross the divide between Rosebud and Little Big Horn, and it would be impossible to do so in the daytime without discovering our march to the Indians; that we would prepare to move at 11:00 p.m. This was done, the line of march turning from the Rosebud to the right, up one of its branches which headed near the summit of the divide.

Major Reno

About 2:00 a.m. of the 25th, the scouts told him that he could not cross the divide before daylight. We then made coffee and rested for three hours, at the expiration of which time the march was resumed, the divide crossed, and about 8:00 a.m., the command was in the valley of one of the branches of the Little Big Horn. By this time Indians had been seen, and it was certain that we could not surprise them, and it was determined to move at once to the attack.

Previous to this, no division of the Regiment had been made since the order was issued, on the Yellowstone, annulling wing and battalion organization. General Custer informed me he would assign commands on the march. I was ordered by Lieutenant W.W. Cooke, Adjutant, to assume command of Companies M, A and G; Captain Benteen, of Companies H, D and K; Custer retaining C, E, F, I and L, under his immediate command, and Company B, Captain McDougall, in the rear of the pack train.

I assumed command of the Companies assigned to me, and, without any definite orders, moved forward with the rest of the column, and well to its left. I saw Benteen moving further to the left, and as they passed, he told

me that he had orders to move well to the left, and sweep everything before him. I did not see him again until about 2:30 p.m. The command moved down the creek toward the Little Big Horn Valley. Custer, with five companies on the right bank, myself and three companies on the left bank, and Benteen further to the left, and out of sight.

As we approached a deserted village, in which was standing one tepee, about 11:00 a.m., Custer motioned me to cross to him, which I did, and moved nearer to his column, until about 12:30 p.m., when Lieutenant Cooke, Adjutant, came to me and said the village was only two miles ahead, and running away. To "move forward at as rapid a gait as I thought prudent, and to charge afterward, and that the whole outfit would support me." I think those were his exact words.

was still standing; besides I could not see Custer or any other support, and at the same time the very earth seemed to grow Indians, and they were running toward me in swarms, and from all directions.

I saw that I must defend myself, and give up the attack mounted. This I did, taking possession of a point of woods, and which furnished, near its edge, a shelter for the horses; dismounted and fought them on foot, making headway through the wood. I soon found myself to the near vicinity of the village, saw that I was fighting odds of at least five to one, and that my only hope was to get out of the wood where I would soon have been surrounded, and gain some high ground. I accomplished this by mounting and charging the Indians between me and the bluffs on the opposite side of the river.

I at once took a fast trot, and moved down about two miles, when I came to a ford of the river. I crossed immediately, and halted about ten minutes or less to gather the battalion, sending a word to Custer that I had everything in front of me, and that they were strong.

I deployed, and, with the Ree scouts on my left, charged down the valley, driving the Indians with great ease for 2 miles. I, however, soon saw that I was being drawn into some trap as they certainly would fight harder, and especially as we were nearing their village which

In this charge, 1st Lieutenant Donald McIntosh, 2nd Lieutenant Benjamin H. Hodgson, 7th Cavalry and Acting-Assistant Surgeon J.M. De Wolf, were killed. I succeeded in reaching the top of the bluff, with the loss of the three officers, and 29 enlisted men killed, and seven men wounded.

Almost at the same time I reached the top, mounted men were seen to be coming toward us, and it proved to be Colonel Benteen's battalion, Companies H, D, and K; we joined forces, and in a short time the pack train came up. As Senior, my command was then Companies,

A, B, D, G, H, K, and M, about 300 men, and the following officers: Captains Benteen, Weir, French and McDougall; 1st Lieutenant DeRudio was in the dismounted fight in the woods, but, having some trouble with his horse, did not join the command in the charge, and hiding himself in the woods, joined the command after nightfall of the 26th.

Still hearing nothing of Custer, and with his reinforcement, I moved down the river in the direction of the village, keeping on the bluffs. We had heard firing in that direction, and knew it could only be Custer.

I moved to the summit of the highest bluff, but seeing and hearing nothing, sent Captain Weir with his company to open communication with the other command. He soon sent back word, by Lieutenant Hare, that he could go no further, and that the Indians were getting around him. At this time he was keeping up a heavy fire from his skirmish line. I at once turned everything back to the first position I had taken on the bluff, and which seemed to me the best.

I dismounted the men, had the horses and mules on the pack train driven together in a depression, put the men on the crests of the hills making the depression, and had hardly done so when I was furiously attacked. This was about 6:00 p.m. We held our ground with the loss of 18 enlisted men killed, and 46 wounded, until the attack ceased, about 9:00 p.m.

As I knew by this time, their overwhelming numbers, and had given up any support from the portion of the regiment with Custer. I had the men dig rifle pits; barricaded with dead horses, mules, and boxes of hard bread, the opening of the depression toward the Indians in which the animals were herded, and made every exertion to be ready for what I saw would be a terrific assault the next day.

All this night the men were busy, and the Indians holding a scalp-dance underneath us in the bottom, and in our hearing. On the morning of the 26th, I felt confident that I could hold my own, and was ready as far as I could be, when, at daylight, about 2:30 a.m., I heard the crack of two rifles; this was the signal for beginning of a fire that I have never seen equaled. Every rifle was with a range that exceeded our carbine, and it was simply impossible to show any part of the body before it was struck.

We could see, as the day brightened, countless hordes of them pouring up the valley from out of the village, and scampering over the high points toward the places designated for them by their Chiefs, and which entirely surrounded our position. They had sufficient numbers to completely encircle us, and men were struck on the opposite side of the lines, from where the shots were fired. I think we were fighting all the Sioux Nation, and also the desperadoes, renegades, half-breeds, and squaw men, between the Missouri and the Arkansas and east of the Rocky Mountains; they must have numbered at least 2,500 warriors.

The fire did not slacken until about 9:30 a.m., and then we discovered that they were making a last desperate attempt, and which was directed against the line held by Companies H and M; in this attack they charged close enough to use their bows and arrows, and one man, lying dead within our lines, was touched by the "coup stick" of one of the foremost Indians. When I say the stick was only about 10 or 12 feet long, some idea of the desperate and reckless fighting of these people may be understood. This charge of theirs was gallantly repulsed by the men on that line, which I accompanied. We now had many wounded, and the question of water was vital, as of 6:00 p.m. of the previous evening until now, 10:00 a.m. (about 16 hours), we had been without.

A skirmish line was formed, under Captain Benteen, to protect the descent of volunteers down the hill in front of his position to reach the water. We succeeded in getting some canteens, although many of the men were hit in doing so; the fury of the attack was now over, and to my astonishment, the Indians were seen going in parties towards the village. But two solutions occurred to me for this movement; that they were going for something to eat, more ammunition (as they had been throwing arrows), or that Custer was coming. We took advantage of this lull to fill the vessels with water, and soon had it by the camp-kettle full; but they continued to withdraw, and all firing ceased, save occasional shots from sharpshooters sent to annoy us about the water.

About 2:00 p.m., the grass in the bottom was set on fire, and followed up by Indians, who encouraged this burning and it was evident it was done for a purpose, which purpose I discovered later on to be the creation of a dense cloud of smoke, behind which they were packing and preparing to move their tepees.

It was between 6:00 and 7:00 p.m. that the village came out from behind the clouds of smoke and dust. We had a close and good view of them, as they fled away in the direction of the Big Horn Mountains, moving in almost perfect military order; the length of the column was fully equal to that of a large division of the Cavalry Corps of the Army of the Potomac, as I have seen it on its march.

We now thought of Custer, of whom nothing had been seen and nothing heard since the firing in his direction

about 6:00 p.m. on the eve of the 25th, and we concluded that the Indians had gotten between him and us, and driven toward the boat, at the south of the Little Big Horn River, the awful fate that did befall him never occurring to any of us within the limits of possibilities.

During the night I changed my position, in order to secure an unlimited supply of water, and was prepared for their return, feeling sure they would do so as they were in such large numbers.

But early in the morning of the 27th, and while we were on the qui vive for Indians, I saw with my glass a dust some distance down the valley. There was no certainty for some time what they were, but finally I satisfied myself they were Cavalry, and if so, could only be Custer, as it was ahead of the time that I understood that General Terry could be expected. Before this time, however, I had written a communication to General Terry, and three volunteers were to try and reach him (I had no confidence in the Indians with me, and could not get them to do anything). If this dust were Indians, it was possible they would not expect anyone to leave. The men started and were told to go as near as was safe to determine if the approaching column was White men, and to return at once in case it was so: but if they were Indians, to push on to General Terry.

In a short time we saw them returning over the high bluff already alluded to. They were accompanied by a scout who had a note from Terry to Custer, saying,

"Crow Scouts had come to camp saying he had been whipped, but that it was not believed. I think it was about 10:30 a.m. that General Terry rode into my lines and the fate of Custer and his brave men was soon determined by Captain Benteen proceeding with his company to his battleground, and where were recognized the following officers, who were surrounded by the dead bodies of many of their men: General G.A. Custer; Colonel W.W. Cooke, Adjutant; Captains M.W. Keogh, G.W Yates, and T.W. Custer; 1st Lieutenants A.E Smith, James Calhoun; 2nd Lieutenants W.V. Reily, of the 7th Cavalry, and J.J. Crittenden, of the 20th Infantry, temporarily attached to this regiment. The bodies of 1st Lieutenant J.E. Porter and 2nd Lieutenants H.M. Harrington and J.G. Sturgis, 7th Cavalry, and Assistant Surgeon G.W. Lord, U.S. Army, were not recognized, but there is every reasonable probability they were killed.

The wounded in my lines were during the afternoon and evening of the 27th, moved to the camp of General Terry, and at 5:00 a.m. of the 28th I proceeded with the Regiment to the battleground of Custer, and buried 204 bodies, including the following named citizens: Mr. Boston Custer, Mr. Redd (a young nephew of General Custer), and Mr. Kellogg, a correspondent of the New York Herald

The following citizens and Indians who were with my command were also killed: Charles Reynolds (guide and hunter), Isaiah (colored), Interpreter: Bloody Knife (who fell from immediately by my side), Bob Tailed Bull and Stab, of the Indian Scouts.

After following over his trail it was evident to me, that Custer intended to support me by moving further down the stream and attacking the village in flank; that he found the distance greater to the ford than he anticipated; that he did charge, but his charge had taken so long, although his trail shows he moved rapidly, that they were ready for him; that Companies C and I, and perhaps part of Company E, crossed to the village, or attempted it at the charge and that they fell back to secure a position from which to defend themselves; but they were followed too closely by the Indians to permit him to form any kind of line.

I think had the regiment gone in as a body, and from the woods in which I fought advanced on the village, that its destruction was certain, but he was fully confident they were running or he would not have turned from me. I think (after the great number of Indians there were in the village), that the following reasons obtained for the misfortune:

His rapid marching for two days and one night before the fight, attacking in the daytime at 12:00 p.m., and

when they were on the qui vive, instead of early in the morning, and lastly, his unfortunate division of the regiment into three commands.

During my fight with the Indians, I had the heartiest support from officers and men, but the conspicuous services of Brevet Colonel F.W. Benteen I desire to call attention to, especially, for if ever a soldier deserved recognition by his government for distinguished services, he certainly does.

I enclose herewith his report of the operations of his battalion from the time of leaving the regiment until we joined commands on the hill. I also enclose an accurate list of casualties, as far as it can be made at the present time, separating them into two lists – "A," those killed in General Custer's Command; "B," those killed and wounded in the command I had.

The number of Indians killed can only be approximated, until we hear through the agencies. I saw the bodies of 18, and Captain Ball, 2nd Cavalry, who made a scout of 13 miles over their trail, says that their graves were many along their line of march. It is simply impossible that numbers of them should not be hit, in the several charges they made so close to my lines. They made their approach through the deep gulches that led from the hilltop to the river; and when the jealous care with which the Indian guards the bodies of killed and wounded is considered, it is not astonishing that their bodies were not found. It is probable that the stores left by them, and destroyed the next two days, were to make room for many of them on their travois.

The harrowing sight of the dead bodies crowning the height on which Custer fell, and which will remain vividly in my memory until death, is too recent for me not to ask the good people posing parties in the field armed, clothed, and equipped by one and the same Government, should not be abolished. All of which is respectfully submitted.

M.A. Reno
Major 7th Cavalry
Commanding Regiment

Major Reno and Captain Benteen Deny Knowledge of Custer's Fate

In his official report Major Reno denied knowing that Custer and the force with him had suffered a terrible defeat or, perhaps, even had been annihilated. Later, at the Court of Inquiry into his conduct at the Battle of the Little Big Horn, which convened January 13, 1879, Reno repeated this view:

That evening, the whereabouts of the Commanding Officer of the Regiment was discussed by Captain Benteen and myself... There was not the slightest belief or suspicion that Custer had been destroyed.

Like Major Reno, Captain Benteen, the third ranking officer of the regiment at the Battle of the Little Big Horn and commander of the reserve battalion, also denied any knowledge of Custer's fate. Benteen, however, added a particular flourish to his denials, and at the Reno Court of Inquiry of 1879 he said:

Captain Benteen

It was the belief of the officers on the hill during the night of the 25th that General Custer had gone to General Terry and we were abandoned to our fate.

In his many denials concerning knowledge of Custer's fate, Captain Benteen was usually diligent in adding the claim that he and other officers of the 7th Cavalry had believed Custer had "abandoned" the rest of the regiment, although he never elaborated on how, or why, Custer, with a force less than half the size of Reno's and Benteen's, could "abandon" them.

Major Reno and Captain Benteen were supported by other surviving officers of the regiment who also said they had no indication as to what had become of Custer after he was last seen riding along the bluffs overlooking the Little Big Horn Valley towards the north.

News Reporter Finerty's Statement

Although badly defeated, the 7th Cavalry's tour of duty on the American frontier was not to end with the Battle of the Little Big Horn. After a few weeks of reorganization on the Yellowstone River they were again on the field in pursuit of the same hostile tribes which had defeated the 7th Cavalry on June 25, 1876. Later that summer Brigadier General George Crook, with another military force also in the field searching for these same hostile tribes, joined General Terry's command.

John F. Finerty, a news correspondent with General Crook's force, regularly dispatched news stories of Crook's campaign to the *Chicago Tribune*. He was an Irishman who had immigrated to the United States in 1864 and had enlisted in the Union Army; it was after his service in the Civil War that he became a news correspondent. As the only newsperson on the spot when Terry's forces joined Crook's, Finerty was able to interview survivors of the 7th Cavalry before any other news representative.

In 1890, Reporter Finerty published a book titled *War*

Path and Bivouac, which was a narrative of Crook's campaign of 1876. Besides detailing Crook's campaign, Finerty also wrote of the Battle of the Little Big Horn, using information told to him by surviving 7th Cavalrymen. Concerning Major Reno's denial of knowledge that Custer had suffered a terrible defeat during the two days Reno's force was besieged, a skeptical Finerty had this to say:

Reno's men felt certain that something dreadful had happened to their comrades because, during the afternoon of the 25th and the morning of the 26th, they had recognized the guidons of the 7th Cavalry which the savages were waving in an ecstasy of triumph....

...It would appear from the statements of Major Reno and other officers engaged in the battle on the bluffs that they were entirely ignorant of the fate of Custer and his five troops until the arrival of Generals Terry and Gibbon.

The author was told by some of the 7th Cavalry that after the commands of Terry and Crook came together in the Rosebud Valley on August 10, 1876, the savages had displayed Custer's guidon and other trophies during the fighting on June 25th and 26th.

It seems strange that Reno could not comprehend Custer's fate until after the arrival of Generals Terry and Gibbon. Where did Major Reno suppose the hostiles procured the uniforms, etc., which they displayed?

It does "seem strange" that the enlisted soldiers who had seen the battle trophies captured by the Indian warriors did not report this information to Major Reno and other officers of the command. The whereabouts of Custer and his command, one would imagine, would have been a topic of interest to those besieged on the bluff, especially Reno and Benteen.

7th Cavalrymen See Custer Uniforms

Captain Thomas M. McDougall, who commanded Troop B of the 7th Cavalry and survived the battle, also spoke of captured cavalry trophies displayed by the Indians in a letter he wrote dated February 26, 1909. He mentioned many of the Indians wearing cavalry uniforms and one in particular who rode back and forth taunting the soldiers until he was finally shot from his horse.

In 1894 a two-part article was published in *Army Magazine*, written by Theodore W. Goldin, an enlisted soldier with Reno's battalion at the Battle of the Little Big Horn. Goldin himself has become controversial with historians concerning various heroics claimed to have been performed by himself during the battle. His personal claims aside, Goldin was at the battle and in his article he made a very interesting statement:

Mounted Indians rode up almost within rifle shot of us, wearing the uniforms of members of Custer's command and waving in their hands guidons and battle flags taken from Custer, all the time taunting us in the most offensive manner.

Battle trophies taken from a defeated enemy were very important to the American Indian warrior of the 19th Century. Unlike the trained soldier of the government armies, the Indian warrior did not regard war as an impersonal venture or simply as an unpleasant job that had to be done. War was a way of life to the plains Indian, a personal adventure that gave the warrior within the tribe self-esteem and status.

Captured war trophies were significant proof of a great warrior and an indication that he was a person to be reckoned with. Taking the uniforms and flags from Custer's soldiers, and then taunting those soldiers besieged on the bluff with those trophies, was totally in character with the Indian warrior and his mode of fighting.

Those who were with Major Reno were not the only soldiers to see evidence of Custer's defeat. Lieutenant Roe was with General Terry's command

and as they marched up the Little Big Horn Valley on June 26, 1876, huge war parties of hostile Indian warriors were seen in front of Terry's force, taunting the soldiers to dare to fight.

In a narrative of his experiences, Lieutenant Roe commented upon the uniforms he saw the Indian warriors wearing:

We could see that some distance in the rear of this skirmish line of Indians was a very large body of mounted men, undoubtedly three or four hundred. While we were looking, from that body of men in the rear of the skirmish line there came out a troop of cavalry to all intents and purposes; they marched by twos and had a guidon flying and were dressed in dark clothes....

I will say here, these apparent troops were Indians dressed in the clothing of General Custer's men whom they had killed.

Private William White, F Troop, 2nd Cavalry, was also with General Terry's column and commented on what he saw:

We didn't know then of the awful thing that had happened to Custer and his men, but as we marched across the valley, we saw many Indians wearing 7th Cavalry uniforms and mounted on Cavalry horses.

Indians Speak of Captured Uniforms

Kate Bighead was a Cheyenne woman living in the Indian village during the Battle of the Little Big Horn. She told how the Indian women, children and old people observed the battle from the western bluffs across the river from the battlefield:

The Indians got guns, cartridges, horses, saddles, clothing, boots, everything the soldiers had with them. During the battle, all of the women and children and old people had been watching from the western hills across the river.... They kept themselves ready to run away if their warriors should be beaten, or to return to the camps if their side should win.

After a long time of this watching, all the time in doubt, they saw a band of horsemen coming across the river and toward them. As the horsemen got into good view, it was seen that all of them had on blue clothing and were mounted soldiers' horses coming to kill the families. Women shrieked, some of them fainted. Mothers and children ran away into hiding.

One woman grabbed her two little boys and set out running up a gulch. She was so excited that in picking them up, she seized their feet and slung them upside down over her shoulders. It soon became known, though, that these men were our own warriors bringing the horses and the clothing of the dead soldiers.

Red Horse, a Sioux warrior who fought Custer on June 25, 1876, in a later narrative also mentioned the fact that many of the warriors dressed in 7th Cavalry uniforms had been captured.

An article appeared in the *Bismarck Tribune* on Wednesday, November 1, 1876, concerning information Captain John W. Smith had on the Battle of the Little Big Horn. Described as "a frontiersman of 20 years experience who speaks Sioux fluently," Smith had spoken to many warriors at the Standing Rock Agency who had participated in the Custer battle. Smith said he had been told:

After wiping out Custer, they returned to Reno, the Indians fighting him with Custer's colors.

Rain in the Face

The victorious Indian warriors were proud they had captured Custer's battle flags and made it a point to tell Smith they had these colors when fighting Major Reno and his command.

From the accounts left by participants it is evident that, after the massacre of Custer and his command, the Indians dressed themselves in the soldiers' clothes and carried off battle trophies, such as cavalry equipment and guidons. Reports of these battle trophies being displayed to the soldiers entrenched on Reno's hill position are plentiful enough, showing that Reno's force did have a good indication of Custer's annihilation. Wherever located on the battle line, Reno's soldiers who saw the ominous displays of captured uniforms and guidons by the Indian warriors surely spoke about this to other soldiers or even reported this information to superiors.

Field Glasses

Another fact that adds to the mystery of Major Reno and Captain Benteen's denial is that many, if not most, of the officers with the command had field glasses, which would have clarified distant figures not necessarily recognized with the unaided eye. Captain Benteen, for instance, wrote of a "pretty good binocular that I always carried."

It was evident to the enlisted men with the unaided eye that the hostile warriors were dressed in soldier's uniforms and carrying cavalry guidons. So what about

the officers who had field glasses such as Captain Benteen? How many times during the two-day siege on the bluff did those surviving 7th Cavalry officers anxiously scan the surrounding terrain carefully for any clues that would reveal the intentions of the hostile Indians or that would indicate the approach of reinforcements?

Lieutenant DeRudio and Private O'Neill's Narrow Escape

Supposing the highly improbable, that no one reported to Major Reno that the Indians were dressed in soldiers' uniforms and displaying captured flags, and that Reno did not actually see these trophies himself, then another source of information concerning Custer's defeat was made available on the night of June 26, 1876.

When Major Reno and his command retreated from the valley, several soldiers were left behind in the wooded area. Some of these men were able to rejoin the soldiers on the bluff that same day but two of them, 1st Lieutenant Charles C. DeRudio and an enlisted soldier, Private Thomas O'Neill, did not make their escape until the night of June 26, 1876. DeRudio later told of an incident before they joined Reno in which he and O'Neill believed they had been rescued:

> *The night* [of June 25-26] *was passed and in the dim light of day, I thought I saw some gray horses mounted by men in military blouses and some in white hats.... I saw one man in a buckskin jacket, pantaloons and top boots and a white hat, and felt quite sure I recognized him as Captain Tom Custer* [General Custer's brother], *which convinced me that the cavalry was of our command.*
>
> *With this conviction, I stepped boldly out to the edge of the bank and called to Captain Custer, "Tom, don't leave us here. " My call was answered by an infernal yell and three or four hundred shots. I then discovered by mistake and found that the savages were clad in clothes and mounted on horses from our men.*

Private O'Neill also wrote of this same incident:

> *The morning was dawning on us before we realized it was growing late. The Indians were coming past in front of us and along the river bank to begin another attack on Reno's command.*
>
> *The Lieutenant had pulled on his boots and I was tugging at mine. He arose and looked out. A column of mounted men were passing us about two or three hundred yards away. Calling to me in a low tone, he excitedly said "O'Neill, I believe it is the command.... " The Lieutenant observed one man dressed in buckskin he believed to be Captain Tom Custer, as he had worn on this expedition. I thought surely it was Captain Tom Custer and was nearly overjoyed at the prospect of soon being with my comrades once more.*
>
> *At the same time, Lieutenant DeRudio stepped boldly out on the river bank and shouted, "Hey Tom Custer! Tom Custer!" The riders stopped and looked in our direction, and then in an instant the war whoop started and a volley of at least 50 shots were fired at us! How we escaped being hit is a miracle, for the bullets cut the brush about us in every direction.*
>
> *The riders were all Sioux Indians dressed in some of the uniforms they had taken, we later learned, from Custer's men in the battle the previous afternoon, and were riding 7th Cavalry horses which they had captured.*

Fortunately, Lieutenant DeRudio and Private O'Neill were able to escape from their perilous situation and when they finally made it into Major Reno's position the night of June 26, 1876, their arrival must have been greeted with astonishment. Undoubtedly, they had been given up for dead. Certainly they were questioned as to their adventures and, as their narratives confirmed, the incident with "Tom Custer" and the Indian warriors dressed as soldiers and mounted on cavalry horses had made an indelible impression upon them. It should have, as it had nearly cost them their lives. Surely, DeRudio and O'Neill mentioned this incident to members of Reno's command, if not to Reno himself.

In fact, when telling of their escape, Lieutenant DeRudio did mention the reaction of members of Major Reno's command when he and Private O'Neill arrived on Reno Hill:

> *After marching two miles, I thought I would go up on a very high hill to look around and see if I could discover any sign of our command; and on looking around, I saw a fire on my left and in the direction where we supposed the command was fighting during the day, probably two miles from us.*
>
> *Of course, we made two conjectures on this fire: it might be an Indian fire and it might be from our command. The only way to ascertain was to approach it cautiously and trust to chance.*
>
> *Accordingly, we descended the hill, and took the direction of the fire. Climbing another, and another hill, we listened awhile and then proceeded on for a mile or more, when, on top of a hill, we again stopped and listened. We could hear voices, but not distinctly enough to tell whether they were savages or our command.*
>
> *We proceeded a little farther and heard the bray of a*

Lieutenant DeRudio

mule, and soon after, the distinct voice of a sentry challenging with the familiar words, "Halt, who goes there?" The challenge was not directed to us, as we were too far off to be seen by the picket, and it was too dark; but this gave us courage to continue our course and approach, though carefully, lest we should run into some Indians again.

We were about 200 yards from the fire and... I cried out: "Picket, don't fire; it is Lieutenant DeRudio and Private O'Neill," and started to run. We received an answer in a loud cheer from all the members of the picket and Lieutenant Varnum. This officer, one of our bravest and most efficient, came at once to me and was very happy to see me again, after having been counted among the dead....

My first question was about the condition of the regiment, I was in hopes that we were the only sufferers, but I was not long allowed to remain in doubt. Lieutenant Varnum said he knew nothing of the five companies under Custer and that our command had sustained a loss in Lieutenants McIntosh and Hodgson....

It was about 2:00 a.m. when I got into camp, and I soon after tried to go to sleep; but though I had not slept for two nights, I could not close my eyes. I talked with Lieutenant Varnum about the battle and narrated to him adventures and a narrow escape I had. Morning soon came and I went to see the officers and told them that the Indians had left....

Sergeant Stanislaus Roy of Company A also mentioned the arrival of Lieutenant DeRudio and Private O'Neill:

That night, Girard and Billy Jackson, DeRudio and Tom came in. I heard DeRudio yell, "Hello," and guard George Bott of A Troop was on post and challenged him, and he answered, "Lieutenant DeRudio," and the officer of the guard gave orders to advance him and he came in. There was great rejoicing as we had supposed they had been killed.

Private John Burkman, who had been with the pack train the day of the battle, later spoke of the arrival of DeRudio and the others:

They told us that whilst they was hidin' by, not fur away, and through the dust and smoke they could see they was wearin' uniforms. Fur a minute, their hearts jumped into their throats. They thought they was some o' Custer's men. One of 'em had on a buckskin coat and a big white hat, and they jumped up and yelled at him thinkin' he was Tom Custer. Then the wind whipped the smoke away a little and they seen the men was Indians.

That bothered us all considerable. We couldn't figger how the Redskins could o' got hold of the 7th's uniforms.

Someone on the bluff must have told Major Reno and the officers with him of Lieutenant DeRudio and Private O'Neill's experience, and the implications of the Indian warriors' wearing of cavalry uniforms was glaringly obvious.

Confronted with the many accounts of Indian warriors seen with the trophies of battle taken from Custer's men, Major Reno's and Captain Benteen's denials of knowledge of Custer's fate appear to be a fabrication. And the uniforms, guidons and cavalry horses were not the only evidence they had of Custer's tragedy.

The Weapons Used by the Indians

2nd Lieutenant Charles A. Varnum later wrote Colonel W.A. Graham, a noted Little Big Horn researcher and author, the following:

Personally, I think and always have, the best guns in the hands of the Indians were the carbines taken from Custer's men and the 70 grain ammunition they got from the same.... On the hill most of the bullets came in with a zap sound. When a zing-g-g sound came, that made you take notice.

The Sioux warrior, Red Horse, also later spoke of the weapons they had captured from Custer's men:

The Sioux took the guns and cartridges off the dead soldiers and went to the hill on which the soldiers surrounded and fought them with guns and cartridges of the dead soldiers.

Theoretically, the Springfield carbine used by the 7th Cavalry at the Battle of the Little Big Horn was actually a superior weapon to most of the Indian warriors' weapons, except for the rate of fire. It had a heavier bullet, a larger charge of powder, and in theory a greater range and accuracy than the warriors' Winchester and Henry repeating

rifles.

When Lieutenant Varnum noted that the use of this weapon by the Indians "made you take notice," he was speaking as an experienced soldier whose life depended on his skill and familiarity with weapons then in use on the American frontier by both the cavalry and the Indian warriors they fought. Major Reno also should have "taken notice" of the use of the Springfield carbine by the Indians. He was on the 1872 Army Board that selected the carbine for use by the cavalry and Reno was as familiar with the Springfield carbine as any soldier.

First Sergeant John Ryan, who was with Troop M at the Little Big Horn, also took note of the use of the Army carbine by the Indians, but in a very different respect than merely the "zing-g-g" that signaled a Cavalry carbine was being fired. Sergeant Ryan wrote the *Hardin Tribune* on June 22, 1923:

> *In regard to the ammunition and the arms that the Indians used on Reno's command, it appears that when Custer's five companies were wiped out of existence, the Indians got all their Springfeld .45 Caliber breech loading carbines.*
>
> *In addition to getting what cartridges the men left in their waist belts, they probably got the 60 extra rounds that each man carried in his saddle bags and also 24 rounds of pistol ammunition Caliber 45. All this ammunition with the carbines were used against Reno's men by the Indians, as a number of our men were wounded with the same caliber ammunition.*

Not only did the Army carbine weapon make a distinct sound, it also made a larger and more frightful wound, something sure to attract the attention of those being fired upon. Because the Army did not issue these weapons to the warring tribes, and because these weapons were too newly issued to the military to have come into general use and circulation as contraband, someone must have asked where the Indians had so recently acquired these Springfield carbines. Surely others besides Lieutenant Varnum and Sergeant Ryan noticed the use of these weapons by the Indian warriors besieging Major Reno's position.

Colonel Gibbon's Account

Colonel John Gibbon was with General Terry's command when it advanced through the Little Big Horn Valley toward Major Reno's position on June 27. In April, 1877, an article was published by *The American Catholic Quarterly Review* by Gibbon about the Army campaign of 1876. In commenting upon their advance through the valley as Terry's command neared Reno's position, Gibbon made some interesting observations. Gibbon said:

> ... *On our left ran the stream bordered with timber and brushwood, and some distance on our right the valley was bounded by low, rolling hills. In our front the stream after cutting into the bluffs crossed the valley from right to left, the timber shutting out all view beyond, save above its top appeared a sharp mountain peak, on the edges of which could now and then be indistinctly made out a few moving figures....*

The "sharp mountain peak" Colonel Gibbon referred to on the Little Big Horn battlefield has since become known as the "Weir Peaks," actually three peaks which join together. These peaks are slightly more than one mile north of Reno's position, about three miles south of the hilltop where Custer's body was found, and also overlook the Little Big Horn valley for many miles in both directions. The Weir Peaks clearly impressed Gibbon for he was to mention them a total of five times in his narrative. Gibbon said:

> *I caught sight of something on the top of a hill, far beyond the sharp peak before referred to, which at once attracted my attention and a closer scrutiny. I sprang from my horse, and, with a field glass, looked long and anxiously at a number of dark objects....*

These "dark objects" were Major Reno's command located a little over a mile south of the Weir Peaks.

At a point further along in his narrative, Colonel Gibbon mentioned observers from Major Reno's command on the Weir Peaks:

> ... *I had observed on the peak before spoken of, and opposite which the advanced guard had now arrived, three horsemen evidently observing our movements and watching us closely....*

Later in his narrative, Colonel Gibbon described the Weir Peaks further:

> ... *Standing on top of the main ridge with my back to the river, I overlooked the whole of the ground to the front; but on turning to my left, the ground was seen to rise higher and higher in successive ridges, which ran nearly perpendicular to the stream, until they culminated in the sharp peak referred to in my description of the previous day, upon which we had seen objects at a great distance down the valley....*

Colonel Gibbon again mentioned the Weir Peaks in his narrative, saying:

> ... *the high peak so often referred to....*

Two of the observers on the Weir Peaks mentioned by Colonel Gibbon have been identified as 2nd Lieutenants Luther R. Hare and George D. Wallace. As these officers were clearly sent to the Weir Peaks as observers, if they themselves did not personally carry field glasses, they surely would have been loaned some. These observers would have had only two purposes; to look for friend, or to look for foe.

Colonel Gibbon was clearly mystified by the length of

time these observers remained on the Weir Peaks as General Terry's column cautiously advanced toward them. Gibbon said:

> ... *They could scarcely, I thought, be white men, for our troops were marching up the valley in two columns, in plain sight of where they sat on their horses, and, if friendly, they surely would have come down and communicated with us. They did finally come slowly down to a lower hill standing nearer to the river, but there they halted again and seemed to question us with their eyes.*

The 7th Cavalry had just fought the greatest alliance of hostile Indians ever before, or after, seen in the American West. About a third of that command, along with the commanding officer, had vanished. The remaining soldiers had been besieged for two days.

From the Weir Peaks some of the white marble headstones which today mark the location of the fallen soldiers on the Custer battlefield are visible to the unaided eye. With even modest field glasses they become even more apparent.

These observers on the Weir Peaks watching General Terry's cautious advance in the Little Big Horn valley had only to rotate their field glasses a few degrees to the right to see the Custer battlefield. Can it be imagined that these observers did not anxiously scan the surrounding hills many times while they were at that position? Where were those Indians anyway? And, once observing the Custer battlefield, how difficult would it have been to dispatch a messenger to Reno's hill position to tell them of what they saw?

Major Reno and Captain Benteen Knew of Custer's Fate

To the soldiers and officers of Major Reno's command, besieged for two days on the bluff, the whereabouts of Custer and his battalion would have been of great concern. That Custer and his men had fought the Indians was not a great mystery. Many soldiers and officers admitted later that they heard gunfire in the direction Custer had gone the afternoon of June 25, 1876. Major Reno himself said in his report of the battle, made just 10 days later:

> *We had heard firing in that direction and knew it could only be Custer.*

At Major Reno's 1879 Court of Inquiry, in narratives, personal interviews, and letters, the survivors of the 7th Cavalry stated clearly that they heard this gunfire. At this inquiry, however, Major Reno and Captain Benteen were to deny that gunfire was heard in the direction of Custer, a contention which, when compared to the statements of numerous survivors of the 7th Cavalry, including Major Reno's report, would appear unbelievable.

Custer and his force had fought the same Indians that had confronted Major Reno and Captain Benteen, and the sound of that battle had been heard at Reno's position. When the Indians later appeared on Reno's front, dressed in soldiers' uniforms, carrying cavalry flags, riding cavalry mounts, and armed with Springfield carbines, it was obvious that Custer's command had suffered an enormous defeat.

Then why did Major Reno at his Court of Inquiry, and Captain Benteen and other officers under their command, deny any knowledge of Custer's defeat?

Although Major Reno's official report of the Battle of the Little Big Horn gave a general picture of the fight, it also contained many obvious distortions and omissions. One of those omissions was that Custer had ordered Reno and Benteen forward to attack the Indian village, and neither of these officers had carried out these orders.

After Major Reno's retreat from the valley, Captain Benteen, and then the pack train, joined him near the final bluff position where a stand had been made by the combined forces. Captain Thomas B. Weir of D Company had made one attempt to advance in the direction that Custer had taken before Reno and Benteen had again withdrawn to the bluff where they made their final stand.

Approximately 210 soldiers had been with Custer, not quite half the soldiers Major Reno and Captain Benteen had under their command at the beginning of the battle, and the obvious fact was that Custer was left alone to fight the Indian warriors while almost two-thirds of the regiment, under the command of Reno and Benteen, failed to come to his assistance, even when the sound of gunfire was heard by them.

One of the basic, indisputable, unchangeable, facts of the Battle of the Little Big Horn is that Major Reno and Captain Benteen disobeyed the orders given to them at the very beginning of the battle. Custer had ordered them to advance to support the planned attack on the Indian camp. They did not advance, and that disobedience may have caused the annihilation, at least partially, of Custer's command. History will never know what the result of that epic battle would have been if all of those in positions of com-

mand had followed the orders given them; perhaps defeat was inevitable. Perhaps not.

The feigned ignorance of Custer's defeat by Major Reno and Captain Benteen was the first step in denial of responsibility for that defeat. It was the first step in a long process of evasions, deceit, and fraud, with the ultimate purpose of casting the blame for the defeat upon Custer. That Custer could have "abandoned" a force almost twice as large as his own, as Benteen was to accuse, is ridiculous.

Yet, the accumulated effect of these accusations, regardless of validity or fact, created confusion and controversy, exactly as Reno and Benteen intended.

Of Custer's annihilation on June 25, 1876, one fact, however, can be safely ascertained. The victorious Indian warriors had flagrantly displayed the evidence of Custer's defeat to those on Reno's hill position. Major Reno knew Custer had been defeated. Captain Benteen knew Custer had been defeated. These two officers also knew that they shared in the responsibility for this defeat.

CHAPTER 2

The Europeans Arrive —— America —— Inter-Tribal War —— A Life of Fear —— Indian Scouts —— Taken Alive —— Experience of Nelson Lee —— Save the Last Bullet for Yourself —— A Frontiersman's View of Warfare Against the Indian —— Revenge —— Sand Creek —— Extermination —— Women and Children Killed —— History of Inhumanity —— The Fate of Prisoners —— Torture and War —— Broken Trust —— The Observations of Granville Stuart —— The Observations of Major Brisbin —— Custer on the Corruption of the Indian Agents —— Bishop Whipple —— Little Robe of the Cheyennes —— Charles Larpenter, Frontiersman on Wars

Sitting Bull

The Battle of the Little Big Horn was not an isolated event. It was one of the countless violent episodes that occurred throughout four centuries of conquest as the native population of North America fought against an onslaught which, in retrospect, might be called a progressing world civilization.

The wars of conquest against the native inhabitants of the American continents began with the landing of Christopher Columbus in 1492 and lasted almost 400 years until the Wounded Knee incident of 1891. These 400 years were witness to wars as cruel and ferocious as any in history, long and dramatic wars of cultures.

The expanding culture of "Western Civilization" had its origins in the Middle East, a crossroads of three continents that had the progressive influences of many races, cultures, and religions that had given these crossroads a dynamic growth. It was an expanding world culture with a philosophy of materialism that made the pragmatic development of the human condition and the world a primary aim. Domestication of animals, dominance of nature for agriculture, and technological advancement, were all results of this philosophy.

At the same time the culture of the Western Civilization was developing at the crossroads of the world on the eastern side of the Atlantic, the culture of the "American Indian" was developing independently on the western side of the Atlantic. The culture of the native inhabitants of the American continents had been isolated from the mainstream of the world for an unknown period of time. There is some evidence that, previous to Columbus, there were Phoenicians, Vikings, the Irish and perhaps others, who had visited the continents, apparently without any permanent impact. Columbus called the native inhabitants "Indians" when he first arrived, with the mistaken belief he had reached India on the Asian subcontinent.

Native tribes inhabited most of the two continents and lived as hunter-gatherers, while the Aztec, Mayan, and Inca cultures were located in Mexico and Peru and had sophisticated, agriculturally based civilizations. At one period there had been massive building of pyramids, and throughout the two continents huge mounds and other structures have been found that indicate, during certain eras, the dominant cultures had been quite vigorous.

Columbus was employed by Spain when he reached the unknown lands and the Spanish were quick to exploit the treasures of what they called "The New World." Within thirty years of the first landing by the Conquistadors, the

Territorial Expansion of the United States

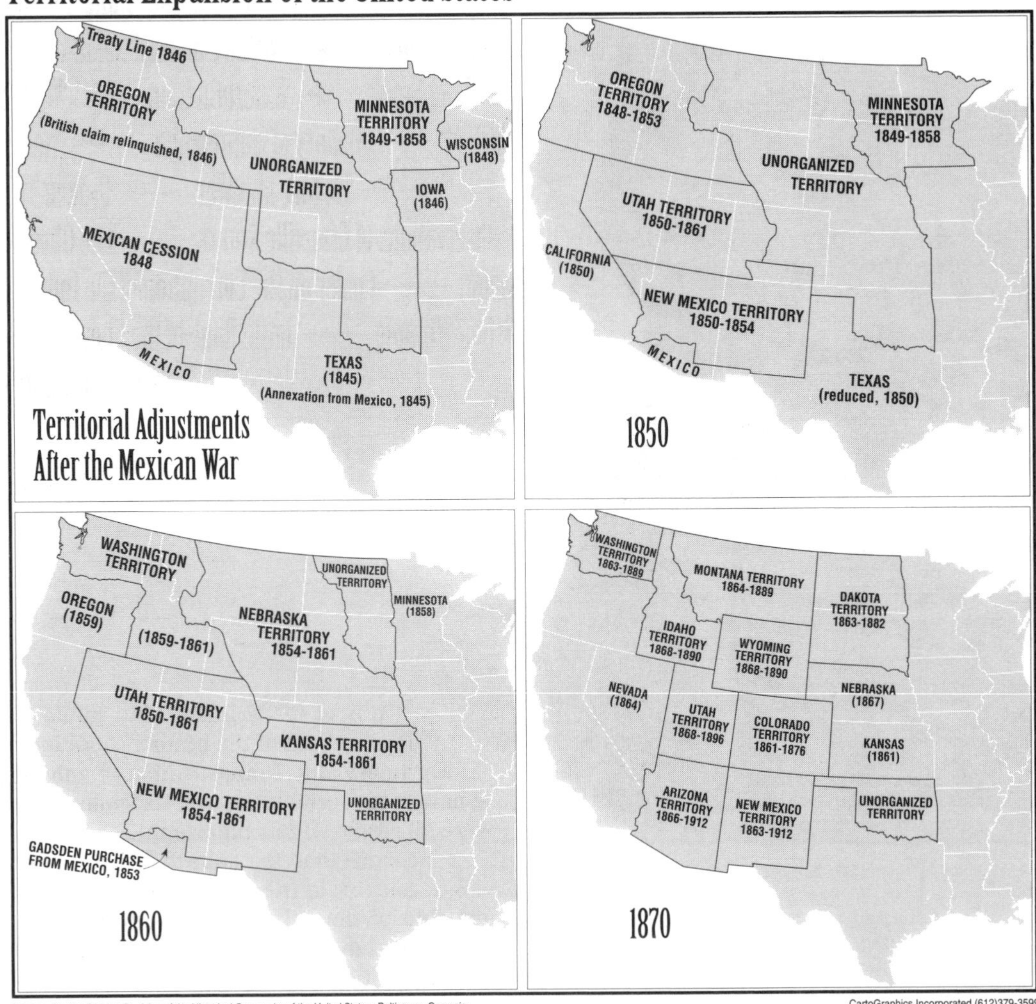

Source: Paullin, Charles O. *Atlas of the Historical Geography of the United States.* Baltimore: Carnegie Institution of Washington and the American Geographical Society of New York, 1932.

CartoGraphics Incorporated (612)379-3599

Aztec culture had been destroyed by the invaders, who were driven forward by the promise of wealth and land.

Iron weapons, firearms, cannons, horses, and huge packs of war dogs trained to kill, proved overpowering to the more numerous Aztecs, who were also impeded by a superstitious dread of newcomers.

The Europeans Arrive

Other European nations quickly recognized the possibilities of the Americas, and by the end of the 16th century the most powerful had established colonies at many locations. The Spanish became dominant in Central and South America, the English along the east coast of what would become the United States, and the French in parts of Canada and the Mississippi Valley.

Many times the American Indians welcomed the newcomers, but invariably that attitude was quickly submerged by the pragmatic intentions of the colonists. They had come to conquer and exploit and, until the entire "New World" had been subjected, that purpose was never deviated from. By the time of the American Revolution of 1776, dramatic inroads had been made from the coastal areas of what would become the United States and the newcomers, in many places, had pushed the American Indians far inland. The encroachments by the newcomers during the period before 1776, and for many years after, were full of bloody battles and massacres, which both sides committed with gruesome frequency.

America

The establishment of the new nation of the United States of America in 1776 soon brought forth a national ideal that

would have significant implications for the American Indians. It was called Manifest Destiny and the belief behind it was that eventually all the land between the Atlantic and Pacific coasts would be one nation.

The "open door" policy to immigration, and the resulting millions of people who came to America, may have made the belief in Manifest Destiny irrelevant; for while the Indian population was constantly being diminished by war and new diseases, there was an endless supply of newcomers, making Manifest Destiny all but inevitable. Europe and America were entering a technological age and advancements in weapons, as well as the enormous numbers of immigrants, placed the Indians at a decisive disadvantage.

Inter-Tribal War

The conquest of North America was to be made a far easier task due to one fact that dominated the existing American Indian cultures. This fact was war. With few exceptions the native tribes lived in a continuous state of war, each tribe waged battles and raids against every other tribe that was not allied with it.

These wars had their origins in the distant past of North America, and as historian Rodman observed in his book *The Far West and Plains in Transition:*

> *Modern anthropologists have concluded that in all probability whites killed fewer Indians than were killed by other Indians in intertribal wars....*

While this fact is buried under the weight of guilt concerning the many injustices the American Indian was subjected to by the newcomers, (and there were many) it is nevertheless a fact that the American Indian was as warlike as any other culture recorded in history.

In discussing why so many American Indians were willing to become scouts for the soldiers of the American West, author Thomas W. Dunlay made the following observation:

> *To present Indian history in terms of Indian-white conflict tends to create the impression that white contact was the only factor of importance impinging on the history of a particular group. Yet the Indians were never simply acted upon by whites. They acted upon the whites as well; furthermore, individual Indians and groups acted on each other. Thus, whites play a less prominent part in Indian reminiscences, even in war stories, than one might expect. [The] Indians' reasons for cooperating with whites were more complex than conscious betrayal and self-aggrandizement.*
>
> *Some tribes saw the whites as useful allies against a strong Indian enemy; if they also saw such cooperation as a means of accommodation to the stronger power, they did not conceive of their actions as betrayal of any group to whom they owed loyalty. Indian history reveals innumerable tribal alliances, and changes of alliance, for reasons not dissimilar to those that move supposedly more sophisticated nations.*
>
> *When Indians fought against other Indians of the same language or culture, they did so for varied reasons, some based on self-interest and some on loyalties they considered of the first importance....*

It was the tradition of inter-tribal conflicts among the American Indians that made their defeat inevitable. Any concentrated action against the invaders was impossible and the result of this was commented upon by author Robert Leckie in his book *The Wars of America*:

> *... Tribe by tribe, outpost by outpost, the dispersed Indians went down before the concentrated white men. It never occurred to Indians of the interior that the tribes of the East Coast were fighting their battle, that they were resisting the white invasion "at the water's edge." No. They went their own way until the white tide flowed over the mountain barriers and engulfed them, too.*
>
> *So each tribe or confederation fought the white man alone, and each time they were conquered, the white man expanded his beachhead, that is, he advanced his frontier farther westward and received more "reinforcements," i.e., immigrants from the Old World....*

By the time of the American Civil War the newcomers had subjected all of the land east of the Mississippi and much of the land on the western coast. Only the land

west of the Mississippi known as the Great Plains still had significant populations of American Indians who retained their original modes of life. The added civilized refinements of firearms and the horse gave these inhabitants of the Great Plains vastly increased mobility and firepower, the basic tools necessary to resist invasion, and yet the ancient conflicts between tribes continued. Historian Anthony McGinnis, in an article on the inter-tribal conflicts of the Great Plains, analyzed the warfare that existed when the new immigrants arrived:

> *When white men first entered the northern plains in the 18th century, they found a complex system of rivalries and alliances. They were amazed to find the tribes almost constantly at war. In the century which followed, the relations between the newcomers and the native Americans were greatly influenced by the phenomenon of inter-tribal conflict.*
>
> *Tribal war was pervasive, and it began to involve traders, travelers, settlers, and government officials. In addition, treaties made between various tribes and the United States government, as well as the methods with which the Indians fought the white man, were influenced by tribal warfare.*
>
> *White people often suffered directly or indirectly from tribal raiding, but most important of all, their opinions of the red man were perhaps determined most by that activity. They often saw the Indians, thus, as murderous and barbarous nomads, living off a seemingly inhospitable land....*

As Mr. McGinnis pointed out, tribal warfare among the American Indians was prevalent across the continent and, with a few notable exceptions, almost every Indian tribe in North America was in a state of almost continuous conflict. Some tribes were allied with others, while other tribes would be singled out as enemies worthy of particular attention.

In an unprejudiced examination of the course events took during the conquest of North America, the role of inter-tribal warfare must be placed in proper perspective.

A Life of Fear

War, for the American Indian of the Great Plains, was primarily an endeavor to obtain plunder, honors, or revenge. Often raids were planned against specific enemies, yet, murders of opportunity, where the lone traveler or small group might inadvertently stumble across an enemy and be killed, were not infrequent.

Author E. Adamson Hoebel, in his writings on the Cheyenne Indians, summarized perhaps best the true situation concerning the life of the American Indians on the Great Plains.

> *Cheyenne feats of bravery are legendary. Yet they are by no means supermen. They live from day to day knowing that every hour exposes them to unannounced attack; every night when they lie down to rest they know that dawn will bring the possibility of an enemy attack on their herds or on their camp.*
>
> *For them, there is no such thing as security – ever. There are no interludes of peace to give* [safety] *from war.*
>
> *When the lurking threat of enemy attacks is not working on them, there is always the knowledge that to qualify as men at all they must themselves go seek out the enemy. Fear haunts them, even though they rarely let it break through to the surface....*

There never could be any lasting peace or security among any of the American Indian tribes on the Great Plains of America as long as the "war path" remained unchanged. These unending wars were without beginning or end and the feud between the Crow, who were scouts for the 7th Cavalry at the Battle of the Little Big Horn, and the Sioux tribes, was one of particular intensity.

The Sioux were especially proficient at terrorizing and otherwise waging successful warfare against their enemies, one reason being that there were more of them. Also, unlike many of the other tribes, the Sioux emulated the military tactics and discipline of the frontier soldiers, at least to a degree.

Those who actually lived on the American frontier and chronicled their experiences recorded many events in the warfare between the tribes of the Great Plains. The new immigrants exploited this warfare, to be sure, although they also attempted many efforts at establishing peace between the tribes. These peace attempts were largely an illusion and temporary at best. Until the wars of the frontier were over near the end of the 19th Century, inter-tribal warfare was a fact in the American West.

Indian Scouts

In a list of battles and skirmishes between the United States Army and the American Indians between 1837 and 1891, published by the Adjutant General's office of the Army in the late 19th Century, participation by Indian scouts is never mentioned prior to 1866. Although in many of these actions Indian scouts certainly were involved, it was apparently not the policy to list them officially prior to the

Scout Curley

American Civil War. Beginning with 1866, however, the phrase "and Indian Scouts" appears repeatedly in the officially listed military actions and, in fact, many of the battles and skirmishes list only "Indian Scouts." The smaller picture of inter-tribal squabbles and conflicts was never, even near the end of the conflicts with the American Indian, able to be replaced by the bigger picture of inter-tribal unity to overcome the invasion by the new immigrants.

Not long after the Battle of the Little Big Horn, an article written by someone with General Crooks command, probably the reporter John Finnerty, was published in the *Chicago Tribune*. In this article the writer made the following observation concerning the Indian scouts with Crook's force.

> *General Crook's Indian allies, remind me that a few notes on their history and peculiar traits may be of interest. Above all other considerations which led the allies to participate in this war, in that of revenge. Looking back even beyond his childhood, the able-bodied Shoshone, Ute, or Crow know nothing of tradition or experience which does not whisper, "War to the knife with the Sioux!"*

In the historical records of the entire conflict between the American Indians and new immigrants, beginning with the Aztec and up to action at Grand River, Montana, in which four soldiers and eight Indians were killed on December 15, 1891, two weeks before the tragic Wounded Knee incident, it would appear that never was any major military action taken against Indians in which Indian allies did not participate. American Indians helped to conquer American Indians, and without that help the "civilization" of North America, if it would not have been impossible, certainly would have been immeasurably more difficult.

Taken Alive

During an archeological examination of Last Stand Hill, bullets from United States army issued .45 caliber Colt Revolvers were found vertically impacted into the ground with particles of human bone. This evidence would indicate that combatants were given final death shots from a government issued firearm.

There has been speculation that at the Battle of the Little Big Horn, Indian warriors took the army issued .45 Colt from wounded soldiers and then killed them with it. Is this an accurate theory, or is there another possibility?

Two factors would seem to indicate an alternative explanation. The first factor is that war was a mystical occupation for the American Indian warrior and, invariably, personal weapons were decorated with mystical symbols and totems. Frequently, these weapons had also been the subject of magical ceremonies to give them special powers over an enemy. It would seem unlikely that an Indian warrior would forego the opportunity to utilize his magical weapon in killing an enemy and, instead, pick up an unfamiliar weapon for this purpose.

The second factor concerning the Colt .45 bullets found vertically impacted on Last Stand Hill is that American Indians were usually in no hurry to kill an enemy, once this enemy had fallen under their power.

An ancient custom of nearly all of the tribes of North America gave an added element of horror to the wars among the American Indians themselves, and also between the Indians and the Immigrants. This was the taking of prisoners for the purpose of torture. Because of this frightful practice by the American Indian, the newcomers frequently responded with a brutality unseen in modern wars on the European continent, although there is considerable precedent in Europe's distant past. Except for isolated acts of sadism and political torture, however, torture was not practiced by the recent immigrants.

A French explorer named Samuel de Champlain witnessed the fate of an unfortunate Iroquois warrior captured by the Hurons and their allies in the 17th Century:

> *Then they tore out his nails, and put the fire on the ends of his fingers and on his privy member. Afterward, they flayed the top of his head and dripped on top of it a kind of gum all hot; then they pierced his arms near the wrists, and with sticks pulled out sinews, and tore them out by force; and when they saw that they could not get them they cut them.*

When invited to participate in the sadistic display, de Champlain declined and explained:

> *We kill them all at once.*

Experience of Nelson Lee

During the 1850s, the Comanche Indians captured a frontiersman named Nelson Lee, along with a Mr. Aikens and two other men, who found themselves confronting a ghastly fate. However, Mr. Lee, to his good fortune, had an alarm clock with him and this device eventually saved him. As the Indians did not clearly understand its purpose, they gave Lee an opportunity to demonstrate it.

Aware of the mystical beliefs of the Indians, Lee made appropriate gesticulations and motions toward the sky and sun while setting the alarm to go off in a few moments. The sudden ringing from the mysterious object had the desired effect of startling the Comanches, and Lee was now in the lucky position of being the object of curiosity and awe concerning this strange power. Two of his companions, named Stewart and Martin, were not so fortunate.

All four victims were hung upright by their arms from specially erected scaffolds, two side-by-side, and facing them the second two were hung. On this occasion Stewart and Martin were to hideously die while Lee and Aikens were forced to watch the dreadful display of their companions being slowly tortured to death. Mr. Lee recorded the fate these two unfortunate men suffered.

> *The Big Wolf* [the tribe chief] *and a number of his old men stationed themselves near us when the war chief, at the head of the warriors, of whom there were probably two hundred, moved forward slowly, silently and in single file.*
>
> *Their pace was peculiar and difficult to describe, half walk, half shuffle, a spasmodic, nervous motion, like the artificial motion of figures in a puppet show.*
>
> *Each carried in one hand his knife or tomahawk, in the other a flint stone, three inches or more in length and fashioned into the shape of a sharp, pointed arrow. The head of the procession, as it circled a long way round, first approached Stewart and Martin.*
>
> *As it passed them, two of the youngest warriors broke from the line, seized them by the hair, and scalped them, then resumed their places and moved on. This operation consists of cutting off only a portion of the skin which covers the skull, of the dimensions of a dollar, and does not necessarily destroy life, as is very generally supposed; in the contrary, I have seen men, resident on the borders of Texas, who had been scalped and yet were alive and well. In this instance, the wounds inflicted were by no means mortal; nevertheless, blood flowed from them in profusion, running down over the face, and trickling from their long beards.*
>
> *They passed Aikens and myself without molestation, marching round again in the same order as before. Up to this time there had been entire silence, except a yell from the two young men when in the act of scalping, but now the whole party halted a half-minute, and slapping their hands upon their mouths, united in a general and energetic war whoop. Then in silence the circuitous march was continued.*
>
> *When they reached Stewart and Martin the second time, the sharp flint arrowheads were brought into requisition. Each man, as he passed, with a wild screech, would brandish his tomahawk in their faces an instant, and then draw the sharp point of the stone across their bodies, not cutting deep, but penetrating the flesh just far enough to cause blood to ooze out in great crimson gluts.*
>
> *By the time the line had passed, our poor suffering companions presented an awful spectacle. Still they left Aikens and myself as yet unharmed; nevertheless, we regarded it as a matter of certainty that very soon we should be subjected to similar tortures.*
>
> *We would have been devoutly thankful at that terrible hour – would have hailed it as a grateful privilege – could we have been permitted to choose our own mode of being put to death. How many times they circled round, halting to sound the war whoop, and going through the same demonic exercise, I cannot tell.*
>
> *Suffice it to say, they persisted in the hellish work until every inch of the bodies of the unhappy men was haggled, and hacked and sacrificed, and covered with clotted blood. It would have been a relief to me, much more to them, could they have only died, but the object of the tormentors was to drain the fountain of their lives by slow degrees.*
>
> *In the process of their torture, there occurred an intermission of some quarter of an hour. During this period, some threw themselves on the ground and lighted their pipes, others collected in little groups, all, however, laughing and shouting and pointing their fingers at the prisoners in derision, as if taunting them as cowards and miscreants.*
>
> *The prisoners bore themselves differently. Stewart uttered not a word, but his sobs and groans were such as only the most intense pain and agony can wring from the human heart. On the contrary, the pitiful cries and prayers of Martin were unceasing. Constantly he was exclaiming – "Oh! God have mercy on me!" "Oh, Father in heaven pity me!" "Oh! Lord Jesus, come and put me out of pain!" – and many other expressions of like character.*
>
> *I hung down my head and closed my eyes to shut out from sight the heart-sickening scene before me, but this poor comfort was not vouchsafed to me. They*

would grasp myself, as well as Aikens, by the hair, drawing our heads back violently, compelling us, however unwillingly, to stare directly at the agonized and writhing sufferers.

At the end of perhaps two hours came the last act of the fearful tragedy. The warriors halted on their last round in the form of a half-circle when two of them moved out from the center, striking into the war dance, raising the war song, advancing, receding, now moving to the right, now to the left, occupying ten minutes in proceeding as many paces. Finally, they reached the victims, for some time danced before them, as it were, the hideous dance of hell, then drew their hatchets suddenly, and sent the bright blades crashing through their skulls.

Mr. Lee was eventually able to escape to write about his unpleasant adventure and Mr. Aikens was never heard from again, probably tortured to death.

Save the Last Bullet for Yourself

The new arrivals on the North American continent, having many centuries separating them from direct participation of such cruel rituals, naturally were appalled at what they viewed as the worst sort of savagery by the American Indians. Unlike the alleged stoic Indian of myth, they had no desire at all to prove their fortitude by being tortured to death and, in fact, held it in the greatest dread. The accounts of the era are full of references of the fear of being taken alive by the Indians and the newcomers considered this the worst possible fate and to be avoided at all costs.

A frontiersman by the name of Henry Bostwick related a fight with the Indians in which he feared he and his companions might be taken alive:

... Geery, Underwood, and myself, who belonged to the "fraternity," had a little side talk which resulted in each one declaring that if he got mortally wounded, he would reserve one shot that should prevent unnecessary sacrifice of the party by remaining to defend a man that must soon die anyway, and also to prevent torture, if captured.

In order to ascertain when we were mortally wounded, we agreed to have Jim examine and decide.

On the other hand, we agreed to remain by and defend each other as long as there was hope of the wounded man living. This understood, we talked it over with Jim, and finally with all the rest, who came to the same agreement.

During the Sioux uprising in Minnesota in 1862, Brigadier General Henry H. Sibley witnessed an incident, which he later wrote about in a letter dated September 19, 1862:

In company with my scouts, we pursued a poor German or Norwegian today supposing him to be an Indian and when he saw he could not escape, he attempted to cut his own throat to avoid being tortured by the Redskins, who he took us to be ... so entirely are these people imbued, naturally enough, with terror of Indians.

Custer, in his book, *My Life On The Plains*, wrote about a Cavalry trooper who was captured by the Indians:

All were too familiar with the horrid customs of the savages to hope for a moment that the captive would be reserved for aught but a slow lingering death from torture the most horrible and painful which savage, bloodthirsty minds could suggest. Such was in truth his sad fate, as we learned afterwards....

... The terrible fate awaiting the unfortunate trooper carried off by the Indians spread a deep gloom throughout the command.

Mrs. Elizabeth B. Custer wrote of an experience she had when Indian raiders had stampeded the mule herd outside Fort Lincoln in a surprise attack. The cavalrymen of the fort quickly mounted their horses and rode off in pursuit, leaving the post dangerously unguarded. Fearing that the raid had only been a ruse designed to draw off the soldiers, Mrs. Custer and the other women of the fort feared an imminent Indian attack. She wrote:

I do not think the actual fear of death was thought of so much as the all-absorbing fear of capture.... One of our members ... called a resolute woman to one side to implore her to promise that when the Indians came into the post, she would put a bullet through her heart....

A Frontiersman's View of Warfare Against the Indian

A book by author Jerry Howe titled, *Great West*, was published in 1851. In a chapter titled "Indian Warfare," Howe discussed his view on the subject, a view probably shared by many of his contemporaries. As the Frontier Army had not yet subdued the American Indians, Mr. Howe's published views have special significance.

The history of man is, for the most part, one continued detail of bloodshed, battles, and devastations. War has been, from the earliest periods of history, the almost constant employment of individuals, clans, tribes, and nations.

If the modern European laws of warfare have softened, in some degree, the horrid features of national conflicts by respecting the rights of private property and extending humanity to the sick, wounded, and prisoners; we ought to reflect that this amelioration is the effect of civilization only.

The Indian kills indiscriminately. His object is the total extermination of his enemies. Children are victims of his vengeance, because, if males, they may hereafter become warriors, or if females, they may become mothers. Even the fetal state is criminal in his view. It is not enough that the fetus should perish with the murdered mother, it is torn from her pregnant womb and elevated on a stick or pole as a trophy of victory and an object of horror to the survivors of the slain.

How is a war of extermination, and accompanied with such acts of atrocious cruelty, to be met by those on whom it is inflicted? Must it be met by the lenient maxims of civilized warfare? Must the Indian captive be spared his life? What advantage would be gained by this course? ... Send a cartel for an exchange of prisoners?

This sequel of the Indian wars goes to show that in a war with savages, the choice lies between extermination and subjugation. Our government has wisely and humanely pursued the latter course.

Mr. Howe undoubtedly expressed a point of view common to many of those who were confronted with, or heard harrowing tails of those who did, the war activities of the American Indian. The subject of captive torture, the "flaming torches to parched limbs" was a very real fear to those who suffered raids by the Indians. As the new arrivals in America were not about to leave, Howe identified only two choices available to his contemporaries concerning the Indian as "extermination or subjectation."

Yet, even after advocating the harshest measures against the American Indian, Mr. Howe apparently still felt a measure of civilized responsibility. In complementing the government for following "wisely and humanely" a policy which, at least, was not one of extermination, even Howe, as harsh as his point of view was, believed there was an alternative to extermination.

Revenge

J.S. Campion published a book in 1878 in which he related a personal experience he had and the effect it had on him and those he was with:

We daily saw the smoldering ruins of burned and gutted stations – busy scenes, when we had last passed that way, of life and motion. Lonely desolation had replaced activity and enterprise.

The unfortunates who had occupied them, then so full of confidence and hope, were murdered. All of them had been our acquaintances, some almost our friends. At one place, the bodies of a family of sixteen strewed the ground, looking ghastly and horrid in the bright light of day.

There they lay, all, from the gray-headed old grandfather to the last infant, the corpses of the sons, their wives and little ones; their sisters, the old man's three marriageable girls; an orphan grandchild all lay there, stripped, mutilated, partly charred. Decently and reverentially we put them "below wolf smell."

More bitter curses than prayers were said I fear over those graves by the rough and hardy mourners who stood round. "Lo the poor Indian" would have received scant mercy at their hands had a chance for vengeance presented itself.

In after years, more than once the memory of that scene has flashed through my mind, and, "Sergeant, pass the word quietly amongst the men that we can not be troubled with prisoners tomorrow," has been the result.

Geronimo

That an individual might find the remains of a massacre or a staked out victim of torture and suddenly become a merciless killer of guilty, or innocent, Indians probably happened many more times than history has recorded. Some even became psychopathic killers, obsessed only with finding and killing Indians. This is what seems to have happened to Captain Albert H. Pfeiffer. He was

witness to the killing of his wife by the Apaches in New Mexico, and in the words of author John Tebbel:

After this frightful experience, Pfeiffer became one of those men occasionally seen on the frontier obsessed with a hatred of Indians and devoting his life to killing them.

These were usually men who, like Pfeiffer, had seen some loved one killed or tortured. Although he continued to command troops and eventually became a Colonel, Pfeiffer went out alone whenever he could to hunt Indians.

He claimed that a wolf pack always followed him, knowing that eventually they would get Indian meat.

Of course, there were many similar situations that happened to the Indians where they had witnessed the killings of their family members and friends and became the mortal enemy of the whites. The Apache chief, Geronimo, had his wife and children killed in an attack on their village. Although he was not at the Battle of the Little Big Horn, he fought longer than any other Indian war chief and Geronimo did not surrender until 1886.

Sand Creek

Perhaps the event which, more than any other, symbolizes the ferocity of the wars of the American West was the attack on the Cheyenne camp at Sand Creek in Colorado on November 28, 1864. "Colonel" John Chivington led the third regiment of Colorado volunteers, which actually was a mob of angry citizens from Denver and not part of the regular Frontier Army, in an attack on an Indian village which, officially, was not at war.

In her book, *A Century of Dishonor*, published in 1881, author Helen Hunt Jackson quoted testimony from the United States Congress concerning what happened at Sand Creek:

Women and children were killed and scalped, children shot at their mothers' breasts, and all the bodies mutilated in the most horrible manner. The dead bodies of females profaned in such a manner that the recital is sickening, Colonel J.M. Chivington all the time inciting his troops to their diabolical outrages....

... I saw a man dismount from his horse and cut the ear from the body of an Indian, and the scalp from the head of another. I saw a number of children killed; they had bullet holes in them; one child had been cut with some sharp instrument across its side. I saw another that both ears had been cut off....

There was one little child, probably three years old, just big enough to walk through sand. The Indians had gone ahead, and this little child was behind, following

after them. The little fellow was perfectly naked, traveling in the sand. I saw one man get off his horse at a distance of about seventy-five yards and draw up his rifle and fire. He missed the child. Another man came up and said, "Let me try the son of a b——. I can hit him." He got down off his horse, kneeled down, and fired at the little child, but he missed him. A third man came up, and made a similar remark, and fired, and the little fellow dropped....

A letter dated Feb. 6, 1880, by W.N. Byers, was printed in the *New York Tribune* and attempted to justify what was known at the time, and also to history, as the "Sand Creek Massacre."

... most of the warriors were engaged in raiding the great Platte River Road, seventy-five miles further north, robbing and burning trains, stealing cattle and horses, robbing and destroying the United States mails, and killing white people. During the summer and fall they had murdered over fifty of the citizens of Colorado.

They had stolen and destroyed provisions and merchandise, and driven away stock worth hundreds of thousands of dollars. They had interrupted the mails, and for thirty-two consecutive days none were allowed to pass their lines.

When satiated with murder and arson, and loaded with plunder, they would retire to their sacred refuge on Sand Creek to rest and refresh themselves, recruit their wasted supplies of ammunition from Fort Lyon – begged under the garb of gentle, peaceful savages – and then return to the road to relieve their tired comrades, and riot again in carnage and robbery....

... in Denver, in the early part of that summer ... the bloated, festering bodies of the Hungate family – father, mother, and two babes – were drawn through the streets naked in an ox wagon, cut, mutilated, and scalped – the work of those same red fiends who were so justly punished at Sand Creek.

Sand Creek was the classic example of how one atrocity gained momentum from previous atrocities. If the statement of Byers is true, then the Indian camp at Sand Creek was the often repeated story of a tribe officially at peace that still had young warriors making raids of opportunity whenever convenient. Brutality on the American frontier was a two-way avenue and at Sand Creek a fearsome massacre resulted. Some sources say up to 450 men, women, and children were killed.

Extermination

The fearful atrocities were mutual, with the exception of the torture ritual, and many western newspapers were vocal in calling for a "final solution" to the "Indian problem." Many western newspapers did not hesitate in calling for the extermination of the American Indians and frequently were joined by the eastern newspapers. After the Battle of the Little Big Horn, many newspapers renewed this demand. The *St. Louis Dispatch* of July 10, 1876, had a chilling editorial:

It would seem that the only recourse left is to declare the hostile element of this race dangerous to the lives and property of good citizens and they should therefore be exterminated as we would exterminate other vampires of the woods.

The *Bismarck Tribune* of July 12, 1876, also carried a lengthy editorial that gave elaborate justification for the harshest measures against the hostile tribes:

What effect the Custer massacre will have upon the country and upon the legislation of Congress remains to be seen. The people will probably realize that they have an Indian war upon their hands of no small magnitude. And if we do not mistake the temper of the Americans, they will demand a prosecution of the war in a manner so vigorous that the fiends of the plains will be glad to surrender their arms as an earnest of their desire for peace.

Let the government establish Indian posts – not agencies – at points where it is most convenient to feed those that justice to distressed humanity requires must be fed, and require them to go there or die of war and famine on the plains.

Let that Christian philanthropy which weeps over the death of a lazy, lousy, lying, stealing redskin, whose hands are still reeking with the blood of defenseless women and children, slain on the frontier, and who are

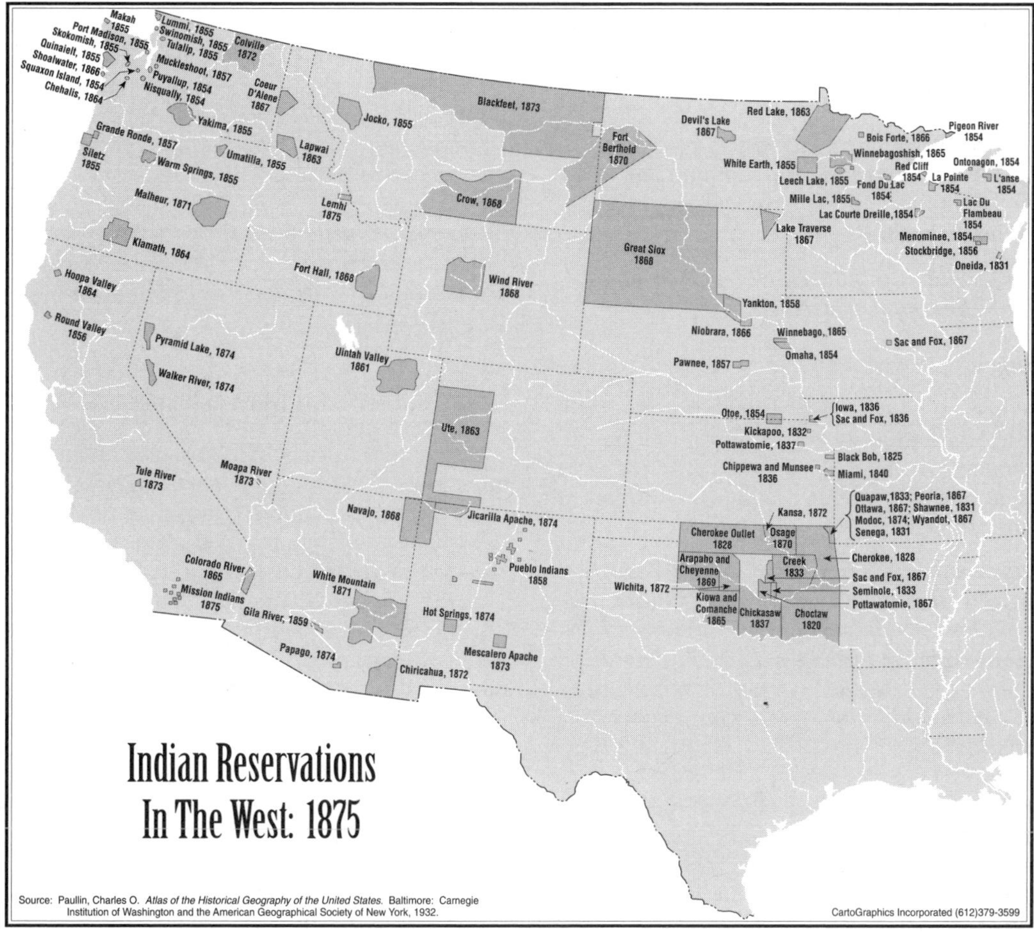

ever ready to apologize for these murderers, take a back seat. Invite the soldier to the front and sustain him while he causes the Indians to realize the power, and these that still live to respect the white man.

Wipe out all treaties, rub out all agencies and reservations, and treat the Indians as they are, criminals and paupers. Feed those that justice to distressed humanity requires should be fed; hang or shoot the murderers, whose crimes are clearly proven; confine those who deserve punishment of a less degree; give the remainder the chance that white men have to gain land, property or a living, and hold them accountable to the same laws that white men and Negroes are required to respect, or cause them to suffer the consequences of a violation of those laws.

Some of the military leaders who fought the Indians also advocated extermination. One of these men was General Torobri, who served in the American west in the period after the Civil War. Concerning attacks on Indian camps, he said:

The confessed aim is to exterminate everyone.

Then, with the icy pragmatism sometimes found among those engaged in war, he added:

... if extermination were not achieved just another burden would be added; prisoners.

Captain Robert G. Carter, who was a member of the 4th Cavalry and fought under Colonel Ranald S. Mackenzie after the Civil War on the western plains of America, spoke of a conference between the Secretary of War, Lt. General Philip H. Sheridan and Mackenzie just before an Indian campaign was launched. The orders given by General Sheridan were:

I want you to be bold, enterprising, and at all times full of energy. When you begin, let it be a campaign of annihilation, obliteration, and complete destruction.... I think you understand what I want done.

Colonel Mackenzie should have understood what Sheridan wanted done, as the words "annihilation, obliteration, and destruction," seem to have left little to the imagination. This campaign, incidentally, involved Mackenzie

crossing the Mexican border under threat of an international incident and destroying Indian camps that were being used as a refuge for raids into Texas. Mackenzie did return with prisoners, so he did not follow Sheridan's shocking orders to the letter.

In an interview published in the *St. Paul Pioneer Press* on July 16, 1876, General Sherman, the Commander of the Army, was asked about the further prosecution of the war with the Sioux and their allies.

> *"Is there any probability that the war will be one of extermination?" Sherman was asked.*
>
> *"It is not unlikely," Sherman replied.*

The many public calls for extermination after the Battle of the Little Big Horn finally became too much for the *St. Paul Pioneer Press*, which responded on July 18, 1876, with an editorial entitled "White Savageism," a part of which is reproduced here.

> *A correspondent wants the Indians exterminated root and branch, old and young, male and female, in revenge for the horrible butchery of our troops on the Little Big Horn and other atrocities which had not the excuse of a state of hostilities. We notice sentiments only a little less bloodthirsty cropping out in several newspapers.*
>
> *We trust the civilized men are few who are really sincere in the utterance of such savage sentiments, or who would not recoil with horror from any attempt to give practical effect to the barbarous vindictiveness they thoughtlessly express.*

The *St. Paul Pioneer Press* was, of course, not the only newspaper that cautioned for moderation toward the American Indian after the Battle of the Little Big Horn. Of all the bloody incidents that occurred during the conquest of America, the defeat of the 7th Cavalry at Little Big Horn was perhaps one of the least worthy of "revenge." The soldiers had, after all, been armed combatants on an expedition in search of the hostile Sioux. The 7th Cavalry had found the Sioux, fought them, and lost.

Women and Children Killed

Many modern sources have often accused the American frontier army of indiscriminately killing Indian women and children. One of the reasons that women and children were frequently killed during the attacks on an Indian camp was the fact that everyone who could fight did, and this included all of the women and most of the children old enough to hold a weapon. Captain Carter commented upon the Indian woman's willingness to fight in an emergency.

> *When cornered, she fought with all the strength of her savage nature and the desperation of a tigress, using her bow and arrows and six-shooter with both of which she was an excellent and most effective shot....*
>
> *... As good as the warrior himself; fighting like a fiend with the same deadly weapons, and mixing in with the former, it was then rarely the case that more or less squaws were not killed and wounded in our attacks upon their villages.*
>
> *There was little or no time for false sentiment, courtesy, or knightly gallantry in the face of a "gun" in the hands of an infuriated squaw intent on "getting" somebody.*

History of Inhumanity

History is replete with inhumanity and no culture is without it in its background. It is a disturbing phenomenon that lurks like an evil shadow throughout human development for which philosophers, and even modern psychologists, have yet to give a satisfactory explanation.

At the height of the development of Western Civilization, during the era of the Roman Empire, huge displays were made of mass torture and execution in the infamous arenas, and it is a much cherished tradition of Christianity that many were put to death there because of their beliefs.

Unfortunately, Christianity, while founded upon the concept of human respect, had also sunk into the depths of human cruelty during the past. During what is known as the "Inquisition," mass torturing and killing took place. Those who did not agree with the theologians, who were also allied with the ruling classes, were brutally murdered.

Concerning torture, however, civilization was able to add one refinement during the Inquisition that primitive cultures were unable to give to their victims, although there is no reason to believe they wouldn't have, had they been able to. This was the added bonus of being charged for the various tortures applied. In Germany the following pricing guide was used in determining the fees for torture that the victim was charged.

> *For terrorizing by showing the instruments of torture – 1 thaler* [a thaler was a medium of exchange].
>
> *For the first degree of torture – 1 1/2 thalers.*
>
> *For arranging and crushing the thumb for this degree – 3 thaler.*
>
> *For the second degree of torture, including setting the limbs afterward, and for salve which is used – 2 1/4 thalers.*
>
> *For cutting out the tongue entirely, or part of it, and afterward for burning the mouth with a red-hot iron – 5 thalers.*
>
> *For cutting off a hand or every finger and for behead-*

ing, all together – 3¹/₄ thalers.

For beheading only 2¹/₂ thalers.

For breaking alive on the wheel – 4 thalers.

For rope and chains for this procedure – 2 thalers.

For beheading and burning, everything included – 5¹/₄ thalers.

While having one's thumb crushed for a mere 3 thalers, or a complete "beheading and burning" for 5¹/₄ thalers, would seem to be a reasonable enough charge, the massive volume of victims made the official torturer a wealthy person who, in one city, rode a horse "like a noble of the court and went clad in gold and silver."

Of course, to make this process legal, the victim must have proper representation which, with diligence, could perhaps spare the victim "everything included," although any confession without torture was considered invalid. How much one would pay to have only a few fingers crushed instead of "everything included" probably depended only upon that person's resources. Good economic sense required this profitable enterprise, like all economic ventures, to have a business plan, and it did. This business plan is described by one author:

The Inquisition required a regular supply of suspects for its survival; therefore, torture was applied to produce the names of accomplices.

Theoretically, the process, once started, would continue until the only people left alive were the lawyers and the torturer.

Had the Inquisition remained in the hands of lawyers and torturers, it might remain a phenomenon today. Fortunately, however, common decency prevailed and at least the torturer has been eliminated from this impenitent duo.

The Fate of Prisoners

The historical fate of prisoners taken in battle has never been a happy one. Plato in 400 B.C. declared that a soldier who gives up in battle deserved whatever fate befell him. However, two occurrences, one of unrecorded origins, the other of the twentieth century, gave a prisoner value, or at least placed restrictions on how he should be treated.

The first, ironically, was the creation of the institution of slavery. Previous to this the life of a prisoner had no value at all to the victor and therefore the prisoner was invariably killed. As civilization progressed, and labor-intensive agriculture increased as part of economies, the value of prisoner labor also increased. While this progression might be considered dubious, given a choice most captives probably would have preferred involuntary labor to being put to death. Slavery, after all, held the possibility of eventual freedom.

The second event occurred in 1907 with the *Hague Regulations*, which provided international rules for the treatment of prisoners of war. The practice of "no quarter" was outlawed as well as providing for humane conditions for prisoners of war. Although the *Hague Regulations* were frequently ignored by warring nations, these regulations were expanded by the *Geneva Convention* of 1929 and subsequent international agreements. It is then only in the twentieth century that the prisoner of war has, if only in theory, been given any guarantee of humane treatment.

The *Geneva Conventions*, the first occurring in 1929 and later ratified by over 150 nations, officially outlawed torture internationally. Primitive torture was a sadistic act. Most modern torture used by governments is for political purposes: terror and information, although any distinction is probably meaningless to the victim. Torture is defined by *Amnesty International* as:

... any act by which severe pain or suffering, whether physical or mental, is intentionally inflicted ... an aggravated and deliberate form of cruel, inhumane or degrading treatment or punishment.

The *Amnesty International* definition of torture is about as good as any, and the fact that civilization has progressed to the point of outlawing this frightful human practice, as well as threatening sanctions for the practice of it, hopefully will give those of the future cause to be appalled at the past, but not doomed to repeat it.

Torture and War

The psychological motivation for humans to inflict deliberate suffering upon others has yet to be adequately defined. Dr. Ronald Markman has been a

psychiatrist extensively involved in modern criminal behavior and has studied deviant behavior in many criminals, including members of the infamous Manson family. In his book *Alone with the Devil Doctor* Markman said:

> *What we may believe is our birthright of civilization and moral behavior is actually a veneer stretched tenuously over a violent, molten core of immense passions, drives, and desires.*

Sabine Baring-Gould, whose accomplishments include the authorship of over 100 books and many songs, including *Onward Christian Soldiers*, made an interesting, if unpleasant, observation of his fellow humans that is similar to that of Doctor Markman. Baring-Gould said:

> *Startling though the assertion may be, it is a matter of fact that man, naturally in common with other carnivores, is actuated by an impulse to kill and by love of destroying life. It is positively true that there are many to whom the sight of suffering causes genuine pleasure and in whom the passion to kill or torture is as strong as any other passion.*

Sabine Baring-Gould's assertion that the urge to kill and cause suffering is a passion is not a pleasant one. The urge to kill is common to carnivores. However, the urge to deliberately cause suffering seems to be a distinctly human characteristic.

It may be, however, that torture practiced for sadistic purposes, as it was by the American Indians, is a learned and not an inherited phenomenon. It is a fact that values and beliefs taught to a child invariably will become part of their personality and in this respect the American Indians were victims of their own culture. How damaging the practice of torture was to the development of the culture of the American Indian can only be speculated.

Torture and war, and revenge for torture and war, created what would appear to have been an endless cycle for the American Indian. There was no escape for any individual and violence was so much a part of the culture of the American Indian that without an outside force acting upon it there is no reason to believe that the twentieth century would have been any different than any preceding century.

The changes that occurred with advancement of Western Civilization into the North American continent may not have been gentle, and could have been more wisely implemented, but these changes were for the better. Certainly America has known an entire century free from outside aggression. In fact, if one excludes the bandit Pancho Villa's raiding of the American southwest, Germany's submarine sinking of American ships off the east coast, and Japan's sending of paper balloons on the atmospheric jet stream with fire bombs attached in an attempt to burn up the United States, war has not touched the North American continent in the twentieth century.

Broken Trust

The defeat of the American Indian was inevitable. Yet, had a wise and uncorrupted policy been consistently followed by the government, the wars with the Indian might have been over by the year 1876 and the Battle of the Little Big Horn might never have occurred.

Many of the authorities who have studied the relationship between the government and the American Indian state that there was never a treaty made between the two that was not broken or violated, most of the time by the government. If this contention is not one-hundred percent true, then it is true enough to be perhaps the mostunfortunate and reproachable element of American history. The way of life of the American Indian, it may be argued, was doomed by the course of world progress and by the isolation of the American continent, long before the first European arrived in the "New World." However, the manner in which "civilization" was brought to the American Indian is in many ways a study in perfidy.

While volumes could be, and have been, written concerning the frauds perpetrated against the American Indian, this unfortunate situation should also be weighed in the context of forces that have shaped American history. The vast opportunities of land and resources that were available in America drew the disadvantaged of Europe like a magnet. There never was an organized or planned conquest of America. No sooner had the eastern coast been settled than new waves of immigrants arrived to push the borders of the original thirteen colonies further west. Innumerable wars followed this western expansion, fought by the American Indians defending their homeland against the unending numbers of new immigrants.

By the end of the American Civil War the government

had implemented a policy of setting aside lands for the American Indian: the reservation system. Also a system of compensation designed to assist them from the transformation of nomadic life to that of a stable domestic environment based upon agriculture was official government policy. Unfortunately, this system was poorly implemented and was subjected to monumental corruption by dishonest government officials as well by many others seeking personal gain.

The Observations of Granville Stuart

Granville Stuart was a gold miner, trader, and rancher in the Montana Territory shortly after the American Civil War. Stuart, as an eye-witness observer, later wrote of the wide-spread frauds perpetrated against the American Indian.

> *There was also the Indian ring. Many persons made huge fortunes furnishing supplies to the government for the Indians and the armies in the country. It was owing largely to the influence of these unscrupulous persons that Indian affairs were conducted as they were....*
>
> *In 1874, Major Maginnis (our then delegate to Congress) explained to an Indian commission why it was that the Indian appropriations were increasing at the rate of a million dollars a year and yet the Indians were dissatisfied and continually on the war path. He said that he had personal knowledge of the operations of the Indian bureau and Indian agents.*
>
> *They will take a barrel of sugar to an Indian tribe and get a receipt for ten barrels. For a sack of flour, the Indians sign a receipt for fifty sacks. The agent will march three-hundred head of cattle four times through a corral, get a receipt for twelve-hundred head, give a part of them to the Indians, sell part to a white man, and steal as many back as possible....*

In the literature of the era there are many commentaries similar or identical with that of Mr. Stuart's. Unfortunately, although the corruption that pervaded the Indian agencies and reservations was well documented, there seemed to be little official action taken by the authorities in the government to stop or prevent the widespread cheating of the American Indian.

The Observations of Major Brisbin

Shortly after the Battle of the Little Big Horn, Major James Brisbin of the 2nd Cavalry was interviewed by a news reporter. He had shortly before walked the field of the Battle of the Little Big Horn and assisted in burying the bodies of those members of the 7th Cavalry killed by Indian warriors. Brisbin was, nevertheless, sufficiently aware of the corrupt practices that had victimized the Indians to remain sympathetic to their legitimate complaints. In this interview Brisbin said:

> *It* [the government] *sends out men who are to act as Agents of the Indians and carry out treaty stipulations, but most of these men spend their time in defrauding, demoralizing, and abusing the Indians in every conceivable manner. I do not believe one-half, possibly not more than one-fourth, of the supplies annually voted by congress ever reach the Indians.*
>
> *The abuses that are perpetrated by these agents are perfectly shameful, and still it goes on from year to year, and there appears to be no relief from these public thieves. Why, if I were an Indian, I would whet my tomahawk and sink it into the brain of the first white man I met. If one has to choose whether he will die by starvation or fall fighting, he had better fight for his rights like a man than starve like a dog.*

Custer on the Corruption of the Indian Agents

Practically every military officer who served on the western frontier of America commented upon the incredible corruption practiced by agents of the government. Prominent among these military men were George Crook, Robert Carter, Nelson Miles, John Gibbon, and Custer. In his book *My Life on the Plains,* Custer wrote about the abuses the American Indian suffered:

> *Under the Constitution of the United States, there are but two houses of Congress, the Senate and the House of Representatives, and most people residing within the jurisdiction of its laws suppose this to be the extent of the legislative body; but to those acquainted with the internal working of that important branch of the government, there is still a third house of Congress, better known as the lobby.*
>
> *True, its existence is neither provided for nor recognized by law; yet it exists nevertheless, and so powerful, although somewhat hidden, is its influence upon the other branches of Congress, that almost any measure it is interested in becomes a law.*
>
> *It is somewhat remarkable that those measures which are plainly intended to promote the public interests are seldom agitated or advocated in the third house, while those measures of doubtful propriety or honesty usually secure the almost undivided support of the lobby.*
>
> *There are few prominent questions connected with the feeble policy of the government which can and do assemble so powerful and determined a lobby as a proposed interference with the system of civilian superintendents, agents, and traders for the Indians.*

Let but some member of Congress propose to inquire into the workings of the management of the Indians, or propose a transfer of the bureau to the War Department, and the leaders of the combination opposed raise a cry which is as effective in rallying their supporters as was the signal of Roderick Dhu.

From almost every state and territory, the retainers of the bureau flock to the national capital. Why this rallying of the clans? Is there any principle involved? With the few, yes; with the many, no. Then what is the mighty influence which brings together this hungry host? Why this determined opposition to any interference with the management of the Indians?

I remember making this inquiry years ago, and the answer then, which is equally applicable now, was: "There is too much money in the Indian question to allow it to pass into other hands." This I believe to be the true solution of our difficulties with the Indians at the present day.

It seems almost incredible that a policy which is claimed and represented to be based on sympathy for the red man and a desire to secure to him his rights, is shaped in reality and manipulated behind the scenes with the distinct and sole object of reaping a rich harvest by plundering both the government and the Indians.

To do away with the vast army of agents, traders, and civilian employees, which is a necessary appendage of the civilian policy, would be to deprive many members of Congress of a vast deal of patronage which they now enjoy. There are few, if any, more comfortable or desirable places of disposing of a friend who has rendered valuable political service or electioneering aid than to secure for him the appointment of Indian agent.

The salary of an agent is comparatively small. Men without means, however, eagerly accept the position; and in a few years, at furthest, they almost invariably retire in wealth.

Who ever heard of a retired Indian agent or trader in limited circumstances? How do they realize fortunes upon so small a salary?

In the disposition of the annuities provided for the Indians by the government, the agent is usually the distributing medium. Between himself and the Indian, there is no system of accountability, no vouchers given or received, no books kept, in fact no record except the statement which the agent chooses to forward to his superintendent.

The Indian has no means of knowing how much in value or how many presents of any particular kind the government, the "Great Father" as he terms it, has sent him. For knowledge on this point, he must accept the statement of the agent.

The goods sent by the government are generally those which would most please an Indian's fancy. The Indian trader is most frequently a particular friend of the agent, often associated with him in business, and in many instances holds his position of trader at the instance of the agent. They are always located near each other. The trader is usually present at the distribution of annuities.

If the agent, instead of distributing to the Indians all of the goods intended for them by the government, only distributes one-half and retains the other half, who is to be the wiser? Not the Indian, defrauded though he may be, for he is ignorant of how much is coming to him. The word of the agent is his only guide.

He may complain a little, express some disappointment at the limited amount of presents, and intimate that the "Great Father" has dealt out the annuities with a sparing hand; but the agent explains it by referring to some depredations which he knows the tribe to have been guilty of in times past; or if he is not aware of any particular instance of guilt, he charges them generally with having committed such acts, knowing one can scarcely go amiss in accusing a tribe of occasionally slaying a white man, and ends up his charge by informing them that the "Great Father," learning of these little irregularities in their conduct and being pained greatly thereat, felt compelled to reduce their allowance of blankets, sugar, coffee, etc., when at the same time the missing portion of said allowance is sagely secured in the storehouse of the agent nearby.

Well, but how can he enrich himself in this manner? it may be asked. By simply, and unseen by the Indians, transferring the unissued portion of the annuities from his government storehouse to the trading establishment of his friend the trader. There the boxes are unpacked and their contents spread out for barter with the Indians.

The latter, in gratifying their wants, are forced to purchase from the trader at prices which are scores of times the value of the article offered. I have seen Indians dispose of buffalo robes to traders, which were worth from fifteen to twenty dollars each, and get in return only ten to twenty cups of brown sugar, the entire value of which did not exceed two or three dollars. This is one of the many ways agents and traders have of amassing sudden wealth.

I have known the head chief of a tribe to rise in a council in the presence of other chiefs and officers of the army, and accuse his agent, then present, of these or similar dishonest practices.

It is to be wondered at that the position of agent or trader among the Indians is greatly sought after by men determined to become rich, but not particular as to the manner of doing so? Or is it to be wondered at that army officers, who are often made aware of the injustice done the to Indian, yet are powerless to prevent it, and who trace many of our difficulties with the Indians to these causes, should urge the abolishment of a system which has proven itself so fruitful in fraud and dishonest dealing toward those whose interest it should be their duty to protect?

Being subject to the authority of the government, it should be noted that Custer, as well as the other military officers who wrote, or spoke out, against the corrupt practices the American Indian was subjected to, did so at risk of their military careers. The fact that these officers chose to publicly voice their concerns is testimony to the legitimacy of their concern as well as to their integrity.

Bishop Whipple

Not long after the Battle of the Little Big Horn a clerical leader of Minnesota, Bishop Henry B. Whipple, wrote a letter to the President of the United States in which he detailed his concern for the policies of the government toward the American Indian. This letter was published in the *Army and Navy Journal* on August 26, 1876.

... The nation left 300,000 men living within our own borders without a vestige of government, without personal rights of property, without the slightest protection of person, property, or life. We persisted in telling these heathen tribes that they were independent nations. We sent out the bravest and best of our officers, some who had grown gray in the service of the country; men whose slightest word was as good as their bond – we sent them because the Indians would not doubt a soldier's honor.

They made a treaty and they pledged the nation's faith

that no white man should enter that territory. I do not discuss its wisdom. The Executive and Senate ratified it.... A violation of its plain provisions was an act of deliberate perjury. In the words of General Sherman, "Civilization made its own compact with the weaker party; it was violated, but not by the savage."

It was done by a civilized nation. The treaty was approved by the whole nation. The people and press approved it, because it ended a shameful Indian war, which had cost us $30,000,000, and the lives of ten white men for every Indian slain. The whole world knew that we violated that treaty, and the reason of the failure of the negotiations of last year was that our own Commissioners did not have authority from Congress to offer the Indians more than one-third of the sum they were already receiving under the old treaty.

Here are two pictures – on one side of the line a nation has spent $500,000,000 in Indian war; a people who have not 100 miles between the Atlantic and the Pacific which has not been the scene of an Indian massacre; a Government which has not passed twenty years without an Indian war; not one Indian tribe to whom it has given Christian civilization, and which celebrates its centennial year by another bloody war.

On the other side of the line there is the same greedy, dominant Anglo-Saxon race, and the same heathen. They have not spent one dollar in Indian war; they have had no Indian massacres. Why? In Canada the Indian treaty calls these men "the Indian subjects of her Majesty." When civilization approaches them, they are placed on ample reservations; they receive aid in civilization; they have personal rights of property; they are amenable to law and are protected by law; they have schools, and Christian people delight to give them their best men to teach them the religion of Christ. We expend more than one hundred dollars to their one in caring for Indian wards....

In essence, the only disagreement between Bishop Whipple and the military men who spoke out on behalf of the American Indian, was whether the Indian Bureau should, or should not, be placed under military command. The Military believed that by placing the Indian Bureau under their direction the corruption could be eliminated, while Bishop Whipple believed making the Bureau a separate department would serve the same purpose, to better advantage.

Little Robe of the Cheyennes

An account exists by Little Robe, who was a chief of the Cheyenne Indians in the 19th Century, in which he recounted the expansion of civilization in the American West and the hardships this had caused the American Indian.

We crowded around the strangers when they made camp and one of our traders told us they were headed for the shore of the big waters far away in the land of the setting sun. We did not see harm in these people passing through our country, so we told them where to find water and grass many days ahead of them.

Not long after we saw these strange people, soldiers came, and their chiefs asked us to make an agreement with them to always allow white people to make a trail through our land to the land of the setting sun. We saw no harm in that, the country was large enough for us all, and they agreed not to tarry in our country and to pass through. These soldier chiefs brought others who said they were sons of a Great White Father who lived many weeks, travel to the East.

We went into conference with them while the soldiers looked on, they gave us presents and our hearts felt good. When they asked us to press our thumbs on a piece of paper to show we made friends with them, we did so, and told all our people to be good to the strangers, and not to molest them.

Soon after the first, we saw many more coming along the trail. We watched them, for they were new to us and we were always curious. When we had the pow-wow with the soldier chiefs and the sons of The Great White Father, we had invited them all to sit in the lodge we had put up. We sat in a circle and The Whirlwind had lit the pipe and passed it to each man on his left.

All had smoked, and we always knew that when any one smoked in the circle under cover of the lodge, he agreed to whatever was spoken of. The Indians felt that way; it was their custom; no one had ever broken such an agreement.

Another day, white soldiers came, who stopped at a point on the new trail. Without explaining, they simply told us they had come to 'sit down' at that spot in our country. We had not known they would do this, else we would not have agreed. When we told the soldier chief, he said the Great White Father had sent them. Our people talked it over and agreed there was some mistake. These soldiers cut down many trees and built a big corral with wooden tepees inside. They had many guns.

Then we knew they were going to stay, and we began to worry. We asked for another council to talk it over and find why our first treaty had been broken. There was not much explanation; they said we must make a new treaty. They asked us to give them some land

along the Platte River to the Big Muddy East, and as far as we owned the hunting ground rights up to the Big Mountains, and a day's travel toward the uphill side of the World.

We were worried and sent runners to the villages of our friends and cousins in the Indian family, the Cut-Throats, Sioux, Cut-Noses, Arapaho, and called them to a pow-wow. Many days we thought of our problem, while we chiefs retired apart and prayed to The Great One Above and listened for his voice in the grass. We decided not to fight yet, but to agree to another treaty.

We sat in conference again and smoked the pipe, than placed our thumbs on a new paper, agreeing to give the land which was asked of us. From that day we knew no peace. More white people came and sat down where we had not agreed.

Our hearts were bad, we painted our ponies for war, took our women, children, and old people away where they were safe, and fought for our land. The Once Below seemed to work his will against us. The Great One Above did not send us any good signs. We were beaten, and signed new treaties because we hoped the whites would become satisfied each time.

We had to save our people. But we were at war all the time; our people could not stay in one spot for a home, even for seven suns. The snows of twenty winters had fallen on us before we came to Sand Creek with our lodges. We had gone to a pow-wow at Fort Bent just before that, they asked us to leave all our new guns and go into camp for the winter. We believed the first Agent, Wyncoop, and did as they said. Black Kettle quieted our young men.

You know what happened. Our camp was attacked and hundreds of unarmed people were killed, and they did not spare our women and children....

The white men lied to us, they were dogs, who called us savages....

The view of Little Robe was undoubtedly shared by many American Indians undergoing the dramatic changes which occurred in the 19th century. Under any circumstances, the change from a nomadic life to one which was "civilized" would have been difficult. However, the perfidious conduct of many of those who came into direct contact with the Indian inevitably caused similar reactions to that of Little Robe.

Charles Larpenter: Frontiersman on Wars

The widespread cheating of the American Indian, frequently with official or semi-official blessing, was not the only injustice suffered by the Indian and also not the worst. Wars are never pleasant and acts of treachery a frequent occurrence. Many times the Indians were, under the pretense of friendship, lured into situations where they were killed. Mr. Charles Larpenter, a frontiersman in the American West prior to the Civil War, left an account of a particularly vicious attack on Indians who were, at least until that point, friendly.

They also got old man Berger to join them. The plot was, when the band came to trade, to invite three of the head men into the fort, where Harvey was to have the cannon in the bastion, which commanded the front door loaded with balls; when the Indians should be gathered thickly at the door, waiting for the trade to commence, at a given signal the three head men were to be massacred in the fort, and Harvey was to kill as many others as he could at one discharge; on which they expected the surviving Indians to run away, abandoning all their robes and horses, of which the three whites were to become the owners, share and share alike.

But it did not happen quite to their satisfaction; for, through some means, the wicked plot was made known in time for the chiefs to run out of the office and escape by jumping over the pickets. Mr. Chardon was quick enough to shoot, and broke the thigh of the principal chief.

Harvey touched off the cannon, but, as the Indians had commenced to scatter, he killed but three and wounded two. The rest quickly made their escape, leaving all their plunder, but saving nearly all their horses, mostof which were at some distance from the fort.

After firing the shot, Harvey came out of the bastion and finished the wounded Indians with his large [dagger]. *I was told he then licked the blood off the* [dagger] *and afterward made the squaws of the fort dance the scalp dance around the scalps, which he had raised himself....*

There are many incidents, some even more horrible than the one recounted by Mr. Larpenter, that were documented during the settlement of the west. It can be imagined that many other similar events were unrecorded. This type of treacherous massacre, however, would have been well known to the Indians of the west and, combined with the swindling and broken treaties that victimized the Indian, it is not surprising that, even by the year 1876, Sitting Bull was able to raise an army of thousands of Indian warriors to challenge the government.

CHAPTER 3

General Custer — Captain Kidd — The American Cavalry in the Civil War — General Lee's Surrender — 7th Cavalry — Officers of the 7th Cavalry — Captain Frederick Benteen — The Scouts — California Joe — Wild Bill Hickok

Lieutenant Charles DeRudio

Custer is well-known to historians as commander of the 7th Cavalry at its defeat at the Battle of the Little Big Horn in 1876. Custer was, however, well-known among his contemporaries previous to this.

The *Dictionary of American Biography* of 1872, published four years before the Battle of the Little Big Horn, contains the following entry by F. S. Drake:

Custer, George A.,
Brev. Major General U. S. A.,
b. New Rumley, OH., Dec. 5, 1839.
West Point, 1861.

Entering the second cavalry, he served in the Potomac Army; was aide to McClellan, and engaged at Yorktown, So. Mountain, Antietam, and Stoneman's raid; was aide to General Pleasonton; Brigadier General of Vols. 29 June, 1863; held with his cavalry brigade the right of the line at Gettysburg; Commander A brigade of the Cavalry Corps in the Richmond campaign, April to August, 1864; and of the 3rd Division Cavalry Corps in Shenandoah Valley, October '64 to March '65.

He routed the rebel rear-guard at Falling Waters; at Winchester, he captured 9 battle-flags, and more men than he had engaged; rendered most important service at Fisher's Hill; Brev. Major General for conduct at Cedar Creek; routed General Rosser, Oct. 9, 1864; and at Waynesboro, captured the remnant of Early's army, ab. 18,000 strong, in Feb. 1865.

In the battles of the campaign ending in the surrender of General Robert E. Lee, Custer commanded a cavalry division, and bore a most important part; distinguishing himself at Dinwiddie C.H., at Five Forks, Sailor Creek, and finally at Appomattox C.H., and April 15, 1865, was made Major General of Vols.

He never lost a gun or a color, captured more guns, flags, and prisoners than any other General not an army commander, and was exceptionally fortunate in his career.

Lieutenant Colonel, 7th Cavalry, 28 July, 1866; Brev. Major for Gettysburg; Lieutenant Colonel for Yellow Tavern, Va., 11 May, 1864; Colonel for Winchester, 19 Sept. 1864; Brigadier General for Five Forks, and Major General U. S. A., for services ending in Lee's surrender.

At the end of the Civil War, like most officers of the regular army, Custer was reduced to his permanent army rank, which was lieutenant colonel. His full title, however, included Brevet Major General of Volunteers and, as a courtesy, Custer was referred to in official correspondence, publications, and by fellow military persons as "General."

General Custer

George Armstrong Custer was born December 5, 1839 in the small community of New Rumley, Ohio. His father, Emanuel, was a blacksmith in the town of Scio, three miles from New Rumley. George Custer's mother, Maria Ward Fitzpatrick, was Emanuel's second wife. Emanuel's first wife died in 1835, leaving him with three children, and Maria had two children by a previous marriage. George was their third child together, the first two having died in infancy. Four more children followed George: Nevin, Thomas, Boston, and Margaret.

All but Nevin were to join George Custer in his last years at Fort Lincoln, Dakota Territory. Thomas and Boston were to die with their brother at the Battle of the Little Big Horn, as well as Margaret's husband, 1st Lieutenant James Calhoun.

Emanuel Custer was a spirited father to his children, playing and scuffling with them as though he were a child himself. The children had been described as being undisciplined, while at the same time having a deep respect and love for their parents. The most marked characteristic of the family was the loyalty and closeness of their relationships.

Young George Custer was a mischievous boy, given to fun and pranks, but not mean-spirited. In school he had been described as excelling "only in the skill in which he evaded study."

An older sister married and moved to Monroe, Michigan, and young Custer was to spend much of his youth with her and her husband, David Reed. One of their children, George Custer's nephew, David Armstrong, would also die at the Battle of the Little Big Horn. The rest of the Custer family eventually moved to Monroe.

In 1856 George obtained the position of school teacher and taught in several small communities.

Somehow, Custer prevailed to gain an appointment to the West Point Academy in the year 1857. There are two versions of how he managed to obtain this coveted appointment. One was that the local congressman John A. Bingham had been favorably impressed with the young man, even though the Custer family was without political influence and Emanuel was a vocal member of the opposing party.

The second version is that an influential farmer intervened on Custer's behalf, stimulated by an interest his daughter had in young Custer. It was this farmer's paternal interest to have Custer as far away from his daughter as possible and apparently the military academy at West Point must have seemed an appropriate distance.

On February 6, 1858, Custer took the oath of allegiance to the United States and received his cadet warrant for West Point. Custer himself described his next four years at the academy as noteworthy only as a bad example not to be followed. He amassed record numbers of demerits for infractions such as laughing in formation, snowball throwing, and similar incidents.

He then added taunting authority, with varied degrees of success, to his previous scholastic skill of avoiding study. One of his classmates observed that never did the officer of the guard appear that Custer did not suspect he was to be the object of that person's attentions.

The growing threat of Civil War caused the term for graduation at West Point to be dropped from five years to four, and in June of 1861 Custer's class prepared to graduate. The young man who would soon be a general ranked 34th in a class of 34 and as if not satisfied with that distinction Custer quickly added another. When his graduation class marched out of the academy Custer was in the guard house.

Apparently, Custer had been the acting officer of the guard when he came across a group of cadets who had surrounded two other cadets who were fighting. Instead of breaking up the fight, as his duty required, Custer ordered the surrounding cadets to "stand back and let them have a fair fight." Perhaps they did have a fair fight, but the result was the arrest of Custer.

President Abraham Lincoln personally signed the note that released Custer from the guard house. The Army needed every trained officer for the coming war and Custer soon found himself in Washington before the Commanding General of the Union Armies, Winfield Scott. Custer was then entrusted to carry a dispatch to the front. The Union Army was gathering near a place called Bull Run and the Confederate Army was nearby. It looked as if there might be a battle and, once he arrived there, Custer was to join

his assigned unit, Company G, 2nd Cavalry.

Custer arrived at Bull Run and delivered his dispatches in time for the battle that would be fought the next day, July 21, 1861. Custer was conspicuous at his first battle and mentioned in reports for his bravery. The first Bull Run was to be a disaster for the Union Army and, when the Confederate Army flanked them, a panicked retreat began back to Washington.

On his own initiative Custer ordered his company to cover the Union retreat over the stone bridge crossing Bull Run Creek and then stemmed the panic at this key bottleneck that, otherwise, could have brought destruction to a large part of Lincoln's new army. At this battle Custer also captured the first battle flag taken by the Union Army in the Civil War.

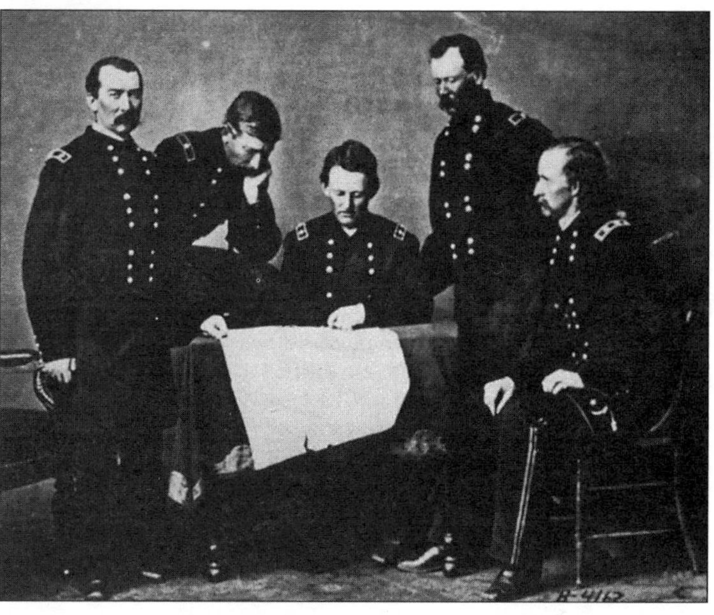

During the next four years Custer's adventures covered over 100 engagements and every major battle the Army of the Potomac fought. In an army where the appointment of officers for political motives was notorious, Custer's military accomplishments merited his promotion to general days before the Battle of Gettysburg. At that famous battle he stopped an effort by the Confederate Cavalry under General J. E. B. Stuart to attack the rear of the Union forces.

At Appomattox Court House where General Robert E. Lee surrendered, it was Custer who cut off the Confederate Army's last avenue of retreat and he received the flag of truce that precluded Lee's official surrender. In between Bull Run and Appomattox, Custer's exploits, if the subject of a novel, would be considered far-fetched. As it is, Custer's war record is part of history and although his contributions to Union victory in the Civil War may be ignored by historians Custer was not ignored by his contemporaries and his accomplishments were recognized.

Concerning Custer's Civil War record, author Gregory Urwin commented on the lack of historical understanding in his book *Custer Victorious*:

> *Academic historians have paid relatively little attention to the Boy General's career and character, and yet as a prominent and enduring figure in America's folklore and popular consciousness, the historical Custer is deserving of closer scrutiny by professional scholars.*

The lack of historical understanding by academics has contributed to the one-dimensional image of the Custer portrayed at the Battle of the Little Big Horn. His Civil War record, however, indicates Custer was an effective American Cavalry leader comparable to other notable cavalry generals of the Civil War such as J. E. B. Stuart and Nathaniel B. Forrest.

Custer author and researcher W. Donald Horn, in his book *Witnesses for the Defense*, documented the comments of many participants of the Civil War, both Union and Confederate, which praised both Custer's leadership and bravery during that conflict. Custer was, by the end of the Civil War, held in high esteem by Ulysses S. Grant, Commanding General Army of the Potomac, who is on record as writing:

> *This will introduce to your acquaintance General Custer, who rendered such distinguished service as a cavalry officer during the war.*
>
> *There is no officer in that branch of the service who had the confidence of General Sheridan to a greater degree than Custer and there is no officer in whose judgement I have greater faith than in Sheridan's.*
>
> *Please understand then that I mean by this to endorse General Custer in a high degree.*

This letter, incidentally, was a recommendation to President Juarez of Mexico whom Custer wished to join in his war against the French occupation of that country. Custer's leave of absence, however, was declined and he remained on duty with the American Army.

By the year 1876, Grant, now president of the United States, would have changed his opinion of Custer dramatically.

Captain Kidd

Captain James H. Kidd was a member of Custer's Civil War command and made an observation concerning a shadow that would haunt Custer throughout his entire career:

> *George Armstrong Custer was undeniably the most picturesque figure of the Civil War. Yet his ability and services were hardly justly appraised by the American people.*
>
> *It is doubtful if more than one of his superior officers –*

if we except Kearny, McClellan and Pleasonton, who knew him only as a subaltern – estimated him at his true value.

Sheridan knew him for what he was. So did the Michigan Cavalry Brigade and the Third Cavalry Division. Except by these, he was regarded as a brave and dashing, but reckless officer, who needed a steady hand to guide him.

Among regular army officers, he cannot be said to have been a favorite. The rapidity of his rise to the zenith of his fame and unexampled success, when so many of the youngsters of his years were moving in the comparative obscurity of their own orbits, irritated them. Stars of the first magnitude did not appear often in the galaxy of heroes. Custer was one of the few.

It is interesting that Captain Kidd commented on Custer's troubled relationships with certain members of the American Army. Jealousy is not a human emotion conducive to impartial judgement and Custer's success apparently made him vulnerable to the small-minded.

The American Cavalry in the Civil War

The tactics and strategies used in tank warfare during World War II has been compared to those used by the cavalry during the American Civil War. German Field Marshal Erwin Rommel was one of the most successful tank commanders of World War II and, like Custer, Rommel preferred to be at the battlefront with his soldiers, always ready to seize an opportunity or make an instant decision based upon the facts before him. Rommel was a successful commander because he knew the value of his personal presence at the front and, while many other generals of his era would be found many miles to the rear in a bombproof shelter, Rommel was willing to risk himself for victory. Field Marshal Rommel said:

The man in command must be the galvanizer of the battle. He must constantly be on the battlefield, in the front line, to exercise his control.

Of course, the impact of such a commander upon their troops is a phenomenon itself. Rommel's soldiers willingly followed him and frequently he was able to overcome the most adverse situations because his soldiers trusted him and were willing to sacrifice unconditionally when called upon to do so.

The American World War II tank general George S. Patton, Jr. was also fond of leading his soldiers from the front echelons. Patton was an extremely effective leader of the American forces in the European theater of war and was so feared by the Germans that they maintained constant surveillance on his location. They knew that, wherever Patton was, the German troops in the vicinity were likely to see action, and probably a lot of it.

In writing about Field Marshal Rommel, author Ronald Lewin analyzed what he believed to be this soldier's secret of success. This formula was also used by General Patton and other successful "calvary" officers. In describing Rommel's methods, Lewin said:

... effortlessly to the management of amount ... he insisted on leading an attack himself ... he made constant use of movement to a flank: by out maneuvering his enemy he was often able to penetrate to the rear, and then to exploit surprise. All these concepts – control from the front, keeping the battle fluid, indirect approach round a flank, the decisively unexpected thrust – provided a recipe for his victories.

His ideas about leadership never changed, essentially: they were always aggressive, dynamic, unpredictable, and founded on the principle that the place of a commander is at the front ... rapid appreciation of a tactical possibility, rapid organization of his troops to exploit it, and personal leadership at the critical point.

General Patton also appreciated the value of his personal presence at the battlefront, and he was frequently there. Patton, however, also appreciated the superiority and abundance of American technology and he was in the enviable position of having total confidence in ultimate victory. Patton understood and exploited that superiority to great advantage.

Patton's personal presence was not, however, always at the battlefront, although he made an attempt for it to seem that way to the soldiers. Patton frequently drove to the battlefront, probably often in some conquering pose in a jeep, and then would quickly hop a small plane back to the rear. The mystifying effect this must of had on his soldiers, Patton always driving to the front, but never returning, can only be imagined.

Like Field Marshal Rommel and General Patton, Custer commanded his soldiers at the

battlefront, but he was not alone. The best soldiers of Custer's command were selected as his personal escort. These soldiers had proven themselves in combat and were the best of a highly motivated command. With this small escort Custer could not only often influence the course of an engagement but also could increase his personal chances of survival. To be honored as a member of the General's escort was a powerful stimulus for his soldiers to excel.

The soldiers of Custer's command also emulated the red tie their General wore. Perhaps the tie was a challenge to the enemy, or perhaps it was merely a colorful addition to the uniform to increase *esprit de corps*. The red tie was the individual marking of a member of Custer's command and it was a shrewd psychological addition that motivated his men.

Custer also had a personal gold medal minted by Tiffany Jewelers in New York City which he awarded to deserving members of his unit. It was a Maltese cross under a general's star, and when Captain Kidd received his he remarked that it was the proudest day of his life. This, of course, was exactly the effect the medal was supposed to have and it was another stimulus for the members of Custer's command to excel.

Another psychological tactic of Custer's was his fondness of the saber charge when it was all but outdated. One of the most unpleasant experiences of a lifetime must have occurred on the receiving end of a thundering charge by cavalrymen brandishing flashing sabers, aware that in moments they would be upon you slashing and cutting in every direction. The psychological impact of such a charge must have been dramatic.

The fact that Custer survived the Civil War also brings forth another observation. Had he been a tyrannical madman who sacrificed his soldiers needlessly, as he has sometimes been accused of, members of his command might have been the first to kill him. This unpleasant truism of combat units is a fact all military commanders have had to confront.

Nat Frankel, in his book *Patton's Best*, commented upon the disdain he felt toward certain types of officers while he was with General Patton's 3rd Army in Europe during World War II.

> *What makes the good ones good and the bad ones bad? What is the difference between an officer for whom he would die and another whom he would just as soon kill? It is, in the long run, the extent to which they share the common lot of their men.*

Enlisted man Frankel's opinion is probably shared by many of the enlisted ranks during any war.

When it comes down to a simple "either-or" choice a seasoned combat veteran will sometimes eliminate an officer he feels regards life cheaply. Because Custer was always at the front, a disgruntled soldier constantly had the opportunity for ending Custer's life, if that soldier wanted to.

General Lee's Surrender

As General Lee and his army retreated from Richmond in the spring of 1865, the Union Army and Custer, now in command of the 3rd Cavalry Division, were in hot pursuit. Lee was headed for Appomattox Station where four trains were waiting, loaded with supplies for his army. Custer arrived there first and captured the trains. Then, advancing toward Appomattox Court House, he secured the road leading to Lynchburg, Lee's last avenue of retreat. The following morning the Confederate Army, finding itself completely surrounded by Union forces, began the process of surrender.

While it is certain that the surrender process began with Custer receiving a flag of truce from the Confederate Army, there are several versions on how this happened. One version is that Captain Simms of General James Longstreet's staff advanced into Custer's lines asking for a truce, which Custer accepted.

Another version is that Custer rode into General Longstreet's lines and met with the Confederate general personally and demanded the Rebel Army surrender. According to this version General Longstreet, who was not about to surrender to a divisional commander, gave Custer a severe browbeating before sending him back to the Union lines.

Whatever happened, the flag of truce was accepted by Custer's division and a few hours later General Lee met General Grant at the Appomattox Court House and surrendered. Custer was there, as were many of the officers of both armies.

After the surrender ceremony General Philip H. Sheridan, who commanded all of the Union Cavalry under General Grant, purchased, as a gift for Mrs. Custer, the table on which the articles of surrender had been signed by Generals Lee and Grant. The note Sheridan sent with it said:

> *I respectfully present to you the small writing table on which the conditions for surrender of the Confederate Army of Northern Virginia were written by Lieutenant General Grant, and permit me to say Madam, that there is scarcely an individual in our service who has contributed more to bringing about this desirable result than your very gallant husband.*

The 7th Cavalry

In May 1865, at the end of the Civil War, over one million soldiers were in service. By year's end this number had been reduced to 38,545, which was quickly to prove inadequate for the army to perform all of its duties.

In the summer of 1866 the Congress authorized the formation of several new regiments of cavalry for service in the West and the 7th Cavalry was one of these.

On September 21, 1866, at Fort Riley, Kansas, the 7th Cavalry was formally organized with Colonel J. Andrew

Smith as commander and Custer as its executive officer.

The officers and enlisted soldiers who were to be part of the 7th Cavalry were those who, for one reason or another, found military life attractive to them. At best the frontier army was a harsh existence with poor food, dreary quarters, and boredom, added to the hardships and deprivations of active campaigning, which made life in a frontier fort anything but pleasant.

The officers, at least, received better treatment, while the routine of the enlisted soldier has frequently been compared to penal servitude with tyrannical discipline and barbaric punishments.

Frequently, only the most dire of economic circumstances, or even the threat of criminal punishment, had driven the enlisted soldier to join the army. Many enlisted only to obtain a horse and weapons with the intention of deserting at the first opportunity.

There were, of course, some who enlisted in the army for idealistic reasons, but many of those in the ranks had been described as a combination of illiterates, criminals, sexual deviants, gamblers, drunkards, and generally antisocial types.

The officers of the 7th Cavalry may have had more in common with the enlisted soldier than not. However, they were characterized as having great experience and ability in leading soldiers in combat and in this respect many could be described as among the best officers in the post Civil War army.

Officers of the 7th Cavalry

Major Marcus Reno was the second in command of the 7th Cavalry at the Battle of the Little Big Horn and had graduated from West Point Military Academy in 1858. Reno entered the Civil War as a lieutenant in the Union Army and, after distinguishing himself on several occasions throughout the conflict was, by wars end, a brevet brigadier general of volunteers.

Major Reno never liked the acting commanding officer of the 7th Cavalry, George Custer, although the reason, or reasons, are not clear. Reno was apparently a chronic inebriate and also had difficulty in getting along with others in the regiment. While he joined Captain Benteen in his dislike for Custer, this seemed to be the only thing in common the two officers had. Benteen would later make some very unflattering comments about Reno, saying:

I had little regard for his opinion in any manner, shape or form....

...I once slapped his face in the club room of a post trader's establishment before quite a crowd of officers....

...I was scarcely on good terms with Reno....

While Captain Benteen's opinion might be considered suspect, Major Reno's conduct during and after the Battle of the Little Big Horn was to earn him the aversion of his fellow officers. In 1880 he would receive a dishonorable discharge from the Army.

While the charges against him had included being drunk, fighting, and window peeping, Reno had never outrun the charges of cowardice at the Battle of the Little Big Horn and many historians believe the actual charges which led to his dismissal from the Army were spurious in nature.

Captain Miles W. Keogh was to be the ranking officer with the two battalions under Custer's command at the Battle of the Little Big Horn. Unlike most of the other soldiers killed with Custer, Keogh's body was not mutilated by the Indians after his death, indicating he had fought courageously and had won their respect.

Captain Keogh was born to a prominent Irish family and at the age of seventeen had found himself a soldier in the St. Patrick's Battalion of the Papal Army. He served with distinction and was eventually appointed commander of that unit, and was also awarded a papal medal which he was to cherish throughout his life. Keogh migrated to America in 1862 and joined the Union Army where he quickly gained a reputation as a soldier.

By the end of the war, Keogh had been promoted to brevet colonel and in 1866 was assigned to the 7th Cavalry as a captain.

Captain Keogh was to command "I" Company throughout his service with the 7th Cavalry.

Captain Keogh also had been described by some as a brutal officer who frequently amused himself by beating up hapless enlisted soldiers. Regardless of his faults, Keogh was doubtless a valued officer, and Custer's selection of him

as the ranking officer under his personal command in the last battle was a deliberate one.

Captain George W. Yates was, like Custer, from Monroe, Michigan, and was a lifelong friend of Custer's. Yates was to command Company F at the Little Big Horn where he and all of his men were to be annihilated with the exception of a small, patrol-sized force which somehow ended up with Major Reno's survivors on Reno Hill. Captain Yates' military career was considered noteworthy enough to be mentioned in a lengthy newspaper obituary after his death at the Little Big Horn.

Captain Thomas W. Custer was a brother to George Custer and several years younger than his famous sibling. Tom Custer had enlisted in the Civil War as a private and by wars end had risen through the ranks to brevet colonel.

Later during the war he served with his brother's Michigan cavalry brigade where he was to win the Medal of Honor twice, one of very few soldiers in America's history to do so. After the war, Tom joined his brother in the 7th Cavalry and at the Battle of the Little Big Horn commanded Company C, which was wiped out with General Custer.

Unlike many of the other officers with the 7th Cavalry, Lieutenant James Calhoun did not have a colorful Civil War record. He was, however, married to Custer's sister, Margaret, and became a close friend and loyal supporter of Custer.

Lieutenant Calhoun commanded Company L at the Little Big Horn and he and the soldiers under him died with Custer's command.

1st Lieutenant Algernon E. Smith had served in the Civil War and had seen extensive action. Although he had not been rewarded with high rank, ending the war as a captain, he did serve as a staff officer with a succession of various generals and became a loyal friend to Custer when he joined the 7th Cavalry.

Smith had been badly wounded during the Civil War and had a shoulder injury which prevented him from raising his arm above his head. Smith commanded Company E at the Little Big Horn with Custer and he was killed with his command.

Captain Myles Moylan had perhaps the strangest career of any officer in the Army. At the opening of the Civil War Moylan had joined the Union Army as an enlisted soldier and after two years of meritorious service was given a commission as a lieutenant. A short time later Moylan was demoted back to the ranks for a minor infraction and the discouraged soldier deserted his unit only to reenlist in another unit under a different name.

Once again, Moylan, who now called himself Charles E. Thomas, rose up from the ranks to be commissioned a Lieutenant and served out the war honorably until discharged in August 1865.

In 1866 Moylan again enlisted in the Army, this time under his correct name. He was soon assigned to the 7th Cavalry where Custer promoted him to the rank of sergeant major of the regiment. With Custer's assistance Moylan now attempted, for the third time, to obtain an officer's commission.

He failed the first written test; however, he did pass it on the second try. Moylan, now a lieutenant once more, was then made the regimental adjutant by Custer until he was later replaced by 1st Lieutenant William W. Cooke in 1871.

At the Battle of the Little Big Horn, Captain Moylan commanded Company A and was with Major Reno during his advance in the valley. Moylan survived the battle and the following year fought at Bear Paw Mountain against the Nez Perces where he was wounded and in 1890 he was awarded a Medal of Honor for this action.

Lieutenant William Cooke was with Custer at the Battle of the Little Big Horn as the regimental adjutant and died next to his commander's side. Lieutenant Cooke was a Civil War veteran who had seen extensive action and ended the war with a brevet rank of lieutenant colonel. He joined the 7th Cavalry in 1866 and at the Washita Battle of 1868 had been in command of a picked company of sharpshooters.

He was later given the position of regimental adjutant and served in this capacity until his death. He may have been Custer's most trusted officer, placing much trust in Cooke's ability and loyalty.

Lieutenant Charles DeRudio served as the 1st Lieutenant of Company A under Captain Moylan at the Battle of the Little Big Horn. DeRudio was a graduate of the Royal Austrian Military Academy, fought in the Italian Civil War, and also as an officer in the French Foreign Legion in Algeria.

On January 18, 1858, DeRudio participated in an assassination attempt on Louis Napoleon of France in which Napoleon (the 3rd) escaped. However, over 100 of Napoleon's guards and bystanders were killed when bombs were thrown at the royal carriage. Two fellow assassins lost their heads on the guillotine while, for some reason, DeRudio escaped this fate and instead was banished to Devil's Island.

Apparently, DeRudio did not care to end his life on that island paradise and, with the aid of a makeshift raft, escaped in time to serve in the American Civil War in the Union Army. DeRudio was assigned to the 7th Cavalry after the end of the war and after the Battle of the Little Big Horn he wrote an account of his adventures during which he narrowly escaped death.

Like so many other officers of the 7th Cavalry, Captain Thomas Weir had been a distinguished Civil War soldier who had received the brevet rank of lieutenant colonel by war's end. Appointed a 1st lieutenant in the 7th Cavalry in 1866, Weir soon became a loyal friend to General Custer.

At the Little Big Horn battle, Captain Weir commanded D Company and was with Captain Benteen's battalion. During the battle he led an unauthorized attempt to go to Custer's aid. The deaths of so many officers at the famous battle left Weir third in rank among the surviving officers. However, when the regiment returned from the field in October 1876, Weir was transferred to New York on recruiting duty.

On December 9th of that year Weir died suddenly, the cause of death reported as "congestion of the brain."

Captain Frederick Benteen

Captain Frederick Benteen was the third ranking officer at the Battle of the Little Big Horn and commanded a battalion there. He had served in the Union Army throughout the Civil War, had been promoted to the brevet rank of lieutenant colonel, and joined the 7th Cavalry in 1866. Benteen took an immediate dislike to Custer and developed a hatred for him that would last until his dying day.

It has been commented upon that Captain Benteen and Custer probably disliked each other at first sight, but it was a letter Benteen wrote for publication after the Washita Battle of 1868, where the Cheyenne camp of Black Kettle was attacked and destroyed by the 7th Cavalry, that brought a simmering feud to a hot boil. This letter was considered slanderous by many members of the 7th Cavalry and created a gulf between Custer and Benteen that would never be bridged. This letter was reprinted in several newspapers and contained emotional passages, apparently deliberately written to cast public disapproval upon Custer and the 7th Cavalry. One passage said:

> *... Take care! Do not trample on the dead bodies of that woman and child....*

This letter enraged Custer, and Captain Benteen later wrote an account of a confrontation he had with his commander over the Washita letter:

> *At Fort Cobb, Indian Territory in winter of '68-'69, officers call was sounded one night from Reg Hdqtrs. I sauntered up, the other officers being mostly there when I arrived. The officers were squatted around the inside of Custer's Sibley tent, (minus a wall), and Custer was walking around the center of the tent with a rawhide riding whip in his hand.*
>
> *When all were assembled, he went on with a rambling story, stammering the while, that it had been reported to him that someone – or parties – had been belittling the fight at the Washita, &c., &c., and that if he heard any more of it, or it came to his ears who had done so, he would cowhide them, switching his rawhide the while.*
>
> *Being right at the door of the tent, I stepped out, drew my revolver, turned the cylinder to see that 'twas in good working order, returned it lightly to holster, and went within.*
>
> *At pause in the talk I said, "General Custer, while I cannot father all of the blame you have asserted, still, I guess I am the man you are after, and I am ready for the whipping promised." He stammered and said, "Capt. Benteen. I'll see you again. sir!"*
>
> *Doubtless you can imagine what would have happened had the rawhide whirred!.... I then went to Randolph Keim, reporter from the N. Y. Tribune (the only man I had spoken to about the matter at all), and told him I wanted him to go with me at once to Custer's tent, taking his notes with him of all I had told him, as a whipping was due somebody, and I didn't want a word I'd said omitted.*

Captain Benteen was notoriously dishonest in many of the statements he made later in his life concerning the years he was with the 7th Cavalry and, if this incident happened the way Benteen said it did, Reporter Keim never mentioned it.

Captain Benteen also gave the impression that he was ready for a gunfight with Custer, had circumstances led him in that direction, for instance, if Custer actually went after Benteen to "cowhide" him.

In reality, Captain Benteen was standing in a tent surrounded by Custer's officers, some of them probably glad Benteen could stand up to Custer, but certainly unwilling to involve themselves in a violent confrontation that would have meant the end of their careers. There were other officers who, had Benteen really made a hostile move, were loyal to Custer and would have brought a sudden end to Benteen's bluster.

It was to be several years before Custer was to settle his score with Captain Benteen concerning the Washita letter. When Custer's book, *My Life on the Plains*, was published Benteen received honorable mention, or so it may have seemed to the unwary reader. Custer wrote:

> *Captain Benteen, in leading the attack of his squadron through the timber below the village, encountered an Indian boy, scarcely fourteen years of age; he was well mounted, and was endeavoring to make his way through the lines. The object these Indians had in attempting this movement we were then ignorant of, but soon learned to our sorrow.*
>
> *This boy rode boldly toward the Captain, seeming to invite a contest. His youthful bearing, and not being looked upon as a combatant, induced Major Benteen to endeavor to save him by making "peace signs" to him and obtaining his surrender, when he could be placed in a position of safety until the battle was terminated; but the young savage desired and would accept no such friendly concessions.*
>
> *He regarded himself as a warrior, and the son of a warrior, and as such, he purposed to do a warrior's part. With revolver in hand, he dashed at the Captain, who still could not regard him as anything but a harmless*

lad. Leveling his weapon as he rode, he fired, but either from excitement or the changing positions of both parties, his aim was defective and the shot whistled harmlessly by Captain Benteen's head. Another followed in quick succession, but with no better effect.

All this time, the dusky little chieftain boldly advanced, to lessen the distance between himself and his adversary. A third bullet was sped on its errand and this time to some purpose, as it passed through the neck of the Captain's horse, close to the shoulder. Making a final but ineffectual appeal to him to surrender, and seeing him still preparing to fire again, the Captain was forced in self-defense to level his revolver and dispatch him, although as he did so it was with admiration for the plucky spirit exhibited by the lad, and regret often expressed that no other course under the circumstances was left him.

Attached to the saddle bow of the young Indian hung a beautifully wrought pair of small moccasins, elaborately ornamented with beads. One of the Captain's troopers afterward secured these and presented them to him. These furnished the link of evidence by which we subsequently ascertained who the young chieftain was – a title which was justly his, both by blood and bearing.

While the passage in Custer's book seems innocent enough, it was perhaps written for one person and one person only, and that was Captain Benteen. While Benteen's letter lamented the deaths of women and children, Custer, in his book, was diligent in pointing out that Benteen himself had killed an Indian youth and then received the dead boy's moccasins as a souvenir of the incident.

That the true intention of this passage was to antagonize Benteen seems to be confirmed by an interview Walter Camp had with Colonel Richard Thompson, who was a lieutenant in the 6th Infantry during the campaign of 1876. Mr. Camp's notes say:

... on the night of June 21, at the mouth of Rosebud, a group of officers, including Custer and Benteen, sat discussing the possibilities of the campaign, and Benteen and Custer engaged in some personalities and recriminations.

Benteen said that if they were to get into a fight, he hoped he would be better supported than he was at the Battle of Washita.

Custer then twitted Benteen of shooting an Indian boy in that battle, and Benteen went on to explain why he had to do so to defend his own life.

Thompson says that the discussion of matters between Custer and Benteen waxed rather warm at this time, and it was plain to be seen that Benteen hated Custer.

The squabble between Custer and Benteen doubtless contained many incidents and took many turns that will never be known. Custer, as the superior officer, was in the dominant position and the endless ways he could have used that position to harass Benteen, and possibly did, placed Benteen in an unenviable situation. Why Benteen did not transfer out of the regiment or why Custer did not have him transferred are unanswered questions.

Were these two so stubborn, and did they so cherish their childish spats, that neither was willing to let go? Or were they prevented from this by higher authorities for clandestine reasons? For instance, was Custer considered a political threat by those in political power? A threat that should be watched closely? If so, who would have been the one person in the regiment who would have eagerly taken the opportunity to inform on Custer to higher authorities?

Had Benteen been asked to assume this role, there can be little question that he would have cheerfully accepted. However, in the absence of proof, this conjecture is mentioned only as a possibility that had the potential to exist.

Captain Benteen was promoted to major in the 9th Cavalry in 1882, six years after the death of Custer. According to some authorities, Benteen attempted to circumvent this transfer to the 9th by circulating a petition in the 7th Cavalry, a petition which most of the officers refused to sign. If this story is true, then apparently Benteen did not have the high esteem of his comrades in the 7th Cavalry that some historians have chosen to believe. In any event, Benteen retired from the Army in 1888 and thereafter resided in Atlanta, Georgia.

After his retirement and before his death in 1898, Benteen began a correspondence with a former enlisted soldier of the 7th Cavalry who was present at the Battle of the Little Big Horn. Private Theodore Goldin was a member of Company G and served in the 7th Cavalry from April 1876 until November 1877, when he was discharged "without honor" because he had been underage at the time of his enlistment.

Private Goldin, however, was able to exploit his fame as a participant at the Battle of the Little Big Horn and he became a lawyer in Janesville, Wisconsin. Goldin also became active in politics and was eventually promoted to honorary colonel in the Wisconsin National Guard. Goldin also, with Benteen's help, was to be awarded the Medal of Honor for his role at the Battle of the Little Big Horn, although this award has remained controversial.

Private Goldin's letters to Benteen apparently have not survived. However, Benteen's letters to Goldin have and these letters contain a detailed and accurate record of how Benteen's mind functioned. Some historians believe that much of what was written by Benteen to Goldin, if not everything, was intended for the "historical record" and eventual publication. If this is true, then Benteen's letters have not had their originally intended purpose which, presumably, was to give validity to Benteen's version of certain events that occurred while he was in the 7th Cavalry.

Historian John M. Carroll said of Benteen's letters to

Goldin:

Benteen presents himself as a paragon of diplomatic virtues and an unparalleled military genius who was mostly misunderstood and envied by all who knew him. Only he, it seems, could easily win at poker against all odds; only he could tell Custer off without bias; and only he could overcome difficulties that defeated other men. At least his letters to Goldin convey this impression.

According to Mr. Carroll, Benteen's letters also revealed him to be a man of:

Monumental vindictiveness and cancerous bitterness toward almost all of his old comrades.

Captain Benteen's letters expose him to have been a person obsessed with spite and petty hatreds, and Benteen made slanderous and mean-spirited comments about nearly everyone he mentioned. This list includes Lieutenant Godfrey, Lieutenant Mathey, Colonel Sturgis, Captain Moylan, Major Reno, General Miles, Lieutenant Gibson (Benteen's second in command of the company he commanded at the Battle of the Little Big Horn), and, of course, Custer.

Most of the letters Captain Benteen wrote contained the usual misrepresentations and fabrications that seem to consistently characterize Benteen. Although there are many revealing passages in these letters, one in particular is typical of what some historians have referred to as "Benteenisms." This passage concerns Lieutenant Godfrey's role at the Battle of the Little Big Horn. In a letter, dated January 6, 1892, Benteen wrote:

... having nothing to do with Moylan or Godfrey, I gave them no orders....

On March 1, 1892, Benteen wrote something much different:

... I ordered Godfrey to take position on the point....

Like most people who have spent a lifetime practicing dishonesty, Benteen thought himself smart enough to fabricate a yarn whenever it was convenient. Yet, like most chronic frauds, Benteen was not smart enough to keep track of these yarns. There are many similar examples contained in Benteen's letters.

Custer had been dead more than 15 years when Captain Benteen began his correspondence with Mr. Goldin. Yet Custer, more than any other person, was the recipient of Benteen's rantings and a few of these are worth mentioning. Concerning Custer, Benteen wrote:

*... what a villain that man was ... he was a murderer ... a bad, bad man ... criminally connected [*with a married woman*] ... a liar ... scoundrel ... thief....*

In his letters to Goldin, Benteen also accused Custer of being a corrupt officer, a card cheat, of sending his men on suicidal missions, of favoritism, and of one offense that particularly bothered Benteen, that of borrowing money from him and not paying it back.

Captain Benteen's written statements, according to him, were:

... gospel truth ... true as holy writ ... all supported with affidavits....

Folk wisdom says that those who frequently shake their finger at others bear close watching themselves. If a validation of this principle has ever existed Benteen is it.

The Scouts

As intrinsic to the 7th Cavalry as any officer were the scouts who were familiar with the West and the various Indian tribes that lived there. Without the skills of these men any success in an operation against the Indians was impossible. They included both native Indians who were in the pay of the government or sought revenge against another tribe, and men from the East who had lived many years in the West until they were almost as familiar with the ways of the frontier as any Indian. In his book, Custer spoke of the value of these men.

... It is usual on the Plains, and particularly during time of active hostilities, for every detachment of troops to be accompanied by one or more professional scouts or guides. These guides are employed by the government at a rate of compensation far in excess of that paid to the soldiers, some of the most experienced receiving pay about equal to that of a subaltern in the line. They constitute a most interesting as well as useful and necessary portion of our frontier population.

Who they are, whence they come or whither they go, their names even, except such as they choose to adopt or which may be given them, are all questions which none but themselves can answer. As their usefulness to the service depends not upon the unraveling of either of these mysteries, but little thought is bestowed upon them. Do you know the country thoroughly, and can you speak any of the Indian languages, constitute the only examination which civil or uncivil service reform demands on the Plains.

If the evidence on these two important points is satisfactory, the applicant for a vacancy in the corps of scouts may consider his position as secured, and the door to congenial employment, most often leading to a terrible death, opens before him. They are almost invariably men of very superior judgment or common sense, with education generally better than that of the average frontiersman.

Their most striking characteristics are love of adventure, a natural and cultivated knowledge of the country without recourse to maps, deep hatred of the Indian

and an intimate acquaintance with all the habits and customs of the latter, whether pertaining to peace or war, and last but most necessary to their calling, skill in the use of firearms and in the management of a horse.

The possessor of these qualifications and more than the ordinary amount of courage may feel equal to discharge the dangerous and trying duties of a scout.

California Joe

Among the scouts that were to serve with the 7th cavalry was a man referred to as "California Joe." His real name seems to have been Moses Milner and he had traveled to the West at the age of 14 in the year 1843. His occupations there included trapper, prospector, cowboy, and scout.

He was to become a lifelong friend of Custer's although, after Custer's death in June of 1876, California Joe was to live only until October of that year when he was shot from behind and killed near Camp Robinson, Nebraska. Of California Joe, Custer wrote:

He was a man about forty years of age, perhaps older, over six feet in height, and possessing a well-proportioned frame. His head was covered with a luxuriant crop of long, almost black hair, strongly inclined to curl, and so long as to fall carelessly over his shoulders. His face, at least so much of it as was not concealed by the long waving brown beard and mustache, was full of intelligence and pleasant to look upon. His eye was undoubtedly handsome, black and lustrous, with an expression of kindness and mildness combined.

On his head was generally to be seen, whether asleep or awake, a huge sombrero or black slouch hat. A soldier's overcoat with its large circular cape, a pair of trousers with the legs tucked in the top of his long boots, usually constituted the outside makeup of the man whom I selected as chief scout. He was known by the euphonious title of "California Joe"; no other name seemed ever to have been given him, and no other name ever seemed necessary.

"Wild Bill" Hickok

Another frontiersman who was to scout for the 7th Cavalry was James Butler Hickok, otherwise known as "Wild Bill" Hickok. "Wild Bill" was to achieve legendary fame as a deadly gunman who, in an interview with Henry Stanley, the same newspaper man who was to track down Dr. Livingston in Africa a few years later, claimed to have killed "over a hundred" men, although none "without good cause."

"Good cause" or not, "Wild Bill" killed quite a number of men and this fact, added to his skills as a scout, apparently elevated him in the eyes of General Custer to that of esteemed peer. Custer wrote:

"Wild Bill" Hickok

Wild Bill was a strange character, just the one which a novelist might gloat over. He was a Plainsman in every sense of the word, yet unlike any other of his class. In person he was about six feet one in height, straight as the straightest of the warriors whoa impeccable foe....

... Of his courage there could be no question; it had been brought to the test on too many occasions to admit of a doubt. His skill in the use of the rifle and pistol was unerring, while his deportment was exactly the opposite of what might be expected from a man of his surroundings. It was entirely free from all bluster or bravado. He seldom spoke of himself, unless requested to do so. His conversation, strange to say, never bordered either on the vulgar or the blasphemous.

His influence among the frontiersmen was unbounded, his word was law; and many are the personal quarrels and disturbances which he has checked among his comrades by his simple announcement that "this has gone far enough," if need be followed by the ominous warning that when persisted in or renewed the quarreler "must settle it with me."

Wild Bill is anything but a quarrelsome man; yet no one but himself can enumerate the many conflicts in which he has been engaged, and which have almost invariably resulted in the death of his adversary. I have personal knowledge of at least half a dozen men whom he has at various times killed, one of these being at the time a member of my command. Others have been severely wounded, yet he always escapes unhurt.

On the Plains, every man openly carries his belt with its invariable appendages, knife and revolver, often two of the latter. Wild Bill always carried two handsome ivory-handled revolvers of the large size; he was never seen without them.

Where this is the common custom, brawls or personal difficulties are seldom, if ever, settled by blows. The quarrel is not from a word to a blow, but from a word to the revolver, and he who can draw and fire first is the best man. No civil law reaches him; none is applied for. In fact there is no law recognized beyond the frontier

> *but that of "might makes right."*
>
> *Should death result from the quarrel, as it usually does, no coroner's jury is impanelled to learn the cause of death, and the survivor is not arrested. But instead of these old-fashioned proceedings, a meeting of citizens takes place, the survivor is requested to be present when the circumstances of the homicide are inquired into and the unfailing verdict of "justifiable," "self-defense," etc., is pronounced, and the law stands vindicated.*
>
> *That justice is often deprived of a victim there is not a doubt. Yet in all of the many affairs of this kind in which Wild Bill has performed a part, and which have come to my knowledge, there is not a single instance men would not be pronounced in his favor.*
>
> *That the even tenor of his way continues to be disturbed by little events of this description may be inferred from an item which has been floating lately through the columns of the press, and which states that "the funeral of Jim Bludso, who was killed the other day by Wild Bill, took place today." It then adds: "The funeral expenses were borne by Wild Bill."*
>
> *What could be more thoughtful than this? Not only to send a fellow mortal out of the world, but to pay the expenses of the transit!*

While Custer commended Hickok for his generosity in paying for the funerals of his victims, it would seem that after the first dozen or so funerals, prudent men would have avoided giving "Wild Bill" reasons to kill them that a "verdict of twelve fair-minded men" would have ruled as just cause.

Hickok only served as a scout for Custer prior to the Washita Battle of 1868. He seems to have been one of those men of the frontier described as afflicted with a perpetual wanderlust, and he traveled extensively throughout the West. Yet, if Hickok had any career plans as a scout for the 7th Cavalry, they came to an abrupt end in August 1870. The 7th Cavalry had been stationed at Fort Hayes, Kansas, while a short distance away in Hayes City "Wild Bill" had set up his headquarters in one of the saloons there.

There are various accounts as to exactly what happened but apparently Hickok had a disagreement with members of the 7th Cavalry and a group of about five soldiers decided to pay him a visit. These soldiers entered the saloon where Hickok was and in the resulting battle two soldiers were shot before Wild Bill "made tracks for the back of the saloon and jumped through a window, taking the glass and sash with him."

And he didn't stop there. A local newspaper reported that Hickok had "made for the prairie and has not been heard of since." It would seem that while Wild Bill was not adverse to shooting one or two 7th Cavalrymen now and then, he was not inclined to take on the entire 7th Cavalry, which probably would have happened.

While Custer and others might have deemed Hickok a noble figure, others familiar with him did not share this impression. A newspaper editorial in a Western paper gave vent to feelings that may have been common to other contemporaries.

> *Doubtless this man* [Hickok] *and his companions have killed more men than any other persons who took part in the late war....*
>
> *They live in a constant state of excitement, one continual round of gambling, drinking, and swearing, interspersed at brief intervals with pistol practice upon each other....*
>
> *How long these Athletes will be able to stand such a mode of life; eating, drinking, sleeping (if they can be said to sleep) and playing cards with their pistols at half cock, remains to be seen. For our self, we are willing to risk them in an Indian campaign for which their cruelty and utter recklessness of life particularly fit them.*

Wild Bill was to continue "gambling, drinking and swearing" until August 2, 1876. Hickok was sitting in a saloon in Deadwood, South Dakota, where he was gambling, drinking, and probably occasionally swearing, when an assassin crept up and, in the preferred mode of killing in the Old West, shot and killed him from behind.

CHAPTER 4

The War with the Sioux —— Report from the Crow Agency —— General Crook's Report —— Hostile Indians Ordered to Surrender —— Winter Campaign —— The Starving Sioux —— Mrs. Custer's Observation —— Colonel Poland's Report —— The War Approaches —— Colonel Gibbon's Campaign —— General Crook's Second Campaign —— The Number of Sitting Bull's Warriors —— The Weapons of the Indian Warriors —— The Cause of the War of 1876

Libby Custer

The year 1876 was an important one in American history. It was the centennial year marking the first one hundred years of the existence of America and extensive celebrations were planned throughout the country. In Philadelphia a centennial exposition took place at which the scientific wonders of the age, as well as other exhibits, were displayed. President Grant and other American leaders, as well as visitors and dignitaries from around the world, attended.

In all these celebrations of the growth of a vigorous new nation, the people of the East were almost oblivious to the problems and conflict on the American frontier.

Unfortunately, the America of 1876 was a nation still at war with the American Indian and vast territories in the West were still dominated by tribes engaged in their ancient tradition of war-making and raiding.

Of the Sioux tribes, the "winter roamers," as they were called because they refused to take assistance or report to the reservations in winter as did the "summer roamers," followed the Chieftain Sitting Bull. These tribes had never been at peace with anyone not directly allied with them and followed a pattern of perpetual war-making.

The War with the Sioux

In a report dated November 9, 1875, Mr. E. C. Watkins, United States Indian Inspector, addressed a report to the Commissioner of Indian Affairs in which he described the state of war that existed on what was then the American frontier:

Washington, D. C.
November 9, 1875

SIR: I have the honor to address you in relation to the attitude and condition of certain wild and hostile bands of Sioux Indians in Dakota and Montana that came under my observation during my recent tour through their country, and what I think should be the policy of the Government toward them.

I refer to Sitting Bull's band and other bands of the Sioux Nation, under chiefs or "head-men" of less note, but no less untamable and hostile. These Indians occupy the center, so to speak, and roam over Western Dakota and Eastern Montana, including the rich valleys of the Yellowstone and Powder Rivers, and make war on the Arickarees, Mandans, Gros Ventres, Assinaboines, Blackfeet, Piegans, Crows and other friendly tribes on the circumference.

Their country is probably the best hunting-ground in the United States, "a paradise" for Indians, affording game in such variety and abundance that the need of Government supplies is not felt. Perhaps for this reason, they have never accepted aid or been brought under control. They openly set at defiance of all law

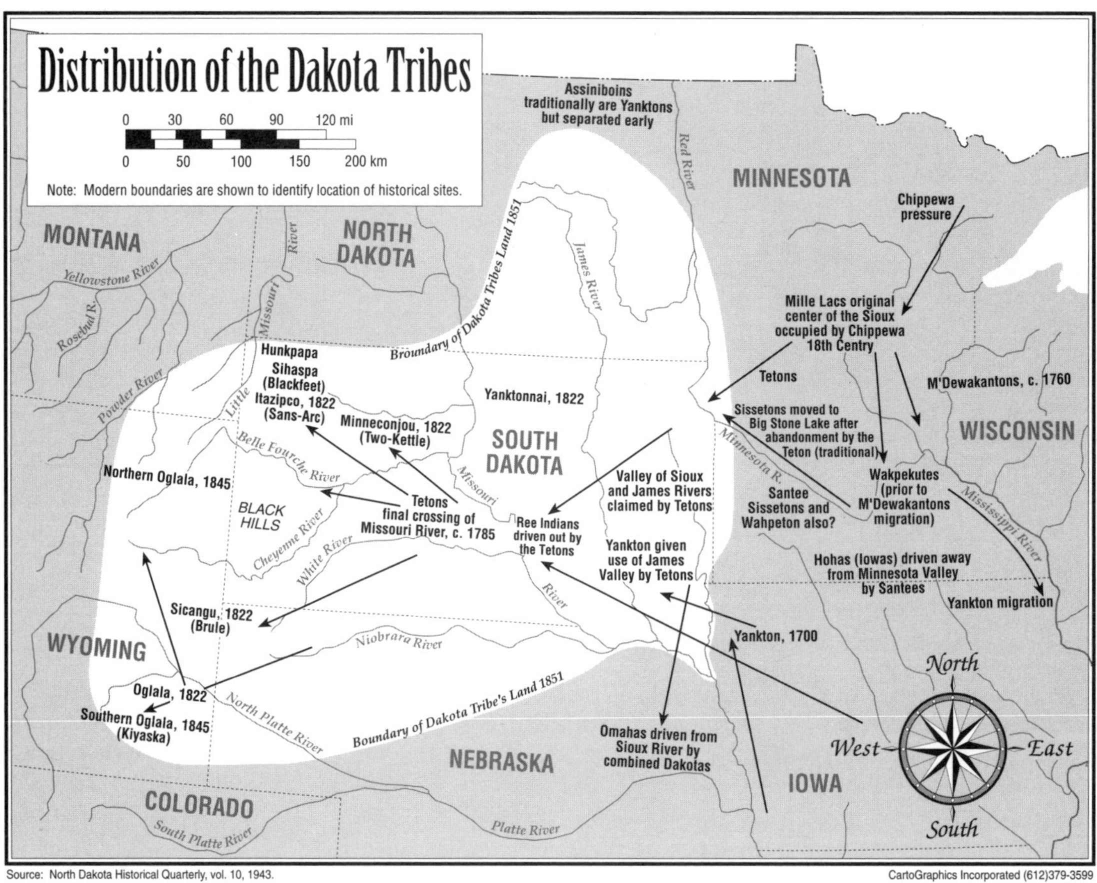

Source: North Dakota Historical Quarterly, vol. 10, 1943.

CartoGraphics Incorporated (612)379-3599

and authority, and boast that the United States authorities are not strong enough to conquer them. The United States troops are held in contempt, and, surrounded by their native mountains, relying on their knowledge of the country and powers of endurance, they laugh at the futile efforts that have thus far been made to subjugate them, and scorn the idea of white civilization.

They are lofty and independent in their attitude and language to Government officials, as well as the whites generally, and claim to be the sovereign rulers of the land. They say they own the wood, the water, the ground, and the air, and that white men live in or pass through their country but by their sufferance.

They are rich in horses and robes, and are thoroughly armed. Nearly every warrior carries a breech-loading gun, a pistol, a bow and quiver of arrows. From their central position, they strike to the east, north and west, steal horses, and plunder from all the surrounding tribes, as well as frontier settlers and luckless white hunters, or emigrants who are not in sufficient force to resist them, and fortunate, indeed, is the man who thus meets them, if, after losing all his worldly possessions, he escapes with his scalp.

And yet these Indians number, all told, but a few hundred warriors, and these are never altogether, or under the control of one chief.

In my judgement, one thousand men, under the command of an experienced officer, sent into their country in the winter, when the Indians are nearly always in camp, and at which season of the year they are the most helpless, would be amply sufficient for their capture or punishment.

The Government has done everything that can be done, peacefully to get control of these Indians, or to induce them to respect this authority. Every effort has been made, but all to no purpose. They are still as wild and untamable, as uncivilized and savage, as when Lewis and Clark first passed through their country.

The injurious effects of the repeated attacks made by these bands on the peaceful, friendly tribes heretofore mentioned cannot be overestimated. No people can reasonably be expected to make progress in the arts of peace, if they must be constantly armed, and prepared to defend their houses and property. No Indians can be expected to "civilize," to learn to cultivate the soil, or the mechanic acts, if, while they have the implements of labor in one hand, they must carry the gun in the other for self-defense. Their natural instincts come to the surface at once, and the Indian agent or missionary who is zealously laboring for the advancement of the people under his care, and to carry out the humane policy of our Government, the only policy worthy of an enlightened Christian nation, finds his labors vastly increased and discouragements multiplied by this state of affairs.

These wild bands are but as a drop in the bucket in number compared to the great body of Indians who have accepted the peaceful policy, made treaties with the Government, and are keeping them, or have been supplied with provisions, goods, and farming-implements, without fair progress in the way of civilization.

In interviews with the Indians along the Missouri River and through Montana, during my recent tour of inspection, they invariably spoke of this subject, and complained bitterly that the Government was not protecting them as it had promised, and frequently closed the case by saying "they might just as well go out and kill white men, as to try to be good Indians, for they get no protection or extra reward for being good." When I told them the Sioux would be punished, they said, "We have heard that before; we'll wait and see."

While I am not disposed to be needlessly alarmed, and do not agree with the writers of articles published in numerous territorial papers of a sensational character on this subject, yet I think there is a danger of some of the young warriors from friendly tribes falling off and joining with these hostile bands, until, with these accessions, they would be somewhat formidable, and might make a simultaneous attack on the white settlers in some localities, if they are thus allowed to gather head.

The true policy, in my judgement, is to send troops against them in the winter – the sooner the better – and whip them into subjection. They richly merit the punishment for their incessant warfare on friendly tribes, their continuous thieving, and their numerous murders of white settlers and their families, or white men wherever found unarmed.

The Government owes it, too, to these friendly tribes, in fulfillment of treaty stipulations. It owes it to the agents and employees, whom it has sent to labor among the Indians at remote and almost inaccessible places, beyond the reach of aid, in time to save. It owes it to the frontier settlers, who have, with their families, braved the dangers and hardships incident to pioneer life. It owes it to civilization and the common cause of humanity.

Very respectfully,
your obedient servant,
E. C. Watkins
United States Indian Inspector

Report From the Crow Agency

On March 10, 1876, Indian agent Dexter Clapp issued a report from the Crow Agency in Montana in which he described the situation of that agency and the events which had occurred in that area from previous summers up to the date the report was issued:

... I have the honor to enclose herewith a report of murders and outrages committed by Sioux Indians in the valley of the Yellowstone since the first of last July.

It shows 17 attacks made by them on parties of whites; nine white men killed and ten wounded, besides a large amount of property stolen or destroyed.

I estimate that they interfered with the building of this agency last summer to the amount of four to six thousand dollars. This is not a new condition of things. For several years, the eastern settlements of Montana have been harassed regularly every summer in the same manner. In fact, a regular predatory warfare has been carried on by the Sioux, and by Sioux that are receiving Government supplies....

... There is another very important consideration. The

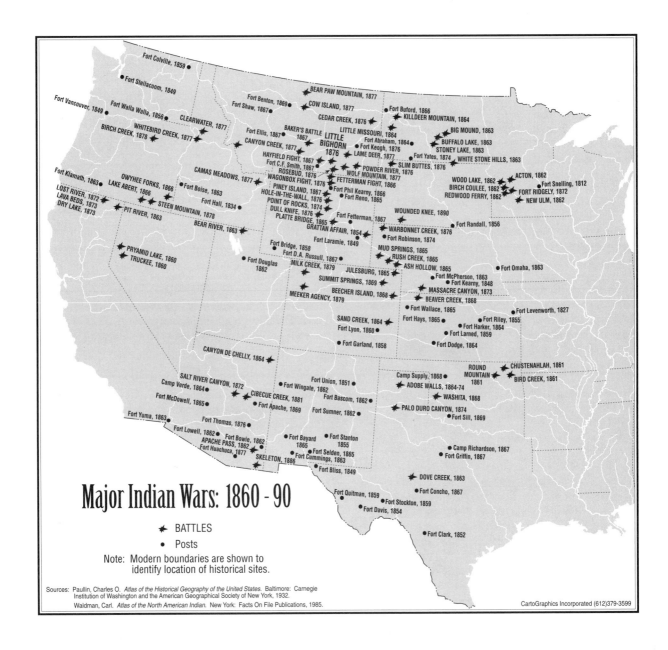

Major Indian Wars: 1860 - 90

Fort Colville, 1859
Fort Steilacoom, 1849
Fort Vancouver, 1849
Fort Walla Walla, 1856
CLEARWATER, 1877
WHITEBIRD CREEK, 1877
BIRCH CREEK, 1878
BEAR PAW MOUNTAIN, 1877
Fort Benton, 1869
Fort Shaw, 1867
COW ISLAND, 1877
CEDAR CREEK, 1876
Fort Buford, 1866
KILLDEER MOUNTAIN, 1864
LITTLE MISSOURI, 1864
Fort Ellis, 1867
BAKER'S BATTLE 1867
LITTLE BIGHORN 1876
CANYON CREEK, 1877
Fort Abraham, 1864
Fort Keogh, 1876
LAME DEER, 1877
Fort Yates, 1874
BIG MOUND, 1863
BUFFALO LAKE, 1863
STONEY LAKE, 1863
WHITE STONE HILLS, 1863
HAYFIELD FIGHT, 1867
Fort C.F. Smith, 1867
POWDER RIVER, 1876
SLIM BUTTES, 1876
CAMAS MEADOWS, 1877
ROSEBUD, 1876
WOLF MOUNTAIN, 1877
WAGONBOX FIGHT, 1876
FETTERMAN FIGHT, 1866
Fort Klamath, 1863
OWYHEE FORKS, 1866
LAKE ABERT, 1866
Fort Boise, 1863
PINEY ISLAND, 1867
Fort Phil Kearny, 1866
HOLE-IN-THE-WALL, 1876
Fort Reno, 1865
WOOD LAKE, 1862
ACTON, 1862
BIRCH COULEE, 1862
Fort Snelling, 1812
REDWOOD FERRY, 1862
FORT RIDGELY, 1872
NEW ULM, 1862
LOST RIVER, 1872
LAVA BEDS, 1873
DRY LAKE, 1873
STEEN MOUNTAIN, 1878
Fort Hall, 1834
POINT OF ROCKS, 1874
DULL KNIFE, 1876
PIT RIVER, 1863
PLATTE BRIDGE, 1865
Fort Fetterman, 1867
WOUNDED KNEE, 1890
Fort Randall, 1856
BEAR RIVER, 1863
GRATTAN AFFAIR, 1854
WARBONNET CREEK, 1876
Fort Robinson, 1874
Fort Laramie, 1849
Fort Bridge, 1858
PYRAMID LAKE, 1860
TRUCKEE, 1860
Fort D.A. Russull, 1867
MUD SPRINGS, 1865
RUSH CREEK, 1865
Fort Douglas 1862
MILK CREEK, 1879
ASH HOLLOW, 1865
JULESBURG, 1865
Fort Omaha, 1863
Fort McPherson, 1863
SUMMIT SPRINGS, 1869
Fort Kearny, 1848
MASSACRE CANYON, 1873
BEECHER ISLAND, 1868
MEEKER AGENCY, 1879
BEAVER CREEK, 1868
Fort Wallace, 1865
Fort Levenworth, 1827
SAND CREEK, 1864
Fort Hays, 1865
Fort Riley, 1855
Fort Lyon, 1860
Fort Harker, 1864
Fort Larned, 1859
Fort Garland, 1858
Fort Dodge, 1864
CANYON DE CHELLY, 1864
ROUND MOUNTAIN 1861
CHUSTENAHLAH, 1861
Camp Supply, 1868
BIRD CREEK, 1861
SALT RIVER CANYON, 1872
Camp Verde, 1864
Fort Union, 1851
Fort Wingate, 1862
ADOBE WALLS, 1864-74
CIBECUE CREEK, 1881
Fort McDowell, 1865
Fort Bascom, 1862
WASHITA, 1868
Fort Apache, 1869
Fort Sumner, 1862
PALO DURO CANYON, 1874
Fort Sill, 1869
Fort Yuma, 1863
Fort Thomas, 1876
Fort Lowell, 1862
Fort Bowie, 1862
APACHE PASS, 1862
Fort Bayard 1865
Fort Stanton 1855
Fort Huachuca, 1877
Fort Selden, 1865
Camp Richardson, 1867
Fort Cummings, 1863
Fort Griffin, 1867
SKELETON, 1886
Fort Bliss, 1849
DOVE CREEK, 1863
Fort Concho, 1867
Fort Quitman, 1859
Fort Stockton, 1859
Fort Davis, 1854
Fort Clark, 1852

✶ BATTLES
• Posts

Note: Modern boundaries are shown to identify location of historical sites.

Sources: Paullin, Charles O. *Atlas of the Historical Geography of the United States.* Baltimore: Carnegie Institution of Washington and the American Geographical Society of New York, 1932.
Waldman, Carl. *Atlas of the North American Indian.* New York: Facts On File Publications, 1985.

CartoGraphics Incorporated (612)379-3599

Crows have always been the fast friends of the whites, and have largely assisted in protecting the eastern settlements of Montana.

The Sioux are now occupying the eastern and best portion of their reservation, and by their constant warfare paralyzing all efforts to induce the Crows to undertake agriculture or other means of self-support.

... four Crows who accompanied General Brisbin's expedition to the mouth of the Big Horn, and remained behind, have just come in, and report that a very large force of Sioux are moving up the north bank of the Yellowstone. Nearly all the Crows have come in much earlier than usual, and report that they expect the Sioux to attack this agency and themselves in large force. They say they have received word from Fort Peck to that effect.

General Crook's Report

General Crook, in a report dated September 25, 1876, stated his views on the war which occurred in 1876 and the causes of it:

... These bands roamed over a vast extent of country, making the Agencies their base of supplies, closely connected by intermarriage, interest and common cause with the Agency Indians, that it was difficult to determine where the line of the peaceably disposed ceased and the hostile commenced.

General Crook

In fact, it was well known that the treaty of 1868 had been regarded by the Indians as an instrument binding on us, but not binding on them. On the part of the Government, notwithstanding the utter disregard by the Sioux of the terms of the treaty, stringent orders, enforced by military power, had been issued prohibiting settlers from trespassing upon the country known as the Black Hills.

... Indians have, without interruption, attacked persons at home, murdered and scalped them, stolen their stock, in fact violated every leading feature in the treaty. Indeed, so great were their depredations on the stock belonging to the settlers, that at certain times they have not had sufficient horses to do their ordinary farming work, all the horses being concentrated on the Sioux Reservations or among the bands which owe allegiance to what is called the Sioux Nation.

In the winter months, these renegade bands dwindle down to a comparatively small number, while in summer they are recruited by restless spirits from the different reservations, attracted by the opportunity to plunder the frontiersman so that by midsummer they become augmented from small band of one hundred to thousands.

While much of General Crook's report was accurate, one element in it must be viewed skeptically:

... the treaty of 1868 had been regarded by the Indians as an instrument binding on us, but not on them.

Sitting Bull and his followers had never signed the treaty of 1868 and naturally felt it placed no restrictions on their continuing warlike activities. Also, the treaty had been violated in many ways, by both white interlopers seeking mineral wealth and land, and by the Government, which also was not fulfilling its treaty obligations to those who chose the "peace road" by residing on the reservations.

In one respect, however, the reports of General Crook, Agent Dexter, and Inspector Watkins pointed out a fact which could not be disputed. This was the continuing raids and activities of war committed against the Crow and other tribes not at war with the Government. An article published in the *New York Herald Tribune* August 15, 1876 described the attitude of these various tribes:

... Letters received here from the Blackfeet Indian agency say that after a full council all the tribes of that nation, namely, the Bloods, Blackfeet and Piegans, have resolved to reject the proposals of Sitting Bull to join in Sioux hostilities against the whites. They have, on the contrary, signified their desire to send a company of scouts to join the Government troops in the war against the Sioux.

The unanimity with which all other tribes desire to go to war against Sitting Bull shows what intense hatred and fear these oppressive and murdering Sioux have created in the breast of the weaker tribes, which have retired before their aggressions. The Crows, the Rees, the Mandans, the Shoshones, the Flatheads, and the Blackfeet are all anxious to join our troops against the tyrants of the plains. It was certainly time for the Government to interfere on behalf of the friendly Indians if not of the whites.

Hostile Indians Ordered to Surrender

In December 1875 the Government demanded that all the Indians in the unceded territory report to the reservations by January 31, 1876, or they would be considered hostile and military action would be taken against them. It was estimated that almost 3,000 people followed the Sioux Chieftain Sitting Bull and, of this number, perhaps 800 were warriors.

The "winter roamers" ignored the Government's demand, and on February 1, 1876, the Secretary of the Interior asked the War Department to take action against them.

Winter Campaign

General Sheridan, commander of the district in which these activities of war were taking place, had hoped for a winter campaign using several columns of soldiers converging on the hostile camps from different directions. However, by February 1, 1876, it was almost too late for this strategy to be successful. If three columns had been launched earlier in the winter, and under the right leadership, the chances of success would have been excellent.

General Miles, Ranald Mackenzie and Custer had the determination and skill to conduct a successful winter campaign and, at one time or another, all did succeed in winter operations. Had these three commanders launched campaigns early in the winter of 1876 there very possibly never would have been a summer war.

One column, under General Crook, did manage to get underway in early March from Fort Fetterman, Wyoming, with about 800 soldiers. Marching northward, an Indian village was discovered and on March 17, 1876, Colonel Joseph J. Reynolds, in command of six companies of cavalry, attacked it. Although he drove the inhabitants from the camp, the Indian warriors rallied and waged a battle to recapture the village from the soldiers.

In an action he would later be court-martialed for, Colonel Reynolds abandoned the camp and instead of destroying the pony herd he had captured, which experience taught must be done, he attempted to bring them with him on his retreat.

That night the Indians raided Colonel Reynolds' camp and recaptured the ponies. The next day, when Reynolds and his six companies of cavalry rejoined General Crook and the main force, Crook then ordered a retreat back to Fort Fetterman and did not take to the field again until May 29, 1876.

General Crook's discouraging expedition accented the leadership crisis that was to mark the military campaigns of 1876. Either Miles, Mackenzie, or Custer personally would have led the attack on the Indian camp and it is unlikely any of them would have abandoned the expedition after a minor setback.

The Starving Sioux

When General Crook resumed his search for the hostile tribes on May 29, 1876, he had an expanded force of more than 1,000 soldiers and almost 300 Crow and Shoshoni Indian allies. In the meantime, Sitting Bull's army of warriors had been growing, as discouraged Indians began leaving the reservations in large numbers.

In one of the great travesties of the Government's relations with the American Indians, the United States had ordered Sitting Bull and his followers to report to the reservations while at the same time failing to provide for those who were already there. As early as February 28, 1876, President Grant was warning the Congress that the Indians on the reservations were in danger of starvation.

By April 28, 1876, the reservations were still not receiving the needed supplies, and on April 29, 1876, the *St. Paul Pioneer Press* published an article on the crisis titled "*Starving Sioux*":

> *Telegrams from Red Cloud and Spotted Tail agencies via Fort Laramie yesterday evening state that no supplies worth mentioning have been issued to the Indians at those points since the 10th inst.*
>
> *The Indians are on the point of starvation, owing to the failure of Congress to vote an appreciation and on the part of the Government to forward the supplies needed. The Indians would undoubtedly have left on a raid here had it not been for the moral effect of the late expedition against Crazy Horse's band, but there can be no question but that they will be forced to raid unless supplies are promptly forwarded.*
>
> *General Crook has been and is now urging the necessity of the supplies and holding to the agencies those Indians who are disposed to be friendly, but is apprehensive that the hostile Indians will be largely reinforced from those at the agencies on account of the lack of supplies....*

Mrs. Custer's Observation

At Fort Lincoln, Dakota Territory, Mrs. Custer wrote of the starvation that faced the reservation Indians, which she had personally witnessed during the spring of 1876:

The Indians came several times from the reservations for counsel, but the occasion that made the greatest impression upon me was towards the spring. They came to implore the General for food.

In the fall, the steamer bringing them supplies was detained in starting. It had hardly accomplished half the required distance before the ice impeded its progress, and it lay out in the channel, frozen in, all winter.

The suffering among the Indians was very great. They were compelled to eat their dogs and ponies to keep from starving. Believing a personal appeal would be effectual, they asked to come to our post for a council.

The Indian band brought their great orator, Running Antelope. He was intensely dignified and fine-looking. His face when he spoke was expressive and animated, contrary to all the precedents of Indian oratory we had become familiar with.

As he stood among them all in the General's room, he made an indelible impression on my memory . . . He described the distressing condition of the tribe with real eloquence.

The storehouses at our post were filled with supplies, and he [Custer] *promised to telegraph to the Great Father for permission to give them rations until spring. Meantime, he promised them all they could eat while they awaited at the post the answer to the despatch.*

Not content with a complaint of their present wrongs, Running Antelope went off into an earnest denunciation of the agents, calling them dishonest.

One of the Indians during the previous summer, with fox-like cunning, had lain out on the dock all day apparently sleeping, while he watched the steamer unloading supplies intended for them. A mental estimate was carefully made of what came off the boat, and compared as carefully afterwards with what was distributed. There was an undeniable deficit. A portion that should have been theirs was detained, and they accused the agent of keeping it.

The General interrupted, and asked the interpreter to say that the Great Father selected the agents from among good men before sending them out from Washington.

Running Antelope quickly responded, "They may be good men when they leave the Great Father, but they get to be desperate cheats by the time they reach us."

I shall have to ask whoever reads, to substitute another more forcible adjective, such as an angry man would use, in place of "desperate." The Indian language is not deficient in abusive terms and epithets.

The answer came next day from the Secretary of War that the Department of the Interior, which had the Indians in charge, refused to allow any army supplies to be distributed. They gave as a reason that it would involve complexities in their relations with other departments.

It was a very difficult thing for the General to explain to the Indians. They knew that both army and Indians were fed from the same source and they could not comprehend what difference it could make when a question of starvation was pending. They could not be told, what we all knew, that had the War Department made good the deficiencies it would have reflected discredit on the management of the Department of the Interior.

The chiefs were compelled to return to their reservations, where long ago all the game had been shot and their famishing tribe, where many of them were driven to join the hostiles. We were not surprised that the warriors were discouraged and desperate, and that the depredations of Sitting Bull on the settlements increased with the new accessions to his numbers.

Colonel Poland's Report

In a report dated July 14, 1876, three weeks after the Battle of the Little Big Horn, Colonel John S. Poland documented what he had personally observed while at his duty station at the Standing Rock agency.

... It has been patent to residents here for months that young men were leaving and the number of arms in the possession of Indians were disappearing very perceptibly since the departure of the troops for the Yellowstone Country....

... The Indians here admit that half their numbers are

out hunting scalps, as revealed by the massacre of June 25, 1876.

I respectfully assert without fear of error or contradictory proof that this agency – by reason of a system of starvation instituted about December '75, and the untamed malevolence of the Indian disposition has furnished 1,500 warriors armed with the best improved Henry and Winchester rifles, each supplied with probably one hundred rounds of ammunition per man – who are now enrolled among Sitting Bull's forces. Rations are issued here to the representatives of nine well known chiefs who are, beyond all doubt, on the warpath with the greater portion of their bands.

Starvation and predisposition led Kill Eagle, chief of the Blackfeet Sioux, with about twenty lodges to go into the hostile camp. He alone it is said carried 3,000 rounds of ammunition with him....

... Permit me to mention one fact in connection with the Indians at this agency. They have been starved for six weeks or two months and are entitled to consideration for not having all left for the prairies where they might at least have procured meat. Eighteen months supplies were sent here in 1875 and before the expiration of fourteen (14) months, these people were starving for six months and they have received less or not more than half rations. This can also be established in a court of justice....

The War Approaches

By June 6, 1876, it was clear a major war on the frontier territories was inevitable and in an editorial on that date the *St. Paul Pioneer Press* discussed its view on the causes of the war. This editorial also reflected the prejudices and misconceptions prevalent at that time against the American Indians:

The public, more especially the west, will await with deep interest the result of the military expeditions recently sent out against the hostile Indians of Dakota.

Since the departure of these expeditions, advises from the Indian country are that the young warriors who had previously remained in quiet at the agencies have joined the hostile bands, and that the war promises to be more serious than at first anticipated. The best authority – the military itself – estimates that Sitting Bull has been reinforced by at least a thousand warriors from Red Cloud agency alone, and that his command now exceeds 2,500 men.

Considering all the natural disadvantages under which the military labor in a campaign so far into the interior of the Indian country, Sitting Bull is no mean foe, and can at least be depended on to cause serious trouble in his subjugation.

Nor are the Indian troubles confined to Dakota alone. The lamentable results of the policy of vacillation and sentimentalism by which the government has attempted to manage the reds, is that, from Texas to Dakota, they have taken to the warpath, and our small army has all that it can do to protect the settlers of the sparsely settled frontiers.

Instead of promising the Indians only what was reasonable and punctiliously fulfilling our engagements, we have promised with a reckless prodigality beyond our power to perform, and encouraged them in extravagant expectations, beyond our power to fulfill. . . .

... Benevolent in intention, the peace policy has been a weak and ruinous one in fact.

So far as the present attitude of affairs with the Sioux nation is concerned, the responsibility rests fairly upon the shoulders of the government in a double sense. After having, by a formal "treaty" with these barbarous reds as independent and sovereign powers, stupidly granted them exclusive and inviolable possession of a vast and valuable territory directly in the path of our western development, the authorities virtually sanctioned the invasion of their conceded rights by sending out a military expedition to explore the country and to set adventurers into a fever of excitement by wonderful stories of the wealth hidden in its hills.

Of course, however, it could not be expected that the Indians would tolerate with patience the incursions of the adventurers, and the complications that have followed will surprise no one.

But our government does not recognize murder as a lawful remedy for an illegal trespass on a right of occupancy, and the Indians should be taught, in a way that they will remember, that what is law for white men is law for red men, and that by making the war on the United States and the citizens of the United States traversing their territory, they have forfeited all rights under treaties with the government, and that henceforth all concerned in the war have no claim on the government except to be dealt with as outlaws and public enemies.

Colonel Gibbon's Campaign

Early in April 1876 a second military column had left Fort Ellis, Montana, and marched east in search of Sitting Bull and his allies. This column was commanded by Colonel John Gibbon and numbered about 450 soldiers and 25 Crow scouts. The scouts were commanded by Lieutenant James Bradley and twice, once on May 16, 1876, and again on May 27, 1876, he pinpointed the location of a hostile village. On both occasions Gibbon failed to press forward with an attack.

On May 16, 1876, the reason was given that Colonel Gibbon's force could not cross the Yellowstone River; and the reason he did not advance on May 27 was not specified. In a dispatch by Colonel Gibbon to General Terry, who was then marching west with the 7th Cavalry, Gibbon, for some strange reason, did not mention that his scouts had spotted an Indian camp. Considering his failure to take advantage of that information, Gibbon may have felt a little reluctant relaying that fact to General Terry, who also happened to be his superior officer.

General Crook's Second Campaign

On June 17, 1876, Sitting Bull's warriors attacked General Crook's army on the upper reaches of the Rosebud Creek. The attack was a surprise and only quick action on the part of Crook's Crow and Shoshoni allies prevented what could have been a terrible disaster.

As Sitting Bull's warriors burst forth from the hills, the Crow and Shoshoni warriors rushed to meet them and held off the attackers long enough for the soldiers to organize a defense. The battle lasted about six hours, yet casualties on both sides were light. About a dozen of Crook's men were killed and twice that many wounded. Although the Indian losses were unknown, they probably suffered a similar number of casualties.

General Crook would claim the Rosebud battle as a "victory" because the battlefield remained in possession of the soldiers. Crook, however, was quick to turn it into a decisive triumph for Sitting Bull. Crook withdrew back to his base camp on Goose Creek and removed his force from active campaigning against the Indians while he awaited reinforcements.

By withdrawing from the campaign, General Crook influenced, perhaps decisively, the upcoming events. The Rosebud Battle took place only 50 miles from the Little Big Horn battlefield and, had he reorganized his command and continued north, Crook could have made contact with the other columns in the field and the combined forces should have been a match for any number of Indian warriors. As it turned out, Crook did not even attempt to contact the other commands, although the information concerning the Rosebud Battle would have been extremely valuable to them.

On the day the Battle of the Little Big Horn took place, John Finerty, the news correspondent with General Crook's command, wrote that evidence of that battle could be seen from Crook's position. Finerty wrote:

> *Colonel Anson Mills, ever restless and enterprising, made an informal reconnaissance from camp on the afternoon of Sunday, June 25th. He went up some distance in the foothills with a small party, and, returning to camp, reported a dense smoke toward the northwest, at a great distance. He called the attention of several to it and all agreed that it must be a prairie fire or something of that kind.*
>
> *It was a prairie fire, sure enough, but it was kindled, as we knew afterward, by the deadly, far-sweeping musketry of the vengeful savages who annihilated Custer and his devoted band on the banks of the Little Big Horn! Even while we gazed, perhaps, the tragedy was consummated, and the American Murat had fought his last battle.*

Apparently, General Crook did not consider the dense smoke worth investigating and on July 1 he left camp with a picked crew of companions on a "hunting and exploring expedition into the mountain ranges." Crook seemed to

have some unique ideas on how to conduct a military campaign.

The Number of Sitting Bull's Warriors

The number of Indian warriors which eventually were to join Sitting Bull by the time of the June 25, 1876 battle with the 7th Cavalry can never be accurately determined, although several researchers and historians have attempted to give reasonable estimates.

It is known that many warriors left the agencies before the battle but, through corrupt motives as well as self-interest, Indian agents underreported these defections. It was in the agents' own interest to overreport the number of Indians on the reservations so as to receive supplies for this number, the surplus then being disposed of for the agents' profit through dishonest means. However, by June 25, 1876, Sitting Bull's army clearly had grown from the original hundreds to many thousands.

Not long after the Battle of the Little Big Horn an article was published in the *Chicago Tribune.* This article contained information which originated from Fort Laramie, Wyoming Territory, July 17, 1876. This article stated:

> *It was estimated that 2,000 warriors left Red Cloud and Spotted Tail (agencies) at the time Gen. Crook started out in May.*

In a subsequent article in the *Chicago Tribune,* information from Fort Buford, dated July 18, was published.

> *Burke, the Agent at Standing Rock, has all along maintained that none of the warriors at that Agency were absent, but Mrs. Galpin, an educated Uncpapa, wrote Captain Harmon, at Fort Lincoln, that of the 2,000 braves not more than 500 had been at the Agency since the 15th of May.*

An article in the *Army and Navy Journal,* dated October 21, 1876, documented the continuing corruption of the Indian agents:

> *The most complete expose of the elastic arithmetic of the "average" Indian agent is made in the result of the last official count of the Indians at Standing Rock agency made by Captain Johnston, First Infantry, in charge and acting as agent.*
>
> *Out of 7,000 – the basis upon which supplies have sent out by the Bureau for the last year or two – only 2,300 are now present and Captain Johnston is satisfied that at no time for many months has there been a larger number than 3,500 present.*
>
> *Yet supplies were recently sent to the agency by the Indian Bureau on estimates for 7,000 souls, and the acting agent says that the quantity received is ample for three years, although intended for one.*
>
> *But the late Indian agent considers the course of the army "usurpation" and "unwarrantable interference."*

Unfortunately, the military authorities would never be given an accurate estimate of these hostile defections from the agencies.

The Weapons of the Indian Warriors

Perhaps one of the most unwarranted statements which had repeatedly appeared in some of the histories of the Battle of the Little Big Horn concerns the weapons used by Sitting Bull's warriors. Many historians claim the warriors had few firearms and were armed mostly with bows and arrows, and they assert that this was the weapon predominantly used during the battle.

This is not true, as the archeological examination of the Custer Hill battlefield area in the mid 1980s demonstrated. Sitting Bull's warriors were well-supplied with firearms and these arms were used at the Battle of the Little Big Horn.

There are also many accounts by those involved which commented upon the fact that Sitting Bull's warriors were armed, not only with firearms, but those of the latest pattern. In the *New York Herald Tribune* of August 19, 1876, an interview with the Sioux warrior Medicine Cloud was published:

> *Medicine Cloud does not know how much ammunition they have, but they have plenty of guns and pistols.*

On October 14, 1876, an interview with Kill Eagle was published. Kill Eagle was in Sitting Bull's camp the day of the battle, but said he was a prisoner and did not fight. :

> *The official report of Capt. Johnston, 1st Infantry, Acting Indian Agent at Standing Rock, has been published. It comprises the statement of Kill Eagle, the greater part of which has already appeared in the* Journal. *As to the arms of the hostiles, the following testimony was given by Kill Eagle.*

Q. Did they have plenty arms and ammunition?

A. They seemed to have. I could not tell, as I had no opportunity to get to see them. All the Indian soldiers who were guarding me had splendid arms.

Q. Did they have needle guns?

A. They had all kinds of arms; Henry rifles, Winchester, Sharps, Spencer, muzzle loaders, and many of them two and three revolvers a piece; all had knives and lances.

Q. Did you hear them say where they got these arms?

A. I heard some of them say where they got them. I heard the Cheyenne Indians say they had always been hostiles, and they captured theirs in battle. This is the only way I heard them say they got their arms.

Q. Did you hear anyone say where Sitting Bull got his ammunition?

A. I was not permitted to run about the camps, and I did not hear about it.

Q. Did the [Indian] *soldiers who were guarding you have plenty of ammunition?*

A. Yes, their belts full, and the best kind of arms, fixed ammunition, metallic cartridges. All of us here had very bad guns. You see what we turned in.

Later, during the summer of 1876, the frontier scout and Eastern showman, William F. "Buffalo Bill" Cody, fought a hand-to-hand fight with an Indian warrior named "Yellow Hand" or "Yellow Bear," in which Buffalo Bill emerged victorious. On August 12, 1876, the *Army and Navy Journal* commented upon the arms carried by Yellow Bear:

... we learn that the chief, "Yellow Bear," who was killed by Colonel Merritt's scout, "Buffalo Bill," recently, was fresh from the agency, and from him as he lay dead on the field, was taken, first, a Winchester repeating rifle of the latest and most improved pattern, with a full supply of ammunition for it; second, the newest style of Smith and Wesson navy revolver, with ammunition; a Colt's old style navy revolver, with ammunition; a heavy knife, shield, and spear.

In a report dated September 25, 1876, General Crook commented upon the fact that many of the hostile Indians were well-armed and the problem this caused the army:

Of the difficulties with which we have had to contend, it may be well to remark, that when the Sioux Indian was armed with a bow and arrow he was more formidable, fighting as he does most of the time on horseback, than when he got the old fashioned muzzle loading rifle. But when he came into possession of the breech loader and metallic cartridge, which allows him to load and fire from his horse with perfect ease, he became at once ten thousand times more formidable.

With the improved arms, I have seen our friendly Indians, riding at full speed, shoot and kill a wolf, also on the run, while it is a rare thing that our troops can hit an Indian on horseback, though the soldier may be on his feet at the time.

The Sioux is a cavalry soldier from the time he has intelligence enough to ride a horse or fire a gun. If he wishes to dismount, his hardy pony, educated by long usage, will graze around near where he has been left, ready when his master wants to mount either to move forward or escape.

Even with their lodges and families, they can move at the rate of fifty miles per day. They are perfectly familiar with the country, have their spies and hunting parties out all the time, at distances of from twenty to fifty miles each way from their villages, know the number and movements of all the troops that may be operating against them, just about what they can probably do, and hence can choose their own times and places of conflict or avoid it altogether.

The Causes of the War of 1876

The causes of the War of 1876 can be described as being as complex and varied as the expanding nation of America of that year. The American Indian had been badly treated and cheated long before the year 1876, and that pattern had continued. The western expansion of America, supplied by millions of immigrants from overseas, as well as by the eastern population, was a force in itself, unstoppable by the Government or the Indian tribes. On the reservations the Indians were being starved and this sent thousands of warriors into

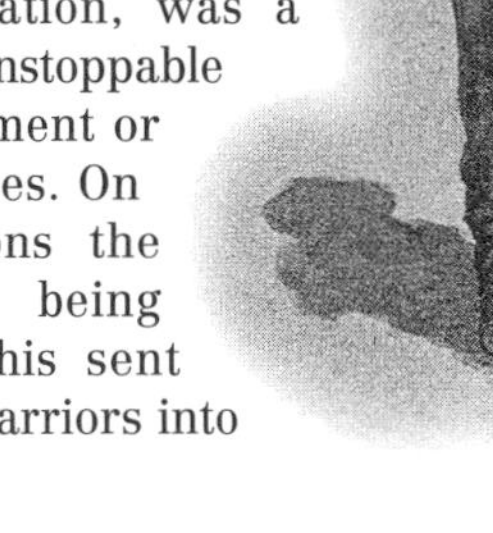

Sitting Bull's war camp.

The warfare among the various tribes of Indians on the Plains had actually increased since the introduction of the horse and firearm, and Sitting Bull and his warriors were just as committed to a life of war as at any time in their past.

The War of 1876 was, however, not caused by the American Frontier Army. Soldiers do not decide where they go, who they fight, or when they fight. This is determined by orders delivered through government authorities, and once ordered to fight a soldier is obligated to do so.

This was the situation in 1876. The Frontier Army had been ordered to seek out and fight Sitting Bull and his army. Although every commander of combat forces that summer: General Terry, Colonel Gibbon, General Crook and Custer, as well as many of the lesser military figures, were to comment at one time or another with great sympathy concerning the unfair treatment of the Plains Indians, they were, nevertheless, obligated to follow the orders given them by the Government.

Unfortunately, unwise and corrupt government practices had assured the soldiers involved in the War of 1876 of two things. First, the Indian warriors which the Frontier Army was ordered to fight were well-armed. Second, there would be a lot of them.

Battle of the Rosebud

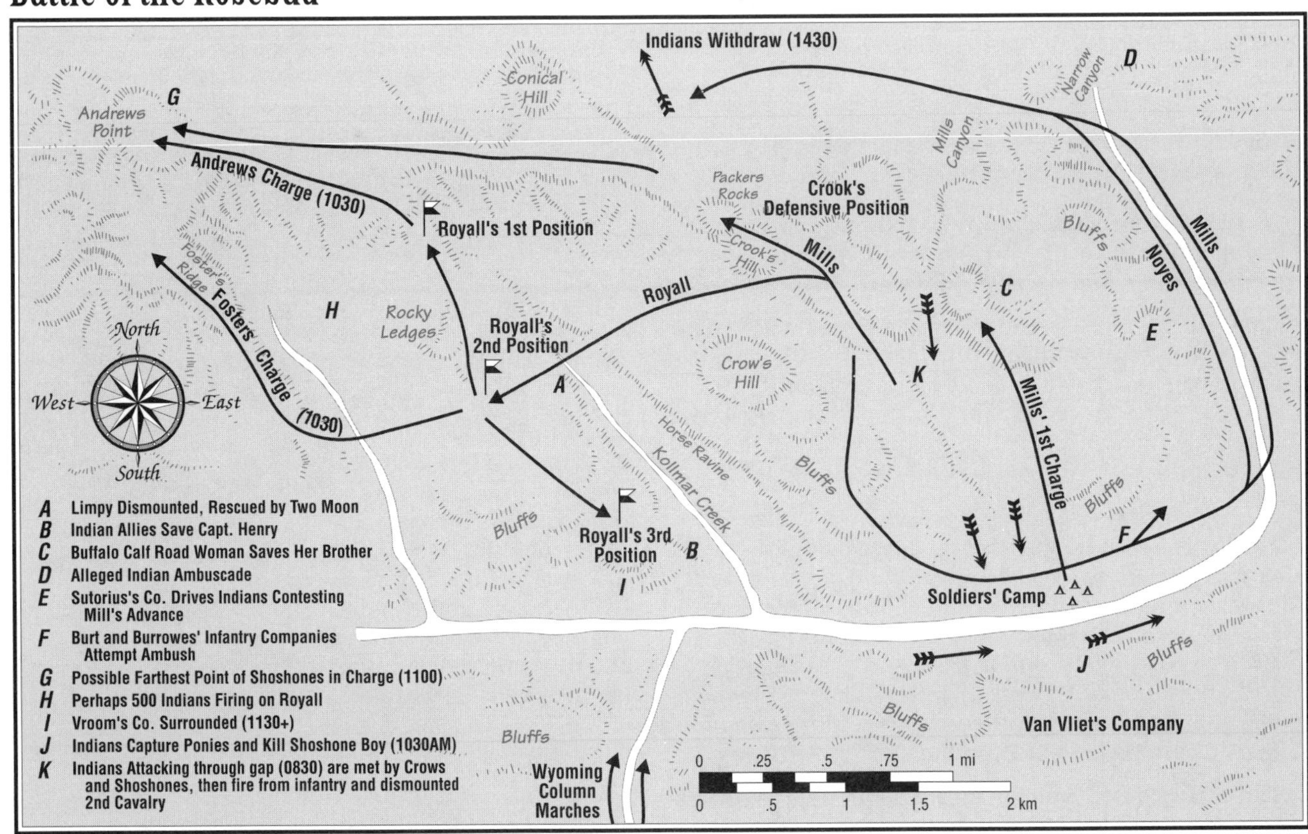

Source: Sarf, Wayne Michael. *The Little Bighorn Campaign.* Hong Kong: Combined Book Inc., 1993.

CartoGraphics Incorporated (612)379-3599

CHAPTER 5

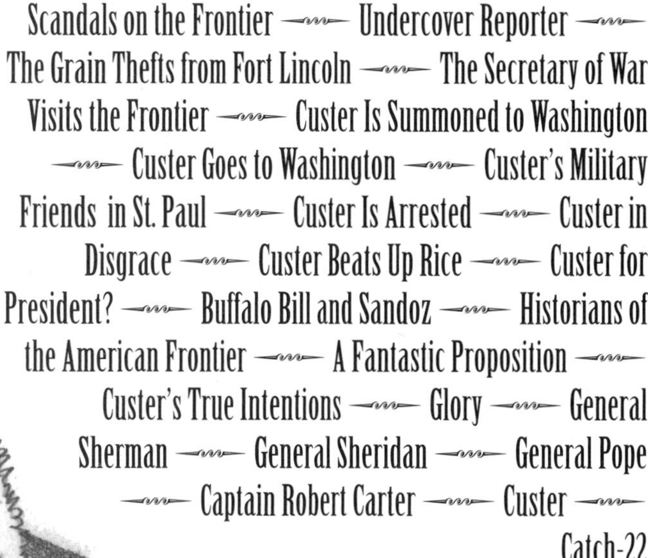

Scandals on the Frontier — Undercover Reporter — The Grain Thefts from Fort Lincoln — The Secretary of War Visits the Frontier — Custer Is Summoned to Washington — Custer Goes to Washington — Custer's Military Friends in St. Paul — Custer Is Arrested — Custer in Disgrace — Custer Beats Up Rice — Custer for President? — Buffalo Bill and Sandoz — Historians of the American Frontier — A Fantastic Proposition — Custer's True Intentions — Glory — General Sherman — General Sheridan — General Pope — Captain Robert Carter — Custer — Catch-22

Chief Gall

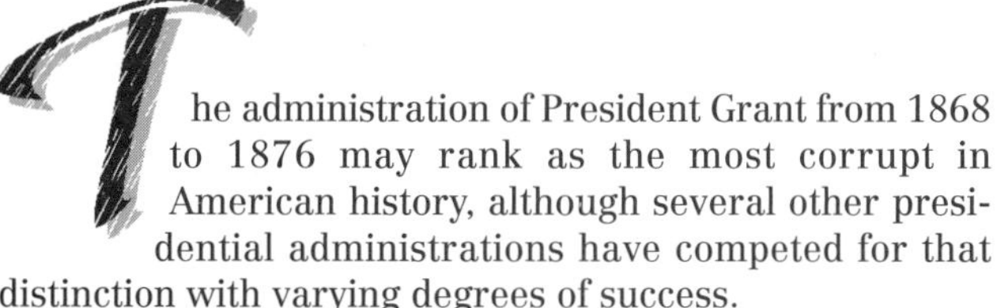

The administration of President Grant from 1868 to 1876 may rank as the most corrupt in American history, although several other presidential administrations have competed for that distinction with varying degrees of success.

The Grant administration, however, ranks with the best, or worst, of them. Historian and author Robert Prickett wrote:

Honesty during Grant's administration was nearly extinct ... virtue in the War and Interior Departments apparently was gone completely.

With the War Department defrauding the settlers and soldiers, and both departments defrauding the Indians, almost everyone on the frontier was contributing money to a large assortment of government officials and politicians.

These conditions, which lasted throughout the two terms of General Grant, became a blot on the pages of every history book of the land.

President Grant has been described by many historians as "personally honest," but an "unfortunate judge of character." Many of those around him were involved in various dishonest schemes and a large number of these shifty characters were eventually caught. However, if Grant could use his poor judgment as an excuse for the many scandals of his administration, then another flaw that plagued him was his refusing to take action when this corruption was brought to his attention. Many of the dishonest dealings of his cronies were widely publicized throughout his administration and, unfortunately, Grant refused to take action unless it was forced upon him. One newspaper described the widespread corruption as:

"Grantism," ... [which] *like a cancer, has sent its poisonous roots through our whole administrative system.*

President Grant himself was publicly insulted as an "imbecile" and vilified almost daily in the newspapers, and yet he would not, or could not, respond by at least attempting to promote honesty in the government.

Scandals on the Frontier

The two scandals which directly affected those on the American frontier were the near total corruption of the Interior Department in its administration of Indian affairs, resulting in widespread unrest among the frontier Indian tribes, and the Post Tradership Scheme which involved, among others, the president's brother, Orvil Grant.

The Post Tradership Scheme was simplicity in itself and involved the basic principle of monopoly. Each military post

President Grant

had a post trader which sold goods to the soldiers stationed there. The pay scale for the soldiers in 1876 was modest, a private started out at a little over $13.00 a month, yet the profits as multiplied by the number of soldiers must have looked attractive to those who were looking for a dishonest way to make a living. The post traderships were "sold" by representatives of Secretary of War William W. Belknap under the condition that the profits were to be divided among various dishonest government officials. Orvil Grant was given the strenuous task of traveling the frontier under military escort to collect Secretary of War Belknap's share of the graft.

In fairness to Orvil, however, it should be mentioned that he eventually did express remorse for his dishonest actions, saying:

> *I do not regret what I did, or getting caught, but that I made so little money at it.*

Honest military officers were outraged and when some of them, including Custer, attempted to circumvent the crooked monopoly by purchasing articles for the soldiers off the military post, an order was received from the War Department directing that the practice be stopped. The soldiers would, under direct order, spend their money at the post trader, regardless of the quality of the goods or the inflated prices which were necessary to pay Orvil Grant, Secretary of War Belknap, and the rest of their pals.

In 1872, General William B. Hazen testified before the House Military Committee concerning the corrupt system used by the post traders and about the same time General Sherman said the system was the "worst possible." Hazen's advice that a commissary system be established was ignored and the entire affair was dropped.

Undercover Reporter

In 1874 an undercover reporter was sent to Bismarck, Dakota Territory to investigate the various frauds. His name was Ralph Meeker and he worked for the *New York Herald*.

Reporter Meeker got a job at Fort Lincoln under the name of J. D. Thompson. The postmaster in Bismarck was Linda Slaughter and she assisted Meeker in forwarding his clandestine reports of the frauds he discovered to a New York newspaper. Apparently, Custer was involved in this investigation and assisted Meeker in developing sources and obtaining undercover employment under an alias at various locations, including Standing Rock reservation and Fort Berthold.

The resulting publicity proved embarrassing to those involved and when it was discovered that Postmaster Slaughter had been forwarding reports through her office, Orvil Grant was quick to tattle to the president. Linda Slaughter was removed from her position but a resulting furor, including a petition by the citizens of Bismarck, caused Miss Slaughter to be reinstated. Reporter Meeker, too, was discovered and in spite of an attempt to assassinate him he managed to escape from the territory alive. His reports and documentation, however, were ignored and the post tradership corruption continued as usual.

The Grain Thefts from Fort Lincoln

Other types of corruption took place at Fort Lincoln, one of them involving the mayor of Bismarck. Mrs. George Yates, the wife of Captain Yates, who was killed at the Battle of the Little Big Horn, related an incident which, if anything, demonstrated the near impunity with which thieves could operate on the frontier.

> *During the Spring of 1875, the grain from the several forage buildings at Fort Lincoln had been steadily disappearing ...*
>
> *... So when, one bright day, just before the breaking up of the river in the Spring, Custer issued orders for the regiment to be in readiness to start at the call of the trumpet for Bismarck, not an officer of his command but was as astonished, and knew as little of what was expected of them as did the citizens of Bismarck when they saw the cavalry, fully armed and equipped, come riding into their little town.*
>
> *The Seventh Cavalry rode to the different places indicated by the General and found the grain at every place pointed out by him, to the surprise and indignation of the honest citizens of Bismarck, who, being in ignorance of the localities the thieves had chosen to secrete*

it, were naturally indignant at the slur cast upon their reputations.

For awhile, loud talking ensued and a riot of no mean pretensions was threatened.

Finally, upon the General insisting, doors were thrown open to him and the stolen grain in every instance was exposed to view, the soldiers turning the bags over and showing the government brand. In the mayor's own warehouse (he being also a prominent merchant at the time), a number were discovered.

You can imagine the good mayor's surprise at this last selection of a repository for these stolen goods.

A number of arrests were made, the mayor now concurring heartily with the military, and for temporary safekeeping, the corn thieves were escorted by the cavalry back to Fort Abraham Lincoln and lodged in the guard house.

Their trial, which took place at Fargo ... occupied many months, and employed numbers of witnesses, the leading actors in the scene shortly afterwards finding their way into the penitentiary.

As Mrs. Yates mentioned in her statement, "the good mayor's surprise" undoubtedly influenced the "good mayor" in "concurring heartily with the military" in learning the location of missing corn and perhaps even being more diligent about preventing similar occurrences, or at least not being caught.

The Secretary of War Visits the Frontier

In 1875 Secretary of War Belknap visited the frontier and one of his stops was to be Fort Lincoln. When Belknap got off the train in Bismarck he discovered that a pamphlet had been printed and distributed to the crowd awaiting him, detailing his connections and alleged connections with various frauds. This rude welcome was to be compounded a short time later when Belknap made an official visit to Fort Lincoln. Protocol called for Custer, as the commander of the post, to meet the secretary of war as he entered the military reservation. Instead, Custer ignored Belknap and awaited him in his quarters.

Robert Seip, the post trader, had sent a basket of wine to Custer with which to entertain Secretary of War Belknap during his visit. Custer returned it with the comment that he did not drink wine and would not serve Belknap even if he did. Another version says Custer made the comment that he was "not that sort of hairpin." Exactly what transpired in Custer's quarters when Belknap made his official visit is apparently not on record, however, it probably was not a very positive meeting for the secretary of war. Custer's treatment of Belknap had already demonstrated he was more than willing to place himself at political risk for what he believed was a just principle and Belknap may very well have received an earful.

Custer Is Summoned to Washington

Matters concerning the post tradership frauds finally came to a head in early 1876, perhaps stimulated by the national elections to be held later in the year. A congressional committee was formed to investigate the accusations against Secretary of War Belknap and his unscrupulous partners. It would meet for nearly four months until June 20, 1876. More than fifty witnesses would be called and the testimony proved that the accusations that had been made for years were indeed true.

Representative Hiester Clymer of Pennsylvania, who headed the congressional committee, knew that Custer, among others, had made accusations against Secretary of War Belknap. Many knew as much, or more, than Custer, concerning post tradership frauds. However, from a political standpoint, Representative Clymer would certainly gain advantages by having Custer testify at the hearings. He telegraphed a summons to Custer to appear, after which Custer, now in the midst of preparations for the coming campaign, telegraphed General Terry for advice. General Terry's reply was:

Dispatch received. You need no order beyond the summons of the committee.

I am sorry you have to go, for I fear it will delay our movements. I should suppose that if your testimony is not as to the facts themselves, and will only point out the witnesses from whom the committee can get the facts, your information might be communicated by letter or telegraph, and that being done, you might ask to be relieved from personal attention without exposing yourself to misconstruction. However, you must use your own judgment....

Your services are indispensable and no thought of a transfer can be entertained.

Custer took General Terry's advice and telegraphed a message to Representative Clymer, attempting to avoid the trip to Washington:

While I hold myself in readiness to obey the summons of your committee, I telegraph to state that I am engaged upon an important expedition, intended to operate against the hostile Indians, and I expect to take the field early in April. My presence here is deemed very necessary.

In view of this, would it not be satisfactory for you to forward to me such questions as may be necessary, allowing me to return my replies by mail.

Custer Goes to Washington

Custer's request to Representative Clymer was refused and the motive for this was commented upon by author Frederick Whittaker:

Custer had telegraphed to Clymer, begging to be excused from attendance at Washington, as an important expedition was about to take to the field in which his presence was necessary. He earnestly begged to be left at his post, but his request was denied. Clymer was bound to have him in Washington for political effect, just as Johnson in old times had been determined to have Custer's name associated with his, in "swinging round the circle."

Representative Clymer was determined to get the publicity that he knew Custer would bring. A newspaper commented on Custer's departure for Washington on March 21, 1876.

General Custer departed for Washington this morning having been subpoenaed to appear before the senate investigating committee, to give testimony will undoubtedly develop such an issue of fraud as will further startle the country.

On April 1, 1876, the *St. Paul Pioneer Press* published a lengthy article concerning Custer's testimony before the congressional committee:

In a very calm style, Custer gave graphic pictures of frontier life and of how the poor boy in blue was constantly robbed by politicians. He knew especially about Sykes, who was trader at Fort Abraham Lincoln, where General Custer is in command.

Sykes, after a time, became tired of the position and told Custer that he was going to resign. Custer at this took him aside and made him confess his reasons for wanting to go. Sykes said that he could not make enough money; that he had to pay a tribute of two-thirds of the profits, and this left him so little that he was obliged to go out of business.

One-third of these profits went to General Hedrick, superintendent of Internal Revenue, and one-third to General Rice, of Washington, an intimate friend of Belknap, who was the same Rice that charged a candidate for a post-tradership $1,000 to introduce them to Belknap. General Custer said it was well known at his post that the post of Fort Buford had to pay the same amount of blackmail to Hedrick and Rice.

Custer's opinion was that in nearly all cases where Indian supplies were given out, this is occasioned by stealing. He had known contractors when on their way to deliver goods at Indian agencies to sell these goodies to settlers on the way.

General Custer's testimony was important from the fact that he gave many details of the petty frauds that were countenanced by the war department. He made a test case by making a report to Belknap of a particular instance of fraud, and when it was ignored, he resolved to no longer waste his time in that direction.

His unhesitating opinion was that both Belknap and Orvil Grant were silent partners in the post-traderships and shared in no end of illicit gain from their transactions.

Custer's Military "Friends" in St. Paul

A series of news articles then marked the testimony of Custer as it grew into a major political controversy which was to culminate in scathing criticism of Custer. By April 16, 1876, Custer was receiving widespread criticism in the newspapers:

As was stated in these dispatches some days ago, General Custer is charged with having inspired the articles in The New York Herald *abusive of Belknap, even if he was not actually their author.*

An attempt was made today in Clymer's committee to find out the truth of the charges. Through the conscientiousness of a Herald *correspondent in reference to stating the business matters of that paper, they were not proven, although his refusal to testify that Custer was not the author leaves the matter in great doubt.*

General Custer's action before Clymer's committee and

elsewhere in giving points against Secretary Belknap and his brother officers has not been regarded favorably by the latter, and they will not be very reluctant to give points on him.

They claim that his official record is quite as available as that of any of the officers he has attacked, and he may be investigated shortly himself. They prefer, however, to make their charges against him in the regular way, and have them tried by a military court of inquiry, and not by the investigating committee.

It is understood that charges will soon be brought against him, which, if substantiated, will be seriously to his detriment.

Among the other charges is one that he has had on his rolls persons who received regular pay as employees, but did not work for the government. As this is one of the charges he has made against other men, his position, if the allegations are proven, will not be enviable. The Captain Harmon who testified today is an ex-army officer who has been a post-trader, an applicant for the tradership at Fort Lincoln.

General Custer in trying to run the Clymer committee so as to break down certain officers whom he dislikes, has placed himself in a position where he is certain to encounter a court-martial.

Some of his statements have already been shown to be false, and his anxiety to break down his superior officers, is now so apparent that whatever he says is received with due allowance.

The newspaper article was published in St. Paul, Minnesota, which was the home duty station of the 7th Cavalry. It is interesting that the article in the *St. Paul Pioneer Press* stated that Custer was:

... in a position where he is certain to encounter a court-martial.

Newspersons do not determine who will receive military discipline; military persons do. Apparently, the newspaper was receiving information from a military person, or persons, stationed in St. Paul.

Custer Is Arrested

After attempting to meet with President Grant several times, and being denied an interview, Custer left Washington for the frontier with what he apparently believed was official permission. When his train arrived in Chicago, however, Custer found himself under arrest for leaving Washington without authorization.

A series of telegrams soon had Custer released and on his way to St. Paul, but he would no longer command the expedition against the Sioux, as had been expected.

Custer now found himself exactly in the position he had feared, which was that of political scapegoat. Author Frederick Whittaker later commented upon President Grant's behavior:

President Grant was once General Grant. As General Grant, he was chiefly distinguished for one virtue, an indomitable resolution and obstinacy in following whatever plan he had resolved on, an iron determination to pursue it at whatever cost. This quality of determination in war had finally conducted him to success because, as a general, his power was absolute. As the executive of a republic, it brought him hatred and ill will, for the successful head of a republic must be an eloquent and persuasive man, who can win others to his side by flattery, and who knows how to yield outwardly, while gaining his ends by craft and subtlety.

Another virtue possessed by General Grant was that of faithfulness to his friends, and this virtue also tended to his success in war, while in peace it operated in exactly the opposite direction. Had it been accompanied by good judgment in the choice of friends, it might not have been so disastrous, but unluckily, Grant seems from the first to have fallen into the hands of very questionable friends, who would have fleeced him had he been a rich man, who were accused of fleecing the nation under his protection, he being a high officer.

The efforts of the Clymer Committee and the House during the Belknap Investigation had undoubtedly been directed towards the injury of Grant and his friends, who formed what was known under the general term of "the Administration"; and the animus of the whole attack was so evident, the persistency of the efforts to find something on which to hang more impeachments so untiring, that they had excited the bitterest indignation in Grant himself.

His very virtues, pride, firmness, faithful friendship, conviction of honesty, tended to embitter his animosity against all connected with the attack on "his administration." He looked on them as mortal enemies, and never forgave them. Amongst these he now counted Custer.

Custer in Disgrace

By May 11, 1876, it had become evident that Custer was in what can be described as very hot water and an article in the *St. Paul Pioneer Press* reflected the public pressure now being vigorously applied to Custer:

He early adopted the theory that military reputation was an affair of printer's ink, and he has made more industrious use of this wonder-working pigment in

keeping his name and exploits before the country than any other American chevalier of our time, except George Francis Train. He is a sort of Dr. Helmbold on horseback, only his Buchu is himself.

He is lieutenant colonel of his regiment; but he is general of the newspaper brigade, which, in his view, is a far more important arm of the military service than either cavalry or infantry.

Whenever he goes into any sort of active service, he has a corps of newspaper correspondents attached to his person, to trumpet his praises, and what they lack in earnestness of obliviation he more than makes up by his own diligence as a newspaper correspondent, and as a prolific contributor to the public journals and periodicals.

Custer is a dashing cavalryman in the field; and he performed some good service during the war, like a good many others; but his vainglorious itching for notoriety and sensationalism, and the general moral lawlessness which is the usual accompaniment of such restless and reckless egotism as his, have manifested themselves in so many offensive forms that he has entirely lost caste in army circles. The means he has taken to manufacture a newspaper reputation for himself have destroyed his reputation in the army itself.

He is regarded simply as a charlatan and a fraud. His recent exploits in the character of a witness before the War Department Investigating Committee have confirmed the uncomplimentary estimate in which he is held in military circles.

Custer is perhaps the only officer in the American army who would have been capable of saying that he is the only man in the army fit to lead an expedition against the Sioux, and then cite General Sherman as authority for this startling assertion.

We have in this statement an average specimen of the extraordinary compound of presumptuous egotism and presumptuous mendacity which make him the reckless and lawless being he is.

Custer Beats Up Rice

One event that was, perhaps, more satisfying to Custer occurred during his unpleasant visit to Washington. As a man of the frontier accustomed to violence he had a chance to exercise a primitive form of retribution on one of the key figures involved in the tradership scandals. He happened to meet a Mr. Rice on a street corner and the result appeared in numerous newspapers:

General Custer was the hero of a severe caning affair, in which E.W. Rice, a claim agent here, was the worsted party.

Rice has long been an intimate friend of General Belknap's, and is believed by a good many to have been the medium through whom a large part of the post-tradership money passed from the buyers to General Belknap.

General Custer's testimony tended to prove this, the General testifying, among other things, that he had been told that in a certain instance a post-tradership was secured through the payment of $5,000 to Rice.

He replied by a newspaper card in which he said that if General Custer did say that any money was ever paid to him [Rice] *for a post-tradership, he was a liar.*

Tonight, Custer met Rice on G street and gave him a very severe caning.

It may have been a chance confrontation, or this meeting may have been planned, at least by Rice, perhaps in an effort to bribe Custer to silence in the congressional hearings. If so, Rice's efforts were quite apparently unsuccessful.

Custer for President?

Despite the fact that spring of 1876 marked the near ruin of Custer's military career, and a very effective scandalizing of him in the newspapers, Mari Sandoz, a later author, developed a theory that Custer had a cunning plan to run for president. This plan required him to win a victory over Sitting Bull and his allies and this victory would have catapulted him into the White House. Mari Sandoz presented this theory in her description of Custer's plan to attack the Indian camp:

And it was a good time now for a military victory, only nine days to the Fourth of July and the national centennial, a hundred years since the Declaration of Independence was signed. It was an excellent time to defeat the warring Sioux, and today the best time of all, with the Democratic Convention opening the day after tomorrow, and James Gordon Bennett of the New York Herald *or his lieutenants surely prepared to stampede the convention for his friend, General George Armstrong Custer. Or Jay Gould of the* New York World *and the western railroads might be as effective.*

Victory now would leave two days and three nights to get the news to the telegraph office and to the Convention at St. Louis. Charlie Reynolds, who had carried Custer's news of gold in the Black Hills out to the world, could reach the telegraph office at Bozeman in less than two days with a terse account that Custer would write.

There would be additional messengers for insurance, Herendeen and others, each taking a different route, Bouyer to spur down to the telegraph at the North Platte River, with Custer himself probably making the run to the Missouri River – Custer for this run and Mark Kellogg.

A victory telegram read at the Convention the morning of the 28th would do it, so he must succeed by sundown this evening, even if the defeated were only a small camp, only the "half a dozen Sioux lodges" that he had told the Ree scouts would make him the Great Father, the President.

Author of several books on Custer, Lawrence A. Frost, as well as other authors and researchers, have disputed Mari Sandoz's theory that Custer had presidential aspirations during 1876 and that this influenced his conduct up to and at the Battle of the Little Big Horn. Frost said:

Sandoz outlined a plan – ludicrous to anyone familiar with convention protocol and political technique, which Custer purportedly had made that would thrust him into the limelight during the Democratic Convention in St. Louis.

Sandoz would have the reader believe that news of Custer's victory over the Sioux would have James Gordon Bennett of the New York Herald *stampeding the convention in an all out effort to get Custer nominated for President.*

She would have one believe that the financier Jay Gould of the New York World *would lend his weight. All Custer would have had to do was "to defeat the warring Sioux."*

The victory would be relayed to a telegraph in Bozeman in two days by the scout Charlie Reynolds. Additional insurance could be added by having George Herendeen and a few other scouts such as Mitch Bouyer head out in other directions with similar messages. Custer, of course, would take the correspondent Mark Kellogg and "make the run to the Missouri River."

To insure his nomination, the victory telegram would have to reach the floor of the Convention by the morning of the 28th of June, so he was forced to finish off the Sioux by the evening of the 25th. Thus, the need to attack Sitting Bull's camp at noon of the 25th, says Sandoz.

Custer may have had political aspirations at one time, but bitter experience had dissipated any such thoughts. He had taken an active part in politics in 1866 by attending the National Union Convention as a delegate. The Convention was held to adopt a doctrine asserting the supremacy of representative government, which they claimed Congress was failing to do.

Custer firmly and even vehemently opposed the election of any individual to office who had supported the Rebellion. In one instance, he publicly opposed a Michigan man because of his efforts to support the South during the Civil War.

It was during this period that Custer was asked to run for Congress, and it was suggested that he become a candidate for Governor. He flatly refused.

As a guest of President Johnson in his "Swing Around the Circle," Custer had every opportunity of observing the professional politician in action and the response to him by inhospitable and radical mobs at some of the stops.

Custer had been exposed to the workup a candidate must undergo to obtain a nomination, the incumbent being no exception. Sandoz surely knew that any aspirant for this office must corral delegates long before a convention. There was no other way. And there is not one shred of evidence that anyone had introduced Custer's name prior to or during the Democratic Convention in St. Louis. A search of the records and of the St. Louis newspapers indicates as much.

Historian and author of the American West Joseph G. Rosa also expressed dismay with Sandoz's research and the methods she used to arrive at far-fetched conclusions. Mr. Rosa attempted to track down another of this author's statements concerning another historical figure, Wild Bill Hickok. In frustration, Mr. Rosa commented:

It is unfortunate that for reasons best known to herself [Mari Sandoz] *was not averse to causing confusion by producing references to historical characters that*

eventually turned out to be fictional, frequently involving others in months of fruitless research.

Buffalo Bill and Sandoz

Historian and author Robert Benjamin Smith published an article in *Wild West* magazine in which he mentioned another problem with Sandoz's conclusions, this time involving William F. "Buffalo Bill" Cody and a one-on-one battle he had with an Indian warrior named Yellow Hair, shortly after the Battle of the Little Big Horn:

> *She* [Sandoz] *described how, in the middle of the fighting at Warbonnet Creek, Yellow Hair (whom she insists on calling Yellow Hand) rode boldly out from the Cheyenne ranks and called a challenge to any bluecoat brave enough to come out and fight hand to hand.*
>
> *At that point, Sandoz claimed, some nameless trooper shot the Indian and lifted his scalp. Later, Bill Cody paid $5 for this souvenir and took credit for the kill as well. Sandoz claimed to have found these "facts" in official military records, though to date those "records" are unknown to any other person on the planet. Still, other writers have accepted her version of the story.*
>
> *Against all this, we have the eyewitness testimony of Chris Madsen. Madsen in later years was a legendary peace officer who, in company with Bill Tilghman and Heck Thomas, helped clean up the Oklahoma Territory.*
>
> *His reputation for truth and honest dealing was beyond question. Madsen saw "Buffalo Bill's" fight with Yellow Hair from start to finish and recalled that "through the powerful telescope furnished by the signal Department, the men did not appear to be more than 50 feet from me."*
>
> *Sergeant Powers saw the same fight, and his account differs from Madsen's in no significant detail.*

Historians of the American Frontier

Historian and author William E. Unrau, in the reference book *Historians of the American Frontier,* also explored Mari Sandoz's concocted theory of Custer's plan to run for president:

> *A large amount of material she had collected for Crazy Horse two decades earlier could be used, and the opportunity to put Custer (whom she intensely disliked) in his proper place encouraged her to write the book. Predictably, nefarious military contractors, ambitious and petty army officers worried about their jobs, bureaucratic snarl and corruption among Indian Office employees, and seething tribal discontent all receive their due.*
>
> *In the final analysis, however, the focus is on Custer himself. Suffering from an aggravated case of egoism and professional insubordination, the catalyst for his stupendous error at the Little Bighorn is his sense of "desperate destiny" and the conviction that a smashing victory over the Sioux would gain him the presidency. "Custer," insists Sandoz, "was very well aware that no one voted against a national hero."*
>
> *Eschewing, as usual, uncryptic documentation by way of footnotes, Sandoz calls attention to certain newspaper accounts, Custer's childhood letters and statements*

"from West Point on," and presumed corroboration provided by Arikara scout Red Star in an interview at the home of Bear Belly, on the Fort Berthold Reservation in August 1912, and published by University of North Dakota Professor O. G. Libby in 1920.

Red Star did, in fact, report Custer's presidential aspirations (although he qualified them by stating that even a minor victory against "only five tents of Dakotas" would do the trick), and there is every reason to believe that Sandoz had read the Libby account sometime prior to her completion of the Little Bighorn book in 1966. But her personal correspondence suggests that the "presidential theory" dates back to the very beginning of her career as a historian, and more important, that the theory has a very personal touch.

A Fantastic Proposition

Throughout the spring of 1876 there is not, in fact, a single word, not even the remotest hint, anywhere, to be found in the newspapers, or any other publication, concerning Custer running for president. Nowhere in any contemporary accounts left by those of the era is this fantastic proposition mentioned either. It simply does not exist.

A New York newspaper, shortly after the Battle of the Little Big Horn, did carry an article about an interview a reporter had with Custer during the spring of 1876, and which may be termed "political," but it concerned a private conversation with Custer and did not appear until after the political conventions had been held:

> *The writer has seen him to speak to him but three times since. The last time was within ninety days, when he occupied the same seat with him in a railroad coach, after his late unpleasantness with the President....*
>
> *... Broaching the subject in relation to his late visit to Washington, I remarked:*
>
> *"It would seem as though the President hadn't treated you fairly, or even delicately, if the telegraph reports are true!"*
>
> *He said, "I can sum it up in a few words. The President has the power, and intends that I shall feel it and be humiliated by him. But Grant probably will not be President much longer, and I hope to live to see the day when my action will be vindicated and my testimony looked upon as being in the cause of right, and feel sure that with a change of administration will be placed in my proper position, both in the army and before the American people."*
>
> *With these remarks, of which I have given the substance, our interview terminated, as it appears, forever. The gallant General has vindicated himself both to the army and in the eyes of the American people.*

There is, of course, a wide gulf between Custer hoping for vindication following a change in the presidency and the possibility that Custer was interested in securing the presidency himself.

Custer's True Intentions

A counter-theory may be proposed concerning Custer's political ambitions which carries as much, or more, credibility than Custer's alleged political ambitions. The only life Custer had ever known was that of a soldier. Every time Custer had dabbled in politics he had suffered unpleasant consequences, the latest being his adventures in Washington D.C. during the spring of 1876. Custer had declined offers to run for political office after the Civil War, when he was at the height of his public fame, and since that time had spent the majority of his time stationed on the western frontier. His friends, family, and the life he chose to live was in the west. Hunting, nature, and the adventure the frontier offered, had drawn Custer to it.

Little about Custer's life indicates that he was a political stooge to be used, as he certainly would have been, in the political arena. He had witnessed the inner workings of politics often enough to know that, however honest or effective a leader he would have been, his enemies, and there would have been many of them, would have spared no effort to destroy him. If scandal could not have been discovered, as was so common in that era of "yellow journalism," it would have been invented. To have given up the freedom of the West for the political quicksand of Washington does not seem to have been a viable option for Custer, even if he had desired it.

One opportunity which was available to Custer, and which he very well may have accepted, was an offer to tour the lecture circuit at the sum of $2,000 a month. This would have required a leave of absence from the Army, but, in 1876, two thousand dollars a month would have made Custer a reasonable fortune. The name of the company which made this offer was "Redpath."

Glory

Adding to the controversy surrounding the Battle of the Little Big Horn, and directly reflecting upon the motives of Custer himself, is Frederic F. Van de Water's book *Glory Hunter*, published in 1934. This book, which burlesques as the "Life of General Custer," was written with the premise that all of the decisions made by Custer leading up to the epic battle were motivated by his desire to attain "glory" by defeating Sitting Bull and his alliance of hostile tribes. Van de Water uses the words "Glory Hunter" frequently throughout this book in reference to Custer, and these words deserve to be examined more closely, as they are a serious accusation and have served as a point of reference for many accounts of the Battle of the Little Big Horn

afterwards.

Custer would have been less than human had he not desired recognition for his accomplishments. To serve as his own "publicist" does not exactly separate him from the mainstream of other public figures, then or now. Custer wrote many articles concerning the frontier for various publications of his era and in 1874 published a book entitled *My Life on the Plains*. Custer was, of course, the "hero" in these stories, which revolved around his exploits on the frontier.

"Image" has become a way of life for modern celebrities, screen actors, politicians, businesses, or, in fact, anyone or any organization which has anything at all to gain or lose from "public perception." The entire field of advertising is directed at manipulating public perception and in modern politics the foremost rule of survival is "perception is reality." In other words, regardless of what reality actually is, what the public believes reality to be is all that really matters.

Custer has been accused of being his own press agent and, consequently, of being guilty of manipulating the newspapers to make himself look good. This determination is necessarily a subjective one but is, nevertheless, probably true. If true, even in the most prolific terms, it only proves Custer was adept in cultivating his own best interests and the only thing that might be identified as unusual about that would be his skill in doing so.

The "Glory Hunter" accusation made by Van de Water actually had the nucleus of its origins shortly after the Battle of the Little Big Horn. Custer was accused of disobeying his orders from General Terry, declining the support of Major Brisbin's squadron of the 2nd Cavalry, rushing forward to the Indian camp with undue haste, and using poor judgement in attacking the camp, all with the purpose of seizing all the "glory" in the battle for himself. The motive for Custer's errors, so this theory goes, was "glory" and nothing else.

General Sherman

Interestingly, many military officers of the Frontier Army made numerous references to the "glory" to be won on the American frontier in fighting Indians. In a letter dated March 5, 1870, the Commanding Officer of the Army, General Sherman, commented upon the paradox which faced every officer in the Frontier Army:

> *There are two classes of people; one demanding the utter extinction of the Indians, and the other full of love for their conversion to civilization and Christianity.*
>
> *Unfortunately, the army stands between and gets the cuffs from both sides.*

On March 24, 1870, General Sherman further elaborated upon his view of the dilemma which confronted the American Frontier Army:

> *The army cannot resist the tide of emigration that is following toward these Indian lands, nor is it our province to determine the question of boundaries. When called on, we must, to the extent of our power, protect the settlers, and, on proper demand, we have to protect the Indian lands against the intrusion of the settlers.*
>
> *Thus, we are placed between two fires, a most unpleasant dilemma, from which we cannot escape, and we must sustain the officers on the spot who fulfill their orders.*

General Sheridan

General Sheridan had a view similar to General Sherman's on the subject of "glory." In the early 1870s he wrote a letter to General Sherman detailing his frustration concerning public perception of the role the Army played on the frontier:

> *It seems strange that there should be such a want of knowledge of the position which army officers have to maintain in reference to Indian affairs.*
>
> *The soldiers do not want to kill Indians. After long years of Indian frontier service, I am satisfied that they are the only good, practical friends the Indians have.*
>
> *We cannot avoid being abused by one side or the other. If we allow the defenseless people on the frontier to be scalped and ravished, we are burnt in effigy and execrated as soulless monsters, insensible to the sufferings of humanity. If the Indian is punished to give security to these people, we are the same soulless monsters from the other side.*
>
> *This is a bad predicament to be in; but, as I have said, I have made my choice, and I am going to stand by the people the government has placed me here to protect.*

General Pope

Brigadier General John Pope was in full agreement with the dilemma of the Frontier Army and is quoted from the United States Congressional Record, House of Representatives as saying:

> *There are no men in the country who are so emphatically peace men, so far as Indians are concerned, as the officers and soldiers of the United States Army. Their lives are passed in that forlorn, desolate country, insufficiently sheltered, with nothing whatever of what is agreeable in life around them, and with the bare necessities of existence and shelter from storms furnished to them.*
>
> *They are bound by every interest and consideration*

that can influence men to preserve the peace. A state of war means for them continual and harassing service.

On the one side denounced by the worthy people of the East, who have but small understanding of the condition of affairs on the frontier, if they do anything to hurt an Indian, and denounced on the other side at the West by the western men if they do not hurt the Indians, they are all men in the most unhappy and unfortunate condition. Peace to them means association with their wives and children. It means freedom from continual exposure and hardship; and it means what perhaps is quite as valuable to them, freedom from outrageous and unjust slander.

There is, therefore, I say, no set of men who are more in favor of peace with the Indians and of preserving it and doing all they can to make it than the officers and soldiers of the United States Army.

Captain Robert Carter

While Generals Sherman, Sheridan, and Pope never actually participated in battles against the Indians, nor an attack upon one of their camps, Captain Robert Carter of the 4th Cavalry did. Captain Carter expressed his opinion a little more directly, as might be expected from a frontline officer. His views were published in his book *On the Border with Mackenzie.*

This is a warfare in which the soldier of the United States had no hope of honors if victorious, no hope of mercy, if he fell; slow death by hideous torture if taken alive; sheer abuse from press and pulpit if, as was often inevitable, Indian squaw or child was killed.

A warfare that called us through the cliffs and canyons on the southwest, the lava beds and labyrinths of Modoc land, the windswept plains of Texas, the rigors of Montana Winters, the blistering heat of Midsummer suns, fighting oftentimes against a foe for whom we felt naught but sympathy, yet knew that the response could be but deathless hate.

A more thankless task, a more perilous service, a more exacting test of leadership, morale and discipline no army in Christendom has ever been called upon to undertake than that which for eighty years was the lot of the little fighting force of regulars who cleared the way across the continent for the emigrant and settler. Who, Summer and Winter, stood guard over the wide "frontier"? Whose lives were spent in almost utter desolation? Whose lonely death was marked and mourned only by sorrowing comrade, or mayhap grief-stricken widow and children, left destitute and despairing?

There never was a warfare on the face of the earth in which the soldier (officer or enlisted man) had so little to gain, so very much to lose. There never was a warfare which, like this, had absolutely nothing to hold the soldier stern and steadfast to the bitter end, but the solemn sense of soldier duty.

Custer

In his book, *My Life on the Plains*, Custer wrote concerning the "glory" in fighting the Indians. If this passage, or any of the similar comments by the soldiers of the era, was ever read by Van de Water, it was ignored:

Provided with but few comforts, necessarily limited in this respect by the amount of transportation, which on the Plains is narrowed down to the smallest practicable, the soldier bids adieu - often a fine one - to the dear ones at home, and with his comrades in arms sets out, no matter how inclement the season, to seek what? Fame and glory?

How many military men have reaped laurels from their Indian campaigns? Does he strive to win the approving smile of his countrymen?

That is indeed, in this particular instance, a difficult task. For let him act as he may in conducting or assisting in a campaign against the Indians, if he survives the campaign he can feel assured of this fact, that one-half of his fellow citizens at home will revile him for his zeal and pronounce his success, if he achieves any, a massacre of poor, defenseless, harmless Indians; while the other half, if his efforts to chastise the common enemy are not crowned with satisfactory results, will cry, "Down with him. Down with the regular army"...

Catch-22

Colonel Gibbon, in his *American Catholic Quarterly Review* article of April 1877, perhaps summed up best the "glory" dilemma of the American Frontier Army:

... "Glory," a term which, upon the frontier, has long since been defined to signify being "shot by an Indian from behind a rock and having your name wrongly spelled in the newspapers."

Speaking strictly within the military there was, of course, "glory" or "honors" in any military victory. Concerning public opinion of 1876, however, any military campaign against the Indians was certain to generate controversy, regardless of its success or failure. Victory would produce the wrath of that segment of the population which believed the Indians were an innocent victim of aggression, while failure would produce anger in the frontier population. The classic "Catch-22" paradox.

When Custer left the conference aboard the steamship

Far West on the evening of June 21, 1876, he would have been well aware that he was about to embark upon a controversial experience. Which would produce the greatest debate: victory or failure?

Custer's uncharacteristic moodiness during the three-day advance to the valley of the Little Big Horn has been documented by Lieutenant Godfrey, as well as others, and perhaps it originated from more than one source. The unknown number of Indians the 7th Cavalry would find, their determination to fight, Custer's political difficulties, and the known disloyalty of his highest ranking officer probably all had a negative psychological influence upon Custer.

The best Custer could hope for was that his superior officers would keep General Sherman's pledge to "sustain the officers on the spot who fulfill their orders." Yet, if these factors were not enough to discourage Custer, he had one more fact to contend with. Win or lose any battle with the hostile Indians, Custer's actions were certain to be controversial.

CHAPTER 6

The 7th Cavalry Leaves Fort Lincoln — Reporter Mark Kellogg — The Location of Indian Camp Unknown — Lieutenant Godfrey's Account of the March up the Rosebud — The Night March of June 24 — Sitting Bull's Camp Is Discovered by the 7th Cavalry — The 7th Cavalry Is Discovered by Sitting Bull's Scouts — Custer's Decision to Attack — Captain Benteen Demands the Advance — Captain Benteen's Scout

Lieutenant Colonel Tom Custer

Finally escaping the political difficulties which had haunted him during the preceding weeks, Custer was able to return to Fort Lincoln and begin preparations in earnest for the campaign against the Indians. On May 9, 1876, the *St. Paul Pioneer Press* commented on the coming expedition:

> *General Terry and staff will leave this morning for Fort Lincoln, a special train at Fargo awaiting their arrival at that point. General Custer will accompany General Terry and will have a command in the column led by General Terry.*
>
> *It is said to be the intention of the government to put this army in motion at once, which will enable its commanders to perform more work than was ever before attempted in one season.... The scope and extent of the new expedition against the Indians are not yet known, but General Terry's movements and those of the other columns cooperating with him will be watched with interest.*

The 7th Cavalry Leaves Fort Lincoln

1st Lieutenant Edward S. Godfrey was to accompany the 7th Cavalry during the campaign in command of Company K and he participated at the Battle of the Little Big Horn. Lieutenant Godfrey joined the 7th Cavalry in 1867 after his graduation from West Point, and remained with that unit for twenty-five years. In 1907 Godfrey retired from the Army as a brigadier general and, of all the survivors of the Battle of the Little Big Horn, he was to become the most respected author and historian of that event.

In 1892 Godfrey's most valuable contribution to the history of the famous battle was published in *Century* magazine. Entitled *Custer's Last Battle*, this account is considered the best narrative by a participant of the entire expedition and the battle of June 25, 1876. Godfrey's *Century* magazine article began as Godfrey, stationed away from Fort Lincoln, received orders to join the 7th Cavalry and continued as the expedition marched west from the Fort:

> *On the 16th of April, 1876, at McComb City, Mississippi, I received orders to report my troop, K 7th Cavalry, to the Commanding General of the Department of Dakota, at St. Paul, Minnesota. At the latter place, about twenty-five recruits fresh from civil life joined the troop and we were ordered to proceed to Fort Abraham Lincoln, Dakota, where the Yellowstone Expedition was being organized.*
>
> *This expedition consisted of the 7th United States Cavalry, commanded by General George A. Custer, 28 officers and about 700 men; two companies of the 17th United States Infantry, and one company of the 6th United States Infantry, 8 officers and 135 men; one platoon of Gatling guns, 2 officers and 32 men (of the 20th*

United States Infantry); and 40 "Ree" Indian scouts. The expeditionary forces were commanded by Brigadier-General Alfred H. Terry, the Department Commander, who, with his staff arrived several days prior to our departure.

On the 17th of May, at 5:00 a.m., the "general" (the signal to take down tents and break camp) was sounded, the wagons were packed and sent to the Quartermaster, and by six o'clock, the wagon train was on the road escorted by the Infantry. By seven o'clock the 7th Cavalry was marching in column of platoon around the parade ground of Fort Lincoln, headed by the band playing "Garry Owen," the Seventh's battle tune, first used when the regiment charged at the Battle of Washita.

The column was halted and dismounted just outside the garrison. The officers and married men were permitted to leave the ranks to say "good-bye" to their families. General Terry, knowing the anxiety of the ladies, had assented to, or ordered, this demonstration in order to allay their fears and satisfy them, by the formidable appearance we made, that we were able to cope with any enemy that we might expect to meet. Not many came out to witness the pageant, but many tear-filled eyes looked from the latticed windows.

During this halt, the wagon train was assembled on the plateau west of the post and formed in column of fours. When it started off, the "assembly" was sounded and absentees joined their commands. The signals "mount" and "forward" were sounded and the regiment marched away, the band playing "The Girl I Left Behind Me."

The 7th Cavalry was divided into two columns, designated right and left wings, commanded by Major Marcus A. Reno and Captain F. Benteen. Each wing was subdivided into two battalions of three troops each.

After the first day, the following was the habitual order of march: one battalion was advance guard, one was rear guard, and one marched on each flank of the train. General Custer with one troop of the advance guard, went ahead and selected the route for the train and the camping places at the end of the day's march. The other two troops of the advance guard reported at headquarters for pioneer or fatigue duty, to build bridges and creek crossings.

The rear guard kept behind everything; when it came up to a wagon stalled in the mire, it helped to put the wagon forward. The battalions on the flanks were kept within five hundred yards of the trail and not to get more than half a mile in advance or rear of the train, and to avoid dismounting any oftener than necessary.

The march was conducted, as follows: One troop marched until about half a mile in advance of the train, when it was dismounted, the horses unbitted and allowed to graze until the train had passed and was about half a mile in advance of it, when it took up the march again; each of the other two troops would conduct their march in the same manner, so that two troops on each flank would be marching alongside the train at all times.

If the country was much broken, a half dozen flankers were thrown out to guard against surprise. The

flankers regulated their march so as to keep abreast of their troops. The pack animals and beef herd were driven alongside the train by the packers and herders.

One wagon was assigned to each troop, and transported five days' rations and forage and the mess kit of the troop; also, the mess kit, tents and baggage of the troop officers and ten days' supplies for the officers' mess. The men were armed with carbine and revolver; no one, not even the officer of the day, carried the saber. Each troop horse carried, in addition to the rider, between eighty and ninety pounds. This additional weight included all equipments and about one hundred rounds of ammunition, fifty in the belt and fifty in saddlebags.

The wagon train consisted in all of about one hundred and fifty wheeled vehicles. In it were carried thirty days' supplies of forage and rations (excepting beef), and two hundred rounds of ammunition per man. The two-horse wagons, hired by contract, carried from fifteen hundred to two thousand pounds. The six-mule government wagons carried from three to five thousand pounds, depending on the size and condition of the mules. The Gatling guns were hauled by four condemned cavalry horses and marched in advance of the train.

Two light wagons loaded with axes, shovels, pick-axes and some pine boards and scantling, sufficient for a short bridge, accompanied the "pioneer" troops. The "crossings" they are termed, were often very tedious and would frequently delay the train several hours. During this time, the cavalry horses were unbitted and grazed, the men holding the reins. Those men not on duty at the crossing slept, or collected in groups to spin yarns and take a whiff at their "dingy dudeens." The officers usually collected near the crossing to watch progress, and passed the time in conversation and playing practical jokes.

... When the haversacks were opened, the horses usually stopped grazing and put their noses near their riders' faces and asked very plainly to share their hardtack. If their polite request did not receive attention, they would paw the ground, or even strike their riders. The old soldier was generally willing to share with his beast.

The length of the day's march, varying from ten to forty miles, was determined in a great measure by the difficulties or obstacles encountered, by wood, water and grass, and by the distance in advance where such advantages were likely to be found. If, about two or three o'clock in the afternoon, a column of smoke was seen in the direction of the trail and a mile or two in advance, it was a pretty sure indication that a camp had been selected. The cavalry, excepting the rear guard, would then cut loose from the train and go directly to camp. The rear guard would send details to collect fuel and unpack their wagons.

The adjutant showed the wing commanders the general direction their lines or tents were to run, and the latter then directed the battalion or troop commanders to their camping places. Generally, one flank of each line would rest near the creek. The general form of the command was that of a parallelogram. The wings camped on the long sides facing each other, and the headquarters and guard were located at one end nearest the creek. The wagon train was packed close to the other end and was guarded by the infantry battalion.

The troops, as they arrived at their places, were formed in line, facing inward, dismounted, unsaddled, and, if the weather was hot and the sun shining, the men rubbed the horses' backs until dry. After this, the horses were sent to water and put out to graze, with sidelines and lariats, under charge of the stable guard, consisting of one non-commissioned officer and three or six privates. The men of the troop then collected fuel, sometimes wood, often a mile or more distant from the camp; sometimes "buffalo chips."

The main guard, or camp guard, consisting usually of four or five non-commissioned officers and twelve or fifteen privates, reported mounted at headquarters, and were directed to take posts on prominent points overlooking the camp and surrounding country, to guard against surprise. Each post consisted of one non-commissioned officer and three privates. The officer of the day, in addition to his ordinary duties in camp, had charge of the safety of the cavalry herds. Sometimes this latter duty was performed by an officer designated as "Officer of the Herd." To preserve the grazing in the immediate vicinity of the camp for evening and night grazing, all horses were required to be outside of the camp limits until retreat.

When the train arrived, the headquarters and troop wagons went directly to the camping place of their respective commands. The officers' baggage and tents were unloaded first; then the wagons went near the place where the troop kitchen was to be located, always on that flank of the troop farthest from headquarters. The teamsters unharnessed their mules and put them out to graze. The old stable guard reported to the troop commander for fatigue duty to put up the officers' tents and collect fuel for their mess.

The troop officers' tents were usually placed twenty-five yards in rear of the line of men's tents and facing toward them. Their cook or mess tent was placed about ten or fifteen yards further to the rear. The "strik-

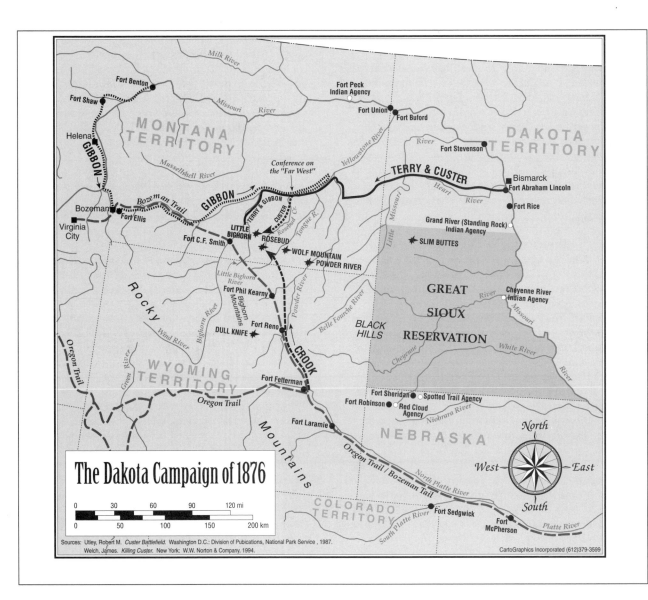

The Dakota Campaign of 1876

0 30 60 90 120 mi
0 50 100 150 200 km

Sources: Utley, Robert M. *Custer Battlefield.* Washington D.C.: Division of Pubications, National Park Service , 1987.
Welch, James. *Killing Custer.* New York: W.W. Norton & Company, 1994.

CartoGraphics Incorporated (612)379-3599

er" made down the beds and arranged the "furniture," so to speak, which generally consisted of a camp stool, tin washbasin, and a looking glass. The men put up their tents soon after caring for their horses. The fronts of their tents were placed on a line established by stretching a picket rope. The first sergeant's was on that flank of the line nearest to the headquarters. The horse equipments were placed on a line three yards in front of the tents. The men were not prohibited from using their saddles as pillows.

A trench was dug for the mess fire and the grass was burned around it for several yards to prevent prairie fires. After this, the cooks busied themselves preparing supper. Beef was issued soon after the wagon train came in, and the necessary number of beeves were butchered for the next day's issue; this was hauled in the wagons. Stable call was sounded about an hour before sunset. The men of each troop were formed on the parade and marched to the horse herds by the first sergeant. Each man went to his own horse, took off the sidelines and fastened them around the horse's neck, then pulled the picket pin, coiled the lariat, noosed the end fastened to the head halter around the horse's muzzle, mounted, and assembled in line at a place indicated by the first sergeant. The troop was then marched to the watering place, which was usually selected with great care because of the boggy banks and miry beds of the prairie streams.

After watering, the horses were lariated outside the vicinity of the camp. The ground directly in the rear of

the troop belonged to it, and was jealously guarded by those concerned against encroachment by others. After lariating their horses, the men got their curry-combs, brushes, and nose-bags and went to the troop wagon where the quartermaster sergeant and farrier measured, with tin cups, the forage to each man, each watching jealously that he got as much for his horse as those before him. He then went at once to feed and groom his horse. The officer whose duty it was to attend stables and the first sergeant superintended the grooming, examining each horse's back and feet carefully to see if they were all right. When a horse's back got sore, through the carelessness of the rider, the man would generally be compelled to lead his horse until the sore was well.

Immediately after the stables, the cooks announced in a loud tone, "Supper!" The men with haversack and tin cup went to the mess fire and got their hardtack, meat, and coffee. If game had been killed, the men did a little extra cooking themselves.

The troop officers' mess kits consisted of a sheet-iron cooking stove, an iron kettle, stewing, frying, baking, and dish pans; a small Dutch oven, a camp-kettle, a mess-chest holding tableware for four persons, and a small folding table. The table in fair weather was spread in the open air. The early part of the meal was a matter of business, but after the substantials were stowed away, the delicacies were eaten more leisurely and time found for conversation.

Custer and scouts

After supper, the pipes were lighted, and the officers, if the weather was cold, went to the windward side of the camp fire. Each man, as he took his place, was sure to poke or kick the fire, turn his back, hitch up his coattail, and fold his hands behind him.

Retreat was sounded a little after sunset and the roll was called, as much to insure the men having their equipments in place as to secure their presence, for it was not often we were near enough to any attraction to call the men away. (In 1876, there was not a ranch west of Bismarck, Dakota, nor east of Bozeman, Montana.) The stable guards began their tours of duty at this time.

The non-commissioned officers reported to the troop commander for instructions for the night; these usually designated whether the horses were to be tied to the picket line or kept out to graze, and included special instructions for the care of sick or weak horses.

At dusk, all horses were brought within the limits of the camp. The picket line was stretched over three wagons in front of the men's tents, or three posts were used when remaining in camp over a day.

During the evening, the men grouped about the fires and sang songs and spun yarns until "taps." The cooks prepared breakfast, which usually consisted of hard bread, bacon and coffee. If beans or fresh meat were to be cooked, the food was put into the Dutch ovens or camp kettles, which were placed in the fire trench, covered over with hot ashes and coals, and a fire was built over them. If the wind blew hard, all fires were extinguished to prevent prairie fires.

The cooks were called an hour or an hour and a half before reveille. At the first call for reveille, usually 4:20 a.m., the stable guard awakened the occupants of each tent and the officer whose duty it was to attend the roll call. Stable call followed reveille and was superintended by an officer. This occupied about three-quarters of an hour. Two hours after the reveille, the command would be on the march. Of course, there were incidents that occasionally relieved the monotony.

Antelope were plentiful, and the men were encouraged by troop commanders to hunt. General Custer had a number of stag hounds, which amused themselves and the command in their futile attempts to catch them.

One morning, they started up a large buck near where the column was marching; Lieutenant Hare immediately followed the hounds, passed them, drew his revolver, and shot the buck.

Nothing of special interest occurred until the 27th of May, when we came to the Bad Lands of the Little Missouri River. On the 30th, General Custer was sent with four troops to make a scout up the Little Missouri, for about twenty miles. He returned the same day, without having discovered any recent "Indian signs." On

the 31st, we crossed the Little Missouri without difficulty. On the 1st and 2nd of June, we were obliged to remain in camp on account of a snowstorm.

Reporter Mark Kellogg

General Sherman had warned General Terry not to bring any newspaper correspondents who, Sherman claimed, caused "mischief," but one did accompany the command anyway. Marcus H. Kellogg, a 43-year-old widower who had worked at various small newspapers, was sent by the *Bismarck Tribune* to write about the expedition. This fact has been used by certain historians and writers to demonstrate Custer's disregard for his superior officer's instructions and some have accused Custer of "disobeying" Sherman's instructions.

This spurious charge ignores the fact that General Terry was in command of the expedition, not Custer, and had Terry not approved of reporter Kellogg, he would not have gone along. This common sense observation is confirmed in an editorial published in the *Bismarck Tribune* on July 19, 1876. It said:

> *Mark Kellogg was the only professional correspondent accompanying* [the expedition] ... *as we are prepared to prove by General Terry himself, of whom the writer obtained for Kellogg permission to go.*

Why General Terry disregarded General Sherman's advice seems apparent. Letters of the Benteen type after the Washita battle were an ever present threat and the best defense against distorted or self-serving accounts of the expedition was to have a news correspondent with them to document events. The reporter, theoretically, would not have a vested interest in presenting a certain point of view.

Considering his experience with Captain Benteen's letter after the Washita battle, Custer would have clearly approved of reporter Kellogg's presence with the expedition. In fact, he very well could have been instrumental in making the arrangements. However, General Terry made the final decision and, considering the circumstances, it was, at least in theory, probably a correct one. Unfortunately, Kellogg would die with Custer and any notes of the day of the battle he had with him and were not recovered.

On the night of June 21, 1876, General Terry, Colonel Gibbon, and Custer held a conference aboard the steamship *Far West* on the Yellowstone River in Montana Territory. The return of Major Reno from his scout had confirmed that large forces of hostile Indians were nearby, perhaps in the Rosebud or the Little Big Horn Valleys, and the three officers formed a plan of action.

Custer and the 7th Cavalry would leave the next day marching south, up the Rosebud Valley and then, presuming no hostile villages had been found, turn west over the divide between the Rosebud and Little Big Horn Rivers into the Little Big Horn Valley. Colonel Gibbon's force would follow the Yellowstone River to the Big Horn River and, at that point, proceed to the Little Big Horn Valley. The written orders given Custer were:

> *Camp at the mouth of the Rosebud River,*
> *Montana Territory,*
> *June 22, 1876.*
>
> *Lieutenant Colonel Custer,*
> *7th Cavalry.*
>
> *Colonel:*
>
> *The Brigadier General Commanding directs that, as soon as your command can be made ready for the march, you will proceed up the Rosebud in pursuit of the Indians whose trail was discovered by Major Reno a few days since.*
>
> *It is, of course, impossible to give you any definite instructions to this movement and were it not impossible to do so, the Department Commander places too much confidence in your zeal, energy and ability to impose on you precise orders which might hamper your action when nearly in contact with the enemy. He will, however, indicate to you his own views of what your action should be, and he desires that you should conform to them, unless you shall see sufficient reason for departing from them.*
>
> *He thinks you should proceed up the Rosebud until you ascertain definitely the direction in which the trail spoken of leads. Should it be found (as it appears almost certain it will be found) to turn to the Little Big Horn, he thinks you should still proceed southward perhaps as far as the headwaters of the Tongue, and then turn toward the Little Big Horn, feeling constantly, however, to your left, so as to preclude the possibility of the escape to the south or southeast by passing around your left flank.*
>
> *The column of Colonel Gibbon is now in motion for the mouth of the Big Horn. As soon as it reaches that point, it will cross the Yellowstone and move up at least as far as the forks of the Big and Little Horn.*
>
> *Of course, its future movements must be controlled by circumstances as they arise, but it is hoped that the Indians, if upon the Little Horn, may be so nearly enclosed by the two columns that their escape will be impossible.*
>
> *The Department Commander desires that on your way up the Rosebud you should thoroughly examine the upper part of Tullock's Creek, and that you should endeavor to send a scout through to Colonel Gibbon's column, with information of the results of your exami-*

nation. The lower part of the creek will be examined by a detachment of Colonel Gibbon's command.

The supply steamer will be pushed up the Big Horn as far as the forks, if the river be navigable for that distance, and the Department Commander, who will accompany the column of Colonel Gibbon, desires you to report to him there not later than the expiration of the time for which your troops are rationed, unless in the meantime you receive further orders.

E. W. Smith, Captain 18th
Infantry.
Acting Assistant Adjutant General.

The Location of Indian Camp Unknown

The orders given Custer by General Terry were necessarily unspecific because no one knew for certain where the Indian camp was located, or in which direction the trail would lead. The plan, however, took into account the best information available to those who attended the conference.

To the west was the Crow Indian reservation, the hereditary enemies of the Sioux. It was unlikely that the hostile Indian trail would lead in that direction. General Crook and his army were somewhere to the south, making any movement in that direction by the hostile tribes risky and unlikely.

To the north, the high waters of the Yellowstone River hindered any movement, although with determination a dangerous crossing could be made. But also, to the north, General Terry was positioning Colonel Gibbon's small army as a blocking force in case the Indians did attempt to move in that direction.

The 7th Cavalry would move south with orders to "feel constantly to the left" and this stipulation reflected General Terry's greatest fear. No one expected that the Indians would stand and fight any of the three military forces in the field now searching for them, and preventing their escape was Terry's greatest concern. The east appeared vulnerable to escape by the hostile Indians, at least on a map, and by "feeling constantly to the left," Custer would insure that none of the hostile tribes escaped in that direction.

Had the main trail of the Indians suddenly turned east, instead of west, Custer's force would then follow the trail in that direction also. In that circumstance, Custer's force would quickly move away from General Terry's command and the plan agreed upon was to be abandoned, if it was necessary to meet such new circumstances. Lieutenant Godfrey, in his 1892 *Century* magazine article, commented on this:

The pack mules sent out with Reno's command were badly used up, and promised seriously to embarrass the expedition. General Custer recommended that some extra forage be carried on the pack mules. In endeavoring to carry out this recommendation, some troop commanders foresaw the difficulties and told the General that some of the mules would certainly break down, especially if the extra forage was packed.

He replied in an excited manner, quite unusual with him: "Well, gentlemen, you may carry what supplies you please; you will be held responsible for your companies. The extra forage was only a suggestion, but this fact bear in mind, we will follow the trail for fifteen days unless we catch them before that time expires, no matter how far it may take us from our base of supplies; we may not see the supply steamer again." And, turning as he was about to enter his tent, he added, "You had better carry along an extra supply of salt; we may have to live on horse meat before we get through."

He was taken at his word, and an extra supply of salt was carried.

General Terry's order to Custer, necessarily inexact, also contained a very important qualification:

It is, of course, impossible to give you any definite instructions in regard to this movement, and were it not impossible to do so, the Department Commander places too much confidence in your zeal, energy and ability to impose on you precise orders which might hamper your action when nearly in contact with the enemy.

It would seem this clause was inserted to cover unforeseen circumstances and to give Custer and the 7th Cavalry the latitude to complete the mission. In a previous campaign on the southern plains, Colonel Mackenzie of the 4th Cavalry had also inserted a similar clause in his orders to subordinates. It had said:

Both columns will disregard any general directions if

any probability offers of overtaking Indians ... endeavor to strike Indian Camps.

The high degree of latitude and discretion allowed by these orders was a measure of the respect and confidence which General Terry accorded to Custer.

Lieutenant Godfrey's Account of the March up the Rosebud

On the evening of June 21, at the conclusion of the conference between General Terry, Colonel Gibbon, and Custer, "officers' call" was sounded for the 7th Cavalry. Custer then informed the officers of the orders Terry had given him. At noon on the following day the 7th Cavalry was to depart on a mission to search for the hostile tribes, and preparations for this departure began immediately.

Lieutenant Godfrey, in his 1892 *Century* magazine article on the Battle of the Little Big Horn, told of the events leading up to the morning of June 25, 1876.

At twelve o'clock, noon, on the 22nd of June, the "Forward" was sounded, and the regiment marched out of camp in column of fours, each troop followed by its pack mules.

Generals Terry, Gibbon and Custer stationed themselves near our line of march and reviewed the regiment. General Terry had a pleasant word for each officer as he returned the salute.

Our pack trains proved troublesome at the start, as the cargos began falling off before we got out of camp, and during all that day the mules straggled badly. After that day, however, they were placed under the charge of Lieutenant Mathey, who was directed to report at the end of each day's march the order of merit of the efficiency of the troop packers. Doubtless, General Custer had some ulterior design in this. It is quite probable that if he had occasion to detach troops requiring rapid marching, he would have selected those troops whose packers had the best records. At all events, the efficiency was much increased, and after we struck the Indian trail the pack trains kept well closed.

We went into camp about 4:00 p.m., having marched twelve miles. About sunset, "officers' call" was sounded, and we assembled at General Custer's bivouacs and squatted in groups about the General's bed. It was not a cheerful assemblage; everybody seemed to be in a serious mood, and the little conversation carried on, before all had arrived, was in undertones.

When all had assembled, the General said that until further orders, trumpet calls would not be sounded except in an emergency; the marches would begin at 5:00 a.m. sharp; the troop commanders were all experienced officers, and knew well enough what to do, and when to do what was necessary for their troops; there were two things that would be regulated from his headquarters, i.e., when to move out of and when to go into camp. All other details, such as reveille, stables, watering, halting, grazing, etc., on the march would be left to the judgement and discretion of the troop commanders; they were to keep within supporting distance of each other, not to get ahead of the scouts, or very far to the rear of the column.

He took particular pains to impress upon the officers his reliance upon their judgment, discretion, and loyalty.

He thought, judging from the number of lodge fires reported by Reno, that we might meet at least a thousand warriors; there might be enough young men from the agencies, visiting their hostile friends, to make a total of fifteen hundred. He had consulted the reports of the Commissioner of Indian Affairs and the officials while in Washington as to the probable number of "hostiles" (those who had persistently refused to live or enroll themselves at the Indian agencies), and he was confident, if any reliance was to be placed upon these reports, that there would not be an opposing force of more than fifteen hundred.

General Terry had offered him the additional force of the battalion of the 2nd Cavalry, but he had declined it because he felt sure that the 7th Cavalry could whip any force that would be able to combine against him, that if the regiment could not, no other regiment in the service could; if they could whip the regiment, they would be able to defeat a much larger force, or, in other words, the reinforcement of this battalion could not save us from defeat. With the regiment acting alone, there would be sure harmony, but another organization would be sure to cause jealousy or friction.

He had declined the offer of the Gatling guns for the reason that they might hamper our movements or march at a critical moment, because of the inferior horses and of the difficult nature of the country through which we would march.

The marches would be from twenty-five to thirty miles

a day. Troop officers were cautioned to husband their rations and the strength of their mules and horses, as we might be out for a great deal longer time than that for which we were rationed, as he intended to follow the trail until we could get the Indians, even if it took us to the Indian agencies on the Missouri River or in Nebraska. All officers were requested to make to him any suggestions they thought fit.

This "talk" of his, as we called it, was considered at the time as something extraordinary for General Custer, for it was not his habit to unbosom himself to his officers. In it he showed concessions and a reliance on others; there was an indefinable something that was not Custer. His manner and tone, usually brusque and aggressive, or somewhat curt, was on this occasion conciliating and subdued. There was something akin to an appeal, as if depressed, that made a deep impression on all present.

We compared watches to get the official time, and separated to attend to our various duties. Lieutenants McIntosh, Wallace (killed at the Battle of Wounded Knee, December 29, 1890), and myself walked to our bivouac, for some distance in silence, when Wallace remarked: "Godfrey, I believe General Custer is going to be killed." "Why? Wallace," I replied, "what makes you think so?" "Because," said he, "I have never heard Custer talk in that way before."

Lieutenant Gibson, in a letter to his wife, dated July 4, 1876, also commented upon this incident:

As we marched along through the strange heat, I could not but recall the rather odd talk we had with Custer on the evening of the twenty-second. When officer's call was sounded, we assembled at his bivouac and squatted in groups about his cot.

He told us that he expected to encounter at least a thousand Indians, and that all precautions for a long campaign must be taken.

He said that until further orders, no trumpet calls would be sounded except in an emergency. General Terry had offered him the additional force of the Second Cavalry, which he had declined, confident that the Seventh could handle the matter alone. He also declined the offer of Gatling guns because they might hamper our movements through such a rugged country.

We were cautioned to husband our mules and ammunition and, finally, he asked all officers to make any suggestions to him at any time. This struck us all as the strangest part of the meeting, for you know how dominant and self-reliant he always was, and we left him with a queer sort of depression. McIntosh, Wallace, Godfrey and I walked back to our tents together and finally Wallace said "I believe General Custer is going to be killed."

"Why?" asked Godfrey.

"Because I never heard him talk in this way before – that is, asking the advice of anyone."

Lieutenant Godfrey continues his narrative of the march up the Rosebud Valley:

I went to my troop and gave orders what time the "silent" reveille should be and as to other details for the morning preparations; also the following directions in case of a night attack: The stable guard, packers, and cooks were to go out at once to the horses and mules to quiet and guard them; the other men were to go at once to a designated rendezvous and await orders; no man should fire a shot until he received orders from an officer to do so. When they retired for the night, they should put their arms and equipments where they could get them without leaving their beds.

I then went through the herd to satisfy myself as to the security of the animals. During the performance of this duty, I came to the bivouac of the Indian scouts. "Mitch" Bouyer, the half-breed interpreter, "Bloody Knife," the chief of the Ree scouts, "Half-Yellow-Face," the chief of the Crow scouts, and others were having a "talk." I observed them for a few minutes, when Bouyer turned toward me, apparently at the suggestion of "Half-Yellow-Face" and said: "Have you ever fought against these Sioux?" "Yes," I replied. Then he asked: "Well, how many do you expect to find?" I answered, "It is said we may find between one thousand and fifteen hundred." "Well, do you think we can whip that many?" "Oh, yes, I guess so." After he had interpreted our conversation, he said to me with a good deal of emphasis, "Well, I can tell you we are going to have a damned big fight."

At five o'clock sharp, on the morning of the 23rd, General Custer mounted and started up the Rosebud, followed by two sergeants, one carrying the regimental standard, and the other his personal or headquarters flag, the same kind of flag he used while commanding his cavalry division during the Civil War. This was the signal for the command to mount and take up the march.

Eight miles out, we came to the first of the Indian camping places. It certainly indicated a large village and numerous population. There were a great many "wicki-ups" (bushes stuck in the ground with the tops drawn together, over which they placed canvas or blankets). These we supposed at the time were for the dogs, but subsequent events developed the fact that they were temporary shelters of the transients from the agencies.

During the day, we passed through three of these camping places and made halts at each one. Everybody was busy studying the age of the pony droppings and tracks and lodge trails, and endeavoring to determine the number of lodges. These points were all-absorbing topics of conversation. We went into camp about five o'clock, having marched about thirty-three miles.

June 24th, we passed a great many camping places, all appearing to be of nearly the same strength. One would naturally suppose these were the successive camping places of the same village, when, in fact, they were the continuous camps of the several bands. The fact that they appeared to be of nearly the same age, that is, having been made at the same time, did not impress us then.

We passed through one much larger than any of the others. The grass for a considerable distance around it had been cropped close, indicating that large herds had been grazed there. The frame of a large "Sun Dance" lodge was standing, and in it we found the scalp of a white man. It was whilst here that the Indians from the agencies had joined the Hostiles' camp.

The command halted here and the "officers' call" was sounded. Upon assembling, we were informed that our Crow scouts, who had been very active and efficient, had discovered fresh signs, the tracks of three or four ponies and one Indian on foot.

At this point, a stiff southerly breeze was blowing; as we were about to separate, the General's headquarter's flag was blown down, falling toward our rear. Being near the flag, I picked it up and stuck the staff in the ground, but it again fell to the rear. I then bored the staff into the ground where it would have the support of a sage-brush. This circumstance made no impression on me at the time, but after the battle, an officer, Lieutenant Wallace, asked me if I remembered the incident. He had observed, and regarded the fact of its falling to the rear as a bad omen, and felt sure we would suffer a defeat.

The march during the day was tedious. We made many long halts, so as not to get ahead of the scouts, who seemed to be doing their work thoroughly, giving special attention to the right, toward Tullock's Creek, the valley of which was in general view from the divide. Once or twice, signal smokes were reported in that direction, but investigation did not confirm the reports. The weather was dry and had been for some time, consequently the trail was very dusty. The troops were required to march on separate trails, so that the dust clouds would not rise so high. The valley was heavily marked with lodge-pole trails and pony tracks, showing that immense herds of ponies had been driven over it.

About sundown, we went into camp under the cover of a bluff, so as to hide the command as much as possible. We had marched about twenty-eight miles. The fires were ordered to be put out as soon as supper was over, and we were to be in readiness to march again at 11:30 p.m.

Lieutenant Hare and myself lay down about 9:30 to take a nap. When comfortably fixed, we heard someone say, "He's over there by that tree." As that described my location pretty well, I called out to know what was wanted, and the reply came: "The General's compliments, and he wants to see all the officers at headquarters immediately."

So we gave up our much-needed rest and groped our way through horse herds, over sleeping men, and through thickets of bushes trying to find headquarters. No one could tell us, and as all fires and lights were out, we could not keep our bearings. We finally spied a solitary candle-light, toward which we traveled and found most of the officers assembled at the General's bivouac.

The General said that the trail led over the divide to the Little Big Horn; the march would be taken up at once, as he was anxious to get as near the divide as possible before daylight, where the command would be concealed during the day, and give ample time for the country to be studied, to locate the village, and to make plans for the attack on the 26th.

We then returned to our troops, except Lieutenant Hare, who was put on duty with the scouts. Because of the dust, it was impossible to see any distance and the rattle of equipments and clattering of the horses' feet made it difficult to hear distinctly beyond our immediate surroundings. We could not see the trail and we could only follow it by keeping in the dust cloud.

The night was very calm, but occasionally a slight breeze would waft the cloud and disconcert our bearings; then we were obliged to halt to catch a sound from those in advance, sometimes whistling or hallooing, and getting a response we would start forward again. Finally, troopers were put ahead, away from the noise of our column, and where they could hear the noise of those in front. A little after 2:00 a.m., June 25th, the command was halted to await further tidings from the scouts; we had marched about ten miles. Part of the command unsaddled to rest the horses. After daylight, some coffee was made, but it was impossible to drink it. The water was so alkaline that the horses refused to drink.

The Night March of June 24

The purpose of Custer's night march may have had little to do with the few miles the regiment advanced. The night march also was effective in simply moving the location of the soldiers' camp.

The 7th Cavalry was following an enormous Indian trail, Indians at war with the United States Government, and these hostile Indians knew already, from two previous battles since the new year, that the Government would send soldiers looking for them.

It can be surmised that Sitting Bull did, in fact, have scouts and spies roaming far and wide across the countryside. In the records of the *North Dakota Historical Society*, Sitting Bull is on record as saying:

We knew the soldiers were coming weeks before the fight.... For three days, our scouts watched Custer marching toward our camp....

The steady defection of "summer roamers" from the reservations, and those driven from the reservations by the starving conditions there, surely were also giving information to Sitting Bull.

Custer had previously experienced more than one dawn attack by hostile Indian warriors. He and the veteran officers and scouts who were with the command were far too competent not to know that the 7th Cavalry had probably been under continuous surveillance by hostile scouts from the very first moment it left Fort Lincoln. A surprise dawn attack by Sitting Bull's warriors, even if modestly successful, would have caused serious difficulties for Custer. Even a few casualties would require a detachment large enough to protect them, and the 7th Cavalry was already on the trail of a force which, Custer had already admitted, would number at least 1,500.

The night march of June 24 and 25 did move the 7th Cavalry perhaps up to eight miles closer to their objective. More importantly, the 7th Cavalry would not be surprised by a sudden Indian attack as General Crook and the southern force had been on June 17.

Sitting Bull's Camp Is Discovered by the 7th Cavalry

After the night march the 7th Cavalry made a temporary bivouac, still on the Rosebud side of the divide, and the scouts were sent ahead to the divide to survey the Little Big Horn Valley. 2nd Lieutenant Charles A. Varnum, the Chief of Scouts, was sent as command of this mission and later wrote an account of it:

With my scouts, I acted as advance guard up the Rosebud and my instructions were, particularly, not to let any trail get away from us without letting Custer know of it. On June 24th, after marching about 20 miles, the command halted and I was sent for and came back to the head of the column.

Custer told me that Godfrey had reported a trail of a part of the Indians had gone up a branch stream to our left about ten miles back, and Custer was rather angry that I had let anything get away from me. I told him of the thoroughness of my work at the front where I had the two Jacksons and Cross and Fred Gerard scattered with my Indians across the whole front, and I did not believe the report.

After discussion, Lieutenant Hare was ordered to report to me as an assistant and I changed horses and went back the ten miles with some of my Rees and found where quite a party had gone up a stream with their travois to find a suitable crossing and ... had worked back to the main trail. I rejoined the command ... and then resumed my place in advance, Hare taking the right front and I the left. We made about ten miles more and went into camp.

Custer came over to the scout camp and had a long talk with the Crows. (Half Yellow Face was still out to the front somewhere so there were only five Crows present.) After a while, he called me in and told me that the Crows reported that between us and the Little Big Horn was a high hill with a sort of Crow nest in the top where the

Crows watched the Sioux when they were on that river and the Crows were on a horse-stealing trip. That their camp could be made out in the clear light of the morning when the daylight broke. The Indian trail we were following led in that direction and the Crows believed their camp was on the Little Big Horn.

Custer said that the Crows were going on at once and he wanted an intelligent white man to go with them and take some Rees for messengers and Bouyer as interpreter and send him back word what we discovered. I said that meant me, but he said it was a tough, mean job, but I insisted that was my place, only I would like to take Charley Reynolds with me for someone to talk to. He told me to do so and to start about 9 o'clock and he would move with the command at eleven and in the morning he would be bivouacked under the base of the hill I was on and he would expect to get word from me there.

I left as directed taking Bouyer, Charlie Reynolds, five Crows (Half Yellow Face, being still away) and eight or ten Rees. The Crows were our guides. Except that we stopped two or three times in the dense undergrowth along a stream to let the Crows smoke cigarettes, we were on the go till about 2:30 or 3:00 a.m. on the 25th, and as daylight broke I found myself in a peculiar hollow like old Crow nest at West Point, near the summit of a high ridge in the divide between the Rosebud and Little Big Horn.

This latter stream was in plain sight about ten miles off. A timbered tributary led down to the Rosebud and up which we had evidently come during the night. Another led down to the Little Big Horn. On this were the two lodges that you know of and which I understand were filled with dead bodies of Indians, probably from Crook's fight of the 17th. . . . I crawled up [the hill] *and watched the valley till the sun rose. All I could see was the two lodges.*

The Crows tried to make me see smoke from villages behind the bluffs on the Little Big Horn and gave me a cheap spy glass, but I could see nothing. They said there was an immense pony herd out grazing and told me to look for worms crawling on the grass and I could make out the herd; but I could not see worms or ponies, either.

My eyes were somewhat inflamed from loss of sleep and hard riding in dust and hot sun, and were not in the best of condition, but I had excellent eyesight and tried hard to see, but failed. About 5 o'clock, I sent the Rees back with a note to Custer, telling him what the Crows reported, a tremendous village on the Little Big Horn. I do not remember the wording of my note, but I was told when the command arrived that Custer got it.

After Custer received Lieutenant Varnum's message, he quickly prepared to ride forward and see for himself the hostile village which Varnum's scouts had reported in the Little Big Horn Valley.

The 7th Cavalry Is Discovered by Sitting Bull's Scouts

The Indian scout Red Star told in an interview of riding with Custer to the Crows' nest:

Custer then told Red Star, through the interpreter, to saddle up at once. "We are going back to where his party are on the hill," he said.

Red Star was not through with his breakfast, but he left his coffee, knocking it over with his foot, saddled up, and joined Custer. In the party were Custer, his bugler, Tom, Red Star, Gerard, Bloody Knife, Bob-tailed Bull, and Little Brave.

They rode hard toward the hill and Red Star heard a bugle as he left camp, blown by Custer's bugler, who turned backward on his horse to do so.

Custer asked by signs of Red Star if the distance was short, and Red Star made signs that it was. When they got to the foot of the hill, Red Star signed that this was the place. They climbed the hill, and came to the scouts.

Charley Reynolds came up and he and Custer went ahead leaving the others behind. Charley Reynolds pointed where Custer was to look, and they looked for some time and then Gerard joined them.

Gerard called back to the scouts: "Custer thinks it is no Sioux camp." Custer thought that Charley Reynolds had merely seen the white buttes of the ridge that concealed the lone tepee. Charley Reynolds then pointed again, explaining Custer's mistake, then after another look, Custer nodded that he had seen the signs of a camp.

Next, Charley Reynolds pulled out his field glasses and Custer looked through them at the Dakota camp and nodded his head again.

Crooked Horn told Gerard to ask Custer how he would have felt if he had found two dead Dakotas at the hill. The scouts had seen six Dakota Indians after Red Star and Bull had left them. Two of them had gone over the ridge down the dry coulee and four of them had ridden into the timber at the foot of the hill.

They thought the two Dakotas were planning to ambush the messengers and they wished to kill them first. They did not do so because they were afraid Custer might not like it. Custer replied that it would

have been all right; he would have been pleased to have found two dead Dakotas.

Then the scouts sat down and one of the Crow scouts, Big Belly, got up and asked Custer through the Crow interpreter what he thought of the Dakota camp he had seen. Custer said: "The camp has not seen our army, none of their scouts have seen us." Big Belly replied: "You say we have not been seen. These Sioux we have seen at the foot of the hill, two going one way, and four the other, are good scouts, they have seen the smoke of our camp."

Custer said, speaking angrily: "I say again we have not been seen. That camp has not seen us, I am going ahead to carry out what I think. I want to wait until it is dark and then we will march, we will place our army around the Sioux camp." Big Belly replied: "That plan is bad, it should not be carried out." Custer said: "I have said what I propose to do, I want to wait until it is dark and then go ahead with my plan."

Red Star, as he sat listening, first thought that Custer's plan was good. The Crow scouts insisted that the Dakota scouts had already seen the army and would report its coming and that they would attack at once, that day, and capture the horses rapidly. Custer replied, "Yes, it shall be done as you say."

The army now came up to the foot of the hill and Custer's party rode down and joined the troop.

In his interview, Red Star spoke of the Sioux scouts that were seen and the fact that Custer's scouts believed that they had been discovered by the Sioux. This discovery of the 7th Cavalry by the Sioux scouts is confirmed in other accounts. The interpreter Fred Gerard told of the discovery of Sioux scouts near the command on the morning of the 25th:

When we went into camp early on the morning of June 25 in the woods, in sort of a narrow valley some miles east of the divide, I threw myself on the ground and soon fell asleep.

I had not slept long, however, before General Custer came up and touched me with his foot, waking me up and saying, "Gerard, get up. Some of the scouts have come in from the high point, and I think we should go up there."

We went up to the high mountain peak, which was about thirteen miles east of the Little Big Horn, and through my glasses I made out a pony herd on the hills or table land beyond that stream. I could distinctly see a large dark spot, or mass, and could even see dust rising, from which I concluded that I was looking at a herd of ponies that were being driven. This was now some hours after daylight, and the light was strong and the atmosphere very clear.

I have heard General Custer criticized for not sending Herendeen to scout Tullock's Fork. General Custer did not overlook this, and the subject came up for discussion while we were on the divide. From the Crow's Nest, we had a good view of the valley of Tullock's Creek, which takes its rise not far from where we were. We could see all over that part of the country, and as no trail led that way, we concluded there were no Indians in that part of the country.

Not long after this, General Custer, finding the Indian scouts had discovered us, decided to attack the camp.

Scout George B. Herendeen also told of the Sioux scouts watching the 7th Cavalry:

Some time during the night, the scouts came in and reported to Custer that the Indian camp was found. We packed up and moved forward at early light.

Mitch Bouyer and Reynolds, who had been out, said the camp was very large. Bouyer said it was the biggest village he had ever seen. Reynolds said there was a heap of them, and Custer replied, "I can whip them." Reynolds said it would take six hours hard fighting to whip them.

About nine o'clock on the morning of the 25th of June and the last day of our march, Custer halted his troops and concealed them as well as he could. He then took an orderly and rode up on the Divide about four miles to where Lieutenant Varnum and Bouyer were. The General was trying to get a look at the village, which was over on the other side of the Divide, on the Little Big Horn.

While Custer was gone, I rode up the Dry Fork of the Rosebud, along which the trail ran, but had not gone

far when I saw two objects going over the hills in the direction of the Little Horn.

Custer was gone perhaps an hour or an hour and a half, and when he came back, Bouyer, who was with him, asked me if I had seen the Indians. I said, "Yes, I had seen what I thought were Indians." Bouyer replied, "You were within 150 yards of them and you surprised them and they have gone to camp as fast as they can go."

In another interview, scout Herendeen further commented upon the fact the 7th Cavalry had definitely been discovered by hostile scouts on the morning of June 25 and was under their observation:

While General Custer was looking for the Indian village, the scouts came in and reported that he had been discovered and that news was then on its way to the village that he was coming.

Another scout said that two Sioux war parties had stolen up and seen the command, and on looking in a ravine nearby, sure enough, fresh pony tracks were found.

In an interview the Crow scout White Man Runs Him said he also observed that the Sioux scouts had discovered the command:

Q. Was it a clear day?

A. Yes, nice and clear. We also saw six Sioux to the northeast over on the other side of Tullock's Creek.

Q. Did you come up on the point with Custer?

A. I went down and reported to Custer what we saw, and Custer came up to see.

Q. What did the scouts say to each other up here on the point?

A. I told Mitch Bouyer it would be a good thing if they would hide here until night and then surprise the camp. Then the two Sioux appeared over there and I said we had better hurry and get over there just as soon as possible.

We did not know whether Custer would listen, but if we hadn't seen the two Sioux, we would have suggested to him to stay here all day and make a night march.

Lieutenant Varnum's narrative continues:

After sending off the Rees, we saw one Indian riding a pony and leading another at the end of a long lariat and some distance behind, an Indian boy on a pony. They were evidently hunting stray stock and were perhaps a mile off toward the Little Big Horn and riding parallel to the ridge we were on. There was a gap in the range to our right and the Crows thought they would cross there and soon discover Custer.

By this time, smoke could be seen in a ravine towards the Rosebud, showing where Custer was. The Crows were mad that he lighted fires.

Bouyer said that White Swan, who seemed to be a sort of leader, wanted us to try and cut him off and kill them where they crossed the range so they would not discover the troops. Bouyer, Reynolds and two Crows with myself started off dismounted to do so.

After perhaps a half mile of hard work through very broken country where we could see nothing, I heard a call like a Crow cawing from the hill and we halted. Our two Crows repeated the imitation but you could easily see they were talking or signaling and we started back. I asked Bouyer what was the matter but he did not know.

On our return, we learned that the Sioux had changed their course away from the pass, but soon after our return they changed again and crossed the ridge. We could see them as they went down the trail towards the command and could then see a long trail of dust showing Custer was moving, but we could not see the column. Before it came in sight, the Sioux stopped suddenly, got together and then as suddenly disappeared, one to the right and one to the left, so we knew that the Sioux had discovered our approach.

About this time ... [six or seven Sioux] *rode in single file along the crest of a ridge forming a divide of the stream running into the Rosebud and in the direction of that stream. That they would soon discover Custer's command we knew, and watched them accordingly. The crest where we were was higher than they were, and as they rode along the crest, reflected against the sky their ponies looked as big as elephants. They rode leisurely, but soon, all of a sudden, they disappeared and soon afterward one black spot took their place. They had evidently ran off to alarm their camp, leaving one man to watch the column.*

The command came in vision about this time and we watched it approach the gap where it halted. I rode down towards the column and soon met the General. He said, "Well you've had a night of it." I said yes, but I was still able to sit up and notice things.

Tom Custer and Calhoun then came up to us and Custer was angry at their leaving the column and ordered them back.

I told the General all I had seen as we rode back toward the Crow nest hill and we climbed the hill together. Custer listened to Bouyer while he gazed long and hard at the valley.

He then said, "Well I've got about as good eyes as anybody, and I can't see any village Indians or anything else," or words to that effect.

Bouyer said, "Well General, if you don't find more Indians in that valley than you ever saw together you can hang me."

Custer sprang to his feet saying, "It would do a damned sight of good to hang you, wouldn't it," and he and I went down the hill together.

I recall his remark particularly because the word damn, was the nearest to swearing I ever heard him come, and I never heard him use that but once before and that was in an Indian fight on the Yellowstone, August 4, 1873.

We rejoined the command and he sent for the officers to assemble, and I hunted for water and grub, as I had none since about 8 o'clock the night before.

Lieutenant Godfrey's narrative continues:

Our officers had generally collected in groups and discussed the situation. Some sought solitude and sleep, or meditation.

The Ree scouts, who had not been very active for the past day or two, were together and their "medicine man" was anointing them and invoking the Great Spirit to protect them from the Sioux. They seemed to have become satisfied that we were going to find more Sioux than we could well take care of.

Captain Yates' troop had lost one of its packs of hard bread during the night march from our last halting place on the 24th. He had sent a detail back on the trail to recover it. Captain Keogh came to where a group of officers were and said this detail had returned and Sergeant Curtis, in charge, reported that when near the pack they discovered an Indian opening one of the boxes of hard bread with his tomahawk, and that as soon as the Indian saw the soldiers he galloped away to the hills, out of range and then moved along leisurely.

This information was taken to the General at once by his brother, Captain Tom Custer.

The General came back and had "officers' call" sounded. He recounted Captain Keogh's report, and also said that the scouts had seen several Indians moving along the ridge overlooking the valley through which we had marched, as if observing our movements; he thought the Indians must have seen the dust made by the command.

At all events, our presence had been discovered and further concealment was unnecessary; that we would move at once to attack the village; that he had not intended to make the attack until the next morning, the 26th, but our discovery made it imperative to act at once, as delay would allow the village to scatter and escape.

As Lieutenant Godfrey's narrative as well as other accounts clearly state, reports to Custer indicated that hostile Indians had discovered the command and the 7th Cavalry was under surveillance. Now the greatest fear was that any delay in attacking the large village would give the Indians time to escape, fleeing to nearby hills by hundreds of trails.

Custer's Decision to Attack

Custer's decision to attack on June 25, 1876, alleged later by some to be motivated by a desire to defeat the Indians alone with the 7th Cavalry, thereby cheating the other column out of the questionable "glory" of that victory, was compelled by the fact that his command had been discovered by hostile scouts.

To have waited until the next day, June 26, would have allowed General Terry's force to reach the mouth of the Little Big Horn River, as planned, but this force still would not have been in a position to assist Custer in his attack on the village. General Terry's force did not arrive on the battlefield until June 27, a day later than Terry was to claim to be the date for the planned simultaneous attack by the two commands.

Lieutenant Godfrey later commented upon the dilemma that faced Custer:

If they [the Indians] *had escaped without punishment or battle, Custer would have undoubtedly been blamed. Included with Custer's orders from General Terry was the clause specifically stating that he had flexibility, if "you shall see sufficient reason for departing from* [the orders]*."*

Discovery of the command by the hostile Indians was not only "sufficient reason" for Custer to deviate from

the orders, it was also absolute necessity if the Indians in the village were not to escape.

What could have happened had Custer not attacked the Indian village after being discovered by the hostile scouts? In his report dated November 25, 1876, General Sheridan said:

If Custer had not come upon the village so suddenly, the warriors would have gone to meet him in order to give time to the women and children to get out of the way, as they did with Crook only a few days before.

In the *Contributions to the Historical Society of Montana* is a comment General Sherman reportedly made concerning Custer's options when the Indian village was discovered. Sherman said:

Custer's attack on the big Indian village was, under the circumstances and according to well-settled principles of Indian warfare neither rash nor desperate, because, having marched into the zone where the Indians were assembled he could do nothing but attack when he found himself in the presence of the Indians.

Had Custer not ordered the attack, not only would the village probably have escaped, but the 7th Cavalry possibly would have been attacked by the Indian warriors at a time and place of their own choosing. Both had happened to General Crook's force only a short time before: the Indian warriors had attacked at a time and place of their own choosing and the village(s) had escaped.

Yet controversy exists on Custer's decision to attack on June 25. *Field Manual 22-100, Military Leadership from HQ Department of the Army,* October 1983 printing, identifies a decision-making checklist for military officers. This checklist contains seven steps, beginning with "*Identify the Problem*" and ending with "*Implement the Plan.*" Using this checklist, at least a framework can be constructed with the known facts and this can be compared to Custer's decision to attack.

1. Identify the Problem.

Custer's written orders were to find and attack the Hostile Indian village.

2. Gather Information.

The scouts of the regiment had unanimously identified an Indian encampment, a big one, about 12-15 miles from the Rosebud divide. Hostile scouts had also been seen by numerous members of the 7th Calvary and the camp would soon be warned.

3. Develop Courses of Action.

Custer had two options; 1.) Conceal the regiment and attack the following day. 2.) Immediate advance and attack.

4. Analyze and Compare.

Custer's first choice, against the advice of the scouts, was to find a suitable location to conceal the regiment and then attack the following day. This choice could have given the men and horses a day to rest, further reconnaissance could have been made, and General Terry and more soldiers were due to arrive about 15 miles to the north of the village the following day. However, the scouts believed if an immediate attack was not made the village would escape and there was also the risk of discovery of the regiment and possible attack by hostile Indian war parties.

The second choice was to immediately advance and attack the village. The disadvantages would be the regiment would not be rested, have the advantage to approach the camp at dawn (if it was still there), further reconnaissance could not be made, and General Terry would be far beyond any supporting range. However, by immediately advancing in broad daylight and executing a swift daylight attack (an unheard of event, according to one historian), the element of surprise might be achieved and the village sucessfully attacked.

5. Make a Decision.

The advice of the scouts was to quickly advance and attack the Indian camp or its escape was inevitable. Only Custer was in favor of waiting a day for the attack . If the unauthorized advance by the regiment, as described by interpreter Gerad, is correct, Custer may have not made the decision to attack at all, but simply acquiesced in it. In any event, Custer gave the order to advance and attack the Indian camp in the Little Big Horn Valley.

6. Make a Plan.

Custer would use the same calvary tactics already successfully used by the Frontier Army; advance quickly, surprise the enemy, and attack from several directions. In every battle or skirmish Custer had with the hostile plains Indians, he had used these tactics successfully.

7. Implement the Plan.

Having made the decision to advance quickly and attack the Indian village, Custer immediately began to implement a plan to attack the Indian village.

Captain Benteen Demands the Advance

Dropping all pretense that the position of the regiment was unknown to the Indians, or perhaps prompted by an unauthorized advance of the regiment which interpreter Girard was later to mention, Custer had "officers' call" sounded by bugle. As the officers gathered, Custer informed them that the location of the village had been discovered and the regiment itself was now under hostile

observation. An immediate advance and attack would be made, and Custer said:

The first company that is ready will have the advance.

The advance was, of course, an honored position and the company commander who had that distinction would lead the 7th Cavalry into what would be the regiment's greatest battle. Lieutenant Godfrey recorded what happened next:

He [Custer] *now ordered that each troop commander inspect his company and equipment, and detail men for the packs, and the first to report would be given the advance and the last would be given the packs.*

Benteen walked off and almost immediately came back and reported his company all right, without having made the required inspection.

Lieutenant Godfrey further elaborated on this incident which, apparently, he found somewhat disturbing:

At the conclusion of his talk, the General ordered us to return to our troops, inspect them, and report when we were ready for the march. He said that the troops would take their places in the column of march in the order of reports. As we dispersed, Benteen and I walked toward our troops together.

We had proceeded not more than fifty yards when, to my surprise, Benteen faced about and reported his troop ready.

In his diary of the expedition, Lieutenant Godfrey wrote:

I thought I certainly would be of the advance, but some company commanders reported without seeing to anything and so got the lead.

Lieutenant Godfrey felt that Captain Benteen's opportunism in snatching the honored advance position was unwarranted, an opinion probably shared by the other company commanders. Benteen's demand for the prestigious position was, perhaps, not only motivated by a desire to enhance his own status in the eyes of his fellow officers, but he also found it an opportunity to irritate Custer. In an account of this incident Benteen hinted as much:

General Custer notified us that the first troop commander who notified him that the requirements of an order issued a few days before were being carried out strictly in the troop, that officer and troop should have the post of honor, the advance.

I notified him at once that in my troop the requirements were being strictly adhered to. I feel quite sure it wasn't expected from me, but he stammered out, "Well Captain Benteen, your troop has the advance."

Of course, no military unit is "always ready," especially to advance directly into combat. There are always last minute preparations and inspections which good judgment and common sense dictate would be necessary. However, Captain Benteen, ever-diligent when it came to a chance to annoy Custer, would seem to have caught Custer off guard this time. As the regiment crossed the divide between the Rosebud and Little Big Horn Valleys, Benteen, perhaps with his chest a little puffed out, was leading the regiment. It was to be a situation that Custer would not long tolerate.

Captain Benteen's Scout

Captain Benteen described the events that followed which proved that Custer, even with the burden of leading his regiment into a critical battle, was never above rising to a challenge from his nimble and malevolent captain.

I had led the regiment but a short distance when General Custer rode up, saying I was setting the pace too fast. He then rode in advance.

The initiative in the little diversion between the two antagonists had passed into the hands of Custer who, even yet, was not quite finished with Captain Benteen.

The regiment had crossed the divide but had not traveled far before a halt was ordered. Custer then divided the regiment into four combat battalions. Major Reno would command three companies, A, G, and M; Captain Benteen would also command three companies, D, H, and K. Like Reno and Benteen, Captain Keogh would command three companies, E, I, and L. The fourth combat battalion would be commanded by Captain Yates and consisted of companies C and F. B Company, commanded by Captain McDougall, would form the rear guard and escort the pack train.

Six soldiers from each company were detailed with the pack train, commanded by 2nd Lieutenant Edward G. Mathey, and this force, together with B company, constituted a fifth reserve battalion of 136 men. The primary purpose of this reserve battalion was the safety of the pack train, however, if the need arose, this force could also be used in combat.

Shortly after the division of the regiment into battalions and after the march had been resumed, Custer sent Captain Benteen an order which has been shrouded in controversy. Captain Benteen said:

I was called up and notified that my command . . . would move to the left to a line of bluffs about two miles away.

In commenting on this order, Captain Benteen also said:

Why I was sent to the left, I don't know.

Some have attempted to justify this order through General Terry's instructions to "feel" to the left during his march, yet this certainly was not Custer's intention. The "left," Terry had referred to, as Custer marched south, was to the east, and the purpose of that advice was to preclude any escape of the Indians in that direction. As the regiment marched toward the Little Big Horn Valley, Custer's left was

Von Clausewitz

now to the south, in the direction of General Crook. Terry was not concerned about an escape by the Indians in that direction.

Two other reasons given for this order have included scouting out any satellite villages and to serve as an advance upon a broad front. Neither of these reasons are supported by the facts. Custer knew the exact location of the Indian village and that also there had not been other villages identified in the direction Benteen was sent. The main force under Custer never deviated from a direct line of march to the Little Big Horn Valley where the village had been seen that morning. Custer knew where to find all the Indians he, or anyone else, wanted to find.

Advancing upon a broad front might have been a prudent course to follow under different circumstances. However, the village was still many miles away and, as yet, there was no reason to deploy the regiment, at least for the military purpose of advancing upon a broad front.

Perhaps the most noted of all theorists on war has been the German Carl Von Clausewitz. He was a military officer during the Napoleonic era of warfare in the early nineteenth century and his impressive textbook, *On War*, is still used by military colleges today and his theories are still a part of military classroom instruction.

Historian Herbert Rosinski described Von Clausewitz's work as "the most profound, comprehensive and systematic examination of war that has appeared to the present day"and, in that regard, it would seem he has no competition. Modern warfare has dated some of Von Clausewitz's ideas, but most of his teachings were applicable during the entire nineteenth century. Even the wars against the Indians in the American West, as unorthodox as they were by conventional military standards, can find definition in Von Clausewitz's teachings.

Carl Von Clausewitz specifically warned against the careless division of forces and Custer's decision to send Captain Benteen to the left of the main force without a clear purpose would appear to fall under Von Clausewitz's principles:

> *There is no higher and simpler law of strategy than of keeping one's forces concentrated. No force should ever be detached from the main body, unless the need is definite and urgent.*
>
> *... incredible though it sounds, it is a fact that armies have been divided and separated countless times without the commander having clear reason for it.*

Strategist Von Clausewitz then terms this separation of forces without a clear and urgent need as: "folly" and "every separation and split an exception that has to be justified.

There was no clear and "urgent" need for Benteen to have been ordered to the left of the main force. Custer himself must have known better than to commit this "folly," and had he been prone to this type of elementary mistake his military career would have suffered long before because of it. What was the phantom military purpose of Benteen's scout to the left, or was there a military purpose to it at all?

Interestingly, Lieutenant Charles Roe, with General Terry's force, had an opinion on Captain Benteen's scout to the left and its reason, according to Roe, was not military. Roe arrived on the battlefield on June 27 and spoke with many surviving officers of the 7th Cavalry. Roe was interviewed by Walter Camp on December 8, 1910, and Camp's notes reveal Custer's order to Benteen could have had no military purpose at all:

> *Roe thinks that Custer's object in sending Benteen to the left from the divide was to keep Benteen out of the fight, as Benteen had the advance and should regularly have been with headquarters.*
>
> *This is the opinion of Benteen's friends, so Roe says.*

Walter Camp also observed that Custer did not send any of the three regimental physicians with Captain Benteen's battalion and this fact could also mean that Custer did not expect Benteen to meet with any opposition on his adventure, nor did he expect him to participate in the initial phase of the attack on the Indian village.

Captain Benteen had audaciously demanded, without deserving, the honored advance position of the regiment and Custer had responded in kind. Benteen, ever the nemesis of Custer, would not only be deprived of the advance, but would be sent on a useless ride to the left of the main force. It was a humiliation to Benteen in front of the entire regiment and one which would have defined Benteen's actual position in the regiment as Custer saw it.

At the Washita battle, Captain Benteen had, at least in the eyes of Custer, betrayed the entire regiment with his vindictive letter that had been published concerning the battle.This had cast a shadow that had never left the 7th Cavalry. On how many other occasions, undocumented in history, had Benteen challenged Custer? How many times had Custer been the victim of Benteen's subterfuge? How many times had Custer responded, or even provoked, mean-minded exchanges? Perhaps both were guilty of petty behavior.

On the morning of June 25, 1876, Custer knew that the 7th Cavalry was going into a great battle. Custer's decision on that fateful day, whether a military or personal judgement, was that Captain Benteen would not be leading the regiment into the Little Big Horn Valley.

CHAPTER 7

Major Reno's Order to Attack the Village — Custer's Advantage — Major Reno's Advance — Major Reno's Halt — Custer's Advance Seen — Messages Sent to Custer — Major Reno's Diversion — Major Reno Retreats to the Woods — Bloody Knife is Killed — Major Reno's Debacle — Was Reno's Retreat Justified? — No Rear Guard — Was There a Rear Guard? — No Defense for Reno

Scout Charles Reynolds

After sending Captain Benteen to the left of the regiment on the "scout" of questionable value, the main force consisting of Major Reno's and Custer's force, followed by the pack train, continued down the divide toward the Little Big Horn Valley. The distance from the top of the divide to the valley has been estimated to be up to fifteen miles and, as the regiment traveled down towards it, it began following a dry stream bed with Major Reno and his battalion on the left side, Custer and his two battalions on the right. They advanced downhill at a trot and the miles passed quickly, although the pack train gradually fell behind and was soon out of sight. As the two battalions neared the valley of the Little Big Horn, the scout, George Herendeen, described what he saw:

> *I was with the scouts and we kept down a creek which led toward the Little Big Horn.*
>
> *When we got near the mouth of the creek, we saw a lodge standing on the bank. We rode up on a hill, so as to flank and overlook the lodge and, soon saw it was deserted.*
>
> *From the top of the hill, we looked ahead down the Little Big Horn and saw a heavy cloud of dust and some stock apparently running. We could see beyond the stream a few Indians on the hills riding very fast and seemingly running away, I said the Indians were running and we would have to hurry up, or we would not catch them.*

Major Reno's Order to Attack the Village

The abandoned tepee contained a dead Indian warrior, apparently killed in the June 17 battle with Crook's force in the Rosebud Valley, not quite fifty miles away. The tepee was set afire and it was at this point, perhaps as close as a mile and a half from the river, that Major Reno was ordered by Custer to advance into the valley and attack the Indian camp. At his 1879 Court of Inquiry, Major Reno said:

> *I received an order from Lieutenant Cook to move my command to the front.*
>
> *I moved forward to the head of the column and shortly after, Lieutenant Cook came to me and said, "General Custer directs you to take as rapid a gait as you think prudent and charge the village afterward and, you will be supported by the whole outfit."*

Custer's promise to support Major Reno's attack has been the subject of much debate and Reno later used this promise to defend his actions. Was it Custer's intention to support Reno's attack in the valley as Reno would later claim? Or did Custer have another plan, one that would have been not only clear to Reno, but one which was as

traditional in cavalry warfare as the stirrup and the saddle. In his report of July 5, 1876, Reno said:

... Custer intended to support me by moving further down the stream and attacking the village in the flank.

Later, Major Reno would drastically alter his original account and claim that he expected to receive support from Custer for his attack on the village from the rear. This new and improved second version had the advantage for Reno of giving the impression that, having failed to give Reno support by following upon his trail, Custer had failed Reno.

Major Reno's first account is undoubtedly correct. In fact, the advantages of a flank attack are so great that it is standard military doctrine that in any military situation in which it can be used, it will be.

The manual *Cavalry Tactics and Regulations of the United States Army* published in 1864 was written by Philip St. George Cook, who was eventually to become an Army General. This manual would have been familiar to Major Reno, Custer, and any experienced cavalry officer.

Regulation 559 of *Cavalry Tactics and Regulations of the United States Army* notes:

... echelons can very readily attack ... in every direction [and] *are maneuvered and changed to lines with great simplicity....*

... while you attack ... [you] *prepare to turn his flank.*

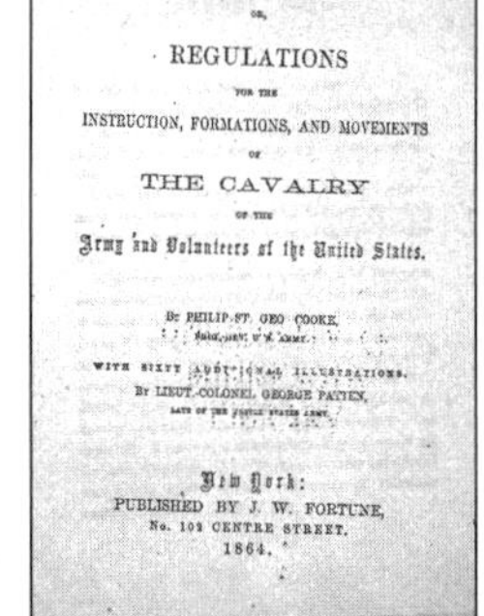

CAVALRY TACTICS:

REGULATIONS

INSTRUCTION, FORMATIONS, AND MOVEMENTS

THE CAVALRY

Army and Volunteers of the United States.

By PHILIP ST. GEO. COOKE,

WITH SIXTY ADDITIONAL ILLUSTRATIONS.

BY LIEUT. COLONEL GEORGE PATTEN,

New York:

PUBLISHED BY J. W. FORTUNE,

No. 102 CENTRE STREET.

1864.

Cavalry Tactics and Regulations of the United States Army, regulation 561:

If possible, at the moment of a charge, assail your enemy in the flank or charge him in the flank when [the enemy] *is engaged in his front.*

Carl Von Clausewitz discussed the principle of the flank attack in detail in *On War*:

Everyone knows the morale effects of ... an attack in flank.

... the risk of having to fight on two fronts and, the even greater risk of finding one's retreat cut off, tend to paralyze movement and the ability to resist and so affect the balance between victory and defeat.

Carl Von Clausewitz not only spoke of the advantage of flank attack, but also rated it as one of the three most important factors he defined as being most critical for victory. In his book *On War*, Von Clausewitz wrote:

Only three things seem to produce decisive advantages: surprise, the benefit of terrain, and concentric [flank] *attack.*

Concentric attack comprises all tactical envelopment, great or small. Its effectiveness is produced partly by the double effectiveness of cross fire, and partly by the fear of being cut off.

General Patton, in his book *War as I Knew It*, described how a flank attack should be conducted. He said:

"Whenever possible ... use a base of fire and a manuevering element. The manuevering element should be the larger of the two forces and should start its attack well back from ... the base of fire."

At the Reno Court of Inquiry the subject of a flank attack by Custer in support of Major Reno's attack was brought up and several officers testified concerning it. Captain Moylan testified:

Q. State whether any attack on that village in flank by another column, or an attack lower down than from where Major Reno was, would or would not have been supporting Major Reno's attack.

A. I think it would have been supporting his attack, that is, to the extent of drawing off the number of Indians necessary to resist it.

Lieutenant DeRudio testified:

Q. State in your opinion as an officer whether an attack by General Custer, as you have described, was an effective support of Major Reno in his attack on that place.

A. If the command to Major Reno was to hold that place, it would probably be an effectual assistance.

James McLaughlin worked and lived among the many of the Indians that had been at the Battle of the Little Big Horn, and in his book, *My Friend the Indian*, wrote:

From what leading Indians in the engagement have told me of the fight, I am of the opinion that if Custer's obvious plan of battle had been carried out, if Reno had struck the upper end of the Sioux camp when Custer struck the village at the lower end, there would at least have been no such disaster as that which overtook the leader of the calvary and the men with him.

I am not at all fearful that this statement of a conviction acquired from the Indians who participated in the fight, and not from any prejudiced military authority, will embroil me in a dispute. The matter admits of no dispute.

There are many other first hand accounts by Indian participants at the battle in which they mention their under-

standing of the diversionary and flank attacks that Custer used. It would seem that they, if anyone, would have understood the tactics of the calvary in attacking a village, as their villages were attacked many time by this identical method.

Concerning Custer's probable intention, Lieutenant Hare testified:

There was plenty of time for him to follow Major Reno and everybody supposed that he would attack the village somewhere, if he did not follow up, he would attack it somewhere else and that was the only other way he had of going to the village and in addition to that I heard firing down there.

Major Reno was a West Point graduate and had been an officer during the Civil War with combat experience. Reno had been a soldier and cavalryman long enough, by any standard, to understand the principle of a flank attack. When Custer did not follow behind Reno, if Reno ever really expected him to, then he also knew that Custer would attack the village from the most advantageous position he could. This would be from the flank on Reno's right.

Custer's Advantage

Custer followed a northwest route along the edge of the bluffs east of Major Reno's advance and overlooking the Little Big Horn Valley. Custer's intention was to support Reno's advance with a flank attack and, in advancing across the high ground, Custer was meeting Von Clausewitz's second principle of a successful attack: the advantage of terrain. Custer had already capitalized on Von Clausewitz's first principle, that of surprise, and the surprise attack by the 7th Cavalry on the village is one of the few details of the Battle of the Little Big Horn upon which most of the Indian accounts agree.

The nearby location of the 7th Cavalry had been known to the Indians, but the regiment's swift advance from the divide between the Rosebud and Little Big Horn Valleys, and Major Reno's sudden attack on the Indian village, accounts by Indian participants agree, had been a surprise. Kate Bighead was a Cheyenne woman in the Indian village the day the 7th Cavalry attacked and she later spoke about the sudden attack by the soldiers. Kate Bighead said:

It was sometime past the middle of the afternoon. Nobody was thinking of any battle coming. A few women were taking down their lodges, getting ready for the move on down the valley that day.

After a while, two Sioux boys came running toward us. They were shouting, "Soldiers are coming!" We heard shooting. We hid in the brush. The sound of the shooting multiplied, pop-pop-pop! We heard women and children screaming.

The Sioux war chief, Crazy Horse, commanded large Indian warrior forces at the Battle of the Little Big Horn. Crazy Horse said:

The attack was a surprise and totally unlooked for . . . the women, papooses, children and in fact all who were not fighters made a stampede in a northerly direction.

The Indian warrior, Iron Thunder, was also in Sitting Bull's camp on June 25, 1876. Iron Thunder said:

I did not know anything about Reno's attack until his men were

so close that the bullets went through the camp and everything was in confusion. The horses were so frightened, we could not catch them.

There are many similar statements made by Indian's who were at the battle. There was not an ambush waiting for the soldiers at the Battle of the Little Big Horn, as would later be claimed by some, nor were the warriors prepared for the sudden attack by the 7th Cavalry. Perhaps the one advantage Custer had sought above all others in making his attack was surprise and, as the Indian participants later agreed, this had been successfully achieved. In moving to the north, across the high ground parallel to Reno's advance, Custer was taking advantage of the high terrain and maneuvering to execute a flank attack.

In the initial phase of the Battle of the Little Big Horn, Custer was, according to Von Clausewitz, entering the battle with some very formidable advantages.

Major Reno's Advance

As the battalions commanded by Major Reno and Custer neared the Valley of the Little Big Horn and the Indian village, Custer ordered Reno to advance into the valley and attack the camp. Reno was ordered to take most of the scouts with him and George Herendeen was among them. Herendeen later described Reno's advance:

Reno took a steady gallop down the creek bottom three miles to where it emptied into the Little Big Horn and found a natural ford across the river. He started to cross when the scouts came back and called out to him to hold on, that the Sioux were coming in large numbers to meet him. He crossed over, however and, formed his companies on the prairie in line of battle and moved forward at a trot, but soon took to a gallop.

The valley was about three fourths of a mile wide. On the left was a line of low, round hills, and on the right the river bottom covered with a growth of cottonwood trees and bushes.

1st Sergeant John M. Ryan was a member of M Company and was with Major Reno's battalion at the Battle of the Little Big Horn. He later gave an account of the crossing of the river and of the advance down the valley. Sergeant Ryan said:

We arrived at the bank of the Little Big Horn River and waded to the other side.

... on the other side of the river, we made a short halt, dismounted, tightened our saddle girths and, then swung into our saddles. After mounting, we came up, Left front into line, Captain French's Company M on the right and Lieutenant McIntosh's company on the left, and, Captain Moylan's in the rear.

We were then in the valley of the Little Big Horn and facing downstream. We started down at a trot and then on a slow gallop. Between the right of my company and the riverbank there was quite a lot of underbrush and bullberry bushes.

Captain French gave me orders to take 10 men off to the right of my company and form a skirmish line, so as to cover the brush from the right of our line to the riverbank, as the Indians might be lurking there. We advanced in that formation from one and a half to two miles.

Doctor Henry R. Porter was a physician assigned to Major Reno's battalion and he testified at the Reno Court of Inquiry concerning Reno's advance down the valley. Doctor Porter said:

Reno started down to the crossing at a trot. Some horses were galloping. We crossed and halted and, some horses were watered. The watering generally was done passing through. The horses generally were in good condition. High spirited – some wanted to run.

Going to the crossing, Reno asked me if I didn't want his gun. He had a fiery horse and had trouble managing him and the gun was in his way. I said, "No."

After we crossed, I heard him command, "Forward!" and they went on down to the woods about two miles, at a lope or trot.

I saw a few Indians and a great many ponies. They seemed to be driving the ponies down the river. There was no opposition.

When we got to the woods, the men dismounted and formed a skirmish line. I was right where I could see them. The horses were led into the woods.

Major Reno had received a direct order to charge the Indian village through the Little Big Horn Valley. Reno then crossed the river, formed his men for a charge, and began his advance down the valley. Although some of the participants reported that the Indian warriors began to advance to oppose Reno's charge, they were apparently not a serious threat because there were no casualties and, as Doctor Porter stated, "there was no opposition."

Major Reno's Halt

Major Reno charged down the valley toward the Indian village, described by participants as several miles away but, after advancing a mile or mile and a half, Reno suddenly halted his charge and dismounted his men in a long line of skirmishers across the Little Big Horn Valley. Scout Herendeen described this maneuver:

He advanced about a mile from the ford to a line of timber on the right and dismounted his men to fight on foot. The horses were sent in to the timber and the men formed on the prairies and advanced toward the Indians.

One company, G, was sent into the wooded area on the right of Reno's line and next to the river with the horses of the battalion. How long the soldiers were on that skirmish line is a debatable question. Herendeen said "a few minutes." The interpreter, Frederick F. Gerard, said five minutes. Doctor Porter later described this maneuver:

When we got to the woods, the men dismounted and formed a skirmish line. I was right where I could see them.

The horses were led into the woods. I watched the fight a few minutes and then led my horse into the woods, looking for my orderly who had the bandages and medicines.

I had been there only a few minutes when the men on the left and right came in.

Concerning the skirmish line, Major Reno testified at his Court of Inquiry:

We were in skirmish line under hot fire for fifteen or twenty minutes.

It would have been to Major Reno's advantage to extend the time his command was on the skirmish line, so his account of fifteen or twenty minutes would seem to be the maximum time the soldiers were on the skirmish line.

Custer's Advance Seen

It was about this time that Custer was seen on the bluffs to the right of Major Reno's line and on the east side of the Little Big Horn River. Lieutenant DeRudio was with Reno's command during the advance in the valley and later said he saw Custer on the bluffs across the river. Lieutenant DeRudio said:

... while I was in the woods, General Custer, Lieutenant Cook, and another man came to the highest point of the bluff and waved their hats and made motions like they were cheering.

Lieutenant Varnum also testified at the Reno Court of Inquiry that he saw Custer's men on the bluffs overlooking Reno's advance on the valley. Lieutenant Varnum testified:

The last time I saw Custer's command was about the time we dismounted in the bottom. I then saw the gray horse company moving down along the bluffs. They were further downstream than the point we struck in crossing [on the retreat Reno was to shortly make].

They were probably three quarters of a mile from where we were in the bottom. They were moving at a trot.

Private Henry Petring was with Major Reno's advance in the valley and also saw Custer on the bluffs:

While in the bottom going on the skirmish line, I saw Custer across the river on the bluffs, waving his hat.

Some of the men said, "There goes Custer. He is up to something, for he is waving his hat."

Many other eye witnesses with Reno saw Custer on the bluffs including the interpreter Fred Gerard and troopers Stanislaus Roy and Thomas O'Neill. However, at his Court of Inquiry, Major Reno denied knowledge of Custer's appearance on the bluff near his advance in the valley. Major Reno testified:

There was no communication to me that Custer's command had been sighted from the timber.

This statement, like so many made by Major Reno, seems absurd. Custer's appearance on the bluffs and, as some reported, the waving of his hat, was a deliberate signal to Reno and his command in the valley concerning Custer's location and intention. It is a reasonable assumption that Custer did not wave a greeting to the Indians in the valley. His intention was to inform Reno of his position, something which, considering the circumstances, might have been of interest to Reno and his command.

It was not only enlisted men with Major Reno's advance who said they had seen Custer, but also officers and it would seem reasonable those officers would have relayed this important information to Reno. This is not to say Reno himself did not see Custer and later misrepresented this fact, as he did many other facts, concerning the Battle of the Little Big Horn.

Messages Sent To Custer

If there had been any doubt whatsoever that Custer intended to support Major Reno's charge with an attack from the flank, then Custer's appearance on the bluff would have eliminated that doubt instantly. Reno's testimony at his Court of Inquiry reveals this to have been a delicate subject for him:

An attack on the flank would not have been a support under the circumstances.

When I said in my report that General Custer meant to support me by a flank attack, it was a conviction formed after the fight. I expected my support to come from the direction I had crossed.

This claimed mystification of where Custer was, and what he intended to do, becomes even more perplexing according to another statement made by Major Reno at his Court of Inquiry:

I sent back word twice: first, by a man named McIlargy, my striker, to say that the Indians were in front of me in strong force.

Receiving no instructions, I sent a second man, Mitchell, a cook.... I still heard nothing to guide my movement.

Both of these soldiers delivered their messages to Custer and subsequently died with him. Custer was definitely known to have sent two messages as he advanced across the bluffs overlooking the Little Big Horn Valley. One message was sent with Sergeant Kanipe to the pack train and ordered it to hurry forward and a second message was sent with Bugler Martin to Captain Benteen and also directing him to hurry forward with the pack train. It is a military principle that orders and messages in a combat situation are of critical, and very frequently of decisive, importance.

Major Reno claimed that he did not receive any instructions at all from Custer apart from the original orders to attack the Indian camp, yet Reno sent two messages that were delivered to Custer. The lines of communication between the two commands were open, at least for a while. It would be truly astonishing if Custer had not responded to Reno's communications. The route which Custer took across the bluffs overlooks the Little Big Horn Valley and Custer certainly would have taken advantage of this to observe the developing situation below him and, according to eyewitnesses with Reno, did.

Common sense, as well as sound military tactics, would seem to indicate that Custer would have communicated with Major Reno, but for Reno to have admitted this would have put him in an uncomfortable, if not untenable, position, especially considering his subsequent actions in the valley.

Actually, one soldier later claimed that he did deliver a message to Major Reno. This person was Theodore Goldin, a private with G Company. Goldin's version of this event is extremely controversial and yet it cannot be proven that it did not happen:

Very shortly after our column headed to the northward,

> *I received a hurriedly scrawled order from the hands of Lieutenant Cook, with the order, "Deliver that to Major Reno, remain with his column until a junction is effected, then report to me at once."*
>
> *I struck out to overtake Major Reno, then perhaps a mile away. I overtook his command just after they had reached the west bank of the river and under shelter of the bluffs they were readjusting their saddles and allowing their tired horses a moment's breathing spell.*
>
> *I at once delivered my message to Lieutenant Hodgson and walked away. I did not read the message, save the last three or four words which were, "We'll soon be with you."*

While Private Goldin's claim is interesting, it is, however, not critical. Custer would have maintained communications with Major Reno and it is just as certain that Reno would deny this happened in order to protect himself. What this message, or messages, said is probably not as hard to surmise as it might seem.

Major Reno's Diversion

When Major Reno began his charge down the valley, he at first had two of his companies on line, with the third behind in reserve. One of the maxims of cavalry warfare, which also applies to any attack, is to "never charge without a reserve."

Cavalry Tactics and Regulations of the United States Army, regulation 562:

> *Formation for attack depends upon the description and disposition of the enemy, upon the nature of the ground, and upon the composition of your force.*
>
> *The first line formed for attack should seldom consist of more than a third of the cavalry; the second, or support, disposed in squadron columns 3 or 4 hundred yards in the rear; the reserve equally to the rear in close column.*

This reserve is used to fall back upon in the event the charge fails, or it can also be used to support the first attacking force with a second wave. Considering that Reno had 175 soldiers with him, counting the scouts, and was confronting a much larger force, the single company he had as a reserve was a questionable military tactic.

As Major Reno continued his charge down the valley he committed what, superficially, appeared to be a fearful blunder. Reno ordered the reserve company into the charging line so his attacking force was merely one thin and fragile line of soldiers. Had Reno continued his charge and reached the village, his line would have been broken in seconds and in a dozen places.

It is a military principle that an attack has a much greater chance of success when it is made on a narrow front and with depth.

Cavalry Tactics and Regulations of the United States Army, regulation 562:

> *Under circumstances which require and admit of a more concentrated attack, the regiment charges in column of squadrons.*

To successfully attack the immense Indian village Major Reno should have charged with one company on line and with the remaining two companies in two succeeding lines. This would have given Reno's attack a narrow front with a depth of three lines. However, the conclusion of Reno's interesting attack is unknown because he halted this unusual maneuver short of the Indian village and dismounted his soldiers as skirmishers.

The formation Major Reno used in charging down the valley, and then the halting of his charge, indicates that Reno was engaging in some complex cavalry maneuvering and, in fact, Reno's attack was a diversionary attack, something which was familiar not only to Custer, but had been an integral part of American cavalry maneuver by many generals, both Union and Confederate, throughout the Civil War.

Custer had the larger force and was advancing at the same time Major Reno was, on a parallel route on the bluffs across the river, and Custer could see everything happening in the valley on Reno's front. It is evident that Reno's primary purpose in the valley was to attract the enemy's attention while Custer moved into position to strike the main blow. Major Reno's attack is a maneuver well known in military doctrine. It was a diversion.

Carl Von Clausewitz described in detail the function of a diversionary attack:

> *The term diversion in ordinary usage means an attack on* [the enemy] *that draws off the enemy's forces from the main objective.*
>
> *In such a diversion, there must be, of course, an objective to attack. Only the value of this objective can induce the enemy to dispatch troops for its protection.*
>
> *The main requirement is that the enemy should withdraw more men from the main scene of operations than are used for the diversion.*

Major Reno's charge was a diversion with the purpose of attracting the attention of the Indians and when the reserve company was ordered onto the charging line it was, in effect, a shrewd bluff. True, if that line actually reached the village, the objective, it would have been a disaster and the small force would quickly be swallowed up and perhaps even annihilated. However, as Reno's battalion charged down the valley the appearance must have been formidable to those in the Indian village.

Major Reno's command, attacking with the element of surprise, would have been a terrifying sight to those in the village and they could not have known what was behind

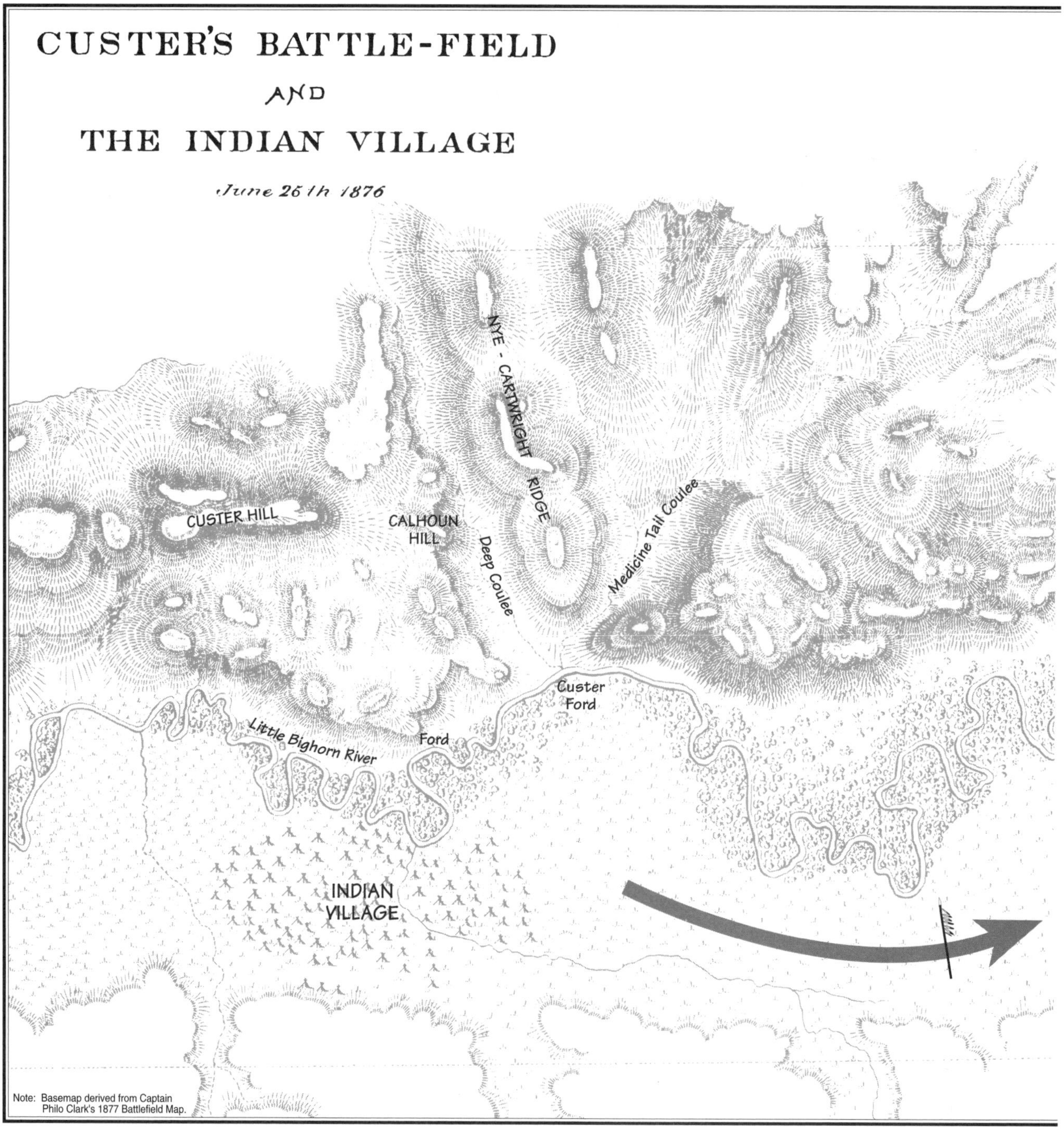

CUSTER'S BATTLE-FIELD
AND
THE INDIAN VILLAGE

June 26th 1876

NYE - CARTWRIGHT RIDGE
CUSTER HILL
CALHOUN HILL
Deep Coulee
Medicine Tail Coulee
Custer Ford
Ford
Little Bighorn River
INDIAN VILLAGE

Note: Basemap derived from Captain Philo Clark's 1877 Battlefield Map.

MAP ONE:

BATTLE OF THE LITTLE BIGHORN

About 2 p.m.: The Indian camp of Sitting Bull has previously been identified from the divide between the Rosebud and the Little Bighorn valleys by scouts of the 7th Cavalry. Custer has divided the regiment into five battalions. Two of them, under Captains Keogh and Yates, are with Custer and are comprised of five companies. One of the remaining battalions is commanded by Major Reno made up of three companies. The fourth battalion is commanded by Captain Benteen and is also made up of three companies. The fifth battalion, made up of one company and six men from each of the other companies, is commanded by Captain McDougall and escorts the pack train.

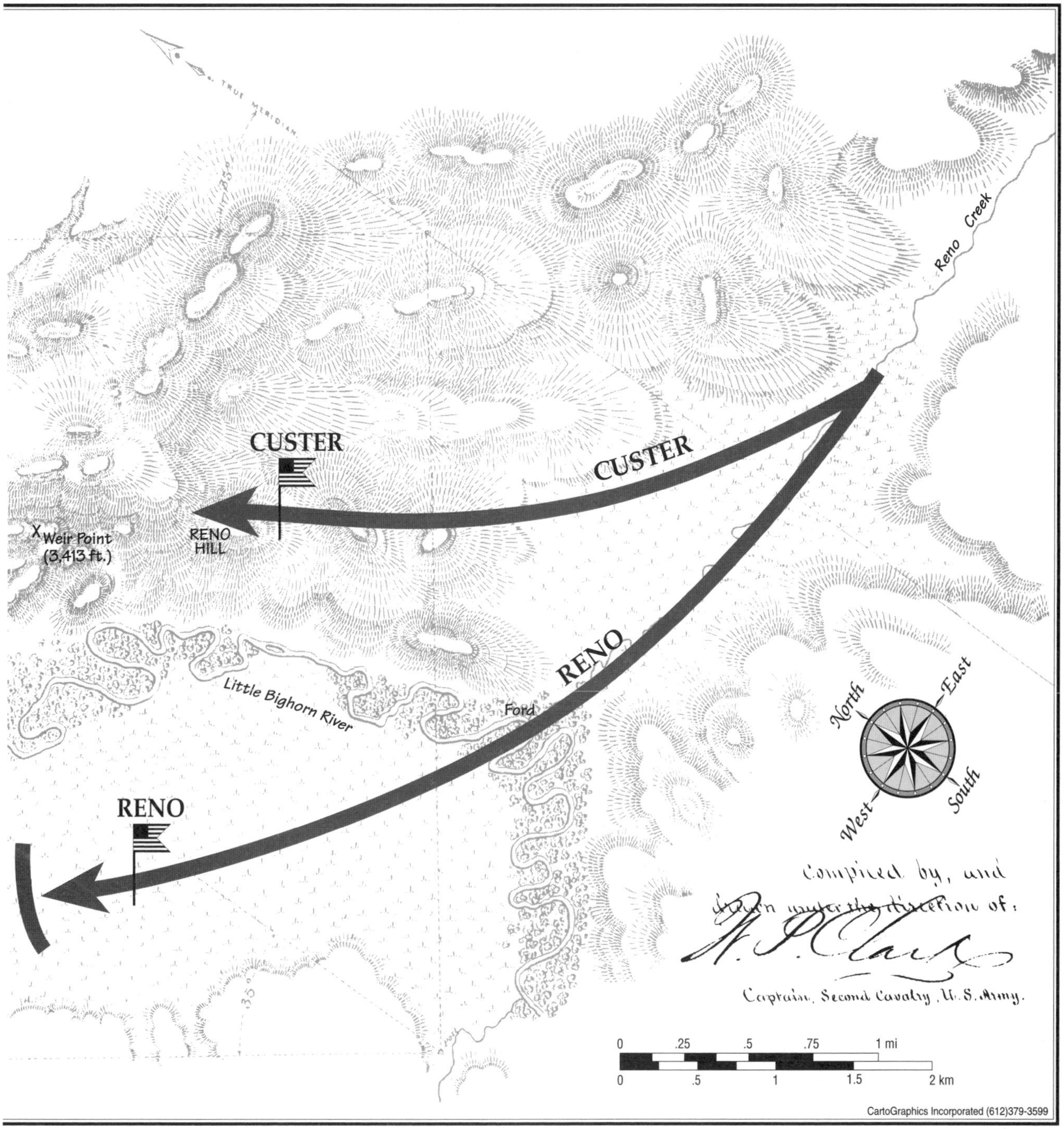

The pack train has fallen several miles to the rear and Benteen has been dispatched on a scout to the left of the main line of the march. Custer and Reno have approached the Indian camp at a trot and, a few miles from it, they separate.

Reno and most of the scouts have been ordered into the valley to create a diversionary attack.

Custer advances across the bluffs parallel to Reno to strike in the flank of the village. Sergeant Kanapie has been dispatched to the rear with an order for Benteen and the pack train to "hurry forward."

The Indians in the village later admitted the attack had been a surprise.

NOTE: Indian and soldier movements and positions are approximate according to testimony and original maps.

that charging line of cavalrymen. Another line with just as many soldiers? Two more lines? The entire regiment of the 7th Cavalry? It is apparent that Reno's charge was, at that point, for psychological effect and this was exactly the sort of brinkmanship Custer and other American cavalry generals had developed into an art form during the Civil War.

Reno's maneuver would seem to indicate that he was an element of a larger plan and was operating under Custer's orders.

Major Reno Retreats to the Woods

When Major Reno dismounted his soldiers the Indian warriors could, for the first time, see the meager force confronting them and they quickly advanced to challenge the soldiers. It was simply impossible that the thin and un-reinforced line of soldiers could have remained in place long, at least in that formation, and they did not. However, Reno's command was still the most visible threat to the Indian village and as long as Reno's force held its position it was like waving a red cape in front of an angry bull. Reno's attack was a classic military textbook example of a diversionary attack.

Two soldiers were, perhaps, wounded on Major Reno's skirmish line before it was ordered into the wooded area next to the river and this demonstrates that the line was never seriously attacked, although it would have been had it remained in position much longer. The number of Indians who were eventually to confront Reno's command was estimated by the participants to be in the hundreds, and some participants claimed nearer to a thousand.

After fighting with the Indians on the skirmish line at most, perhaps, fifteen minutes, the soldiers on the skirmish line were withdrawn into the woods where the horses and G Company had been sheltered. The wooded area itself was a strong position and, if needed, could have been defended for a considerable length of time. There are numerous precedents during the wars against the Indians in the west where even a small force held out against huge numbers of Indian warriors: the Hayfield fight, the Adobe Walls fight, Beecher's Island and the Wagon Box fight, to name a few.

The bravery of the Indian warrior was legendary, but his concept of warfare was ambush and raiding. To have followed a battalion of soldiers into a wooded area, with its resulting nasty fight and large casualties, was not an attractive proposition to any Indian warrior. And it is also unlikely that any Indian war chief would have led his warriors into such a confrontation. Lieutenant Hare was in the wooded area with Major Reno, and later said:

> *If the Indians had charged us in the timber we could not have stood it but a few minutes; but Indians don't do that.*

Lieutenant DeRudio was also in the timbered position with Major Reno's command, and he later said:

> *Major Reno could have held his position in the timber three or four hours by careful use of ammunition.*

The purpose in ordering the men to the wooded area, however, was not defensive. The soldiers passed the word that they were going to remount and charge. Sergeant Culbertson, who was with Major Reno's command, testified at the Reno Court of Inquiry:

> *We fired three or four shots from the edge of the woods and then someone called to me to get to our horses.... They said we were going to charge.*

Bloody Knife is Killed

The soldiers were gathering their horses and mounting them when Bloody Knife, the Indian scout who had spent many years as Custer's friend and companion, approached Major Reno. At his Court of Inquiry, Reno said:

> *I was trying to get from him* [Bloody Knife] *by signs where the Indians were going.*

Suddenly, a hostile bullet struck Bloody Knife in the head and sent a bloody shower of gore into Reno's face.

If any single incident affected the course of the Battle of the Little Big Horn, if one bullet could win or lose a battle, then the shot that struck Bloody Knife was it. Before the incident Major Reno, to all appearances, had at least been in control of the situation he was confronted with. Afterwards, Reno lost his presence of mind entirely and abandoned any military duty. Scout George Herendeen

later commented on this incident:

I thought at the time it demoralized him a great deal when Bloody Knife was killed.

From a non-military viewpoint it is possible to sympathize with Major Reno. He was already in the unenviable position of fighting the greatest concentration of hostile Indians ever seen in the American West, an enemy who would show no mercy to a defeated foe. Then, dramatically adding insult to the situation, Bloody Knife's head exploded into Reno's face. It can be imagined that this would be enough to rattle anyone's nerves.

Major Reno, however, did not have the privilege of reacting to that situation, or any other military situation, from anything other than a military perspective. Reno was a soldier and any situation with which he was confronted as a soldier required he exercise the obligation of military duty. At the Battle of the Little Big Horn, Reno was not only a soldier, but also the commander of a battalion of 175 soldiers and scouts. The lives of these men were Reno's responsibility. How Reno reacted to any situation during the battle, regardless of how unpleasant that situation was, would directly affect the members of his command, as well as the course the battle would take. But it was fear, all too human fear, and not military duty, which now determined the actions of Reno.

Major Reno's Debacle

Defying all military doctrine, as well as common sense, Major Reno now committed a fearful blunder, which would not only remove his command from any effective participation in the battle, but also nearly destroy it. Lieutenant Varnum later told of what happened:

When I got to the right of the line, I met Gerard and Reynolds and talked with them about three minutes, when I heard cries: "Charge! Charge! We are going to charge!"

There was confusion and I jumped up and said, "What's that?" and started down the woods and grabbed my horse. Everybody was mounted. I didn't hear any orders.

The men passed and I followed out and let my horse race to the head of the column, which was then halfway to the place we crossed soon after.

I came up on the left side of the column and saw no officer at the head and supposed the column had met some Indians and had wheeled and started for them and the others had followed. I yelled to them to stop. I then saw Major Reno and Captain Moylan and they went on to the crossing.

Immediately on the other side, there is a high bluff and they climbed that. The horses were tired and panting and could hardly make it....

As the command rode out and across, the men were using revolvers–they had to jump the horses into the river; it was a straight bank, four or five feet high; the other side was a little better; but my horse nearly threw me as he jumped on the other side; the water was about four and a half feet deep.

When I got across, I started up a ridge to the left, but some men called me back. Evidently, they saw some Indians there, because Dr. DeWolf started up that ridge and was shot.

There were Indians on the hill we went to. The command started its retreat in columns of fours at a fast gallop. The crossing was not covered.

Everybody I saw was considerably excited when they got on the hill. They were excited when they went in, for that matter. The command was demoralized to a certain degree. They left a great many behind–the organization was not as good as when it went in. A great many men were missing.

Doctor Henry R. Porter also described Major Reno's retreat:

At the time I heard Reno say we would have to get out and charge them, he moved out and the men followed from all directions.

They had a great deal of trouble finding their horses, but as soon as they mounted, they went out.

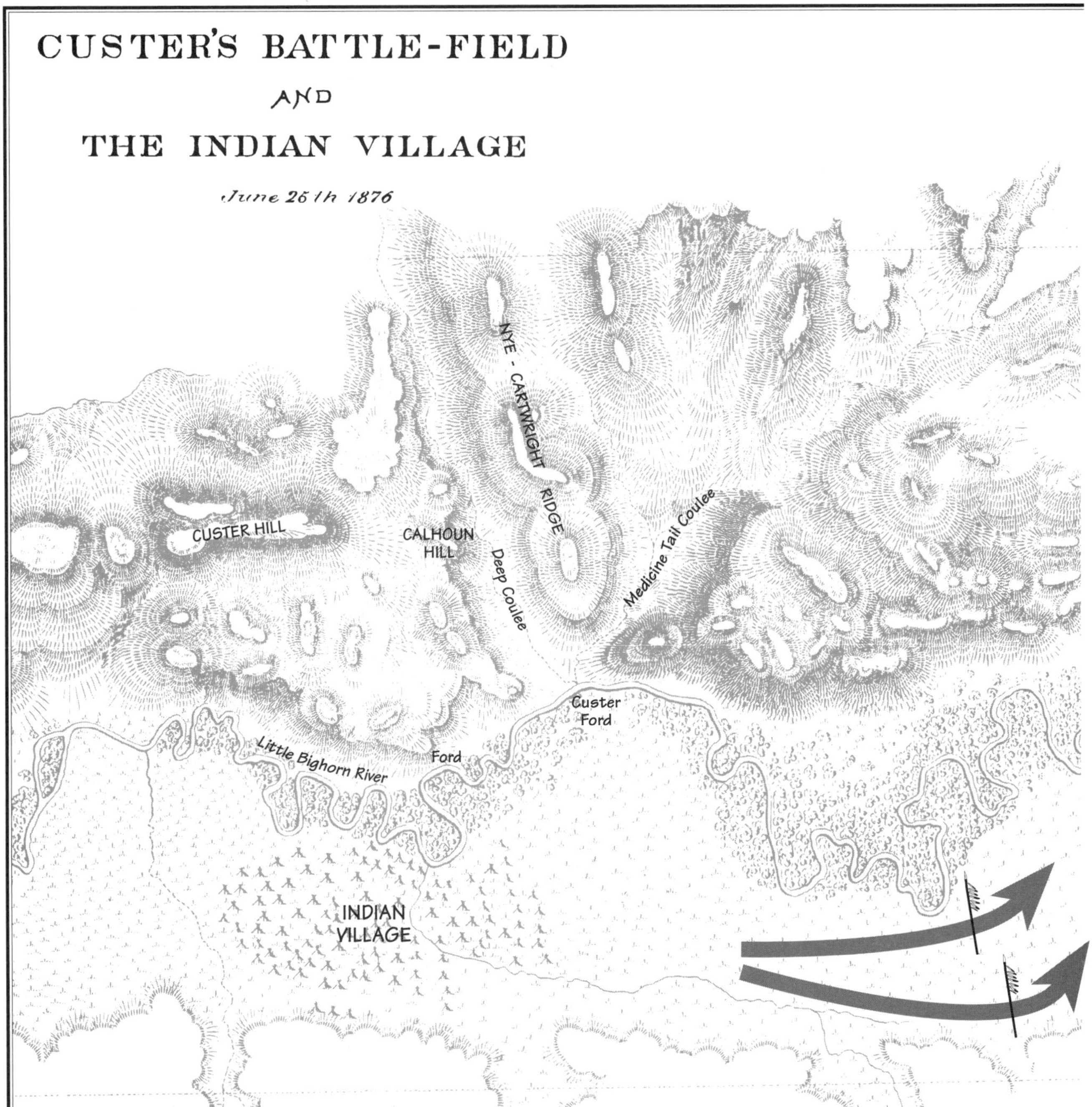

CUSTER'S BATTLE-FIELD

AND

THE INDIAN VILLAGE

June 26th 1876

NYE - CARTWRIGHT RIDGE

CUSTER HILL

CALHOUN HILL

Deep Coulee

Medicine Tail Coulee

Custer Ford

Ford

Little Bighorn River

INDIAN VILLAGE

Note: Basemap derived from Captain Philo Clark's 1877 Battlefield Map.

MAP TWO:

BATTLE OF THE LITTLE BIGHORN

Major Reno halts his advance and briefly forms a skirmish line. The Indian warriors advance to meet the attack and begin to out-flank Reno's left. Reno then withdraws his command into the wooded area next to the river. Two messages have been sent to Custer by Reno. Custer has been seen on the Weir Points waving his hat to Reno's men in the valley.

While on the Weir Points Custer has dispatched Bugler Martin to Benteen ordering him to advance and "be quick." Custer continues to advance toward "Custer Ford" with the intention of supporting Reno's diversion in the valley with an attack from the right flank.

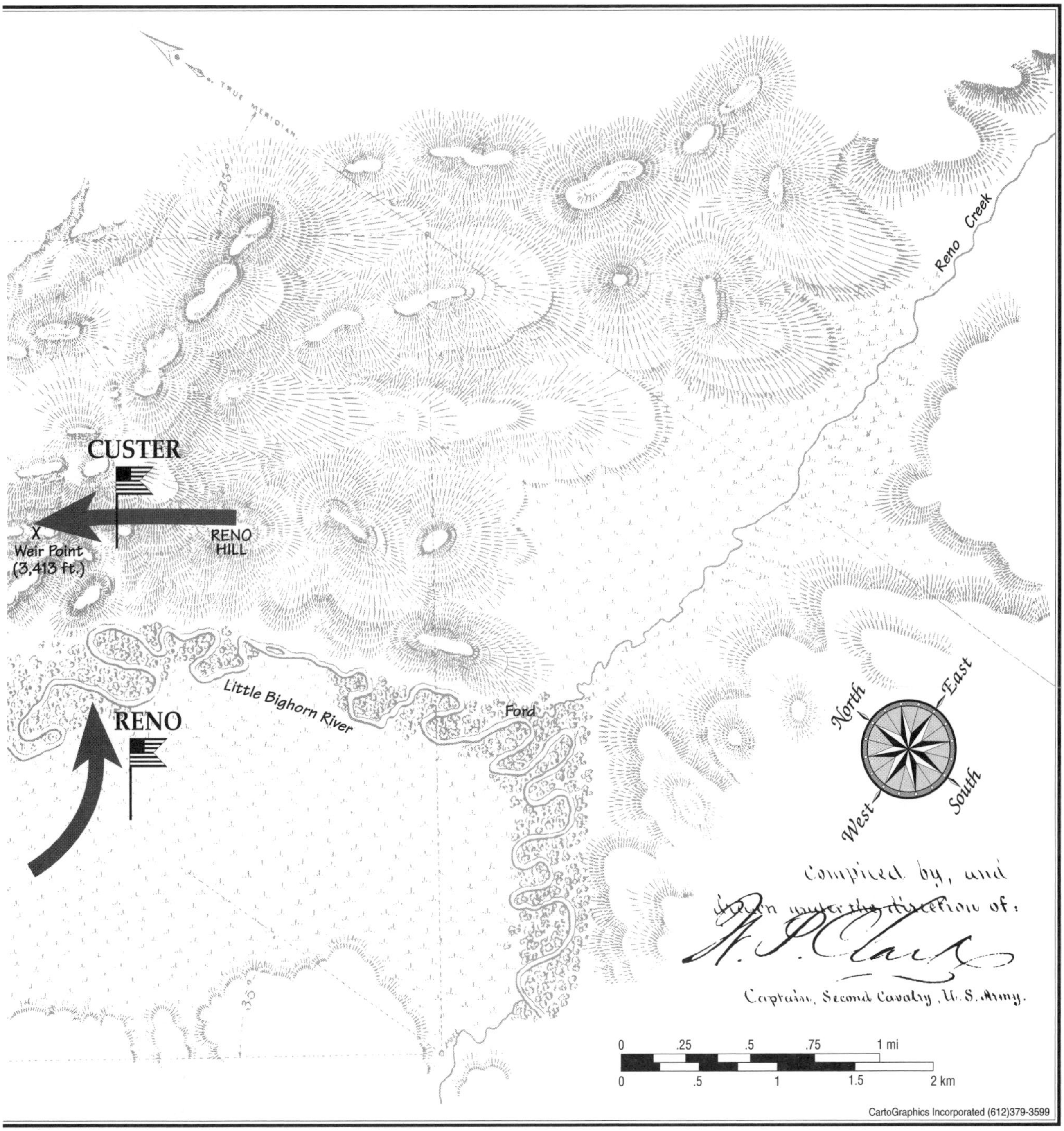

Benteen and the pack train continue to advance towards the battlefield.

I stayed a few minutes with the wounded man and when I got out, the men were all running and the Indians, too, within a few yards of me. There were a few Indians between me and the command.

I went out expecting to see the command charging the Indians but, instead, the Indians were charging the command. They were all on the run. I let my horse out and got to the edge of the river and he jumped in and crossed with the rest. There was a great deal of dust, [yelling] *and confusion. The wounded man was left in the timber.*

The first officer I saw on the bluffs was Lieutenant Varnum. He had his hat off and said "For God's sake, men; don't run. There are a good many officers and men killed and wounded and we have got to go back and get them."

The scout, George Herendeen, was left behind during the disorganized retreat, but witnessed much of it, which he later described:

Major Reno was sitting on his horse in the [clearing]. *The troops were in line, in close order, their left toward the river.*

I heard him order, "Dismount," and there was a volley [more acurately described as a "mass fire" as the Indians did not fire organized vollies] *fired by the Indians; I judge the ones I had seen coming in and had fired at.*

There was an Indian named "Bloody Knife" standing in front of Major Reno, within eight feet from him, and he and a soldier were hit. The soldier yelled and then Major Reno gave the order to dismount and the soldiers had just struck the ground when he gave the order "Mount", and then everything left the timber on the run.

Major Reno started out and the line broke to get out as far as I could see; they were getting out at any place they could find. There was dense underbrush and not more than one man could pass at a time, so they had to go single file on a trail that had been made by buffalo or some [other] *animals.*

That volley and the man hollering seemed to startle everybody and they ran. I followed. I was not frightened at first, till after I got dismounted. I was not in the timber and thought I had a good position and, there was nothing to get frightened at.

I started and got to the edge of the timber. The men were passing me and all going as fast as spurs will make a horse go; and I started my horse.

There was a dense dust and I could not see where I was going. I got about 150 yards and my horse went down and I went off. Men were passing me all the time and everybody running for his life. Some Indians almost ran over me as I fell, about twenty of them.

I got up and turned and went right back into the timber.

Was Reno's Retreat Justified?

Concerning his retreat at the Battle of the Little Big Horn Major Reno offered an explanation at his Court of Inquiry:

I had no doubt that I could explain the retreat from my position; but I did not give it a thought. I never thought it would be questioned.

This fanciful statement on the part of Major Reno was made possible only by the fact that Custer was dead. Had Custer lived, Reno would have been assured that his retreat would have been "questioned." The wooded area was a strong one for defense, and the losses his battalion had suffered up to the point of his retreat were tragic enough, but did not number more than half a dozen soldiers, if indeed there had even been that many.

Lieutenant McClernand was with General Terry's command and, of course, did not participate in the disastrous retreat. In his account of the battle he did describe Major Reno's retreat and his account of it would have come directly from those who survived it. As McClernand also gave his opinion of this retreat as a military officer who was on the Battlefield only days later, this opinion can be given some credence. McClernand said:

Reno's casualties were three officers, including Dr. DeWold, and twenty-nine enlisted men and scouts killed; seven enlisted men wounded, and one officer, one interpreter and fourteen soldiers and scouts missing. Nearly all the casualties occurred during the race for the hills. The Crow scout remained with the command, but the Rees continued their flight to Powder River.

As Reno's disorganized units regained the bluffs, they had a breathing spell, for about this time the foe began to withdraw to meet, as it was later learned, Custer's onslaught. It may be too much to say that Custer prevented the annihilation of Reno's command at this period, but certainly his blow fell none too soon to prevent further disorganization and probably additional heavy losses. Had Reno shown a bolder spirit in the timber and greater confidence in his leader, he

might at this moment from that position have changed to fortunes of the day; at least he might have saved Custer's command from annihilation without incurring his own. He left the woods at the worst possible time both for himself and Custer, even though the latter had not moved to his immediate support, he should have known his chief would strike soon. It was not in the nature of the man [Custer] *to turn his back to the foe, and a diversion on any part of the field would have contributed to his lieutenant's relief. A short distance through the woods from the old bed of the river would have enabled Reno to fully see the village into which a withering fire might have been poured, while many of its defenders were confronting Custer, and with a most demoralizing effect.*

Historians have debated Major Reno's retreat, and at times even justified it. Yet Reno was under direct orders from his commanding officer and Reno did not have a choice, none whatsoever, but to carry out those orders. Reno's orders did not include a panicked retreat from the battlefield.

No Rear Guard

Lieutenant Varnum later commented on Major Reno's retreat from the Little Big Horn Valley:

In such a movement, the troops must be kept well closed up and, if there is any delay in crossing, some disposition must be made to cover it.

Lieutenant Varnum's statement is true. While an attempt can be made to justify Major Reno's retreat by himself, or others, how that retreat was conducted cannot, in any way, be explained away. Concerning any retreat during a battle, Carl Von Clausewitz is clear in his book *On War* as to the necessity of a rear guard:

In order to utilize any weakness or mistake on the part of the enemy, not an inch more ground that the force of circumstances requires [should be given up] ... *in order to keep morale as high as possible, it is absolutely necessary to make a slow fighting retreat, boldly confronting the pursuer whenever he tries to make too much of his advantage.*

The retreats of great commanders and experienced armies are always like the retreat of a wounded lion. . . .

The first movements have to be almost imperceptibly short and, it must be a general principle not to let the enemy impose his will.

This principle cannot be put into practice without fighting fierce engagements with the pursuing enemy, but it is a principle worth the cost. Otherwise, the pace is bound to increase till withdrawal turns into rout. More men will be lost as stragglers than would have been lost in rear guard actions. And the last vestiges of courage will have disappeared.

The only way to prevent a retreat from becoming a rout, according to Von Clausewitz, is:

... a strong rear guard, made up of the best troops, led by the most courageous General and supported at crucial moments.

Having a strong rear guard during any retreat is, in fact, standard military doctrine in any trained army, anywhere, and a military maxim. The United States cavalry manual of 1864 describes how a retreat, when necessary, should be conducted.

Cavalry Tactics and Regulations of the United States Army, regulation 560:

... retire by alternate squadrons.... [The first squadron] *having retired the distance ordered, or at the signal HALT.* [The second squadron now withdraws covered by the first squadron.]

This "leap-frog" retreat allows one squadron to provide covering fire while the other squadron retreats and vice-versa.

Was There a Rear Guard?

Actually, there may have been a "rear guard" for Major Reno's retreat, although self-appointed and doomed. The last words of the scout, Charles A. Reynolds, according to Doctor Porter, was a condemnation of Reno's retreat with "what dumb fool move is this."

This would seem to indicate Reynolds knew Reno was about to invite disaster upon his command. This scout would have had two choices: retreat with the main force, or join the others who remained behind in the relative safety of the wooded area. Yet, Reynolds apparently did neither and his body was found near the skirmish line.

Likewise with the black scout, Isaiah Dorman, who had joined the expedition by special request of Custer. Little is known of Dorman other than he had been on the frontier at least since the Civil War, and perhaps earlier. He had lived among the Indians himself and had a Sioux wife. Like Reynolds, Dorman was found near the skirmish line.

Scout Isaiah Dorman

Certainly, the scouts Reynolds and Dorman had the experience and skills to save themselves. They had only to retreat to the wooded area for safety, but they did not. Did these two scouts deliberately forfeit their lives to give Major Reno's retreat a few added moments of protection? Considering that, had these two been prone to

making foolish mistakes, they probably would have died on the frontier long before the Battle of the Little Big Horn, it would seem possible, even probable, that they did. Reynolds was known to have been a deadly shot, Dorman probably was also, and these two scouts may have prevented Major Reno's retreat from becoming a much worse disaster than it actually was.

No Defense for Reno

Major Reno did not post a rear guard when he left the woods. Reno did not have a rear guard during his retreat to the river. At the river crossing Reno again did not post a rear guard. The result of Reno failing to have a rear guard was a rout, as Carl Von Clausewitz so accurately predicted in his book *On War*, and resulted in terrible loss of life to Reno's battalion and which, not surprisingly, also caused his entire command to become thoroughly demoralized.

By the time Reno's battalion reached the bluff top, almost one third of his command was either killed, wounded, or missing.

It may be chosen to defend Major Reno as a human being, that his actions were no worse than many people, if not most, would have taken in a similar situation. From the standpoint of accepted military doctrine, however, Reno's retreat is clearly beyond any reasonable defense.

CHAPTER 8

Messages Sent by Custer — Major Reno and Captain Benteen Disobey Orders — Custer's Plan — Custer's Drifting Trail — General Tom Rosser — Custer's Style of Combat — Captain Benteen's Letter — Accounts by the Indians — Distance of Major Reno's Battalion from the Indian Camp — Gunfire Heard by Major Reno's Command — Private Theodore Goldin's Statement — Custer Seen in Valley — Other Evidence — Sound Testing by Professor Flower — The Facts — The Truth Distorted

Rain in the Face

After separating his command from Major Reno's, Custer and the two battalions with him turned to the right and proceeded north. Two maps are known to have been drawn of the battlefield immediately after the Battle of the Little Big Horn. One of the maps was drawn when General Terry's command arrived on the battlefield on June 27, 1876. At the Reno Court of Inquiry, 1st Lieutenant Edward Maguire, who was the engineering officer with Terry, and in charge of drawing this map, spoke of this map:

I was General Terry's Staff Engineer.... We arrived at Reno's hill position about 10:00 a.m., June 27, 1876. In my official capacity as Engineer, I had measurements of the Little Big Horn battlefields made by a sergeant who accompanied me.

In September, 1876, a map of the Little Big Horn battlefield, drawn by Lieutenant Maguire, was forwarded to Headquarters, Military Division of the Missouri. A version of this map was presented at the Reno Court of Inquiry in 1879.

Captain Benteen also drew an unofficial map which he sent with a letter to his wife shortly after the battle. The Maguire map and the Benteen map are the only two maps known to have been drawn of the battlefield on the spot and while the evidence was fresh at hand. Both maps clearly show Custer's route, after separating from Major Reno, to have been north, following the bluff tops on the east side of the Little Big Horn River.

Revisionist accounts which claim Custer's movements were different, perhaps further east by a mile or more, contradict not only the original maps, but also the numerous eye witnesses who were with Major Reno and saw Custer on the bluffs across the river.

It would seem, this was the logical route for Custer to follow. From these bluffs Custer could observe Major Reno's advance, the opposition Reno was confronted with, and, as Custer proceeded north, the Indian village. To have advanced to battle further east, where Major Reno's advance would not have been visible, and to where the Indian village also could not have been seen, defies common sense, as well as military doctrine. As Custer proceeded northward it is obvious that he intended to support Reno's advance with an attack on the flank of the village.

Messages Sent by Custer

As Custer advanced north along the bluffs, overlooking the Little Big Horn Valley, he sent back two messages to the rear battalions, and he also received two messages from Major Reno. Sergeant Daniel A. Kanipe delivered Custer's first message and, through this good fortune, sur-

vived the Battle of the Little Big Horn. In an account he left of the battle, Sergeant Kanipe told of the advance of Custer's two battalions across the bluffs and of the message with which he was sent back:

When we reached within a quarter of a mile of the junction of Benteen's Creek with the Little Big Horn, I sighted Indians on the top of the range of bluffs over the Little Big Horn River.

I said to First Sergeant Bobo, "There are the Indians."

General Custer threw up his head about that time and we [the] *troops, C, E, I and F, headed for the range of bluffs where we had seen the Indians.*

Tom Custer, brother of the General, was Captain of my troop, C. We rode hard, but when we reached the top, the Indians were gone. However, we could see the tepees for miles.

The Crow Indian scouts with our outfit wanted to slip down and get a few ponies. Some of them did slip down, but they got shot for their pains.

Chief Scout Mitch [Bouyer], *Curley, a Crow, and "Bloody Knife" Reeve* [Ree] *stayed up in the bluffs with us.*

It is interesting that Sergeant Kanipe mentions seeing the scout Bloody Knife with Custer's command, as there are several accounts of this scout being with Major Reno's command. Certainly, most of the members of the 7th Cavalry would later have known of the fact that Bloody Knife had been killed next to Major Reno, including Sergeant Kanipe, and it must be surmised his addition of Bloody Knife to his narrative was deliberate. Sergeant Kanipe also said:

I was riding close to Sergeant Finkle. We were both close to Captain Tom Custer. Finkle hollered at me that he couldn't make it, his horse was giving out. I answered back: "Come on Finkle, if you can." He dropped back a bit.

Just then, the Captain told me to go back and find McDougall and the pack train and deliver to them orders that had just been issued by General Custer.

"Tell McDougall," he said, "to bring the pack train straight across to high ground–if packs get loose, don't stop to fix them. Cut them off. Come quick. Big Indian camp."

The urgency of the message sent back with Sergeant Kanipe made it clear; Custer wanted every soldier forward as quickly as possible, and also Custer ordered these soldiers to seek the advantage of terrain, "the high ground." Kanipe was sent while Custer was on the bluffs overlooking the Little Big Horn Valley and Major Reno's advance, before reached the prominent Weir Peaks. Nevertheless, at least part of the Indian camp was visible, and it was apparent to Custer that the 7th Cavalry was entering a major battle.

Custer continued his advance across the bluffs and, minutes after sending Sergeant Kanipe to the rear, a second message was dispatched from the Weir Peaks with Bugler John Martin. This message was addressed to Captain Benteen and it said:

Benteen, come on. Big village. Be quick. Bring packs. W.W. Cooke. P.S. Bring packs.

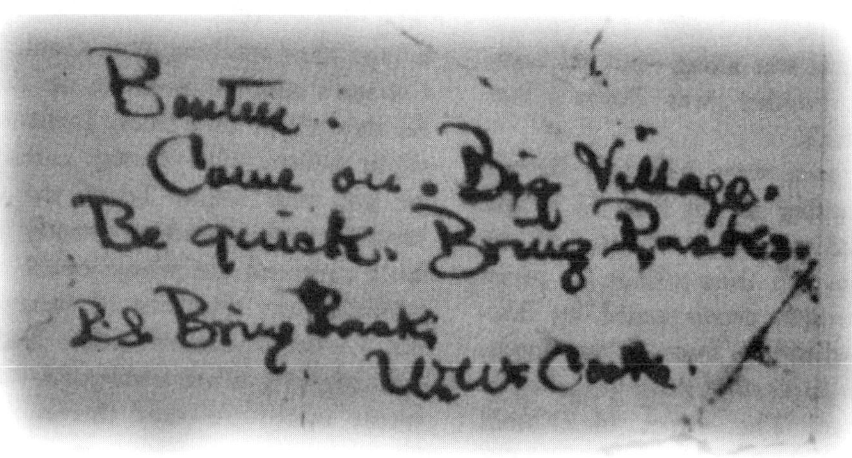
Benteen.
Come on. Big Village.
Be quick. Bring Packs.
P.S. Bring Packs.
W.W. Cooke.

Bugler Martin told about his ride back to Benteen with what would be Custer's last known communication:

General Custer's column moved always at a gallop. It was about a mile and a half from the watering place to the point on the ridge where we could see the village.

After he [Custer] *saw the village, he pulled off his hat and gave a cheer and said "Courage, boys, we will get them, and as soon as we get through, we will go back to our station."*

We went more to the right from the ridge and down to a ravine that led to the river.

At the time General Custer passed the high place in the ridge, or a little below it, he told his Adjutant to send an order back to Captain Benteen. I don't know what it was. Then the Adjutant called me...

He said, "Orderly, I want you to take this dispatch to Captain Benteen and go as fast as you can." He told me if I had time and there was no danger to come back, but otherwise to remain with my company which was with Captain Benteen.

My horse was tired and I went through as fast as he

could go. The Adjutant told me to follow the same trail we came down. After I started back, I traveled five or six hundred yards, perhaps three quarters of a mile, and got on the same ridge where General Custer saw the village.

I looked down and saw that Major Reno's battalion was engaged. I went on to about three or four hundred yards above the watering place and met Captain Benteen.

I delivered my dispatch to him and told him what Lieutenant Cooke had told me.

Captain Benteen read the dispatch and put it in his pocket and gave me an order to Captain McDougall to bring up the pack train and keep it well up.

Bugler Martin

Captain Benteen asked me where General Custer was. I said I supposed that by that time, he had made a charge through the village. I said nothing about Major Reno's battalion. He did not ask about it.

Once again the urgency of the second message emphasized that every soldier was needed forward quickly. The "bring packs" order did not pertain only to the ammunition packs; Custer's command had not yet fired a shot. Each of the soldiers with Custer had 100 rounds for the carbine with them and another 24 for the pistol, which was adequate for the initial phase of the battle.

Custer wanted the 125 soldiers in Captain Benteen's battalion, and the 136 soldiers with the pack train, forward with all possible speed to support the diversionary attack Major Reno was now making in the valley and the flanking attack Custer was about to make.

Why the second message was addressed directly to Captain Benteen, instead of the "if you can find him" instructions given to Sergeant Kanipe and the first message, can be observed from the Weir Peaks from which the message was sent. This cluster of three peaks is the most prominent geographical position on the Little Big Horn battlefield and from it the back trail on which Benteen and the pack train were approaching is visible for many miles.

Captain Benteen arrived at Major Reno's hill position as Reno's soldiers were still straggling up to it. This indicates Benteen was never as far to the rear as he wanted others to believe. Aided by field glasses, Custer saw Benteen advancing down the trail and, for this reason, he addressed the second message directly to him. When the first message was sent Custer had not yet reached the Weir Peaks and he could not yet see Benteen's advance.

Major Reno and Captain Benteen Disobey Orders

Captain Benteen did not obey the spirit of Custer's last order to "bring packs." Custer's intention, as he clearly stated in the order, was for Benteen's battalion to assist the pack train, stampeding the mules as fast as possible, and advancing on Custer's trail across the bluffs right into the Indian village where they would then join the Custer and Reno battalions. If a resolute defense was needed in the village, the mules could have been shot for barricades.

In an interview with Walter Camp, Captain McDougall, who commanded the rear guard with the pack train, mentioned the possibility of using the mules for barricades, if necessary:

When he got within sight of Reno Hill, the top of it was covered by men and he did not know whether they were Indians or White men. He was now moving with one platoon ahead of packs and one in rear.

He now put ammunition packs together and gave orders that in event of attack the head platoon should deploy and try to stand them off, and, if unsuccessful, the details of enlisted men with the ammunition packs would immediately lead the animals in a circle, shoot them down and then lie behind them and fight as long as they could. They could live on mule meat for a few days.

Custer knew General Terry and his command were due at the mouth of the Little Big Horn River the following day, June 26. This was about fifteen miles away from the Little Big Horn battlefield and hardly a half day's normal march away. The objective had been reached, the Indian camp, and if the 7th Cavalry had successfully attacked and destroyed the village, their mission would have been accomplished. The ammunition packs were important, as any member of the 7th cavalry would have understood, and these packs would have been protected.

However, with resupply only half a day's march away at the mouth of Little Big Horn River, and the Indian village located and about to be attacked, the mules and most of the supplies on them would then have been expendable and secondary to the accomplishment of the mission. In the opening phase of the battle Custer needed soldiers, not supplies. "Hurry forward and don't stop to fix any broken packs, cut them loose." If the mules had to be shot for defense, then they too were expendable.

What Custer wanted, what he clearly ordered in his last two known messages, was the pack train and the soldiers with it, as well as Captain Benteen and his battalion, to advance as quickly as possible to assist in the attack on the Indian village.

Major Reno denied ever receiving any further instructions from Custer beyond the original order to advance. The lines of communication were open, as proven by the two messengers Major Reno sent to Custer. These messengers made it to Custer and died with his command. Custer

Benteen's Map of the Battle of the Little Big Horn

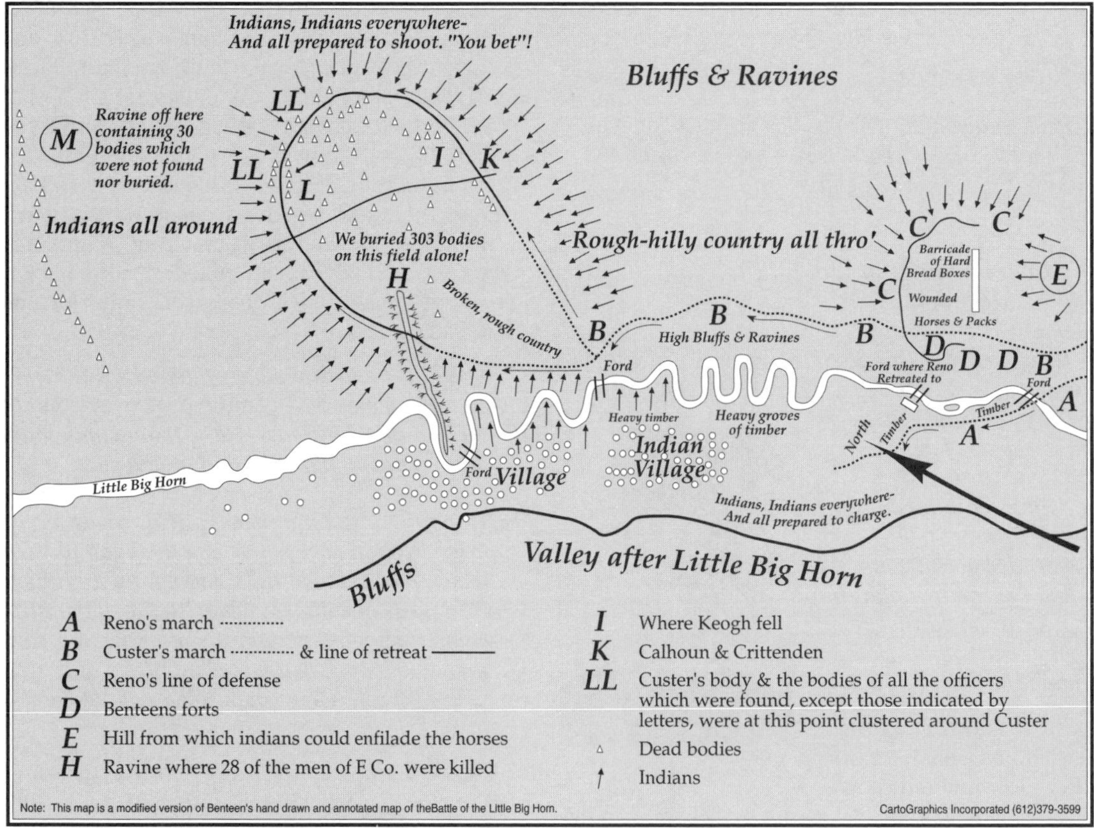

also sent back two messages to the rear and these messages were delivered as well.

It would seem unlikely that Custer could not have communicated with Major Reno when the lines of communication were open; Custer received two messages from Reno, so the lines of communication were open. Simple logic would dictate a response from Custer. However, for Reno to have admitted receiving further instruction from Custer would have made any defense of his later actions untenable. Major Reno said at his court of inquiry:

It was impossible to have victory over the Indians. . . .

This was a statement which, as many of Major Reno's and Captain Benteen's statements did, cast the blame for the defeat on Custer and his poor judgement in ordering an attack on the village.

Custer's Plan

Some have claimed that Custer did not have a "plan." From the Weir Peaks Custer had sent back his last known messages. From the Peaks, Custer had full view of Major Reno's diversionary attack in the valley and the Indian camp. Custer had seen Captain Benteen on the back trail and he knew the pack train would not be much farther behind Benteen.

Custer had not been able to approach the village at night and deploy the 7th Calvary carefully for a dawn attack, as would have been preferred. The plan had to be improvised immediately, as conditions demanded, which was exactly what a cavalry officer was trained to do. This plan, however, would be nearly identical in execution to every other attack the cavalry made on an Indian camp.

Custer was not attacking a position of entrenchments and bunkers. He was attacking an Indian camp with the objective to capture and destroy it and, if possible, to capture and destroy the pony herd. This was the plan used by the Frontier Army over and over again to successfully defeat the hostile Indian tribes of the plains and one which forced the Indians to return to the reservations. A key element for success was surprise and, in this respect, all of the Indian participants who later spoke of the battle agree that the sudden attack on the village by the 7th Cavalry was a surprise.

In essence, Custer's "plan," as he developed the final touch on the Weir Peaks, was to exploit the element of surprise, get every soldier in the regiment into the Indian camp as quickly as possible, and then destroy the camp.

Cavalry Tactics and Regulations of the United States Army, regulation 561:

Meeting an enemy by surprise, the cavalry should instantly charge... every effort of impetuosity should be used.

From the Weir Peaks, Custer's trail led directly to a river ford about one mile to the north. This was the closest ford available for Custer to cross the river and attack the village, thus supporting Major Reno's diversionary attack. Immediately after the battle there was apparently no dissention that this, in fact, had been Custer's route, as shown by the battle maps of Lieutenant Maguire and Captain Benteen. Supposing that Custer's trail could have led anyplace other than directly to the ford would seem to be absurd.

For Custer to have taken his force further away from the Indian village, for instance directly to the final hill position where the bodies of his command were later found, would only have further scattered an already dispersed regiment. Custer would not have made this foolish mistake, and it is unlikely that any inexperienced lieutenant would have either.

Reaching the river ford the question arises, "Why wouldn't Custer have crossed it to support Major Reno's attack?" The Indian participants of the battle, almost without exception, agree the sudden attack by the 7th Cavalry was a surprise, so there would not have been an ambush waiting for Custer at the ford. Major Reno's diversionary attack was the visible and immediate threat to the camp, exactly as it was intended to be, and this diversionary attack attracted the attention of the Indian warriors while Custer advanced to execute a textbook military attack on the flank further downstream.

Had there been an ambush waiting for Custer at the river ford, evidence would have been found later in the form of dead cavalry horses and possibly dead soldiers, although every effort would have been made to carry the dead soldiers off to prevent the demoralizing mutilations which the Indians would have inflicted on the bodies. Neither dead cavalry horses nor the bodies of soldiers were found at the crossing, so there was neither an ambush waiting, nor was there any repulse there.

Custer's Drifting Trail

At the Reno Court of Inquiry Captain Benteen attempted to mislead the court into believing the trail of Custer's command had never come close to the ford, and as "evidence" he used the fact that dead horses and soldiers were not found there. Captain Benteen testified:

In my opinion, the route taken by General Custer is not properly indicated on the map, though until recently I had believed it was; but I could never account for the fact that there were no dead bodies at that ford, for if he had gone down to the river and was attacked there, there would have been horses and men killed there, but there were none.

Lieutenant McClernand commented on the fact that those who examined Custer's trail just days after the battle believed that it had led to the river ford:

When the battlefield was carefully gone over and studied by Gibbon's command and the remnants of the 7th Cavalry, I cannot recall that there was any dissenting opinion about Custer having descended from the bluffs by following down a large coulee that led to the river not far from the center of the village.

If he entertained any intention to strike at the hostiles, or their camps, when he reached this coulee, it certainly invited him to descend, for it offered the first good opportunity for his command to reach the valley, after it commenced to bear to the right from Reno's column.

When questioned at the Reno Court of Inquiry concerning Custer's trail, Lieutenant Godfrey said:

Q. State if you made any examination of the point "B" or near it.

A. I went down to that ford and thought I saw evidences of where shot horses had gone across the ford, and I made up my mind at the time that General Custer had attempted to cross there.

At the Reno Court of Inquiry Lieutenant Wallace mentioned the changing official version of Custer's route on the battlefield. Lieutenant Wallace testified:

On June 28 when we moved out to bury the dead, I was told we followed his trail, but have since been told we did not.

Just who it was that told Lieutenant Wallace that they had not followed Custer's trail on June 28 was not identified. It must be wondered exactly how difficult it would have been to follow a trail of over 200 cavalry horses and how this trail, over the years, was able to move about so mysteriously.

There was no "dissenting opinion," as Lieutenant McClernand pointed out, concerning Custer's route directly after the battle, so it must be concluded that this drifting trail was, like so many other issues, a manufactured "fact," designed to deliberately confuse objective observers and to protect certain surviving officers.

General Tom Rosser

Thomas L. Rosser was a former Confederate cavalry general whose success in the Civil War made him quite qualified to render an intelligent judgement concerning what may have happened at the river ford. In an article printed in the *New York Herald Tribune* on August 22, 1876, Rosser pointed out:

I have heard that someone has advanced the theory that Custer was met, at this point where he first struck the river, by overwhelming numbers, and so beaten that his line from that point was one of retreat. This is simply ridiculous.

Had Custer been repulsed at this point, his column would have been driven back upon the line on which he had approached and the proposition is too silly to be discussed.

Of course Tom Rosser was correct. A repulse at the river ford would have sent Custer retreating over his back trail to rejoin the other elements of the regiment. When Major Reno retreated from the valley battle that is exactly what he did. He fell back to rejoin the battalions that were advancing to the battlefield. To suppose that Custer would have done anything other than retreat toward reinforcements is, as Rosser said, "ridiculous" and "silly."

Custer's Style of Combat

Then what did happen at the river ford where Custer's trail so clearly led if he was not repulsed there? One clue, almost conclusive in itself, was Custer's style of combat, which was to attack fiercely and at the first opportunity.

Cavalry Tactics and Regulations of the United States Army, regulation 561:

The charge is the decisive action of cavalry.... Meeting an enemy by surprise, the cavalry should instantly charge.

The Indians admit to a surprise attack by the 7th Cavalry, which the evidence seems to prove. Custer did reach the ford and was unopposed there, which the evidence also seems to prove. The mission objective and Major Reno were on the other side of the river and, with these facts at hand, Custer would have done the obvious. He would have crossed the river and attacked the objective. Anyone acquainted with Custer's military history, military theory, or the use of calvary in battle, would recognize this as probable. Interestingly, in Major Reno's report of the battle he made a statement in which he acknowledged that Custer may have crossed the river:

After following this trail, it is evident to me that Custer intended to support me by moving further down stream and attacking the village in the flank; that he found the distance greater to the ford than he anticipated,

that he did charge ... that Companies C and I and perhaps part of Company E crossed into the village or attempted it.

Only later did Major Reno change this view, undoubtedly because of the unflattering implications for himself. If Custer did cross the river, he would have been not much farther than a mile from Reno's most advanced position in the valley. Custer would then have been in the rear of the Indian warriors on Reno's front and thus given him the support promised. The two forces would have been separated by only a few short minutes by cavalry charge and, with an unexpected attack materializing in their rear, it is almost certain that the Indians on Reno's front would have quickly melted away.

Captain Benteen's Letter

Like Major Reno, Captain Benteen at first said that Custer's command had crossed the river into the Indian camp. Benteen wrote a letter to his wife, dated July 4, 1876:

I am of the opinion that nearly all, if not all, of the five companies got into the village.

The letter to his wife actually was written over a span of several days, and before it was sent Captain Benteen had added the following:

The latest and probably correct account of the battle is that none of Custer's command got into the village at all.

By the time of the Reno Court of Inquiry, Captain Benteen had refined this "latest and probably correct" version even further:

I can't think he got within three furlongs [about 3/8ths of a mile] *of the ford.*

This evolving version of Custer's trail by Captain Benteen contradicts every known account of Custer's route made by those who were on the battlefield only days afterwards, and it also contradicts the map which Benteen himself drew. Benteen's obviously false testimony reveals Custer's movements to have been an extremely sensitive subject for him, as well as for Major Reno.

Captain Henry B. Freeman was an infantry officer with the reinforcements that arrived on the battlefield with General Terry on June 27, 1876. In Freeman's personal diary he mentioned that some of the surviving officers of the 7th Cavalry believed that at least a portion of Custer's command had crossed the Little Big Horn River and attacked the Indian camp.

Whoever these officers were, for some reason, they apparently did not make a determined issue of this point. There are no references to Custer's crossing the river in any of the newspaper accounts published after the Battle of the Little Big Horn, nor did this subject come up, except indirectly, at the Reno Court of Inquiry.

However, Dr. Holmes Paulding of General Terry's command did make an interesting comment in a letter he wrote dated July 8, 1876. Dr. Holmes said:

Finally on reaching the ford they were met by an immense body of Indians fighting on foot. They crossed in the face of this terrible fire but were driven back, dismounted, and put in one or two vollies, remounted and retreated alternately. [Calvary Tactics and Regulations ... Regulation 560]

The brother-in-law of the Crow scout Goes Ahead, who was with the Custer battalion, Frank Behune, made a statement recorded in the South Dakota Historical Collections. Behune said he had been told many times by Goes Ahead that:

They were going to ford the river at the south end of the timber on the island. The gray horse troop got across. They dismounted. They got orders to fire and did fire. The first one killed was an Indian woman, hit in the left breast.

When the Indians from below saw the flag, they came upon the ponies and joined the Indians that were here. An officer took a book out and wrote a note, and sent a soldier down the river. (He indicated that it was thought to be an attempt to reach the commander, meaning Terry.) The soldier went ahead across the river.

It is interesting that Behune mentions that Goes Ahead told him that Custer sent a message from the river crossing, but there does not appear to be any corroborating statements by the other Crow scouts with Custer.

Accounts by the Indians

Puzzling accounts by Indians who were in the village cannot be reconciled with any fact other than, at some point during the Battle of the Little Big Horn, soldiers entered the village and fought there. These Indian accounts speak of women and children killed and tepees burned. Chief Gall of the Sioux said that the soldiers:

... killed my two squaws and three children, which made my heart bad.

Red Horse, who was, like Gall, a Sioux chief, was in the Indian camp the day of the Battle of the Little Big Horn. Red Horse also said:

The attack was made on the camp about noon. The troops were divided, one party charging right into camp.

Red Horse also said:

The troops set fire to the lodges.

Kill Eagle was in Sitting Bull's hostile camp on the day the 7th Cavalry attacked, although he claimed later he had not been at war with the government and had been an unwilling witness to the battle. Kill Eagle said:

Before retiring across the creek, the soldiers got into camp and set fire to some of the lodges.

A Sioux woman by the name of Moving Robe Woman, who was a member of Sitting Bull's Hunkpapa camp the day of the battle, later described the attack on the Indian village by the 7th Cavalry:

The soldiers began firing into our camp.... I heard a terrific volley of carbines. The bullets shattered the tepee poles.... I saw a warrior ... grasping his tomahawk. He started running towards his horse when he suddenly recoiled and dropped dead. He was killed near his tepee.

Captain Poland, stationed with the 6th Infantry, interviewed many of the Indian participants of the Battle of the Little Big Horn. In a report issued from Standing Rock Agency, Dakota Territory, dated July 24, 1876, Poland stated he had been told by Indians who had returned to the agency that Custer had crossed the river into the Indian camp.

They reported that he [Custer] *crossed the river, but only succeeded in reaching the edge of the Indian camp. After he was driven to the bluffs, the fight lasted about an hour.*

A map of the Little Big Horn Battlefield was published in the *New York Herald Tribune* on November 16, 1877, which had been drawn with the collaboration of Sitting Bull. This map clearly shows that the path taken by some of the soldiers went right through the Hunkpapas camp next to the ford. While the person who drew the map identified these soldiers as belonging to Major Reno's battalion, was this actually the case?

Sitting Bull later responded to questions asked about the Battle of the Little Big Horn and described what he identified as an attack by Custer's command. In his interview, Sitting Bull said:

Q. Did any of the chiefs see him [Custer]?

A. Not here [Reno Valley fight], but there [pointing to the place where Custer charged and was repulsed on the North bank of the Little Big Horn].

Q. Was there any heavy fighting after the retreat of the soldiers to the bluffs?

A. No, not then, not there.

Q. Where then?

A. Way down here.

... and Sitting Bull indicated with his finger the place where Custer approached and touched the river. That said he was where the big fight was fought a little later.

In a discussion with A.G. Shaw, a Sioux warrior by the name of Thunder Hawk discussed what he described as Custer's attack on the Indian village:

Custer crossed the river at the mouth of Reno Creek [west] *of Calhoun Hill, then he swept down with all his command along the river on the west side and passed his tent and was shooting into the Indian camp.*

Who were these Indians speaking of when they spoke of soldiers in the camp, tepees burned, and women and children shot? Could it have been Major Reno's command?

Distance of Major Reno's Battalion from the Indian Camp

Accounts by the members of Major Reno's command say his charge was halted long before the battalion reached the Indian camp. The actual distance from the village was estimated to be up to, and even over, a mile. At the Reno Court of Inquiry Lieutenant Varnum said:

Our skirmish line was about two miles from the first crossing and about 800 yards from the nearest part of the village.

Interpreter Fred Girard estimated the distance from Major Reno's line to the Indian camp as:

... a mile or half a mile away.

Doctor Porter said:

I did not see the village until I got in the woods and then saw it through a clearing ... the nearest tepee was one quarter mile away.

In fact, there seem to be no accounts in narratives, testimony, or otherwise, by members of Major Reno's battalion who say they (the person giving the account) were in the Indian camp, the burning tepees, or of the killing of women and children. Reno's men may not have been quick to admit they had killed women and children, but someone should have mentioned the burning of tepees, if any had been burned by members of Reno's command.

Gunfire Heard by Major Reno's Command

After Major Reno retreated from the valley to the hill position and was joined by Captain Benteen, many members of the combined command mentioned hearing the sound of gunfire in the direction Custer was known to have taken. The only exceptions to this were Reno and Benteen who, defying credibility, claimed at the Reno Court of Inquiry not to have heard this gunfire. Significantly, the gunfire that was heard on Reno Hill was said to have originated "down there" and there are even references to its having come from the village. At the Reno Court of Inquiry Lieutenant Wallace testified:

I heard scattering shots in the bottom ... it was apparently in the village.

The civilian packer, B.F. Churchill, was with the pack train when it arrived at Reno's hill position. At the Reno Court of Inquiry Mr. Churchill testified:

The firing I heard appeared to come from the lower end of the village. Others heard it and spoke of it.

Lieutenant Hare also testified at the Reno Court of Inquiry and he said:

I heard firing down there just after Benteen came up.

At the Reno Court of Inquiry those who were on Major Reno's hill position and would mention hearing this gunfire included Captains Moylan and McDougall, Lieutenant Godfrey and 2nd Lieutenant Winfield S. Edgerly, and Sergeant Ferdinand A. Culbertson. Nearly everyone else who was on Reno's hill position and testified also mentioned hearing this gunfire.

Custer's final position was not "down there" in the valley, or anywhere near the village. It was "over there," nearly four miles from Major Reno's position and the Weir Peaks also blocked the view of Custer's final position. It is likely that this geographical formation would have distorted the sound of any firing on Custer Hill if, in fact, it could have been heard at all.

The interpreter Fred Gerard had, along with others, been left behind in the wooded area when Major Reno had retreated out of the valley. These men were hiding from the Indians when they heard gunfire that was so close they debated actually leaving the woods to join with what they believed was Custer's attack. Gerard said:

I heard continuous firing clear on down as if there was a general engagement, down to where I afterwards went to General Custer's battlefield. And I heard firing to the left of the village; three or four volleys as if there were 50 to 100 guns at a volley.

Lieutenant DeRudio was with me and he said "By God, there's Custer coming; let's go and join him."

I told him to wait, that we had plenty of time, that when the firing got opposite we could go out and join him, that he was now too far away. I heard the volleys during the firing down there, after the heavy firing that sounded like a general engagement.

There was a continuous scattered fire all the time until it got down below where Custer's battlefield was and then it became heavy. There was a skirmish fire all the way down from where I first heard it.

In an interview with Walter Camp, Gerard further elaborated on the strange pattern of firing he heard. According to Mr. Camp's notes, Gerard believed he heard a detachment of Custer's battalion fighting its way through the Indian village, and he was certain he heard firing down near the river. Gerard also stated that he had heard volleys fired, as did many others, although Custer's command on the final hill position was discovered to have fought and died in skirmish formation in which the soldiers do not fire as a unit, but as individuals.

Volley firing would only occur when the soldiers were in close formation and under the command of an officer who would be directing their fire at a specific target.

Private Theodore Goldin's Statement

Private Theodore W. Goldin, who was with Major Reno's command, made an interesting claim in a letter he wrote concerning the sound of gunfire heard from Reno's hill position:

I met a retired officer who served in the country soon after the battle, and he told me that several years after the fight, and while his company was stationed at Old Fort Custer [at the mouth of the Big Horn River], *there was quite an argument over this same question and it was decided to settle the matter by an experiment.*

He took his entire company and marched to monument hill, while another group of officers, after carefully comparing watches, proceeded to the knoll on which the officers of Reno's command were gathered, and that at a certain agreed time, he caused his men to fire three volleys at specified intervals, and that the firing could

not be heard on the knoll.

Several years after the battle, during a Fourth of July celebration, a news reporter by the name of H.L. Knight made an observation which would seem to confirm Private Goldin's statement:

> *Not half a mile from the Custer battlefield was an encampment of the Crow tribe ... the minute gun* [a cannon], *a twelve pounder, ... was being fired at regular intervals ... , and we stood right on the spot where Reno's camp was made fourteen years ago* [and this cannon could not be heard on Reno's position].

Custer Seen in Valley

The most astonishing statements made by those of the 7th Cavalry who survived the Battle of the Little Big Horn, however, did not concern what they heard, but rather what they saw. When Sergeant Edward Davern testified at the Reno Court of Inquiry, he said:

> *Shortly after reaching the top, I heard volley firing from downstream. It was not very distinct, but you could tell it was volley firing. No shots between the volleys.*
>
> *I could see Indians circling around in the bottom on the right, away down and raising a big dust. I could not tell on which side of the creek, there are so many bends in it.*
>
> *I spoke to Captain Weir about it. I said, "That must be General Custer fighting down in the bottom." He asked me where and I showed him. He said, "Yes, I believe it is."*

At another point in his testimony Sergeant Davern said:

> *When I saw the dust and heard the firing, I remarked to Captain Weir, "General Custer must be fighting the Indians, they are circling in the bottom."*
>
> *He said "Why do you think so?" I said, "I hear the firing, and see the dust, and see, the Indians have all left us."*

Lieutenant Edgerly also testified at the Reno Court of Inquiry that he had seen Custer in the valley during the Battle of the Little Big Horn. Lieutenant Edgerly said:

> *Shortly after I got on the hill, almost immediately, I heard firing and remarked about it, heavy firing, by volleys, down the creek.*
>
> *Captain Weir came to me and said General Custer was engaged and we ought to go down.*
>
> *I said I thought so too. He went away, walking up and down anxiously. I heard the fire plainly.*
>
> *The First Sergeant came up then and I saw a large cloud of dust and thought there must be a charge, and said, "That must be General Custer, I guess he is getting away with them."*
>
> *He said, "Yes sir, and I think we ought to go there."*

When further questioned, Lieutenant Edgerly said:

> *Q. You heard firing from the field below?*
>
> *A. Yes, sir.*
>
> *Q. The dust you saw was not from the Custer battlefield?*
>
> *A. No, sir.*
>
> *Q. Was it from the same side of the river that the Indian village was?*
>
> *A. Yes, sir.*

In a statement made at Fort Adeste in 1881, Lieutenant Edgerly repeated his observation made at the Reno Court of Inquiry and he described what he saw while on Reno's hill position.

> *... loads of dust, horsemen rushing back and forth on the opposite side of the river and about four miles away.*

Lieutenant Mathey, who was with the pack train, also saw evidence of a battle taking place in the Indian village and this is particularly significant. If, when the pack train arrived, Custer was still fighting in the village and there were no Indian warriors on Major Reno's front at all, then what was to stop this combined force from advancing down the valley to support Custer's attack?

Lieutenant Mathey, when questioned at the Reno Court of Inquiry, said:

> *Q. What hostile Indians did you see on your arrival and how did you acquaint yourself with it and where did you see them?*
>
> *A. I saw a few scattered Indians on the bottom, not in any numbers at all.*
>
> *Q. Was there firing around Major Reno's position?*
>
> *A. No, sir.*
>
> *Q. Did you observe at that time any movement of Indians at a distance?*
>
> *A. Someone gave me a glass and I saw off at a distance of three miles or more, and could see Indians circling around but no soldiers.*

Q. Where was that?

A. Downstream, about where the village was.

Q. Could you tell on which bank it was?

A. On the left bank.

Q. At the time how did it impress you and the others about you?

A. I can only answer for myself and my first sergeant. We both thought that General Custer was charging the Indians.

It is apparent from the statements of Sergeant Davern, Lieutenant Edgerly, and Lieutenant Mathey that, as Major Reno and Captain Benteen vacillated on the Reno hill position, a battle was being fought in the Little Big Horn Valley. The sound of this battle was clearly heard and it was also visible to those on Reno Hill.

Other Evidence

The body of a soldier with Custer's battalion was found on the site of the Indian village. This was Sergeant James Bustard of I Troop. The interpreter Gerard also noted:

I saw several dead horses in the village marked U.S. 7th Cavalry; they were to the right of some lodges.

There could be explanations for Sergeant Bustard and the cavalry mounts being found in the village, but there is yet other evidence that cannot be easily resolved. Tangible evidence has been found on the site of the Indian village indicating cavalry troops may have fought there. This evidence is in the form of spent U.S. Army shell casings.

In 1965 Author Jesse W. Vaughn received a letter from Mr. Roy Nagashina who owned a home on the site of the old Indian encampment of 1876. Mr. Nagashina explained what he found on his property:

... *a great many cartridges of that* [army] *description.*

According to Mr. Vaughn, Nagashina noted the locations of his findings:

... *the relics were found on the bench north of the bend ... and in the bottom land where the Indian village was located along the river.*

These army shell casings were found too far north to have come from Reno's skirmish line in the valley or his wooded position, although there are other possibilities as to their origin.

Sound Testing by Professor Flower

On May 10, 1995, Professor Terry Flower of the *College of St. Catherine*, St. Paul, Minnesota, completed a sound analysis of firearms similar to the ones used by the cavalry at the Battle of the Little Big Horn. Previous to this date, Professor Flower fired the government-issued Springfield Carbine with cartridges loaded with black powder similar to that used by Custer's command.

Sound levels were recorded and then projected to determine where the sound of gunfire heard by Reno's command could have, or could not have, originated from. Without taking into account the major terrain feature of the Weir Peaks or the background noise of Reno's command, but rather only the distance involved, Professor Flower concluded:

Thus, volleys [heard] *at Reno Hill could only marginally be heard from the campground sight* [near where the village was located] *and most likely not heard at all from the final Last Stand Hill.*

To be reasonably certain of this issue, on-site acoustical testing is needed.

The Facts

Major Reno and Captain Benteen were experienced cavalrymen and they realized the significance of Custer's successful attack on the Indian camp; Custer had reached the objective. This fact, if known at the time, would have completely altered the perspective held of the Battle of the Little Big Horn, with extremely unfavorable implications on the conduct of Reno and Benteen and the course the battle might have taken. Reno and Benteen, to protect themselves, had to distort the evidence and change the facts concerning the battle and a key fact to be distorted was Custer's attack on the village.

The original opinions of both Major Reno and Captain Benteen were that Custer had crossed the Little Big Horn River and attacked the Indian camp. Captain Freeman recorded that other officers of the 7th Cavalry shared this belief. Accounts by the Indians confirm that soldiers were in the village and had burned tepees and women and children were killed. Eye-witness observations by soldiers on Reno's hill position place Custer in the village, and the sound of gunfire heard by Reno's men supports this observation.

The Truth Distorted

The belief that Major Reno and Captain Benteen wanted to instill concerning the Battle of the Little Big Horn was that there was not a "plan," and, as a result of Custer's misjudgments, the battle had been a hopeless endeavor from the very beginning. It was Custer who had "abandoned" Reno and Benteen, and Custer's errors alone that had brought destruction upon his command. Any personal responsibility Reno and Benteen had for the disaster was insignificant.

Custer's plan had been simple and had been the same as every other attack by soldiers on an Indian camp: charge

CUSTER'S BATTLE-FIELD

AND

THE INDIAN VILLAGE

June 26th 1876

NYE - CARTWRIGHT RIDGE

CUSTER HILL

CALHOUN HILL

Deep Coulee

Medicine Tail Coulee

CUSTER

YATES

Custer Ford

Ford

Little Bighorn River

CUSTER

INDIAN VILLAGE

Note: Basemap derived from Captain Philo Clark's 1877 Battlefield Map.

MAP THREE:

BATTLE OF THE LITTLE BIGHORN

While the scout Bloody Knife confers with Reno, he is killed. Reno panics and retreats out of the wooded area toward the bluffs to his rear. It is a disorganized retreat and Reno loses one third of his command either killed, wounded or missing.

Captain Benteen arrives on the battlefield and sees Reno's retreat. Benteen's command joins with Reno on the bluffs and the pursuing Indians vanish. Gunfire is heard by members of both commands downstream.

Custer arrives at Custer Ford and crosses with one battalion, Keogh's, while Yates with two companies rides further downstream to create another diversion. Yates' battalion may or may not have

crossed the river.

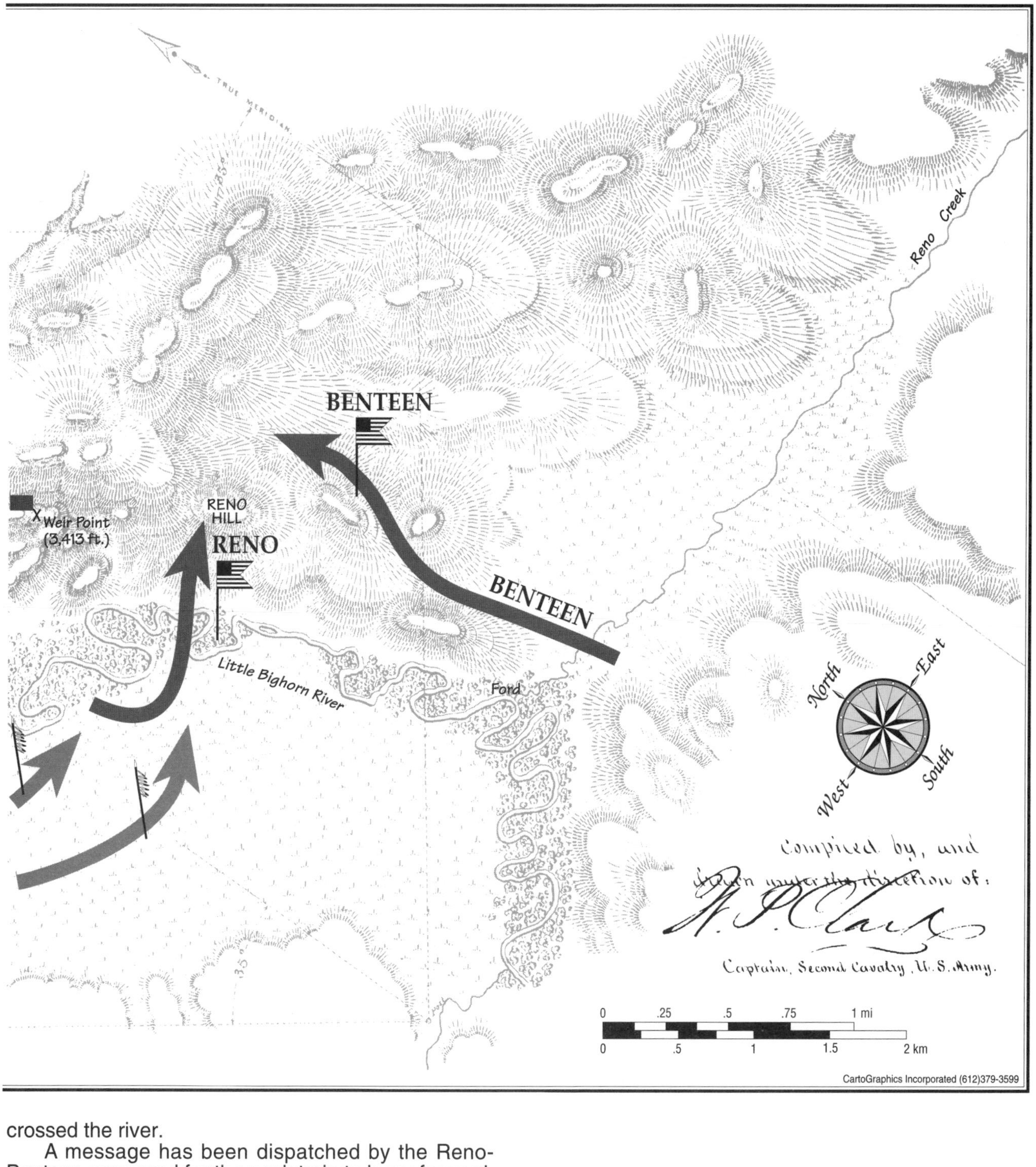

A message has been dispatched by the Reno-Benteen command for the pack train to hurry forward.

the village, capture it, and then destroy it. To accomplish this plan required that all those in command positions follow the orders given them by Custer and that the entire regiment advance as quickly as possible and assist in the attack.

Custer had ordered Major Reno to charge the village. He also advised Captain Benteen of a "big village" and ordered him to "be quick" and advance to the front. The pack train had been ordered to hurry forward and "if any packs come loose, don't stop to fix them." Custer's orders to the supporting battalions were absolutely clear. The objective was also absolutely clear. Only Custer achieved the objective, which was to attack and enter the village. The other battalions of the regiment, which numbered almost two-thirds of the total, failed to advance and support Custer's attack as they had been ordered to do.

If Custer had been successful in entering the Indian camp, then what if Major Reno and Captain Benteen had carried out the orders given them and advanced to support Custer's position in the village? Could the Indian warriors, even numbering in the thousands, have rallied from the sudden attack, which they all admit was a surprise, and could they have managed to drive an entire regiment of cavalry from the village? The great advantage the soldiers had over the Indian warrior in this type of battle was the unit discipline and training of the soldiers.

Under the direction of competent officers, company or battalion-sized volleys would have had a devastating effect on any attempt to drive the soldiers from the Indian village. There is simply no record in the history of the wars in the American West of any number of Indian warriors, under any circumstances, confronting that volume of firepower in an open battle. Historians can only speculate as to the outcome of the Battle of Little Big Horn had the Indians set a precedent and confronted an entire United States Army regiment in open battle.

There can be little question that on June 25, 1876, a terrific battle would have been fought between the United States 7th Cavalry and Sitting Bull's alliance of Indian tribes at war with the U.S. Government. It would have been a battle resulting in many casualties on both sides and, in any event, one of historic proportions. Yet, the battle may have taken another course for the 7th Cavalry had Custer's orders, or indeed the spirit of military duty, been carried out by Major Reno and Captain Benteen.

CHAPTER 9

Captain Benteen's Statement — Captain Benteen's Arrival — The Indians Vanish — The Pack Train Arrives on the Battlefield — The Decisive Role — Captain Weir's Advance — The Weir Peaks — The Lost Patrol — Others Soldiers Follow Captain Weir — The Weir Peaks Abandoned — Who Gave the Evacuation Order? — Captain Benteen Gave the Order

Captain Fredrick Benteen

John Martin, the bugler who had been sent back to Captain Benteen with Custer's last known message, witnessed the final part of Major Reno's retreat on his ride across the bluffs overlooking the Little Big Horn Valley with Captain Benteen's advance:

We followed General Custer's trail until we got on the same ridge where I saw Reno engaged [on his ride back with Custer's message].

About the time we got there we saw Reno's battalion retreating to the same side of the river we were on. We joined Reno.

Captain Benteen's Statement

In describing his arrival on the battlefield Captain Benteen said the following:

I met Trumpeter Martin, who brought a written order, which I have. It has no date.

It says: "Benteen, come on – big village – be quick – bring packs. P.S. Bring packs. W.W. Cook."

It was about two miles from where Major Reno first crossed the Little Big Horn that Martin met me, and about two and a half miles from the burning tepee. I did not know whose trail I was following. I asked Martin, after reading the note, about the village. He said the Indians were all "skedaddling;" therefore, there was less necessity for me to go back for the packs. I could hear no firing at that time. I was then riding four to five hundred yards in advance of the battalion with my orderly. Captain Thomas B. Weir was about two hundred yards in my rear. I waited till he came up and handed him the note. I asked him no questions and he did not volunteer advice.

When the command came up, I ordered a trot and went on ahead to the crossing of the Little Big Horn at the ford "A." That was my first sight of it. There I saw an engagement going on and supposed it was the whole regiment. There were twelve or thirteen men in skirmish line that appeared to have been beaten back. The line was then parallel with the river and the Indians were charging through those men. I thought the whole command was thrashed and that was not a good place to cross.

To my right, I noticed three or four Indians four or five hundred yards away from me. I thought they were hostile, but on riding toward them found they were Crows. They said there was a big "pooh poohing" going on. Then I saw the men who were up on the bluff and I immediately went there and was met by Major Reno.

I did not consider it necessary for me to go back for the

pack train as it was coming, and the Indians could not get to it except by me.

Captain Benteen's arrival with his battalion, just as Major Reno's soldiers were retreating from the valley, demonstrates how close behind the main force Benteen's command had been. At the Reno Court of Inquiry Benteen would later attempt to exaggerate the distance he had covered on his scout, saying:

I was separated from Reno possibly fifteen miles when at the greatest distance.

Captain Benteen's claim is false. "Fifteen miles" would have placed Benteen several hours away from the battlefield, an impression he wanted to give, but which is contradicted by his arrival in time to see Major Reno's men fighting in the valley. 2nd Lieutenant Winfield S. Edgerly of Captain Weir's D Troop was to give a more realistic version, saying:

I don't think we were more than two and a half miles from the general direction of the trail at any time.

From the accounts of the soldiers with him it is apparent that at no time during his advance did Captain Benteen hurry forward, even after receipt of two messages from Custer directing him to do so. His indifference had even provoked Captain Weir, as Lieutenant Godfrey noted, to leave the morass ahead of the rest of the battalion, taking the lead position, whereas Weir's company had actually been second in the line of the march.

Had Captain Benteen moved quickly forward after the messages had been delivered from Custer he could have arrived on the battlefield much sooner. Even a few minutes could have had an influence on Major Reno's retreat.

Custer had humiliated Captain Benteen by removing him from the advance position of the regiment and then sending him on a useless scout. Benteen was smarting under that treatment. Benteen's sulky attitude and dilatory advance can probably, at least in part, be attributed to Custer's malevolence.

Yet, for Captain Benteen there seemed to be a precedent for tardy actions at the Battle of Little Big Horn. During the Washita Battle of 1868, Captain Albert Barnitz commanded a battalion of which Benteen's company was part. In an account he left of the battle, Barnitz detailed how he and his command cautiously advanced in the predawn darkness to their assigned position and he also commented upon one other instance of Benteen's tardiness. Captain Barnitz said:

We found to our surprise that the [regimental] band, which should have remained with General Custer, was, through some misconception of orders, following us, and that [Captain] *Benteen's squadron, which should have accompanied us, had not yet come up. The band was sent back.... Benteen having at length arrived.*

Courage could very well not have been the deciding element concerning Captain Benteen's apparent reluctance to fight Indians, especially when attacking a village full of women and children. His letter after the Washita Battle, which spoke of dead women and children, could have been a sincere expression of Benteen's feelings and not merely an attempt to defame Custer and the 7th Cavalry. His Civil War record and his subsequent actions in organizing a defense on Reno's hill position seem to preclude, at least occasionally, any question of his courage. Benteen's true motivations, whatever they were, will unfortunately never be known.

Captain Benteen's Arrival

Arriving at Major Reno's position on the bluffs, Captain Benteen halted his ordered advance to assist Reno's disorganized battalion. A momentary pause by Benteen was justified. Reno badly needed support, and not only in the form of material aid. Reno and his men were demoralized by the rout in the valley and the psychological impact of Benteen's arrival helped to calm the panic of those who had survived the terrifying retreat. Yet, Benteen was still under orders to advance and the need for his battalion at the front was magnified by Reno's removal of his battalion from the attack. This left Custer and his command somewhere on the battlefield unsupported by the majority of the regiment.

At the Battle of the Little Big Horn this was the moment of ultimate decision for Captain Benteen, for his actions could, and did, prove a decisive influence on the course of the battle. Unfortunately for Custer and his command, Benteen rose to the occasion by doing nothing. Benteen joined Major Reno on the hilltop position and refused to advance one inch further.

The two excuses Captain Benteen used to justify his inaction were the need to assist the wounded and the necessity for more ammunition. Both of these excuses defy the facts.

The wounded who had not been able to cling to their horses during Major Reno's retreat had been left behind in the valley. A bold charge down the bluffs might have saved some of these soldiers, but an effort to assist them was never attempted. The wounded soldiers in the valley were abandoned to their fate. Lieutenant DeRudio, left behind and hiding in the wooded area during Reno's retreat, witnessed what happened to some of these soldiers:

I had not been in this hiding place more than 10 minutes when I heard several pistol shots fired in my immediate vicinity, and shortly thereafter came the silvery, but to me diabolical voices of several squaws.

I raised my head with great caution to see what the women were at, and to discover their exact location. I found the women at the revolting work of scalping a soldier who was perhaps not yet dead. Two of the [women] *were cutting away, while two others performed a sort of war dance around the body and its*

mutilators.

I will not attempt to describe to you my feelings at witnessing the disgusting performance ...finally the squaws went away, probably to hunt for more victims, and I employed the time thinking of my perilous position.

The other excuse used by Major Reno and Captain Benteen to justify their inaction was the need to distribute ammunition to Reno's command. This excuse, however, does not withstand the weight of the evidence. It would seem the battle in the valley had not been of long enough duration to have seriously depleted the 100 rounds of carbine ammunition each soldier had carried, and Lieutenant Godfrey commented upon this fact:

It seems most improbable, in view of their active movements and the short time the command was firing, that "most of the men" should have expended one hundred fifty [actually one hundred] *rounds of ammunition per man.*

B.F. Churchill, a packer, also testified at the Reno Court concerning the ammunition packs. Churchill and another packer named Mann had been ordered forward with the mules carrying the ammunition packs and when questioned Churchill said:

Q. What was done with the ammunition you brought up at the time you brought it up?

A. The boxes were unpacked at the time and we packed them up again.

Q. Where was the other mule that was sent forward with ammunition?

A. I did not see him.

Q. Were the boxes of ammunition brought up at that time opened?

A. Not at that time.

Q. When were they opened?

A. After we moved down the river and back again and the mules were unpacked.

Q. What was the object of unpacking the ammunition when you first came there?

A. We supposed they wanted it immediately and we unpacked it for their use.

Q. Why was it not used, if you know?

A. I don't know.

Lieutenant Mathey, the officer in charge of the pack train, was also asked at the Reno Court of Inquiry about the ammunition packs:

Q. Did you see that ammunition taken out of the boxes?

A. Not that I remember.

George Herendeen, the scout left behind in the wooded position after Major Reno's retreat, was asked during the Reno Court of Inquiry about how much ammunition those with him had.

Q. State if the men you found in there had any ammunition.

A. Yes, sir, they all appeared to have plenty. There were 7 or 8 horses in there. About half the men were mounted and about half dismounted. The men who had horses had plenty of ammunition in their saddlebags.

Why it was necessary to manufacture the ammunition

issue was also brought out at the Reno Court of Inquiry. Lieutenant DeRudio who, like the scout Herendeen, had been left behind in the wooded area after Major Reno's retreat, made an interesting observation when questioned:

Q. State if that timber could have been held with the number of men he had, and how long?

A. He could have held it as long as he had ammunition.

Q. If the ammunition had been handled coolly and carefully and had not been fired away rashly and at random, how long would that much ammunition have lasted?

A. Probably 3 or 4 hours, depending on circumstances.

The shortage of ammunition later claimed as a reason for the failure of Major Reno and Captain Benteen to advance is another manufactured "fact" of the Battle of the Little Big Horn.

The Indians Vanish

With the arrival of Captain Benteen's command on Major Reno's hill position, the Indian warriors broke off their pursuit of Reno and his soldiers and soon after they began to disappear back down the valley toward the village. Lieutenant Godfrey noted the retreat of the Indians from near Reno's position:

They all seemed to go down the river not more than 10 minutes after our arrival.

Lieutenant Hare confirmed Lieutenant Godfrey's observations:

As soon as the command got to the top of the hill, all the Indians left, about 100-150, and went downstream. Those that stayed in the bottom were taking care of their dead and wounded. We were too far away to tell whether they were warriors or old men and women.

Many other officers on the Reno Hill position noted the fact that the Indian warriors vanished with the arrival of Captain Benteen's battalion, including Lieutenant Varnum and Lieutenant Edgerly. The most telling fact, however, which confirms that the Indian warriors had left Major Reno's front with the arrival of Benteen's battalion, is that after Benteen reached the hill neither command was to suffer a single casualty until much later in the battle. The failure of Reno and Benteen to regroup quickly and advance, perhaps, could have been justified had they been confronting a large force of warriors, or at least a few. The astonishing fact is, however, they were confronted by none.

From the statements of those on the Reno Hill position it is clear that Captain Benteen's arrival was only partially responsible for the disappearance of the Indian warriors. For it was at this time that the sound of gunfire was heard downstream, the gunfire that everyone at the Reno Court of Inquiry was to admit hearing, with the exception of Major Reno and Captain Benteen. This gunfire could only have been the sound of Custer making an attack. While Reno and Benteen vacillated on the hill position the Indian warriors, who had previously been forced to confront Reno's advance, were now free to fight Custer unhindered by the other battalions of the regiment. Captain Benteen clearly recognized the significance of this issue and attempted to confuse it by saying:

I am convinced that when the order brought by Martin reached me General Custer and his whole command were dead.

This self-serving falsehood by Captain Benteen defies all known facts. His eagerness to obviously distort the truth reveals, once again, Benteen knew his own conduct at the Battle of the Little Big Horn to have been something he had to cloak with mistruths. Many soldiers heard the gunfire from the Little Big Horn Valley, which could have originated only from Custer's command doing battle with the Indians. Reno and Benteen were still under orders to advance and the spirit of their military duty called for them to "march to the sound of the guns."

Major Reno understood this issue perfectly, as did Captain Benteen. At his Court of Inquiry, Reno said:

If I had heard the firing as they represent the firing, volley firing, I should have known he [Custer] *was engaged while I was on the hill, but I heard no such firing.*

Lieutenant Varnum was questioned at the Reno Court as to what the duty of the command on Reno Hill would have been when this volley fire was heard:

Q. When a fight is going on and an officer in charge of a column has no orders to remain away or at a certain position, and he hears the sound of firing, what is it his duty to do always?

A. I suppose he would take his command and go there to find out what was going on and help or send and find out what the matter was.

This gunfire was heard in "volleys" and this confirms it could only have been the sound of Custer making an attack. Major Reno testified at his Court of Inquiry:

Indians never fire by volleys. It's every man for himself.

There is, in fact, no record of the Plains Indian warriors ever firing by organized volleys during battle. Yet, as the sounds of battle were heard on Reno Hill, Sergeant Davern testified at the Reno Court of Inquiry about the action taken by Major Reno and Captain Benteen:

Q. Refresh your memory about what was done by any part of the command right away after that firing was heard.

A. Nothing was done.

In the account he wrote of the Battle of the Little Big Horn, Lieutenant McClernand gave his view of the lack of action by Major Reno and Captain Benteen. McClernand wrote:

> *Reno himself has been ordered to charge the village, but he had not done so. Custer's instructions to his lieutenants indicated that he contemplated positive and aggressive action. So far as they were concerned he did not get it. No one who knew him could have doubted that he intended to push the fighting. Such was his nature.*
>
> *Not having supported his Chief in the valley, every rule of warfare dictated that Reno should strike hard when he gained the top of the bluffs. He now had half of the regiment with him, and McDougall's troop coming on; in all seven troops against Custer's five. His own battalion was, it is true, badly shaken, but neither Benteen nor McDougall had been engaged. Reno stood still.*
>
> *Some of his officers looking down from the edge of the bluff at the large number of mounted warriors in the bottom below, observed that the enemy suddenly started down the valley, and that in a few minutes scarcely a horseman was left in sight. Reno's front was practically cleared of the enemy. Among the officers on the bluff the question of "what's the matter with Custer, that he don't send word what we shall do," was being asked.*
>
> *If Custer could have heard and replied we may imagine his saying – "I was counting on aggressive and helpful action from Reno, and but a short time ago Benteen was ordered to come on, to be quick, and to bring the packs. The extra ammunition, as you know, is on the packs. You hear heavy firing in the direction I disappeared. You must know I am fighting. You know it is my rule to act quickly and vigorously in battle. You are my subordinates. Why do you not observe the spirit of my instructions and act?"*
>
> *It is not sufficient to say that there was no serious doubt about Custer being able to take care of himself. He had gone downstream with five troops, heavy firing was heard in that direction, it was evident a fight was on for neither Custer nor the Indians would be wasting ammunition by shooting at a mark, and yet Reno with six troops and another approaching stood still, thus ignoring the well known military axiom to march to the sound of guns.*

Beyond this point in the Battle of the Little Big Horn it could be debated that any responsibility for the defeat of the 7th Cavalry disappears from Custer. Mistakes Custer may have made, but it would have been utterly impossible for him, or any other military commander, to have won a victory without the cooperation of almost two-thirds of his force. This simple and obvious truth would later be commented upon by General Nelson Miles, as well as other military officers, and also many historians. This fact must be placed above all other reasons that have been given for the defeat of the 7th Cavalry at the Battle of the Little Big Horn.

The Pack Train Arrives on the Battlefield

Captain Thomas M. McDougall, who commanded the rear guard and was behind the pack train, described his advance from the divide:

> *We started about 20 minutes after the command left. Lieutenant Mathey in advance with the mules made the trail, and we followed in the rear.*
>
> *We proceeded along till we came to a kind of marshy watering place where I found five or six mules mired. I dismounted my company to assist the packers and got them out in about 20 minutes. We adjusted the packs and proceeded.*
>
> *About four miles from there, we came to a tepee. I dismounted and looked inside and found three dead Indians and a fire built around. From that point, I saw in the distance a large smoke and told Lieutenant Mathey to halt for a few minutes till we could close up and prepare for action.*
>
> *About a mile from there, Lieutenant Mathey sent word that the fight was on. I told him to hurry with the mules as fast as possible. I went on about two miles and saw black objects on the hill in a mass and thought they were Indians.*
>
> *I told my company we would have to charge them and get to the command. We drew pistols. I put one platoon in front and one in rear of the train and charged to where those persons were.*
>
> *I found that it was Major Reno and his command.*

Captain McDougall also identified the most difficult elements to resolve concerning the battle of the Little Big Horn. At the Reno Court of Inquiry Captain McDougall testified:

> *I can form no idea of the times or distances.*

Considering the expected confusion that would occur during any battle, Captain McDougall's statement is understandable. Attempts to estimate time and distance accurately during the battle, regardless of the best efforts of the

participants, would have been difficult. However, at the Battle of the Little Big Horn there were not only honest mistakes concerning time and distance, but deliberate distortions.

The arrival of the pack train is one of the events of the battle that was deliberately distorted, with the advantage of making the regiment look much more scattered than it actually was. Captain Benteen attempted to distort the arrival time of the pack train by saying:

I should think it was an hour and a quarter to an hour and a half before it [the pack train] *arrived.*

Major Reno also attempted to distort the arrival of the pack train, by saying:

In about an hour the pack train arrived.

The pack train had been ordered by Custer to hurry forward with the message sent with Sergeant Kanipe and Kanipe said:

On my route back to Captain McDougall, I saw Captain Benteen about half way between where I left General Custer and the pack train. He and his men were watering their horses when first seen.

Captain McDougall and the pack train went directly to the bluff where I left Custer's five troops. When we reached there, we found Reno with a remnant of his three troops and Benteen with his three troops.

Bugler Martin, who had been sent back with the second and last known message from Custer, commented on the proximity of the pack train:

I joined my troop [with Benteen after delivering his message], *and rode with them. The pack train was not very far behind them. It was in sight, maybe a mile away, and the mules were coming along.*

Packer B.F. Churchill had been ordered to hurry ahead of the pack train with the ammunition mules and was asked how long it was until the rest of the pack train arrived. Churchill said:

It came up pretty quick. They kept stringing along a few at a time, but it was only a short time till all were up.

Churchill also commented upon arriving in time to see Major Reno's troops still retreating from the valley. He said:

I saw some coming up the hill, some mounted and some on foot.

Sergeant Davern, who was with Major Reno's command, corroborated Churchill's statement and said:

I saw the pack train come up soon after I got on the hill.

On his way back to deliver his message to Captain Benteen, Bugler Martin was also passed by Boston Custer, the General's youngest brother. Boston had been with the pack train and was on his way forward to join his brother's battalions. Boston joined and died with his two brothers, General Custer and Captain Tom Custer.

Bugler Martin later mentioned passing Boston Custer:

Just before I got to the hill, I met Boston Custer. He was riding at a run, but when he saw me, he checked his horse and shouted, "Where is the General?" and I answered, pointing back of me, "Right behind that next ridge you'll find him." And he dashed on.

That was the last time he was ever seen alive.

It is interesting that one person was able to join Custer and three battalions would fail. It is also significant that Sergeant Kanipe and Bugler Martin place the pack train not far behind Captain Benteen. Captain McDougall also said he had heard gunfire during his advance and reported it to Major Reno. McDougall said it was "volleys," something which Reno never directed to be fired, nor do any of the men with Reno or Benteen speak of volleys being fired by them at any time. Significantly, McDougall and the pack train were so close to the battlefield that McDougall actually heard the fire from Custer's command fighting.

The "hour and a quarter to an hour and a half" before the arrival of the pack train, as claimed by Captain Benteen and Major Reno, is unfounded. Its actual arrival was much sooner. The arrival of the pack train gave the combined battalions almost 400 soldiers, including over 250 who had not yet fired a single shot and still, astonishingly, no attempt was made to assist Custer's command.

The Decisive Role

Custer made two critical mistakes at the Battle of the Little Big Horn. The first was to send Captain Benteen on a militarily useless scouting mission to the left of the regiment during its advance to the Little Big Horn Valley. This humiliating errand had the effect of taking Benteen down a few notches, but it also gave Custer a resentful subordinate on whom he would potentially have to depend later. Custer was, considering the circumstances, taking a risk for which the consequences were unforeseen. Even so, had Custer not made the second mistake the first might have remained insignificant.

There can be little doubt that Custer intended to, and did, play the decisive role at the Battle of the Little Big Horn. When Custer divided the regiment into battalions the two he placed under his personal command included his most trustworthy and loyal officers: Captains Keogh, Yates, and his brother Tom; Lieutenant Smith, and his brother-in-law, Lieutenant Calhoun. This was Custer's second mistake.

These officers were among the best in the regiment and would have ranked high among the most qualified officers in the Army. They were true soldiers to whom the principle of loyalty was an absolute code of life and they possibly combined more combat experience together, proportionately, than had ever been joined together in an American battle, perhaps any battle. When he made the decision to have these officers with him, Custer knew at the critical point in the coming battle he would be able to depend upon these soldiers unconditionally.

The scenario of Major Reno and Captain Benteen vacillating on the hill position while the sounds of nearby battle were heard would have been quite different had a few of Custer's more loyal officers been there. They simply would not have allowed it to happen.

Captain Weir's Advance

As it was, one officer with Major Reno and Captain Benteen attempted to fulfill his military duty, and at great risk to himself. This officer was Captain Thomas Weir, who commanded D Company, part of Benteen's battalion. Various accounts exist of what was to be the only attempt to support Custer, however, all accounts agree that it was Weir who initiated this advance. Private Theodore Goldin left an account of what some historians have called "the Weir Advance." Private Goldin said:

> *Soon after the pack train arrived, I walked over toward the edge of the bluffs with Lieutenant Wallace, trying to point out to him the location of the body of Lieutenant McIntosh.*
>
> *Near where we were standing, quite a group of officers had gathered and stood looking down into the valley, talking earnestly together. Just who made up this party I am not certain, but as I now recollect it, Major Reno, Captain French, Captain Weir, Captain McDougall, and possibly some of the other officers were in the group.*
>
> *While Lieutenant Wallace and I were still talking, Captain Weir hastily left the group, and as he passed us, I heard him say something like "By God, if you don't go, I will, and if we live to get out of here, somebody shall know of this." To whom he addressed his remarks, or the particular occasion for them, I never heard, as I never heard the matter mentioned after that.*
>
> *A few moments after this, I saw Captain Weir mount his horse and move rapidly down the river toward a high bluff that hid our view of the valley to the northward, followed by Lieutenant Edgerly, with D Troop.*
>
> *This move on the part of Captain Weir was, as I afterward learned, unauthorized by his battalion commander, and came very near costing us the lives of Lieutenant Edgerly and the whole troop.*
>
> *Just as soon as this move came to the knowledge of Captain Benteen, he mounted the two remaining troops of his battalion, and accompanied by Captain French, with M Troop and detachments from other troops of the command, moved out toward the high point of bluffs, behind which Captain Weir and his troop had already disappeared.*
>
> *After Captain Benteen and his command moved out, Major Reno had his trumpeter repeatedly sound the halt, but no attention was paid to it by the advancing column, which continued its forward move in column of fours, until they reached the high point above referred to.*

Lieutenant Edgerly of Captain Weir's D Company also

described Weir's advance:

Captain Weir, my Captain, came to me and asked me what I thought we ought to do.

I thought we ought by all means to go down to Custer's assistance. He thought so too, and I heard the first sergeant express himself to that effect.

He then asked me if I would be willing to go down with only D troop, if he could get permission to go. I told him I would.

He then walked towards Colonel Reno and Benteen, and very shortly came back, mounted his horse, took an orderly with him and went out in the direction from which we had heard the firing and which had then almost wholly ceased.

I supposed that he had received permission to go out with the troop (though he afterwards told me he had not, and had not even asked for it), so I mounted the troop and followed him.

After going a few hundred yards, I swung off to the right with the troop and went into a little valley which must have been the one followed by Custer and his men, or nearly parallel to it, and moved right towards the great body of the Indians, whom we had already seen from the highest point.

After we had gone a short distance down the valley, Colonel Weir, who had remained to our left on the bluff, saw a large number of Indians coming toward us, and motioned with his hand for me to swing around with the troop to where he was, which I did.

When I got up on the bluff, I saw Colonel Benteen, Captain French and Lieutenant Godfrey coming toward us with their troops.

Captain Benteen also had a version, actually several versions, of Captain Weir's advance:

I followed, with the remaining two troops of my battalion, the trail Weir had "sallied on," he having no orders to proceed, some ten minutes later perhaps; anyway, just as soon as I learned of his insubordinate and unauthorized movements.

While en route to the highest point on the bluffs in that vicinity, Major Reno kept his trumpeter pretty busily engaged in sounding the "Halt" for the purpose of bringing my command to a stand. However, I paid no heed whatever to the signal, but went to the highest point of the bluffs.

Captain Weir

Interestingly, Captain Benteen wrote to his wife with a dramatically different story shortly after the Battle of the Little Big Horn:

I must tell you now what I did. When I joined up with Reno's command, we halted for the packs to come up and then moved along the line of bluffs towards the direction Custer was supposed to have gone in. Weir's company was sent out to communicate with Custer, but was driven back.

Who was Captain Benteen telling yarns to this time? Was Captain Weir "sent out," or had he "sallied on" without orders? As there are numerous accounts which confirm Weir made his advance without, or even against, orders, it would appear this time Benteen was telling falsehoods to his wife. Why Benteen felt the need to misrepresent Weir's advance to her is anyone's guess.

The Weir Peaks

Captain Weir advanced northward following Custer's trail toward the cluster of peaks now named after him. It was from this position, the Weir Peaks, that Custer had been seen by Major Reno's men in the valley and from where Bugler Martin had been dispatched with the "be quick" order for Captain Benteen.

The Weir Peaks overlook the Indian village in the valley and Custer Hill, where Custer and his command were found massacred, is also visible. A slight rise on the ridge leading back to Reno's hill position prevents a clear view of it from the Weir Peaks, but visibility continues almost to that point. Of all the positions on the battlefield the Weir Peaks are clearly the most important, if only for observation purposes.

There are three points in the Weir Peaks group, and they are connected by ridges. A natural basin is formed between them. To the west, facing the Indian village and the Little Big Horn River, the peaks drop off almost vertically. From this direction the position is invulnerable to an attack. The north facing side, and also the east side, rise up from the surrounding ground, making them also an extremely formidable position for defense. In fact, in many respects the Weir Peaks almost give the impression of an artificial fortification and if it were to be turned into such there would be little that could be done to improve it, at least by 19th century standards. Carl Von Clausewitz recognized the importance of high terrain such as the Weir Peaks concerning defense:

Undeniably, in a mountainous area a small post in a favorable position acquires exceptional strength.

A unit that on open ground can be dispersed by a couple of cavalry squadrons and will think itself lucky if it

can escape capture or annihilation by rapid retreat, can face an army in the mountains....

A small post can acquire extraordinary strength in mountainous terrain.... this tactical result needs no further proof ... the battalion defend(s) the mountain and the mountain defend(s) the battalion.

Von Clausewitz's description of the "mountain" fits the Weir Peaks exactly, if not in size, then certainly in description. It is a position of tremendous natural strength and, as added importance, it overlooked the entire village and all of the Little Big Horn Battlefield, with the exception of Reno's hill position. If any position on the Little Big Horn battlefield can be termed a "key" position, it is the Weir Peaks.

As Captain Weir and his orderly advanced toward the Weir Peaks alone something amazing happened. Or didn't happen. Author Evan Connell commented on this incident:

Captain Weir, enraged and disgusted by Reno's timidity, left the hilltop bunker without permission and, followed by an orderly, rode northward along the bluffs to see what he could see.

Considering that these two men must have been visible to hundreds of Sioux, it is surprising they were not cut off and butchered.

"Surprising" is, if anything, an understatement. It is true that Custer and his command were somewhere, either alive or dead. If already dead, then the Indian warriors would have been able to, at the very least, watch the Reno-Benteen-McDougall combined force which was still, if one omits the leadership, a potentially dangerous threat. If Custer's command was still a viable threat, then, considering the large number of Indian warriors on the battlefield, the Weir Peaks become even more important because by the Indian warriors' occupying them the Reno and Custer forces would have been divided.

It is also astounding, regardless of Custer's status, that the Indian warriors, so legendary in their skillful use of terrain in warfare, would have left the Weir Peaks unoccupied. Astounding unless, of course, there was a reason the Weir Peaks were not occupied by the Indian warriors. After all, Custer himself had passed over the Weir Peaks and, like the Indian warriors, he too was legendary in his use of terrain in warfare. Custer would have seen, at a glance, the importance of the Weir Peaks and it is unlikely he would have failed to have taken advantage of them.

The Lost Patrol

Besides the fact that Captain Weir and his orderly had been able to advance unmolested to the peaks, there was another fact which amazed Author Connell:

Quite a few soldiers assigned to Custer's battalion[s] somehow appeared on Reno's hilltop, but with so many officers and non-commissioned officers dead, it became impossible to learn why or when these men defected.

For instance, 24 men from Captain Yates' F Company joined Reno while the rest died with Custer. This is particularly strange. It might not be puzzling if Yates' company had formed the tail of the column because one man after another could lag behind, ease out of sight, but it appears that Yates may have been leading the way.

How could 24 men desert in the shadow of old Iron Butt [Custer] *himself?*

How indeed could this large number of soldiers have deserted from Custer's command? Even if F Company had been at the rear of the column it is common practice for

military formations on the move to have a rear guard of trusted soldiers, one duty of which it is to encourage deliberate laggards and potential deserters along. Considering Custer's long experience in the military it is unlikely that he would have overlooked this important detail.

Custer would have ordered a rear guard. How then could this large number of soldiers who were with Custer escape the destruction which their fellow soldiers with Custer suffered?

Some soldiers were legitimate stragglers from Custer's command, soldiers who had a reason for falling behind the main force and which also gave them the opportunity to later join Major Reno's force. A Crow scout named Soldier, who was following in the rear of Custer's command, spoke of cavalrymen whose horses gave out:

> *I, White Eagle and Bull, followed Custer...we came upon a white soldier whose horse had given out and he was kicking the horse and striking him with his fist and saying, "Me go Custer, Me go Custer."*
>
> *I soon came across a second soldier whose horse was down, overcome by heat, and he could not get him up and was swearing...*

Some of these legitimate stragglers have been identified as Privates John Brennan, Peter Thompson, and James Watson of Company C, and Gustave Korn of I Company.

A number of other soldiers from throughout the five companies with Custer survived the battle and their eventual appearance on Reno Hill is a mystery. One soldier, a private named Frank Hunter of Company F, was said to have ridden through the Indian camp on a terrified horse and then joined up with Reno's command. If this story is true, and Hunter did survive the battle, then it must have been a fascinating, and certainly unforgettable, ride. Interestingly, later that summer when Private Hunter's enlistment expired, he did not reenlist. Apparently, Hunter's experience at the Battle of the Little Big Horn had satisfied any military aspirations he may have had.

Companies E and F, however, seem to have had an unusually large number of soldiers who did not die with their units on Custer Hill. Historian Robert B. MacLaine researched this strange fact and he concluded that these soldiers must have been left behind at the Powder River camp, although he admitted there is no evidence to support this theory:

> *The muster roll* [for E and F Companies] *does not indicate anyone as being at the supply depot on Powder River, but does not give any other explanation for the* [surviving] *men.*

MacLaine identified seven soldiers from Company E and ten soldiers from Company F as somehow ending up on Reno Hill without a suitable explanation of how or why they got there. As baffling as the large number of survivors from E and F Companies is also the fact that the blacksmith, farrier, and saddler, the entire horse maintenance team of E Company, were also among these survivors. These three men, whose skills would have been in great demand on the marches Custer planned, certainly would not have been left at the Powder River camp. Also included with this sizeable force was a sergeant and a corporal. These facts, added to the horse maintenance team, indicate these survivors could have been a fairly organized force and, adding these soldiers to the Crow scouts and stragglers, the size of this improvised unit is nearly as strong as a platoon.

It would seem this force was too large in number and too well organized to have simply straggled away from Custer's command without a purpose. Instead of these soldiers' simply wandering about the battlefield, an alternative explanation can be offered: that these soldiers did have a purpose and a very important one at that.

Lieutenant Godfrey commented, under questioning, about his arrival with Captain Benteen's battalion on the battlefield at the Reno Court of Inquiry and an observation he made:

> *Q. State what view you had of the bottom and describe the march from that place to where you joined Major Reno's command on the hill.*
>
> *A. I saw a good many horsemen in the bottom and saw smoke from the burning prairie. We did not stop long enough to take a good view, but I thought from what I saw and what the sergeant had said that they were burning the village and did not look particularly to see.*
>
> *Q. Did you see troops on the hill about that time?*
>
> *A. Soon after bearing to the right and passing out there I did. I suppose they were troops put out for a picket guard as a protector to the working parties.*
>
> *Q. Why did you have that impression?*

A. I knew from General Custer's habit. He had put out troops to protect the command at other times.

One possible explanation to the large number of survivors is that Custer deliberately positioned this force at a place which he considered important and which also allowed them to survive the destruction of Custer's command. There is only one position on the battlefield which meets this criterion. This position is the Weir Peaks. This could be the reason that the Indian warriors had not occupied this important position from which they could have observed any advance from Reno Hill, where there was a still dangerous force numbering almost 400 soldiers. This could only be the reason Captain Weir and his orderly were able to advance to this position from Reno's Hill alone and unmolested.

Any view of the battlefield confirms that the Weir Peaks are a key, if not the key, position on the battlefield and that during this epic battle of the American West, certainly someone, either the soldiers or the Indian warriors, would have occupied them. By not leaving a patrol-sized force to hold this position, Custer would have risked the advance he had ordered for the pack train which had been told to "keep to the high ground." Custer also would have risked being cut off from the regiment in that direction.

The Weir Peaks were also the perfect rallying point should Custer have had to retreat, and they were also a key element in the high ground across the river. Every soldier is taught the importance of occupying the high ground on a battlefield. Custer had passed over this important position and it would seem inconceivable that he, or any other military commander, would have overlooked the significance of the Weir Peaks, or would have failed to take advantage of them.

Other Soldiers Follow Captain Weir

The other company commanders on Reno Hill, perhaps shamed by Captain Weir's courage and determination, followed him to the peaks in the belated effort to join with Custer and reunite the regiment. It is not clear how many companies actually reached the Weir Peaks, but it is certain that the other two companies of Captain Benteen's battalion, H and K, did. Also, probably at least two companies, A and B, never reached the peaks at all. However, because the Weir Peaks did not remain long occupied by the soldiers, the fact that companies A and B did not reach the peaks is inconsequential. Captain McDougall described the advance of his company and the fact that it never reached the Weir Peaks:

I mounted up and followed the command in single file toward a high mountain [the Weir Peaks] *downstream.*

After going about a quarter of a mile, Captain Moylan met me and said he could not keep up on account of the wounded. I told him if he would take the responsibility, I would let him have one of my platoons. He said "all right" and I took the second platoon in person down to where he was. Upon returning I saw the men "left about" to go back to our original position.

The Weir Peaks Abandoned

What Captain McDougall describes as the "left about" is perhaps the strangest and most extraordinary event of the Battle of the Little Big Horn. The Weir Peaks, the "mountain that protects the battalion," a key battlefield position, the position that had apparently previously been protected by only an improvised force left by Custer, was now ordered abandoned. Not a single soldier had been killed or wounded during the advance to it, nor while it had been occupied, and yet this nearly invulnerable and key position was now evacuated.

That the soldiers were not driven from the Weir Peaks is clear, not only by the fact the record shows there were no casualties suffered while the position was occupied, but also by the statements of those who participated. Lieutenant Godfrey commented upon the fact that the soldiers were not driven from the peaks by the Indian warriors:

At the time we got to the advanced point no Indians confronted us...there was no severe engagement at that point, no casualties until we started back, which was soon after the deployment.

The Indians only fired occasional shots.

At the Reno Court of Inquiry Lieutenant Godfrey was questioned concerning the position of the soldiers on the Weir Peaks:

Q. When you got down to that advanced position, were there Indians confronting the command or engaging it at that time?

A. No, sir.

Q. Was the engagement severe in and around there, or was there any engagements at all resulting in any casualties?

A. No, sir, no severe engagement at all.

Q. What were the casualties during that advance before the troops started back?

A. I don't think there were any before they started back.

Q. Was there much firing on the part of the Indians down at that point up to the time the command started to go back?

A. No, sir.

Lieutenant Wallace was also questioned at the Reno Court of Inquiry concerning the opposition which confronted the soldiers on the Weir Peaks:

Q. Did any part of the command actually engage the enemy?

A. I know there was heavy firing on Captain Weir's company, and I know Captain Godfrey's company acted as rear guard when the command fell back and they got a heavy fire. There was no firing on the point I occupied at that time.

Q. Was there any other firing there?

A. I don't remember any.

Q. What were the casualties there?

A. The only one I heard of was a man wounded and left of Captain Weir's company.

Lieutenant Edgerly testified at the Reno Court of Inquiry and corroborated Lieutenant Godfrey's account:

Q. State if the Indians drove the command from that position.

A. They did not. The orders were to fall back and we fell back....

The soldier Lieutenant Wallace mentioned was not killed during the advance to the Weir Peaks or while that position was occupied. This soldier actually was killed during the retreat from the peaks back to Major Reno's first hill position. The battlefield marker, which shows where he fell, is on the south side of the Weir Peaks and between that position and Reno's Hill position. This soldier was Vincent Charley of D Company.

Who Gave The Evacuation Order?

Who gave the order to abandon the Weir Peaks? Many historians believe Major Reno himself never advanced as far as that position. If Reno was not there to give the evacuation order, then someone else must have given the order. There are conflicting statements concerning with whom, or how, this order originated. Lieutenant Godfrey said:

Lieutenant Hare [then came to me and] *told me the command was ordered back.*

Lieutenant Hare said:

Benteen suggested to Reno that they fall back.

Major Reno said:

Lieutenant Hare came back and said he had taken the responsibility of using my name and ordered the return of the command.

Captain Benteen's testimony at the Reno Court of Inquiry was pure "Benteenism." Benteen said:

I don't know who gave the order.

Captain Benteen Gave the Order

The phantom order to evacuate the Weir Peaks was certainly given because the position was evacuated. Yet, it was apparently a sensitive subject since no participant wanted to admit who had given the order.

It also seems inconceivable that Captain Benteen, who commanded the only organized battalion on the Weir Peaks, would not have known where the order to evacuate the position came from. His "I don't know who gave the order" is an astounding statement, or would be, if it hadn't originated from Benteen.

However, there are a few accounts of this order that seem to indicate that Captain Benteen did know where the order originated. Lieutenant Gibson, the second in command of Benteen's H Company, mentioned a comment made by Benteen while on the Weir Peaks:

This is a hell of a place to fight Indians. I am going to see Reno and propose that we go back to where we lay before starting out here.

Private George Glenn claimed to have actually heard a comment made by Benteen to Reno:

Major Reno, we cannot fight them here. We had better fall back and make a stand somewhere.

Major Reno never ordered the advance to the Weir Peaks, nor is there any indication that he exercised any command at all once it got there. Reno possibly never even reached the peaks, which would have left command of the position to the next ranking officer, the only one who commanded an entire battalion on the Weir Peaks.

The order to evacuate the Weir Peaks could have come only from, or confirmed by, the ranking officer who commanded on the spot: Captain Benteen.

CHAPTER 10

General Terry's Confidential Report —— Newspaper Coverage —— Military Leaders Endorse the Disobedience Charge —— The Problem of Finding the Indians —— Major Brisbin's Letter —— Conference on Far West —— Reporter Kellogg's News Article —— Lieutenant Bradley's Diary —— What Custer's Order Really Meant —— Who to Blame for the Defeat —— The Actual Plan —— General Terry's Statement

Crazy Horse

On June 27, 1876, two days after the Battle of the Little Big Horn, General Terry wrote the following official report:

Headquarters Department Of Dakota,
Camp on Little Big Horn River, Montana,
June 27, 1876

To the Adjutant General of
the Military Division of the Missouri,
Chicago, Ill., via Fort Ellis:

It is my painful duty to report that day before yesterday, the 25th instant, a great disaster overtook General Custer and the troops under his command. At 12 o'clock of the 22nd, he started with his whole regiment and a strong detachment of scouts and guides from the mouth of the Rosebud. Proceeding up that river about twenty miles, he struck a very heavy Indian trail which had previously been discovered, and, pursuing it, found that it led, as it was supposed it would lead, to the Little Big Horn River.

Here he found a village of almost unexampled extent, and at once attacked it with that portion of his force which was immediately at hand. Major Reno, with three companies, A, G and M of the regiment, was sent into the valley of the stream, at the point where the trail struck it.

General Custer, with five companies, C, E, F, I and L, attempted to enter it about three miles lower down. Reno forded the river, charged down its left bank, dismounted, and fought on foot until finally, completely overwhelmed by numbers, he was compelled to mount, recross the river, and seek a refuge on the high bluffs which overlooked its high bank.

Just as he recrossed, Captain Benteen, who with three companies, D, H and K, was some two miles to the left of Reno when the action commenced, but who had been ordered by General Custer to return, came to the river, and rightly concluding that it would be useless for his force to attempt to renew the fight in the valley, he joined Reno on the bluffs.

Captain McDougall, with Company B, was at first some distance in the rear, with the train of pack mules; he also came up to Reno. Soon, this united force was nearly surrounded by Indians, many of whom, armed with rifles of long range, occupied positions which commanded the ground held by the cavalry ground from which there was no escape.

Rifle pits were dug and the fight was maintained, though with heavy loss, from about half past 2 o'clock of the 25th till 6 o'clock of the 26th, when the Indians

withdrew from the valley, taking with them their village.

Of the movements of General Custer and the five companies under his immediate command, scarcely anything is known from those who witnessed them for no officer or soldier who accompanied him has yet been found alive.

His trail, from the point where Reno crossed the stream, passes along and in the rear of the crest of the bluffs on the right bank for nearly or quite three miles. Then it comes down to the bank of the river, but at once diverges from it as if he had unsuccessfully attempted to cross; then turns upon itself, almost completes a circle, and ceases. It is marked by the remains of his officers and men and the bodies of his horses, some of them dotted along the path, others heaped in ravines and upon knolls, where halts appear to have been made.

There is abundant evidence that a gallant resistance was offered by the troops, but that they were bested on all sides by overpowering numbers.

The officers known to be killed are: General Custer, Captains Keogh, Yates, and Custer, Lieutenants Cooke, Smith, McIntosh, Calhoun, Porter, Hodgson, Sturgis, and Riley, of the cavalry; Lieutenant Crittenden, of the Twentieth Infantry; and Acting Assistant Surgeon DeWolf, Lieutenant Harrington, of the cavalry, and Assistant Surgeon Lord are missing; Captain Benteen and Lieutenant Varnum, of the cavalry are slightly wounded. Mr. Boston Custer, a brother, and Mr. Reed, a nephew of General Custer, were with him and were killed. No other officers than those whom I have named are among the killed, wounded and missing.

It is impossible as yet to obtain a nominal list of the enlisted men who were killed and wounded; but the number of killed, including officers, must reach 250; the number of wounded is 51.

Mr. Reed, Custer's nephew

At the mouth of the Rosebud, I informed General Custer that I would take the supply steamer Far West up the Yellowstone to ferry General Gibbon's column over the river; that I should personally accompany that column; and that it would, in all probability, reach the mouth of the Little Big Horn on the 26th instant.

The steamer reached General Gibbon's troops, near the mouth of the Big Horn, early in the morning of the 24th, and at 4 o'clock in the afternoon, all his men and animals were across the Yellowstone. At 5 o'clock, the column, consisting of five companies of the Seventh Infantry, four companies of the Second Cavalry, and a battery of three Gatling guns, marched out to and across Tullock's Creek. Starting soon after 5 o'clock in the morning of the 25th, the infantry made a march of twenty-two miles over the most difficult country I have ever seen.

In order that scouts might be sent into the valley of the Little Big Horn, the cavalry, with the battery, was then pushed on thirteen or fourteen miles further, reaching camp at midnight. The scouts were sent out at half past 4 in the morning of the 26th.

They soon discovered three Indians who were at first supposed to be Sioux, but, when overtaken, they proved to be Crows who had been with General Custer. They brought the first intelligence of the battle. Their story was not credited. It was supposed that some fighting, perhaps severe fighting, had taken place; but it was not believed that disaster could have overtaken so large a force as twelve companies of cavalry.

The infantry, which had broken camp very early, soon came up, and the whole column entered and moved up the valley of the Little Big Horn. During the afternoon, efforts were made to send scouts through to what was supposed to be General Custer's position, to obtain information of the condition of affairs; but those who were sent out were driven back by parties of Indians, who, in increasing numbers, were seen hovering in General Gibbon's front. At twenty minutes before 9 o'clock in the evening, the infantry had marched between twenty-nine and thirty miles.

The men were very weary and daylight was fading. The column was therefore halted for the night, at a point about eleven miles in a straight line above the mouth of the stream. This morning the movement was resumed, and after a march of nine miles, Major Reno's entrenched position was reached.

The withdrawal of the Indians from around Reno's command and from the valley was undoubtedly caused by the approach of General Gibbon's troops.

Major Reno and Captain Benteen, both of whom are officers of great experience, accustomed to see large masses of mounted men, estimate the number of Indians engaged at not less than twenty-five hundred.

Other officers think that the number was greater than this. The village in the valley was about three miles in length and about a mile in width. Besides the lodges proper, a great number of temporary brush-wood shelters was found in it, indicating that many men beside its proper inhabitants had gathered together there.

Major Reno is very confident that there were a number of white men fighting with the Indians. I have as yet received no official reports in regard to the battle; but what is stated herein is gathered from the officers who were on the ground then and from those who have been over it since.

Alfred H. Terry
Brigadier General

General Terry's Confidential Report

Simultaneous with his first report General Terry also included a "confidential" report. Upon reaching Washington this second report remained "confidential" for as long as it took General Sherman, Commanding General of the Army, to hand the report to a newsperson. It was an explosive document, as it was undoubtedly intended to be, and in many newspapers the two reports appeared simultaneously.

July 2nd, 1876.

I think I owe it to myself to put you more fully in possession of the facts of the late operations. While at the mouth of the Rosebud, I submitted my plan to General Gibbon and to General Custer, and they approved it heartily. It was that Custer with his whole regiment should move up the Rosebud till he should meet a trail which Reno had discovered a few days before, but that he should not follow it directly to the Little Big Horn, but that he should send scouts over it and keep his main force further to the south, so as to prevent the Indians from slipping in between himself and the mountains.

He was also to examine the headwaters of Tullock's Creek as he passed it, and send me word of what he found there. Scouts were furnished him for the purpose of crossing the country to me.

We calculated it would take Gibbon's column until the 26th to reach the mouth of the Little Big Horn, and that the wide sweep which I had proposed Custer should make would require so much time that Gibbon would be able to cooperate with him in attacking any Indians that might be found on the stream.

I asked Custer how long his marches would be. He said they would be at first about thirty miles a day. Measurements were made and calculations based on that rate of progress. I talked with him about his strength and at one time suggested that perhaps it would be better for him to take Gibbon's cavalry and go with him. To this suggestion, he replied that he would prefer his own regiment alone – as much could be done with it as with the two combined.

He expressed the utmost confidence that he had all the force that he could need, and I shared his confidence.

The plan adopted was the only one which promised to bring the infantry into action, and I desired to make a sure thing of getting up every available man. I offered Custer the battery of Gatling guns, but he declined, saying that it might embarrass him and that he was strong enough without it.

The movements proposed by General Gibbon's column were carried out to the letter, and had the attack been deferred till it came up, I cannot doubt but we should have been successful. The Indians had evidently nerved themselves for a stand.

I learned from Captain Benteen that on the 22nd the cavalry marched 12 miles. On the 23rd, 35 miles from 5:00 a.m. to 8:00 p.m. On the 24th, 45 miles, 10 miles further, then after resting, but without unsaddling, 23 miles to the battlefield. The proper route was not taken, but as soon as the trail was discovered it was followed. I cannot learn that any examination of Tullock's Creek was made.

I do not tell you this to cast any reflections upon Custer for whatever errors he might have committed; he has paid the penalty and you cannot regret his loss more than I do, but I feel that our plan must have been successful had it been carried out, and I desire you to know the facts in the section yourself.

So far as I can make out, Custer acted under misapprehensions. He thought that the Indians were running, and for fear that they might get away, he attacked them without getting all his men up, and divided his command so that they were beaten in detail.

I do not at all propose to give the thing up here, but I think that my troops require a little rest, and in view of

the strength which the Indians have displayed, I propose to bring up what little reinforcements I can get. I should be glad of any that you can send me. I can take two companies of infantry from Powder River, and there are a few recruits detailed whom I can get for the cavalry. I ought to have a larger mounted force than I now have, but this I fear cannot be obtained.

I hear nothing from General Crook's operations. If I could hear, I should be able to form plans for the future more intelligently.

Alfred H. Terry
Brigadier General Commanding

Charles Varnum

General Terry's second report clearly cast the responsibility for the Little Big Horn defeat on Custer because he had "disobeyed" the orders given to him by Terry and had failed to carry out the agreed upon "plan." It can be speculated that this accusation for disobedience of orders was eagerly endorsed by Colonel Robert P. Hughes (Terry's chief-of-staff), by Major James S. Brisbin of the 2nd Cavalry, and especially by Major Reno and Captain Benteen.

Newspaper Coverage

When the news of the defeat was first made public the only source of information available to the newspapers was that which was being telegraphed to them and the charge against Custer of disobedience of orders was accepted as fact.

In the days immediately after the news of Custer's defeat became public, the headlines of papers around the country read "Custer's Fault," "Custer's Blunder," and "Custer's Mistake," echoing the disobedience charge made by General Terry, in his second report. Without any conflicting information this charge was, at first, accepted as fact. The *St. Louis Dispatch* of July 7, 1876 said:

The movement so far as General Gibbon's column was concerned was carried out in every particular, but General Custer reached the point of attack before the time agreed upon, made the charge single-handed in the absence of the support of Gibbon's column – hence the disaster – a slaughter which has shocked the nation.

The *St. Paul Pioneer Press* of July 8, 1876, stated:

Custer did not follow his instructions or the route laid out for him. As soon as he struck the trail to the Little Big Horn instead of passing to the south of it, he followed the trail until he came upon the Indian Camp. Without communicating with Terry or waiting until Gibbon's column could be brought up according to the plan agreed upon, he threw his regiment in two separate detachments into a hand-to-hand fight with three thousand Indians. The disastrous result, which has carried mourning into so many households, is known.

Military Leaders Endorse the Disobedience Charge

In newspaper articles unnamed military leaders were also quick to add to the disobedience charge, either out of sincere belief, or perhaps other motives. An article in the *Boston Globe* of July 7 quoted military leaders on the disobedience charge:

The movement made by Custer is censored to some extent at military headquarters in this city, the older officers say it was brought about by foolish pride.

The *New York Herald Tribune* of July 8 said:

The higher army officers, not withstanding their sorrow at General Custer's fate, agree that he was violating orders and that even if he had been victorious, he would have been in danger of court-martial.

With this type of news coverage, and without any surviving member of Custer's command to dispute the disobedience of orders charge, it is not surprising that the blame for the defeat became set in much of the public's mind as Custer's alone. The wording of the actual order given Custer, however, when examined by qualified authorities, is subject to other interpretations.

The Problem of Finding the Indians

General Nelson Miles had a distinct opinion on the disobedience of orders accusation against Custer and in his memoirs said the following:

It will be observed that General Custer was directed to move up the Rosebud in pursuit of the Indians. The next sentence, it will be noticed, leaves no question that it was expected that his command would come in contact with the Indians; and surely when this command was directed to move by a course in which they would be placed from 40 to 50 miles distant from any other, confidence was reposed in the knowledge, zeal, and ability of the commander to exercise his best judgement.

It is folly to suppose that either a small or a large band

of Indians would remain stationary, and allow one body of troops to come up one side of it while another body came up on the other side and engage it in battle. It is fair to give the Indians credit for a reasonable amount of intelligence.

Other military officers expressed views similar to General Miles concerning the disobedience of orders charge against Custer. A soldier experienced in combat against the Plains Indians, Captain Robert Carter of the 4th Cavalry commented upon the order given to Custer:

It was simply a letter of instructions, and a very elastic one at that.... It does not order Custer to do what a battle order would actually compel him to, so . . . General Terry regarded it as a letter of instructions and not an order.

All this is an endeavor to herd (enclosing and capturing), 4,000 or 5,000 savages, the finest light cavalry this world has ever seen – across the country in the hope of corralling them in the near vicinity of either Gibbon or Terry, and then by Custer closing in on them, capture or destroy the entire Indian outfit – an anomalous condition, an absurdity, and something unheard of in the annals of Indian warfare in this country.

Captain Carter's comment upon the absurdity of the plan, as later defined by General Terry, is emphatic and, as an experienced soldier of the American Frontier, he was qualified to render an informed judgement, and he was correct. The Indian village never would have stood still as two converging columns of soldiers leisurely closed in on them. In his memoirs, General Miles repeatedly asserted the following:

It is fair to give the Indians credit for a reasonable amount of intelligence.

In his report dated November 25, 1876, General Sheridan said:

... Long experience had taught me how difficult it is to catch an Indian in the summer season.

As General Terry and Custer saw it, and all Frontier Army officers would have understood it, the real concern was the escape of the Indian village and it was a problem recognized by their contemporaries in the military, as well as those on the frontier. On June 20, 1876, five days before the Battle of the Little Big Horn, an article published in the *St. Paul Pioneer Press* commented upon the problem of actually finding the hostile Indians:

... there is not much probability of these cunning rascals being caught by our more slow-moving forces, for they can break up and fly in a thousand different directions and hide away among the hills and gullies, every foot of which is to them familiar ground.

A letter sent by a member of General Terry's command, dated June 23, 1876, two days before the defeat of the 7th Cavalry, was published in a newspaper on July 11, 1876. This letter confirmed that the issue of the Indians escaping was a problem that concerned the command:

... General Terry deserves success from his energy and the dispositions he has made of his troops to close the retreat of the Indians, yet the country from its mountainous nature affords so many secure and undiscoverable [locations] *that their escape is not impossible.*

Like General Miles and Captain Carter, Lieutenant Godfrey did not believe Custer had disobeyed his

orders and expressed his opinion in his 1892 *Century* article on the battle:

A battle was unavoidable. Every man in Terry's and Custer's commands expected a battle; it was for that purpose, to punish the Indians, that the command was sent out, and with that determination Custer made his preparations.

Had Custer continued his march southward – that is, left the Indian trail – the Indians would have known of our movement on the 25th, and a battle would have been fought very near the same field on which Crook had been attacked and forced back only a week before; the Indians never would have remained in camp and allowed a concentration of the several columns to attack them.

If they had escaped without punishment of battle, Custer would undoubtedly have been blamed.

A careful examination of the orders issued to General Custer will show that he was given practically a free hand. If any supplemental instructions were given, they were never revealed to the public. General Terry had no practical experience in Indian warfare.

General Custer had that practical experience; he was a student of Indian characteristics; had intimated observations, both in peace and war. He knew that in our centuries of Indian warfare, there were more escapes than punishments inflicted for outrages and depredations; that most of these escapes resulted from failure to give vigorous pursuits in following the Hostiles; that the way to find the Hostiles was to follow the trail, stay with it; that success usually depended on surprise attacks; that forewarned approaches resulted in scattering into groups or by families and thus escape punishment, [and pursuit opted to disorganized] ...

Lt. James Calhoun

It was an absurdity to think that two commands, of 700 and 400, separated by from 50 to 100 miles, could coordinate their movements in that open country and hold the Hostiles for a cooperative attack. In such a case, and the Hostiles had escaped, who would have shouldered the blame?

... the country toward Tullock's Fork was under surveillance, and it is reasonable to suppose that had circumstances not caused a change of plans for a daybreak attack on the 26th, that Scout Herendeen would have been sent to General Terry's headquarters with information as to plans, etc.

There could not have been any understanding, as contended by some, that the two commands of Custer and Gibbon were to meet at or near the mouth of the Little Big Horn on June 26th.

Major Brisbin's Letter

Major James S. Brisbin of the 2nd Cavalry, and part of General Terry's force which arrived on the battlefield June 27, 1876, and whose apparent dislike for Custer seems to have been matched only by that of Captain Benteen, wrote a letter to Lieutenant Godfrey in 1892. In this letter, Brisbin referred to Custer as an "insufferable ass." Brisbin was also prolific in his insults and accusations against Custer. The cause of this dislike is uncertain but, unlike Captain Benteen, who had served under Custer and had been given ample reason to dislike him, Brisbin was never a member of Custer's command.

Major Brisbin also quoted part of General Terry's last order to Custer in a letter to Lieutenant Godfrey and Brisbin's version of this order contained an important addition that was not in the original order as it had been published in the newspapers shortly after the battle:

You will remember that after Custer fell, Terry appointed me chief of cavalry. I looked over all the papers affecting the march and battle of the Little Big Horn, and took a copy of the order sending you up the Rosebud. That order now lies before me, and it reads:

"You should proceed up the Rosebud until you ascertain definitely the direction in which the trail above spoken of leads. (Terry had referred to the trail Reno followed.) Should it be found, as it appears almost certain that it will be found, to turn toward the Little Big Horn, he thinks (that is, the Department Commander thinks) that you should still proceed southward, perhaps as far as the headwaters of the Tongue River, and then (then underscored in order) turn toward the Little Big Horn,

feeling constantly, however, to your left, so as to preclude the possibility of the escape of the Indians to the south or southeast by passing around your left flank."

"It is desired that you conform as nearly as possible to these instructions, and that you should not depart from them unless you shall see absolute necessity for doing so."

In his letter Major Brisbin also added:

The absolute necessity here meant following the Indians alone or attacking them alone with your meager force.

Colonel W.A. Graham corresponded with Lieutenant Godfrey, who eventually became a General, over the course of many years. In 1923 Godfrey sent Graham the original Brisbin letter. This letter aroused Graham's interest and he began an investigation to either prove or disprove Brisbin's version of the order. Graham commented on the results of this investigation:

I asked General Godfrey whether he had checked the Brisbin version of the instructions above quoted against General Terry's Department Headquarters records. He replied that he had never made any effort to do so, being satisfied that Brisbin was mistaken.

I considered such a check important, for if the last sentence, as quoted by Brisbin was correct, it came close to establishing Custer's disobedience as a fact, whereas the official version raised merely an implication.

For that reason, a search began for Terry's Headquarters records for 1876. It took some time and considerable effort to find them, but they were at length located at Ft. Snelling, Minnesota, in storage. The Quartermaster custodian was prevailed upon to dig out the desired information, and I received from him a certified copy of General Terry's letter of instructions to Custer as it appeared in those records.

The document proved General Godfrey to be correct. General Brisbin was in error.

While Colonel Graham mildly refers to Major Brisbin's version of the order as "in error," he also identifies the addition quoted by Brisbin as close to establishing Custer's disobedience as a fact. Since this version of General Terry's order to Custer has never appeared elsewhere, and is in direct contradiction to the known original order, it must be concluded that Brisbin's version was a fabrication. In other words, Brisbin was so desperate to prove that the "insufferable ass" had disobeyed orders at the Battle of the Little Big Horn that Brisbin was willing to invent his own version of the order to prove the disobedience charge. This is remarkable considering the fact that, unlike many others involved in the battle. Major Brisbin had absolutely nothing to gain or lose by this fabrication except to satisfy his own personal motives, whatever they were.

Conference on Far West

The fact that General Terry's order to Custer is subject to so many interpretations must be considered in defense of Custer's own interpretation of them. If an argument can be made one way or another, after careful scrutiny by experts, then could these orders have been any more clear to Custer? At best, the order must be considered ambiguous and Custer was to use his own judgement as the circumstances dictated, just as was stated in the order itself.

However, setting aside the controversy over the written order, there was the conference between General Terry, Colonel Gibbon, and Custer, the night of June 21, 1876, on the steamship *Far West,* anchored in the Yellowstone River. At this conference the issues involved, as well as the various possibilities, were certainly discussed, perhaps in detail, and a verbal understanding also reached.

Colonel Gibbon was to support General Terry's statement of the "plan," and Custer never lived to give his interpretation. However, in Custer's last letter to his wife, written just before he left June 22, on his last mission, he wrote what he apparently believed to be Terry's intentions in the order:

I send you an extract from General Terry's official order, knowing how keenly you appreciate words of commendation and confidence, such as the following:

"It is of course impossible to give you any definite instructions in regard to this movement; and were it not impossible to do so, the Department Commander places too much confidence in your zeal, energy, and ability to wish to impose upon you precise orders, which might hamper your action when nearly in contact with the enemy."

Clearly, in his letter to his wife, Custer believed he had been given nearly a free hand in conducting the expedition. To support this belief were other letters written shortly before the 7th Cavalry separated from General Terry on June 22. Because these letters were sent by lengthy mail routes across vast distances, and the first reports of the battle were telegraphed, these letters did not appear in the newspapers until several days after the first reports of the battle had been published.

Reporter Kellogg's News Article

Mark Kellogg, the news correspondent with Custer, wrote the following report dated June 21, 1876. It was his final contribution as a news reporter and also contained the ominous prophecy that he would be "in at the death." Kellogg's prophecy proved to be correct and he would die with Custer.

A new campaign is organized, and tomorrow, June 22,

General Custer with twelve cavalry companies, will scout from its mouth up the valley of the Rosebud until he reaches the fresh trail discovered by Major Reno, and move on that trail with all rapidity possible in order to overhaul the Indians, whom it has been ascertained are hunting buffalo and making daily and leisurely short marches.

In the meantime, General Terry will move on the steamer to the mouth of the Big Horn River, scouting Pumpkin Creek en route, with General Gibbon's cavalry as well as infantry, which are marching toward the Big Horn on the north side of the Yellowstone. This part of the command will march up the Big Horn Valley in order to intercept the Indians if they should attempt to escape from General Custer down that avenue.

The hope is now strong and I believe, well founded, that this band of ugly customers, known as Sitting Bull's band, will be gobbled and dealt with as they deserve.

In his article Reporter Kellogg identified the role of General Terry's column, which was to prevent the escape of the Indians should they have retreated down the Little Big Horn Valley. He did not mention a "plan" to attack the camp simultaneously by the two separate columns.

Another letter was sent to the *New York Herald Tribune* dated June 22, 1876. This letter also did not mention a specific "plan" for the two forces to attack the Indian camp simultaneously, and also implied that Custer was given a free reign to follow the Indians wherever they went. It has been speculated that this letter was actually written by Custer.

Yesterday, Terry, Gibbon and Custer got together, and, with unanimity of opinion, decided that Custer should start with his command up the Rosebud Valley to the point where Reno abandoned the trail, take up the latter and follow the Indians as long and as far as horse flesh and human endurance could carry his command.

Custer takes no wagons or tents with his command, but proposes to live and travel like Indians; in this manner, the command will be able to go wherever the Indians can.

Gibbon's command has started for the mouth of the Big Horn. Terry in the Far West starts for the same point today, with Gibbon's force, and the Far West loaded with thirty days' supplies, he will push up the Big Horn as far as the navigation of that stream will permit, probably as far as old Fort C.F. Smith, at which point Custer will reform (rejoin?) the expedition after completing his present scout.

Custer's command takes with it, on pack animals, rations for fifteen days. Custer advised his subordinate officers, however, in regard to rations, that it would be well to carry an extra supply of salt because, if at the end of fifteen days the command should be pursuing a trail, he did not propose to turn back for lack of rations, but would subsist his men on fresh meat-game, if the country provided it; pack mules if nothing better offered.

A very interesting letter appeared in the *Pioneer Press* of St. Paul, Minnesota, on July 4, 1876. Printed before the news of the disaster had been received, this letter, like the Kellogg and "Custer" letter, did not mention a specific plan and also stated Custer might follow the Indians for great distances and away from General Terry:

Bismarck, D.T., July 3 – The mail of date of June 25, the first from the expedition arrived here this afternoon via Buford.

Custer was to leave on the 22nd with twelve companies of cavalry and proceed up the Rosebud to the headwaters of the Little Big Horn. He took the trail where Reno left it, and intends to follow it up, with the expectation of overtaking the hostiles within two or three days.

General Terry and staff went on the 21st with the steamer Far West to the mouth of the Big Horn, and will supply Custer from that point, should the pursuit of the Indians lead him that way. In case they should take another course he may go to [Fort] *Fetterman for supplies.*

Lt. William Cooke

The telegraphed report containing the disobedience of orders accusation against Custer quite naturally outran the labored overland mail originating on the Yellowstone River. However, several days after the first reports of the Battle of the Little Big Horn were received by telegraph, more letters began appearing in the newspapers, letters that had been written before Custer separated from General Terry.

One of these letters was printed in the *New York World*, July 11, 1876, and was dated June 21, 1876. The author was described as a 7th Cavalry officer and it was printed under the heading, "*Custer Justified: the command under General Custer expecting to attack alone.*"

The six companies of the Seventh Cavalry

which, under the command of Major M.A. Reno, were directed to scout up Powder River to the junction of the Little Powder, and from that point to the Tongue River, scouting down it to its mouth, where the main column was to be rejoined, returned on the 10th instant.

Owing to a misinterpretation of the order, Major Reno, instead of scouting down Tongue River, after reaching that point, moved in a southwesterly direction to Rosebud River, where he expected to find a large village of hostile Indians and establish a reputation as an Indian fighter.

The hostiles, however, had moved their village to some point further south, but from the large trails seen, it was supposed they had only been gone about two weeks and that there were about three hundred lodges in the party, making a total of about nine hundred warriors. Everything indicated that they were moving in a very leisurely manner and were not aware of the presence of such a large number of troops in their immediate vicinity. The Crow scouts with General Gibbon's command think they have gone to Little Horn River, and that they can be reached in six or seven days.

Immediately after the return of Major Reno, General Custer was directed to move against the hostiles with his entire regiment. Camp was at once moved to this point, and tomorrow at 12 o'clock the Seventh Cavalry will once more take up the line of march, proceeding up Rosebud River on the Indian trail, and following it until the village is reached.

Fifteen days rations are to be taken on pack mules, which are liable to be made to last twenty or twenty-five days, should circumstances require it, for when General Custer finds an Indian trail, he generally becomes acquainted with those who made it.

The best guides in the country have been procured, and everything looks as if a grand success was to be made of this scout.

This morning, six Crow Indian scouts from General Gibbon's command joined General Custer for duty with his raid. Officers well acquainted with the different tribes of Indians say they are brave and anxious to meet the Sioux. Besides being well acquainted with the country, they will be of immense value to the command.

When they reported, they said to the General they were glad they were going out with him; that they would take him to the Sioux village, and that in case they should be killed, after their bodies have been eaten by the wolves, all the white people would know of it and would say they had died as white men die. The General complimented them very highly and said they were the finest looking Indians he had ever seen.

The effect of this remark was rather ludicrous. As soon as it was made, an Indian brought out from his breast a large looking glass and proceeded to make an elaborate toilet. After it was completed, the glass was passed the next, and so on until the entire party had added to their appearance in one way and another. Vanity of vanities, all is vanity.

The wagon train of this command was left at the mouth of Pewan River, guarded by the infantry and dismounted cavalry men. General Terry had established his headquarters on the steamer Far West, where he will remain during the summer, moving up or down the Yellowstone River as his presence may be required.

General Gibbon's command is ordered to the mouth of Big Horn River, from which point the companies of the Second Cavalry with him will scour the country in that direction.

An article dated July 8, 1876, appeared in the *Boston Globe* on July 10, 1876. This article was telegraphed from the Dakota Territory by someone who had apparently returned to Fort Lincoln on the steamship *Far West* when the wounded were evacuated from the battlefield. Interestingly, this author made a point to disagree with the now official version of Custer's disobedience of orders:

A special telegraphing from Dakota Territory, describes the plan of action which had been arranged between the several commanders, clearly showing that General Custer was strictly within the line of his duty, and acting in obedience to the orders of his superior. He says:

"It was believed the Indians were on the head of the Rosebud, or on the Little Horn, a divide or ridge only fifteen miles wide, separating the two streams. It was announced by General Terry that General Custer's column would strike the blow, and General Gibbon and his men received the decision without a murmur."

There was great rivalry between the two columns, and each wanted to be in at the death. General Gibbon's cavalry had been in the field since the 22nd of last February, herding and watching these Indians, and the infantry had been in the field and on the march since early last March. They had come to regard the Yellowstone Indians as their peculiar property, and have worked and waited five months until the Indians could be concentrated and Generals Crook and Terry got into position to prevent their escape.

The Montana column felt disappointed when they learned that they were not to be present at the final capture of the great village, but General Terry's rea-

sons for according the honor of the attack to General Custer were good ones.

First, Custer had all cavalry, and could pursue if they attempted to escape, while Gibbon's column was half infantry, and in rapid marching in approaching the village, as well as in pursuing the Indians after the fight, General Gibbon's cavalry and infantry must become separated and the strength of the column be weakened.

Second, General Custer's column was numerically stronger than Gibbon's, and General Terry desired the strongest column to strike the Indians; so it was decided that Custer's men were, as usual, to have the post of honor, and the officers and men of the Montana column cheered them and bid them God speed.

On June 21, General Custer encamped at the mouth of the Rosebud, on the south bank of the river, and General Gibbon at once broke up his camp on the north bank and marched up the Yellowstone.

On the next day, June 22, at 12 o'clock, Custer announced himself ready to start, and drew out his column. It consisted of the whole of the Seventh United States Cavalry, twelve companies, having fourteen officers, with 185 pack mules loaded with fifteen day's rations of bacon, sugar, coffee and short forage. General Terry reviewed the column in the presence of Generals Gibbon and Brisbin, and it was pronounced by all in splendid condition.

The men were in the best of spirits, and mounted on the finest horses that could be bought in the East. General Custer, dressed in a suit of buckskin and mounted on a magnificent blooded mare, rode proudly at the head of his regiment, and looked every inch a soldier.

The last goodbye was said, the officers clustered around General Terry, their idolized department commander, for a final shake of the hand, and in the best of spirits, filled with high hopes, they galloped away to their death.

General Custer lingered behind a little for General Terry's instructions, and with a grip like iron and a God bless you, Terry turned back to the boat. Custer was proud of his regiment, but his face wore a sad expression. I had known him for sixteen years, and I never saw Custer so nervous and sad as he was when we last met.

Lieutenant Bradley's Diary

Lieutenant James H. Bradley was chief of the scouts with General Terry's force. Bradley kept a diary of his experiences on the campaign and he made a very revealing entry for June 21, 1876, as Custer prepared to leave:

> *It is understood that if Custer arrives first, he is at liberty to attack at once, if he deems prudent. We have little hope of being in at the death as Custer will undoubtedly exert himself to the utmost to get there first.*

Like the correspondence dated before the battle, it was

Lieutenant Bradley's understanding that Custer and the 7th Cavalry probably would fight the Indians alone.

What Custer's Order Really Meant

Once the Indian trail was discovered Custer made known his intention to follow it wherever it led and for however long it took. The 7th cavalry was taking rations for fifteen days and Custer warned his troop commanders to carry along an extra supply of salt because they might end up living off mule meat. General Terry also would have known of these preparations and they reflected the concerns that Custer's force possibly would have to make unforeseen movements before the hostile Indians were found.

Colonel Gibbon's force, with the infantry, would be far less mobile than the 7th Cavalry, and the fact that Custer was clearly expected to be the one to do the actual fighting was reflected in that Major Brisbin's battalion of 2nd Cavalry was offered to Custer. Also offered was the battery of gatling guns, but both Brisbin's cavalry and the "shoot 'em all day guns," as the Indian warriors referred to them, were declined.

Six of Colonel Gibbon's Crow scouts, however, were also offered to Custer and eagerly accepted. The scouts were intimately familiar with the area to be searched because it had once been Crow tribal land before the Crow were driven from it by the Sioux.

The acceptance of the gatling guns and Major Brisbin's cavalry would have rendered Colonel Gibbon's force nearly useless. The infantry themselves were effective in battle, but unable to successfully pursue the Indians in summer. They could be used as a blocking force at the head of the Little Big Horn or Rosebud Valleys, but this was the only role they could realistically be expected to fill. Clearly, and without doubt, General Terry, and the other officers involved, expected the 7th Cavalry to do the fighting.

From the available correspondence dated before the Battle of the Little Big Horn, and from that which originated after the battle, a clear contrast emerges. The correspondence dated before the battle does not mention the clearly defined plan claimed in Terry's confidential report after the battle. If this "plan" existed in the form General Terry and his supporters claimed it had, then why was it a total mystery to Custer, Reporter Kellogg, and many of the other officers and men of the expedition?

Why, if this "plan" existed, is there no mention of it in any of the correspondence dated before the battle? The answer to this question: there was no such specific plan in existence before the Battle of the Little Big Horn. It was created afterwards as an expedient to protect the survivors from possible criticism concerning the failure of the campaign.

Who to Blame for the Defeat

Lieutenant Edgerly of the 7th Cavalry commented on the true motives of the disobedience charge:

The fact is that a great disaster having occurred, some people believed that either Terry or Custer had to be the scapegoat.

The following statement appeared in the *St. Louis Dispatch* on July 8, 1876, and gives an indication of the criticism General Terry and others feared:

Custer was simply acting as Colonel of the Seventh Cavalry, which composed the main body of the expedition. He was not, like Crook and Gibbon and Terry placed in a responsible position.

For the general mismanagement of the campaign against the Sioux he [Custer] *cannot therefore be held responsible.*

Only the most cautious and skeptical journalist could see through the manufactured controversy and identify the underlying truth of the issue. General Terry was the expedition commander and Custer had departed June 22, under his instructions. Terry, like all the survivors of the expedition, as well as the entire nation, was shocked at the Little Big Horn massacre and it was inevitable for the commander of the expedition to have felt a measure of guilt and responsibility for the disaster. In reality, Terry had made his decision in conjunction with Custer and Colonel Gibbon, using the best information they had available.

The defeat was not General Terry's fault. Yet, Terry, and those close to him, felt compelled to invent the disobedience of orders charge to protect themselves from possible criticism on the decision to separate Custer's and Gibson's commands. This calculated accusation was effective in its purpose and instead of an outpouring of criticism concerning Terry's conduct of the expedition, there was only a mild murmur of the type voiced in the *St. Louis Dispatch* article of July 10, 1876. Terry, with the support of Colonel Gibbon, Colonel Hughes, Major Brisbin, and especially Major Reno and Captain Benteen, effectively created a smoke screen which diverted attention from their own conduct to a manufactured digression on the part of Custer.

The Actual Plan

The actual plan, if it may be so defined, existed only in the most general sense and, in principle, Custer was to pursue and fight the Indians wherever they might be found. The role of the plan for the second force, that of General Terry and Colonel Gibbon, burdened with the slow moving infantry, was for them to arrive at the mouth of the Little Big Horn River on June 26 so as to block any escape of the Indians in that direction. Lieutenant Roe, of Colonel Gibbon's command, quoted General Terry as saying the night of June 25:

I am very anxious to push on tonight as I have agreed with General Custer to be at or near the mouth of the Little Big Horn River on the morning of the 26th.

Another member of General Terry's command, Lieutenant McClernand, also confirmed that it was General Terry's intention to cooperate with Custer's command at the mouth of the Little Big Horn River. Lieutenant McClernand said:

> *My understanding, as a staff officer to Colonel Gibbon, was that after crossing the Yellowstone he* [Gibbon], *was to push for the Little Big Horn, near its mouth, so as to get below the Indians, if they were on that stream, while General Custer struck them from above.*
>
> *... the Montana Column had the longer route assigned to it and a big and high river to cross, and few, if any, thought General Custer would wait for us.*

The scout Herendeen commented on his own understanding of the plan:

> *... on the 21st of June and soon after Colonel Gibbon left the boat Major Brisbin came out of the cabin and I asked him where his Cavalry would probably be in the next few days so I could find him, and he replied at about the mouth of the Little Big Horn.*

Lieutenant Edward Maguire, in his report of the expedition, said:

> *These instructions were supplemented by verbal information to Custer that he could expect to find Gibbon's column at the mouth of the Little Big Horn no later than the 26th.*

The date of June 26th was not that of simultaneous attack on the Indian village, but rather the date Colonel Gibbon's force was to be at the mouth of the Little Big Horn River and in position to block any escape of the Indians in that direction. That was the actual plan and the only one which had a reasonable chance of success.

As it was, General Terry did not actually arrive at the site of the Battle of the Little Big Horn, and where the Indian village had been shortly before, until June 27, one day later than was claimed to be the date of the simultaneous attack on the village by the two forces. Had Custer interpreted his orders differently, and had he determined to wait until June 26 for the attack, the 7th Cavalry still would have fought the Indians alone.

General Terry's Statement

The 7th Cavalry was rationed for fifteen days and Custer had warned his troop commanders to carry along an extra supply of salt because the regiment would follow the Indian trail wherever it led. Custer was given the six Crow Scouts familiar with the vast country over which the 7th cavalry was to travel, and was also offered Major Brisbin's 2nd Cavalry battalion and the gatling guns.

In all the correspondence dated before the Battle of the Little Big Horn, not a word was said of the "plan" in the scope it was later claimed to exist. Custer's order contained the statement, "unless you shall see sufficient reason for departing from them," which clearly gave him flexibility in carrying out the order. With the known facts, the case against Custer claiming disobedience of orders should be accepted for what it really was: a diversion. It was simply an expedient to protect the living, at whatever expense to the memory of the dead.

However, there is one final fact which confirms General Terry's intent when Custer and the 7th Cavalry departed June 22. This evidence comes from the most irrefutable source of all, General Terry himself, and is contained in a communication addressed to General Sheridan dated June 21, before Custer and the 7th Cavalry had departed on their mission. Terry said:

> *My only hope is one of the two columns will find the Indians.*

General Terry got his wish. One of the two columns did find the Indians. It was General Custer and the 7th Cavalry.

CHAPTER 11

General Terry's Arrival on the Battlefield — Major Reno's Report — Captain Benteen's Report — General Terry's Report — Lack of Newsmen with the Command — The Theories of Custer's Defeat — Tom Rosser Enters the Fray — Interview with Reno and Benteen — General Miles' Statement — General Sheridan's Report — President Grant's Role — The Captain Hughes' Fabrication — Whittaker Book — Whittaker's Reply to Captain Benteen — Whittaker's Next Move

General Alfred Terry

A cover-up occurred after the Battle of the Little Big Horn. This cover-up was not an organized, Machiavellian type of conspiracy, with shadowy characters meeting behind closed doors to plot and scheme a course of action. Instead, this coverup was more like a stone cast into a pond with ripples spreading out until the entire subject of the Battle of the Little Big Horn had been touched in one way or another by distortion, dishonesty, and fraud. The participants were many, their motives varied, and each contribution was like adding a brick to a wall to hide the truth.

General Terry's Arrival on the Battlefield

The arrival of General Terry and his command on the battlefield on June 27th, began the cover-up. Like guileless children, Major Reno, Captain Benteen, and other surviving officers, had gushed their innocent concern on where the impetuous Custer might be. Why had Custer left them all alone to fight the Indians? Why had Custer "abandoned" them?

These officers conveniently ignored the evidence before their eyes, the cavalry uniforms the warriors had been seen wearing, the guidons they waved, the army carbines that were fired at them. This was all to be hidden from General Terry while Captain Benteen, always quick to point his finger, was swift to reproach Custer, claimed he believed Custer had "abandoned" them and gone to join Terry's force.

This claim of ignorance concerning the fate of Custer and the soldiers with him was to establish a pattern that would spiral throughout the cover-up and demonstrated what was to become an essential and pervading element of it. The best defense, it is said, is a good offense, and to cast the blame upon Custer for having "abandoned" Major Reno and Captain Benteen was a calculated maneuver designed to confuse the real issues. This pattern of casting blame on Custer, now conveniently dead and unable to respond to any accusation, no matter how misleading, was to be used to great advantage, especially by Captain Benteen.

Major Reno's Report

Major Reno's report of the battle, dated July 5, 1876, required him, as the now acting Commander of the 7th Cavalry, to give a detailed account of the action. This report contained a self-serving version of the Battle of the Little Big Horn in which Reno attempted, to the best of his ability, to evade his responsibility for the defeat.

Major Reno's report contained many obvious mistruths and glaring omissions. Reno had written his report before the "official" version of the battle had a chance to develop, and there were also many facts in it which Reno would later regret writing, facts he would later attempt to change when the Military Court of Inquiry was held into his conduct at the battle a few years later.

Some historians believe Major Reno wrote his report

with the assistance of Captain Benteen, and it would be difficult to imagine Benteen not involving himself in the creation of this document which, Benteen knew, would have implications concerning his own conduct. Major Reno's report was another brick added to the wall to hide the truth.

Captain Benteen's Report

Captain Benteen also wrote a report on the Battle of the Little Big Horn:

Camp Seventh Cavalry,
July 4, 1876.

Sir:

In obedience to verbal instructions received from you, I have the honor to report the operations of my battalion, consisting of Companies D, H and K, on the 25th ultimo.

The directions I received from Lieutenant Colonel Custer were, to move with my command to the left, to send well-mounted officers with about six men who would ride rapidly to a line of bluffs about five miles to our left and front, with instructions to report at once to me if anything of Indians could be seen from that point.

I was to follow the movement of this detachment as rapidly as possible. Lieutenant Gibson was the officer selected, and I followed closely with the battalion, at times getting in advance of the detachment. The bluffs designated were gained, but nothing seen but other bluffs quite as large and precipitous as were before me.

I kept to these and the country was the same, there being no valley of any kind that I could see on any side. I had then gone about fully ten miles; the ground was terribly hard on horses, so I determined to carry out the other instructions, which were, that if in my judgment there was nothing to be seen of Indians, Valleys, ... in the direction I was going, to return with the battalion to the trail the command was following.

I accordingly did so, reaching the trail just in advance of the pack train. I pushed rapidly on, soon getting out of sight of the advance of the train until reaching a morass; I halted to water the animals, who had been without water since about 8:00 p.m. of the day before.

This waiting did not occasion the loss of fifteen minutes, and when I was moving out the advance of the train, commenced watering from that morass. I went at a slow trot, until I came to a burning lodge with the dead body of an Indian in it on a scaffold. We did not halt.

About a mile further on, I met a sergeant of the regiment with orders from Brisbin Lieutenant Colonel

Custer to bring it to the front with as great rapidity as was possible.

Another mile on, I met Trumpeter Morton [Martin], *of my own company, with a written order from First Lieutenant W.W. Cook to me, which read:*

"Benteen, come on. Big village. Be quick. Bring packs. W.W. Cook."

"P.S. Bring Packs."

I could then see no movement of any kind in any direction; a horse on the hill, riderless, being the only living thing I could see in my front. I inquired of the trumpeter what had been done, and he informed me that the Indians had "skedaddled," abandoning the village.

Another mile and a half brought me in sight of the stream and plain in which were some of our dismounted men fighting, and Indians charging and recharging them in great numbers. The plain seemed to be alive with them.

I then noticed our men in large numbers running for the bluffs on the right bank of the stream. I concluded at once that those had been repulsed, and was of the opinion that if I crossed the ford with my battalion, that I should have had it treated in like manner; for from long experience with cavalry, I judged there were 900 veteran Indians right there at that time, against which the large element of recruits in my battalion would stand no earthly chance as mounted men.

I then moved up to the bluffs and reported my command to Major M.A. Reno.

I did not return for the pack train because I deemed it perfectly safe where it was, and we could defend it, had it been threatened, from our position on the bluffs, and another thing, it savored too much of coffee-cooling to return when I was sure a fight was progressing in the front, and deeming the train as safe without me.

Very respectfully,
F. W. Benteen
Captain Seventh Cavalry
Lieutenant Geo. D. Wallace
Adjutant Seventh Cavalry

Unlike Major Reno's report, in which Reno had attempted to explain away in detail his responsibility for the defeat, Captain Benteen was much more clever. Benteen realized that Reno, as the ranking surviving officer, naturally would bear the brunt of any criticism concerning the conduct of the survivors, and the shrewd move for Benteen would be to remain in the background as much as possible. Benteen's report reflected this strategy and actually was not a report of the battle at all. It was a report of his advance to the battlefield and it ended with his arrival at Major Reno's hill position. The advance made by Captain Weir in his attempt to join with Custer, for example, was omitted entirely, and thus any examination of this sensitive subject avoided. Captain Benteen did not lie in his report, he simply failed to tell the truth. Benteen's report was to be another brick in the wall.

General Terry's Report

General Terry wrote two reports of the battle. His second "confidential" report, accusing Custer of disobedience of orders, had been quickly routed to the newspapers and the fabricated charge was echoed across the country. Had this accusation truly been the issue it was later made out to be, and not an afterthought designed to protect others, it should have been made in the first report where it belonged.

Author and researcher Dr. Charles Kuhlman believed he traced the origin of the disobedience of orders charge to General Terry's Chief of Staff, Captain Robert Hughes, who, aided by Major Brisbin of the 2nd Cavalry, Colonel Gibbon, and, of course, Major Reno and Captain Benteen, convinced Terry to write the second report containing the accusation against Custer.

Interestingly, General Terry's second report contained a statement which may have pinpointed the original instigator of the disobedience charge against Custer beyond the broad brush painted by Dr. Kuhlman:

I have learned from Captain Benteen that on the 22nd the cavalry marched 12 miles.

On the 23rd, 35 miles from 5:00 a.m. to 8:00 p.m.

On the 24th 45 miles, 10 further, then, after resting, but not without unsaddling, 23 miles to the battlefield.

What General Terry had "learned" from Captain Benteen was that the 7th Cavalry had marched a total of 125 miles from June 22 until the day of the battle, June 25. This charge implicated Custer in disobedience of orders by claiming that Custer and the 7th Cavalry hurried to the battlefield in order to win a victory over the Indians. It also implied that Custer had carelessly exhausted his men and horses during this rushed advance.

Lieutenant Maguire was the chief of engineers with General Terry and on July 10, 1876, submitted a report which reaffirmed a statement in Terry's report concerning the distance the 7th Cavalry had marched:

I proceed to give the details of Custer's march from the Rosebud, and of the battle, as I have been able to collect them up to the present time.

On the 22nd, they marched 12 miles; on the 23rd, they

marched 35 miles; on the 24th, they marched from 5 a. m. till 8 p. m. , or about 45 miles; they then rested for four hours. At 12 they started again and proceeded 10 miles. They were then about 23 miles from the village. They reached the village about 2 p.m. on the 25th.

They had made a march of 78 miles in a day and a half, and, Captain Benteen tells me, without a drop of water.

2nd Lieutenant George D. Wallace was the official internist of the 7th Cavalry during the span of time covered by the 125 miles Captain Benteen "informed" General Terry and Lieutenant Maguire of, and Wallace's itinerary has the following entries:

June 22, 12 miles
June 23, over 30 miles
June 24, 28 miles
June 24-25 [night march], *8 miles*
June 25, 8 miles from the Rosebud divide to the battle field.

Captain Benteen created an extra 39 miles! Had he been concerned with informing General Terry of the truth all he had to do was show Terry the official record kept by Lieutenant Wallace. General Terry was duped, again, by Captain Benteen. The 7th Cavalry had marched a total of 86 miles, by Lieutenant Wallace's record, between June 22nd and June 25th. According to Benteen, however, they had:

Marched 78 miles in a day and a half and, Captain Benteen tells me, without a drop of water.

Years after the battle, when he wrote an account of the Battle of the Little Big Horn, Benteen must have forgotten his original version of the lengthy forced march to the battlefield without water, because he wrote:

My battalion reached the trail Custer had followed, just in advance of the pack-train, and pretty close to a boggy place where I thought water for the animals could be gotten. So, perhaps fifteen minutes were consumed in watering them.

Just as my battalion pulled out on the trail from the watering-place, the advance mules of the pack-train floundered into the bog....

The itinerary kept by Lieutenant Wallace contains the following entries:

June 24, We followed the right bank of the Rosebud, crossing the first two running tributaries seen ... camped 7:45 p.m. on the right bank of the Rosebud.

In Lieutenant Godfrey's narrative he commented upon the advance of Benteen's battalion from the Rosebud divide to the battlefield:

Some time after getting on the trail, we came to a water hole, or morass, at which a stream of running water had its source, Benteen halted the battalion. While watering, we heard some firing in advance, and Weir became impatient at the delay of watering and started off with his troop, taking the advance, whereas his place in column was second.

The rest of the battalion moved out very soon afterward and soon caught up with him. We were now several miles from the Reno battlefield or the Little Big Horn. Just as we were leaving the water-hole, the pack train was arriving, and the poor thirsty mules plunged into the morass in spite of the efforts of the packers to prevent them, for they had not had water since the previous evening.

Captain Benteen's claim of a 78-mile march without water is another "Benteenism."

Lack of Newsmen with the Command

News reporter Mark Kellogg had been with the 7th Cavalry and his death with Custer's personal command was to be one of history's great losses. Mr. Kellogg's notes, unfortunately, were not recovered and this invaluable record probably was either captured by the Indians who, even to this day, may have them buried in a sacred medicine bundle hidden some place, or these notes could have been deliberately destroyed by members of the 7th Cavalry.

Because Reporter Kellogg had died with Custer the newspapers used surviving members of the 7th Cavalry, as well as officers who were with General Terry's command, to provide them with information and stories of the battle. As these soldiers were all personally involved in the battle, in one way or another, the first stories which appeared in the newspapers cannot be characterized as objective.

Numerous articles appeared in the newspapers soon after the battle, whose authors were identified only as "officers" with the expedition. Major Brisbin has been identified as one of the officers who wrote news stories, and his well documented dislike of Custer probably influenced his version of the event.

Later, Major Brisbin also fabricated the fraudulent addition to Custer's controversial order from General Terry in an attempt to "prove" the disobedience charge, and this documented dishonesty makes anything Brisbin contributed to the newspapers particularly suspect.

The lack of a qualified, and hopefully objective, news correspondent with the command after the battle proved to be a serious obstacle to obtaining the truth. The various unidentified officers who wrote stories about the Battle of the Little Big Horn could have had, and some probably did, personal motives which influenced their accounts. These officers might also have been swayed by others with personal agendas.

With Major Reno and Captain Benteen now the ranking officers in the command, one would imagine that not only

would they have frowned upon unfriendly accounts of the battle, but that Reno and Benteen would also, at the same time, have encouraged versions that they approved.

The Theories of Custer's Defeat

In the first days after the news of the battle had been made public the newspapers presented two theories to explain the destruction of Custer's command.

The first theory was that Custer had blindly ridden into an ambush and his force had quickly been destroyed. However, the place for this ambush, had one occurred, would have been the river ford as Custer and his command had approached the village. As there were no bodies of soldiers or dead cavalry horses found at the river ford to support the ambush theory, and since the ridges and hilltops where Custer and his men were found is simply not ambush terrain, the ambush theory seems unlikely.

Any lingering doubt of this would appear to be dispelled by the archeological examination of the battlefield during 1984 and 1985. The evidence indicates Custer's men fought long and hard in orderly skirmish lines along well chosen positions, not in a disorganized rout that would indicate an ambush.

Although there is little to support it, the second theory was Custer's command was destroyed in a retreat. Either of these theories were acceptable to Major Reno and Captain Benteen, and neither of these men were about to present any facts which would have contradicted these two theories.

Tom Rosser Enters the Fray

One man, however, identified an important point in the first reports of the battle. This was Tom Rosser, the former Confederate cavalry general who had crossed swords with Custer in open battle during the Civil War.

On July 8, 1876, the *St. Paul Pioneer Press* published a letter written by Mr. Rosser and this letter pointed out many discrepancies in Major Reno's account of the Battle of the Little Big Horn:

From what I can gather from General Terry's instructions to General Custer, it is quite evident that it was expected, if not expressed, that Custer should attack the savages wherever found, and as to the manner of attack, of course that was left to the discretion and judgment of General Custer; and, viewing the circumstances of this fatal attack from my standpoint, I fail to see anything very rash in the planning of it, or reckless in its attempted execution.

On the contrary, I feel that Custer would have succeeded had Reno with all the reserve of seven companies passed through and joined Custer after the first repulse.

I think it quite certain that General Custer had agreed with Reno upon a place of junction in case of the repulse of either or both of the detachments, and instead of an effort being made by Reno for such a junction, as soon as he encountered heavy resistance, he

took refuge in the hills and abandoned Custer and his gallant comrades to their fate.

It is useless to say that Custer should have amused those Indians as soon as he reached them, or diverted their attention until General Terry could come up with reinforcements, for, although it is as stated that General Terry was only 20 or 30 miles off, and he moved by forced marches, he did not reach the scene of the disaster until three days [actually two] *after its occurrence.*

The Indians were running, and it is very evident to my mind that General Terry expected them to make every possible effort to escape, and Custer was doubtless ordered to pursue them, cut off their retreat to the south, and to drive them back upon Terry and Gibbon, and, thus hemmed in between these commands, they were to be crushed. To do this, it was necessary for Custer to strike them wherever found, and by vigorous blows and hot pursuit, he was to drive them into the trap which Terry had set for them.

Infantry on expeditions against Indians can only be used as guards for supply-trains, and in the pursuit of Indians upon a mission such as Custer's, they are as useless as foxhounds in pursuit of wild geese.

It was expected when the expedition was sent out that Custer and the Seventh Cavalry were to do all the fighting, and superbly did a portion of them do it. As a soldier, I would sooner today lie in the grave of General Custer and his gallant comrades alone in that distant wilderness, that when the last trumpet sounds, I could rise to judgment from my part of duty, than to live in the place of the survivors of the siege on the hills.

I knew General Custer well; have known him intimately from boyhood, and, being on opposite sides during the late War, we often met and measured strength on the fields of Virginia, and I can truly say now that I never met a more enterprising, gallant or dangerous an enemy during those four years of terrible war....

Interview with Reno and Benteen

Tom Rosser's letter voiced the same criticism that was to follow Major Reno throughout his life and into posterity, and that being Reno had failed in his military duty at the Battle of the Little Big Horn. Reno "took refuge in the hills and abandoned Custer and his gallant comrades to their fate." Since this was exactly what Reno had done it was impossible for him to explain his actions, although he gave it his best effort in an article published August 10, 1876, in the *Chicago Tribune*. Someone identified as a "correspondent" interviewed Reno and Benteen. Once again, Benteen's involvement is apparent in the formation of what was to become the "official" version of the Battle of the Little Big Horn:

When I read the first part of your letter, published in the Pioneer Press of the 8th inst., as copied from the Minneapolis Evening Tribune, my thought was that your motive had only the object of a defense of a personal friend – a gallant soldier against whom you fought, but after reading all of it, I could no longer look upon it as the tribute of a generous enemy, since through me, you had attacked as brave officers as ever served a Government, and with the same recklessness and ignorance of circumstance as Custer is charged with in his attacks upon the hostile Indians.

Both charges – the one made against him and the one made by you against us – are equally untrue. You say:

"I feel Custer would have succeeded had Reno, with all the reserve of seven companies, passed through and joined Custer after the first repulse," and after confessing that you are firing at long range, say further:

"I think it quite certain that Custer had agreed with Reno upon a piece of junction in case of the repulse of either or both detachments, and, instead of an effort being made by Reno for such a junction, as soon as he encountered heavy resistance he took refuge in the hills and abandoned Custer and his gallant comrades to their fate."

As I shall show, both the premises are false, and consequently all the conclusions of your letter fall to the ground, including your hifalutin talk about the last trumpet.

Benteen, with his battalion, was sent far to my left by Custer's order. When I went into the fight, he was out of sight.

My battalion was to the left and rear when we approached the village, but was brought to the front by Custer.

The only official orders I had from him were about five miles from the village when Colonel Cooke, the Regimental Adjutant, gave me his orders in these words:

"Custer says to move at as rapid a gait as you think prudent, and to charge afterwards, and you will be supported by the whole outfit."

No mention of any plan, no thought of junction, only the usual orders to the advance guard to attack by the charge.

When the enemy was reached, I moved to the front at a fast trot, and at the river halted ten minutes or less, to gather the battalion.

I sent word to Custer that I had the enemy in my front very strong, and then charged, driving the reds before me about three miles or less, to within a short distance of their village, supposing my command, consisting of 120 officers and men and about 25 scouts and guides, followed by the columns under Custer.

As I neared the village, the Indians came out in great numbers, and I was soon convinced I had at least ten to one against me, and was forced on the defensive. This I accomplished by taking possession of a point of woods where I found shelter for my horses.

I fought there, dismounted, and made my way to within 200 yards of the village, and firmly believe that if, at that moment, the seven companies had been together, the Indians could have been driven from their village.

As we approached near their village, they came out in overwhelming numbers, and soon the small command would have been surrounded on all sides, to prevent which I mounted and charged through them to a position I could hold with the few men I had.

You see by this I was the advance and the first to be engaged and draw fire, and was consequently the command to be supported, not the one from which support could be expected.

All I know of Custer from the time he ordered me to attack till I saw him buried is, that he did not follow my trail, but kept on his side of the river and along the crest of the bluffs on the opposite side from the village and from my command; that he heard and saw my action I believe, although I could not see him, and it is just here that the Indians deceived us.

At this time, I was driving them with ease, and his trail shows that he moved rapidly down the river for three miles to the ford, at which he attempted to cross into the village, and with the conviction that he would strike a retreating enemy.

Trumpeter Martin of Company H, and who the last time of any living person heard and saw General Custer, and who brought the last order his Adjutant, Colonel Cooke, ever penciled, says he left the General at the summit of the highest bluff on that side, and which overlooked the village and my first battlefield, and as he turned, General Custer raised his hat and gave a yell, saying they were asleep in their tepees and surprised, and to charge.

Custer's disaster was not the defeat of the Seventh Cavalry, who held their ground for 36 hours with a force outnumbered ten to one.

The Indians made him over-confident by appearing to be stampeded, and, undoubtedly, when he arrived at the ford, expecting to go with ease through their village, he rode into an ambuscade of at least 2,000 reds.

My getting the command of the seven companies was not the result of any order or prearranged plan. Benteen and McDougal arrived separately, and saw the command on the bluffs and came to it. They did not go into the bottom at all after the junction.

They attempted to go down the trail of General Custer, but the advance company soon sent back word they were being surrounded. Crowds of reds were seen on all sides of us, and Custer's fate had evidently been determined.

I knew the position I had first taken on the bluff was near and a strong one. I at once moved there, dismounted, and herded the pack train, and had just time to do so when they came upon me by thousands.

Had we been 20 minutes later effecting the connection, not a man of that regiment would be living today to tell the tale.

As you have the reputation of a soldier, and, if it is not undeserved, there is in you a spirit that will give you no rest until you have righted, as in your lies, the wrong that was perpetrated on gallant men by your defense of Custer, I request that you will publish this letter with such comments as that spirit will dictate.

The correspondent then cited Captain Benteen:

After proceeding through a rough and difficult country, very tiring on the horses unnecessary fatigue, I decided to return to the main trail.

Before I had proceeded a mile in the direction of the bluffs, I was overtaken by the Chief Trumpeter and the Sergeant Major with instructions from General Custer to use my own discretion, and, in case I should find any trace of Indians, at once to notify General Custer.

Having marched rapidly and passed the line of bluffs

on the west bank of a branch of the Little Big Horn River, which made into the main stream about two and a half miles above the ford crossed by Colonel Reno's command, as ordered, I continued my march in the same direction. The whole time occupied in this march was about an hour and a half.

About three miles from the point where Reno crossed the ford, I met a sergeant bringing orders to the commanding officer of the rear guard. Captain McDougall, Company B, to hurry up the pack trains.

A mile further, I was met by my trumpeter, bringing a written order from Lieutenant Cooke, the Adjutant of the regiment, to this effect: "Benteen, come on; big village; be quick; bring packs." And a postscript saying. "Bring packs."

A mile or a mile and a half mile further on, I first came in sight of the valley and Little Big Horn. About twelve or fifteen dismounted men were fighting on the plains with Indians, charging and recharging them. This body numbered about 900 at this time.

Captain Reno's mounted party were retiring across the river to the bluffs. I did not recognize till later what part of the command this was, but it was clear they had been beaten. I then marched my command to their succor.

On reaching the bluff, I reported to Colonel Reno, and first learned that the command had been separated, and that Custer was not in that part of the field, and no one of Reno's command was able to inform me of the whereabouts of General Custer.

While the command was awaiting the arrival of the pack mules, a company was sent forward in the direction supposed to have been taken by Custer. After proceeding about a mile, they were attacked and driven back.

During this time, I heard no heavy firing, and there was nothing to indicate that a heavy fight was going on, and I believe that at this time, Custer's immediate command had been annihilated.

As I neared the village, I saw Indians passing from the hill behind my left flank. I knew no support could be coming, so I dismounted and took possession of a point of woods about half a mile upstream from the village, sheltered my horses, and advanced to the attack, reaching within 200 yards of the village.

Tom Rosser replied to Major Reno's letter publicly and again Rosser repeated his charges, this time more directly:

The errors which I believed that you committed in that engagement were attributed to what I believed to have been a lack of judgement and a want of experience in Indian Warfare, as I understand you have seen but little service with your regiment on the Plains; and, in looking over your plan of attack, I could see no good reason for your gently pushing a line of skirmishers down toward a mounted force of Indians, when it was expected that you would attack vigorously with your entire command.

The fact of your dismounting, and taking to the point of timber to which you refer, was an acknowledgment of weakness, if not defeat, and this, too, when your loss was little or nothing. This was an act which I condemned.

You had an open field for cavalry operations; and I believe that, if you had remained to the saddle and charged boldly into the village, the shock upon the Indians would have been so great that they would have been compelled to withdraw their attacking force from Custer, who, when relieved, could have pushed his command through to open ground, where he could have maneuvered his command, and thus greatly have increased his chance of success.

But, if you had charged into the village and been repulsed, could you not have fallen back upon Benteen in good order, and thus have saved the disaster which befell you in the confusion and haste with which you were forced to recross the river?

You must remember that your situation was very different from the one in which Custer was placed. You had an open field in which you could handle your command, while Custer was buried in a deep ravine or canyon, and, as he supposed, stealthily advancing upon an unsuspecting foe, but was, by the nature of the ground, helpless when assailed on all sides by the Indians, in the hills above him.

Captain Benteen says:

"When I first came in sight of the Valley of the Little Big Horn, twelve or fifteen dismounted men were fight-

ing on the plain with Indians, charging and recharging them. Colonel Reno's mounted party was retiring across the river to the bluffs. I then marched my command in line to their succor."

Now, in reading this account at this distance, would one be blamed for supposing that those dismounted men had been cruelly abandoned to their fate, and were only saved by the timely arrival of the gallant Benteen?

From your letter, I infer that your entire command was not called into action in your attack upon the village, and that your loss was but trifling until you began your retreat.

Now, to the reporter of the New York Herald, you state that you made a reconnaissance in the direction of Custer's trail about 5 o'clock. The Indians appear to have withdrawn from your front as soon as you recrossed the river.

Why then could you not have gone in pursuit of Custer earlier? When you did go, you say that you heard "chopping shots." Do you not think that, even then, by a bold dash at the Indians, you might have saved a portion, at least of Custer's perishing command?

While Custer's command was making its way through these gorges towards the enemy, he himself, climbing the hillsides wherever he could, and peeping over their broken crests, was observing the condition of the village, and believing his approach undiscovered, he is heard to exclaim (I suppose to a messenger to you):

"Charge! They are asleep in their tepees."

I have heard that someone has advanced the theory that Custer was met, at this point where he first struck the river, by overwhelming numbers, and so beaten that his line from that point on was one of retreat. This is simply ridiculous.

Had Custer been repulsed at this point, his column would have been driven back upon the line on which he had approached, and the proposition is too silly to be discussed.

I claim that the part which Custer acted in this engagement was that of a bold, earnest man, who believed that he had before him a rare opportunity to strike the Indians a blow which, if successful, would end the campaign, and it was worth the bold effort; and, although he was unsuccessful, he was not, in my opinion, rash, and risked no more than he had often hazarded before and had won.

He did that which in 99 cases out of 100 will succeed, but this by chance was the fatal exception, yet the recruit does not impair the value of the rule.

You know that, even in civilized warfare, the boldest movements are generally successful, and the General who plans for the enemy and is counseled by his fears is sure to fall.

General Miles' Statement

The Reno-Rosser exchange of accusations draws attention to a fact which was to be the cornerstone in the coverup of the details of the Battle of the Little Big Horn. General Miles would later point out this poignant fact and, as he later became the Commander of the United States Army, his observation stretches beyond the common sense meaning readily apparent even to nonmilitary people:

> *The loss of 262 men under such circumstances would have caused a very searching investigation in almost any country, and it is strange that there has never been any judicious and impartial investigation of the causes that led to that disaster.*

General Miles was, of course, correct. The magnitude of the defeat alone demanded an investigation, not to mention the mysterious and disputed circumstances that surrounded the event. A responsible and impartial investigation, however, could have addressed questions which many people would not have wanted answered. The political tone that was to develop around the Battle of the Little Big Horn was demonstrated by a news article shortly after the defeat became public, already mentioned but repeated here:

> *The higher army officers, not withstanding their sorrow at General Custer's fate, agree that he was violating orders, and say that even if he had been victorious, he would have been in danger of court-martial.*

This statement by "higher army officers," who remained unidentified, was ridiculous. A single precedent of a "victorious" general being court-martialed, for any reason, is a historical nonoccurrence. The disobedience charge itself was a fraud, invented after the defeat and, had Custer met with success, a success that would have invariably made General Terry look the wise commander, there would have been no need for the fabricated disobedience of orders charge.

General Sheridan's Report

General Sheridan might have been expected to have

pressed for an investigation. However, his involvement was limited to a simple statement which met the political expedient of blaming Custer:

I fear it was an unnecessary sacrifice, due to misunderstanding and superabundance of courage, the later being extraordinarily developed in Custer.

At this stage of his life General Sheridan has been labeled by some historians as a political stooge, which he may have been. However, it is noteworthy that in his annual report dated November 25, 1876, Sheridan did not mention the disobedience of orders charge directly, although he did repeat General Terry's version of Custer's orders. It may have been this charge was omitted out of past affection for Custer, or even consideration for his still living wife.

Yet, it is a rare occurrence when ethical reasons will outweigh pragmatic ones when a political issue is involved. Perhaps General Sheridan knew in his heart the disobedience charge was a sham and was reluctant to attach his name to something he might regret later.

President Grant's Role

The real power behind the ordering, or not ordering, an official investigation rested not with "higher army officers," regardless of who they were, but with the President, Ulysses S. Grant. President Grant, however, had numerous reasons for not allowing any unbiased inquiry into the defeat. One reason, which had already been the basis for many other decisions concerning Custer, was Grant's personal animosity toward the dead cavalry commander. Custer had been a real thorn in his side while alive and the last thing Grant would have wanted would have been to elevate Custer to martyrdom, or even to have cleared him of blame.

There were also the very real issues Custer had been involved with shortly before his death. The wholesale corruption of Grant's government, including the cheating of both the Indian and the frontier military, was not something President Grant would have wanted to attract further attention to. Added to this was the entire failure of Grant's policy toward the Indians which was, to a large degree, a direct cause of the conflict.

The year 1876 was also an election year and the Presidential contest of that year was to be especially virulent and controversial. A detailed examination into the defeat, with all of its satellite issues, would have proven embarrassing to Grant's political allies, although they had long since decided to cast aside any thought of a third term for Grant himself, and the President undoubtedly felt political pressures to not take action on the issue. In fact, President Grant limited his public involvement in the issue to a vindictive statement which only served the purpose of further confusing the facts:

I regard Custer's massacre as a sacrifice of troops brought on by Custer himself, that was wholly unnecessary – wholly unnecessary.

He was not to have made the attack before effecting the junction with Terry and Gibbon.

He was notified to meet them on the 26th, but instead of marching slowly, as his order required in order to effect the junction on the 26th, he enters upon a forced march of 83 miles in 24 hours and thus had to meet the Indians alone.

The "83 miles in 24 hours," as President Grant said, was such an outrageous distortion of the truth that it must be wondered if it was a deliberate falsehood or if Grant was honestly confused. Regardless, the spiteful tone of Grant's remarks was deliberate and it served the political purpose of casting the blame for the defeat entirely upon Custer.

It also accomplished another purpose and that was it assured those further down the chain of command, General Terry, Major Reno and Captain Benteen, that any distortions of the truth were under official approval by the highest authorities in the government.

Captain Hughes' Fabrication

Captain Robert Hughes had been General Terry's chief of staff during the Little Big Horn campaign and years later he wrote a widely published article concerning the battle. Among the other "facts" Captain Hughes included in his article to support his contention that Custer disobeyed orders, was his own version of the march of the 7th Cavalry to the battlefield. Hughes wrote:

... the trail of the Indians was followed directly to the village, and with such extraordinary haste that there can be no reasonable doubt that Custer had deliberately formed the purpose to follow the trail and attack the village upon reaching it, regardless of where Gibbon's column might be, and without considering that force as a factor in the action!

The actual facts are that Custer had intended to wait until June 26 to attack the village, as numerous eyewitnesses with the command noted, and the attack of June 25 was only ordered because the command had been discovered by hostile scouts.

In his article Captain Hughes also managed to add 26 miles to the march, making it 112 miles instead of the 86 actually marched. Dr. Charles Kuhlman noted this discrepancy and what particularly disturbed him was the fact that Captain Hughes apparently had Lieutenant Wallace's official report of the march before him, and quoted from it, so the correct distance would have been available to Hughes. Dr. Kuhlman also lamented the:

... innocent readers who believed that Captain Hughes was writing in good faith, as did the present writer, until he was alerted by certain passages that did not square with known facts ... involving the grossest kind

of distortions and flat falsehoods ... he knew he was not telling the truth.

Dr. Kuhlman also caustically observed that the Hughes article was:

... a poor compliment to his readers, not all of whom were morons.

Dr. Kulhman's observation, however, should be qualified by modification of the word "readers." The casual reader of Captain Hughes' article should not have been expected to shuffle through military documents to verify the statements made by Hughes.

Dr. Kulhman also proposed an alternative scenario to the Battle of the Little Big Horn, one which might have taken place had Custer done exactly what Captain Hughes thought he should have, and that is continued his march toward the headwaters of the Rosebud River.

The accounts by some Indian participants of the battle say that the village was preparing to move June 25 when it was suddenly attacked by the 7th Calvary. They say they were planning to move north toward the mouth of the Little Big Horn River. The morning of June 26 found Major Brisbin and his four companies of cavalry, about 160 men, near the mouth of the Little Big Horn River while the infantry was still several miles away. There can be little question that Brisbin's small force, directly in the path of the moving village, would have been attacked with, most likely, unpleasant results for Brisbin's command. If Brisbin's force had not been annihilated, it certainly would have been badly mauled.

Had this event occurred, which would have also included the escape of the village, the question might be asked as to who would then have been made the scapegoat of the disaster? Would Custer's orders have been re-examined, except this time with fresh attention brought to the "when nearly in contact with the enemy" clause of his orders from General Terry, and with what results? Had Major Brisbin's force been attacked, it can be easily suspected that Captain Hughes, and certainly Brisbin, would have discovered a new meaning to Custer's orders, and this new meaning, most likely, would not have been favorable to Custer.

Whittaker Book

Not long after the Battle of the Little Big Horn a former Civil War cavalryman and author by the name of Frederick Whittaker began a biography of Custer and near the end of the year 1876, *The Complete Life of General G.A. Custer* was published. This book was written with the collaboration of Mrs. Custer, who felt her dead husband was being treated unjustly by the newspapers and members of the military and government. The book has suffered criticism by both contemporaries and historians as being far too laudatory to Custer. Nevertheless, Whittaker's book raised legitimate questions and, for the first time, Captain Benteen found his own role at the battle under close scrutiny:

Looking at all the testimony impartially from this distance of time, the conduct of Benteen is far worse than that of Reno.

The Major did his best in his fight, and it was nothing but want of experience in command and in Indian warfare that caused his defeat. Benteen's case is different. He was an old Indian fighter, a man of remarkable personal courage, as he proved in the subsequent battle, had often fought under Custer, and knew his business perfectly.

That he should have, as his own testimony confesses, deliberately disobeyed the peremptory order of Custer to "come on," argues either a desire to sacrifice Custer, or an ignorance of which his past career renders him incapable.

Custer told him to "come on" and he "reported to Colonel Reno." Well then, it may be said, what did Benteen do afterwards? The rest of his testimony shows what he did. He says:

"While the command was awaiting the arrival of the pack mules, a company was sent forward in the direc-

tion supposed to have been taken by Custer. After proceeding about a mile, they were attacked and driven back. During this time, I heard no heavy firing, and there was nothing to indicate that a heavy fight was going on, and I believe that at this time Custer's immediate command had been annihilated."

"The rest of the story you must get from Colonel Reno, as he took command and knows more than anyone else."

It is curious in Benteen's evidence how his only estimate of time comes in before the battle. Afterwards, there is not a word about time.

Who would think that this brief paragraph covered from 2:30 to 6:00 p.m. If the one company was sent forward, why was it not supported by the whole outfit? Why was Custer left alone with his battalion, while the other battalions were out of danger?

The answer to the questions is given by Reno and Benteen in their evidence, almost unassisted by others. The reasons were, Reno's incapacity and Benteen's disobedience.

Captain Benteen, having already manipulated the facts of the Little Big Horn battle with such contributions as the accusation of Custer "abandoning" them, his distortion of the distance marched by the 7th Cavalry, and various other distortions, was not about to allow Author Whittaker to come along and spoil it for him by calling attention to the facts.

In the January 20, 1877, issue of the *Army and Navy Journal*, a rebuttal to Whitakker's book, entitled *How History is Manufactured*, authored by Captain Benteen, was published:

1st. Had Reno fought as Custer fought, and Benteen obeyed Custer's orders, the battle of the Little Big Horn might have proved Custer's last and greatest victory.

I put right here, without fear of contradiction: yes, and his first Indian victory too! "The battle of the Washita" is comprised in this grand total. (I do not mean to include Custer's war record in this assertion.)

I say here that Colonel Reno and I thought during the siege of June 25th and 26th at the Little Big Horn, that he, Reno, was the abandoned party, and spoke of it as another "Major Elliott affair;" thinking that General Custer had retreated to the mouth of the river, where the steamboat was supposed to be, and that Reno's command was left to its fate.

I am accused of disobeying Custer's orders. Nothing is further from the truth in point of fact, and I do not think the matter of sufficient importance to attempt to vindicate myself... when I have the consoling belief that the contrary is so well known by all my military superiors and comrades.

I have one child – a ten year old boy; if he learns from his father's daily life, what his character is, as he must, will it make much difference to him in after years, in stumbling across Whittaker's book, to see his father quoted as having neglected the first duty of a soldier?

No sir; as I hope to demonstrate to him by daily life, that the assertion was altogether without foundation, and I have no idea that any pain will be ever caused him should he in afterlife not find the contrary confirmed by weightier evidence than Whittaker's book.

There was a slight undercurrent in the 7th Cavalry which you, as a public organ, might know, and which

knowledge may throw some light on matters of which Mr. O'Kelly, the Herald reporter, wrote, and from which Whittaker obtained his cue ...

Most certainly, Colonel Reno asked me not for counsel in preparing his report. However, the report when

received by the regiment drew from one officer the exclamation in public, "But he doesn't mention me!" (calling out his own name.)

From that moment can be said, the Society for Mutual Admiration was organized in the regiment and assiduously did they work – Colonel Reno being the chief objective point, I the second, from being unfortunate enough to have been specially mentioned by Colonel R. in his official report.

The meetings of the society have been held in secret; no 1st class men were contributing members; none of them can bear the test of light and truth; but still they don't want their light hidden under a bushel, and they have succeeded in getting vile slanders into public print, through the greatest organ this country has, and yet they are not happy! Now, through Whittaker, the story goes into history(?)

With the benefit of perspective concerning Captain Benteen's role in confusing the issues of the Battle of the Little Big Horn, his accusation of "vile slanders" by others has all the credibility of a toad with the most warts calling everyone else in the forest ugly. However, looking beyond Benteen's usual twisting of the facts, his skillful use of poetry, and his talent in somehow finding a way to include an innocent ten year old child to support his argument, Benteen also accomplished something he did not intend.

For the first time Captain Benteen acknowledged his own role at the Battle of the Little Big Horn and he also admitted that there was "a slight undercurrent in the 7th Cavalry." Of course, those who were not in agreement with Benteen were not "1st class men," while those who did support Benteen obviously were. And while those who did not support Benteen were unable to "bear the test of light and truth," Benteen obviously could.

A cynic might observe that Captain Benteen's talents were wasted on the frontier and his true calling was that of politician, a phrenologist, or of a traveling medicine show proprietor–fields where he could have written new chapters on how to befuddle and hoodwink those people unwary enough to believe a single word he said.

Whittaker's Reply to Captain Benteen

Mr. Whittaker was up to the challenge of Captain Benteen's letter and the following issue of the *Army and Navy Journal* contained his response:

I had said my say in the book, and was willing to stand or fall thereby. Captain Benteen seems disposed to reopen the case in another manner, and bring into the controversy matters entirely extraneous, which require a reply, in the name of justice towards a gallant officer, now in his grave and unable to defend himself. This is General Custer, late of the 7th Cavalry, a brother officer of Captain Benteen, and of the same regiment.

In considering the letter of Captain Benteen, I divide its matter into the three paragraphs in which it appeared, and shall consider them separately, and I hope with temperance and justice.

I. The first of these paragraphs asserts that had Custer won the battle of June 25, 1876, it would have been "his first Indian victory," and Captain Benteen proceeds to say, "The battle of the Washita is comprised in this grand total:" "I say here that Colonel Reno and I thought, during the siege of June 25th and 26th at the Little Big Horn, that he, Reno, was the abandoned party, and spoke of it as 'another Major Elliott affair;' thinking that Custer had retreated to the mouth of the river, where the steamboat was supposed to be, and that Reno's command was left to its fate."

There can be no question, I think, that Captain Benteen wishes to convey in these words the idea that General Custer unnecessarily abandoned Major Elliott to his fate, and further that the Indians defeated Custer in the battle of the Washita.

Captain Benteen closes this paragraph with the expression of a belief that his conduct is endorsed by his "military superiors and comrades," but I hardly think he can claim a like endorsement for his opinions on the conduct of Custer at the Washita. The terms of General Field Orders No. 6, Nov. 28, 1868, Headquarters Department of Missouri, in which General Sheridan alludes to that battle as a "defeat of a large force of Cheyenne Indians," a "signal success," and offers "special congratulations" to Custer, for "efficient and gallant services rendered," forbid such a presumption.

The historical results of Custer's famous campaign of 1868-9, recorded in the files of the Army and Navy Journal at the time; the pacification or conquest by him of the Cheyennes, Arapahos and Kiowas, in seven months from the time he took the field; the famous request, signed by Sherman, Sheridan, Sully, and the officers of the 7th Cavalry, which recalled Custer from suspension to immediate command; these and many other facts, familiar to the Army and the world, are Custer's best defense against the assertions of Captain Benteen's letter, which should have been made, if made at all, in 1868, while facts and witnesses were there to confront them.

Whether Captain Benteen's conduct of June 25, 1876, will bear the same tests as those applied to Custer's in 1868, time will show.

Further, it is consoling to know where the "first-class men" of the 7th Cavalry are to be found, and who compose the second-class, and so on downwards.

Whittaker's Next Move

The publication of Frederick Whittaker's reply to Captain Benteen's letter did not signal the end of the intrepid author's battle with either Major Reno or Captain Benteen. Whittaker's book on Custer may be devalued by those who dislike Custer, but Whittaker was yet to make a contribution to history which would prove to be a major source of information on the Battle of the Little Big Horn.

It would take Mr. Whittaker some time to make his next move, but that it was coming Major Reno and Captain Benteen would have been well aware. Whittaker was not finished with them yet.

CHAPTER 12

Whittaker's Letter to Congressman W.W. Corlett — Major Reno Takes Action — The Reno Court of Inquiry — The Witnesses — Testimony of Major Reno Compared to His Report — Captain Benteen's Testimony — Benteen and the Guidon — Major Reno's Report — The Court's Findings

Major Marcus Reno

General Nelson Miles' observation concerning the Battle of the Little Big Horn, which was both poignant and a fact which cannot be overlooked as a primary cause to the mystery surrounding the event, is repeated here. Miles said:

The loss of 262 men under such circumstances would have caused a very searching investigation in almost any country, and it is strange that there has never been any judicious and impartial investigation of all the causes that led to that disaster.

There was no substitute for an investigation of some kind and one man was determined to stimulate official action of one sort or another. Frederick Whittaker had generated controversy with his hurried biography of Custer and after its publication he remained involved in the issues.

Whittaker's Letter to Congressman W.W. Corlett

In a letter addressed to Delegate William W. Corlett of the Wyoming Territory, dated May 18, 1878, Mr. Whittaker requested official action:

Mount Vernon, N. Y.,
May 18, 1878
Hon. W.W. Corlett, M. C.

Dear Sir:

Having been called upon to prepare the biography of the late Brevet Major General George A. Custer, U.S.A., a great amount of evidence, oral and written, came into my hands, tending to prove that the sacrifice of his life and the lives of his immediate command at the battle of the Little Big Horn was useless, and owing to the cowardice of his subordinates.

I desire, therefore, to call your attention, and that of Congress, through you, to the necessity of ordering an official investigation by a committee of your honorable body into the conduct of the United States troops engaged in the battle of the Little Big Horn, fought June 25, 1876, otherwise known as the Custer Massacre, in which Lieutenant Colonel Custer, Seventh United States Cavalry, perished, with five companies of the Seventh Cavalry, at the hands of the Indians.

The reasons on which I found my request are as follows:

First: Information coming to me from participants in the battle, written and oral, to the effect that gross cowardice was displayed therein by Major Marcus A. Reno, Seventh United States Cavalry, second-in-command that day; and that owing to such cowardice, the orders of Lieutenant Colonel Custer, commanding offi-

cer, to said Reno, to execute a certain attack, were not made.

That the failure of this movement, owing to his cowardice and disobedience, caused the defeat of the United States forces on the day in question; and that had Custer's orders been obeyed, the troops would probably have defeated the Indians.

That after Major Reno's cowardly flight, he was joined by Captain F.W. Benteen, Seventh United States Cavalry, with reinforcements, which were placed under his orders, and that he remained idle with this force while his superior officer was fighting against the whole force of the Indians, the battle being within his knowledge, the sound of firing audible from his position, and his forces out of immediate danger from the enemy.

That the consequences of this second exhibition of cowardice and incompetency was the massacre of Lieutenant Colonel Custer and five companies of the Seventh United States Cavalry.

Second: The proof of these facts lies in the evidence of persons in the service of the United States government, chiefly in the army, and no power short of Congress can compel their attendance and protect them from annoyance and persecution if they openly testify to the cowardice exhibited on the above occasion.

Third: The only official record of the battle now extant is the report written by Major Reno, above named, and is, in the main, false and libelous to the memory of the late Lieutenant Colonel Custer, in that it represents the defeat of the United States forces on that occasion as owing to the division by Custer of his forces into three detachments, to overmanning his forces, and to ignorance of the enemy's force, all serious charges against the capacity of said Custer as an officer; whereas the defeat was really owing to the cowardice and disobedience of said Reno and to the willful neglect of said Reno and Captain Benteen to join battle with the Indians in support of their commanding officer when they might have done it, and it was their plain duty to do so.

Fourth: The welfare of the United States Army demands that in case of a massacre of a large party troops, under circumstances covered with suspicion, it should be officially established where the blame belongs, to the end that the service may not deteriorate by the retention of cowards.

Fifth: Justice to an officer of the previously unstained record of Lieutenant Colonel Custer, demands that the accusation under which his memory now rests, in the only official account of the battle of the Little Big Horn now extant, should be proved or disproved.

I have thus give you, as briefly as I can, my reasons for asking this investigation, and the facts I am confident of being able to prove.

My witnesses will be all the living officers of the Seventh United States Cavalry who were present at the battle of June 25, including Major Reno and Captain Benteen; myself to prove statements of an officer since deceased, made to me a few days before his death; F.T. Gerard, Indian Interpreter to the United States forces; Dr. Porter of Bismarck, D.T., contract surgeon at the battle in question; Lieutenant Carland, Sixth Infantry; Sergeant Godman, now of the Signal Service, and others whose names I can find in time for the committee's session, should the same be ordered.

Trusting, dear Sir, that this letter may result in an investigation which shall decide the whole truth about the battle of the 25 June 1876, and the purgation of the Service.

I am your obedient servant,
Frederick Whittaker

Major Reno Takes Action

Major Reno could see the handwriting on the wall and, shortly after Whittaker's letter became public, he too wrote a letter to a Congressman, Henry B. Banning of Ohio to support an investigation. Unfortunately, the much needed congressional investigation did not materialize and, instead, a Military Court of Inquiry, also requested by Major Reno, was ordered by President Rutherford Hayes (elected

in the fall of 1876) to convene in January 1879. Major Reno's letter, dated June 22, 1878, requested that the President take official action:

Harrisburg, Pa.,
June 22, 1878
His Excellency,
The President,

A letter addressed to Hon. W.W. Corlett, Delegate of Congress from Wyoming Territory, and by him referred to the House Committee of Military Affairs, and thus made semi-official, appeared in the press of the 13th inst.

As the object of this letter was to request an investigation of my conduct at the battle of the Little Big Horn River, and was also the first time various reports and rumors had been put into definite shape, I addressed a communication to the same committee, through its chairman, urging that the investigation be resolved upon.

The Congress adjourned without taking any action, and I now respectfully appeal to the Executive for a "Court of Inquiry" to investigate the affair, that the many rumors started by camp gossip may be set at rest and the truth made fully known.

The letter to Mr. Corlett which is referred to, is hereto attached.

I am, Sir
Very respectfully,
Your obedient Servant
M. A. Reno
Major 7th Cavalry

Major Reno's request for a Military Court of Inquiry was a shrewd move on his part. His request was accepted by a Special Order dated November 25, 1878. Had there not been a Military Court of Inquiry to investigate Reno's conduct, there very well may have been a Congressional investigation which would have been unlimited in its scope in examining the issues. As it was, the Military Court was to "officially" confine itself to examining only Reno's conduct.

The Reno Court of Inquiry

The Reno Court of Inquiry convened January 13, 1879, in Chicago, Illinois. If there was any question that it was Frederick Whittaker who had instigated the proceedings, this was dispelled during the opening remarks of the court when Whittaker was referred to as the "accuser" of Major Reno. The court ruled that Whittaker was to be officially notified that the Court proceedings had begun and Whittaker then attended the procedures.

1st Lieutenant Jesse M. Lee was the official recorder of the Court. While Lee's role was similar to that of prosecutor, he severely limited himself, or was limited, throughout the proceedings, failing to press cross-examinations of the witnesses and limiting his introduction of evidence that might have proved embarrassing to Major Reno.

Major Reno selected as his counsel Attorney Lyman D. Gilbert. Mr. Gilbert vigorously conducted Major Reno's defense, primarily through objections to questions that were not directly relevant to Reno's conduct. It was an effective strategy and numerous times Mr. Gilbert circumvented any deviation into the overall issues of the Battle of the Little Big Horn.

The Witnesses

Of the 23 witnesses who were called before the Court, there were only a few who did not support Major Reno's version and conduct at the battle. Some of the civilian witnesses, such as the scout George Herendeen; an interpreter, Fred Gerard; and a civilian packer, John Frett, were openly critical of Reno. Doctor Porter also was blunt with the truth which, had he been diligently questioned by Recorder Lee, might have exposed further facts with which Attorney Gilbert would have had serious problems.

Other witnesses, such as Lieutenant Godfrey and Lieutenant Varnum, seemed to hint at the truth, but again Recorder Lee failed to press the pertinent questions. When examining the testimony it seems Godfrey and Varnum knew more than they were willing to say and would have been willing to tell more, perhaps much more, had they been "forced" through questioning to do so.

There also were a number of witnesses who energetically supported Major Reno. Captain Moylan, the man whom Custer had helped promote, for the third time, from the enlisted ranks to officer, might have been expected to defend his former commander, but Moylan's loyalties apparently were confined to the living and he was surpassed perhaps only by Captain Benteen as the witness most favorable to Reno.

The entire Court proceeding, and the testimony of those who testified before it, can be characterized as an evasion of responsibility. This is clearly illustrated by the statements of Captain McDougall, who commanded the rear guard with the pack train, and Lieutenant Mathey, who commanded the pack train itself. This testimony concerns the order brought back by Sergeant Kanipe.

Captain McDougall testified:

I received no notification to hurry up the packs. I think Lieutenant Mathey got that order.

Lieutenant Mathey testified:

I received no orders from Custer, Reno or Benteen on that march. Only from Captain McDougall. No sergeant reported to me with orders.

The order in question was the one sent back with Sergeant Kanipe telling the pack train to hurry forward.

One of these two officers received the order, and the other would have known of it within moments, yet neither Captain McDougall nor Lieutenant Mathey admitted receiving this order. Why were they compelled to deny the receipt of Custer's order when neither was on trial? Was it a fear of admitting any responsibility at all during the battle? Or could it have been a sense of guilt that many of the surviving officers felt and the desire to tell the court as little as possible, even to the extent of irrelevant perjuries?

Sergeant Kanipe, incidentally, said he delivered the message to Captain McDougall; however, it would have made little difference to whom the order was given. The other officer would have quickly known of the order.

At the Reno Court of Inquiry, one fact which stands out is that for many statements made by one witness, a conflicting statement exists by another. It would be possible to write several stories of the Battle of the Little Big Horn, each different, by picking between the various accounts. At least some of these conflicting statements can be explained as legitimate confusion with the memory of the event which, it can be imagined, had an indelible psychological impact on the survivors.

Concerning the problem of memory, the book *Evidence* by John M. Maguire, says:

One of the most common difficulties encountered in the handling of witnesses is the lapse or loss of recollection....

Speaking in particular of the problem of memory in remembering a traumatic event, Psychiatrist Lenore Terr, who has researched this phenomenon, is quoted as saying:

Terrifying incidents are particularly susceptible to memory mistakes because the horror and confusion interfere with the memory process.

Accepting that legitimate confusion would exist in the memories of survivors, certain facts may always remain unclear. However, by comparing the known facts with the testimony of the witnesses, it is possible to sort out some of what seems to be deliberate distortions from legitimate confusion.

Testimony of Major Reno Compared to His Report

There are many discrepancies between Major Reno's report and the testimony he gave at the Court of Inquiry.

In his report, Major Reno said:

We heard firing in that direction and knew it could only be Custer.

At the Court of Inquiry, Reno was to say:

I do not remember anybody reporting to me that he heard firing ... I heard no such firing.

In his report, Major Reno said:

In a short time, the pack train came up.

At the Court of Inquiry, Major Reno testified:

In about an hour and a half, the pack train would come up.

In his report, Major Reno said:

Custer intended to support me by moving further down the stream and attacking the village in the flank.

At the Court of Inquiry, Major Reno said:

I had no reason to believe that General Custer would support me in other manner than from the rear.

An aggressive prosecutor might have asked Major Reno to clarify which of the statements he made were the truth and which were not. Did Reno lie on his official report, a military offense, or was he giving false testimony before the court, also an offense?

There were many other statements made at the Court of Inquiry by Major Reno that were obviously untrue or a manipulation of the facts in a deceitful manner. In fact, Reno's entire testimony can be characterized, as can Captain Benteen's, as flagrant distortions and mistruths. A few of Reno's more obvious violations of the known facts and incredulous statements illustrate his distortion of the truth:

It did not occur to me that Custer with 225 men needed anyone quickly.

I consider that the results of the battle justified my every act.

I consider that I obeyed orders.

I did everything I could to assist and cooperate with General Custer.

I believe that when I came out of the timber, Custer's command was all dead.

These statements by Major Reno defy common sense. Why would Custer, with only about one-third of the regiment engaged in an attack, not need support? Reno did not obey his orders and it has been argued by many that Reno and Captain Benteen caused the results of the battle. Reno's statement that Custer's command was dead by the time he left the timber is extraordinary considering the fact that, minutes before, Custer had been seen alive on the Weir Peaks overlooking the Little Big Horn Valley. There is no testimony at the Reno Court of Inquiry, or in any other accounts of the Battle of the Little Big Horn, that Reno did anything after his retreat from the valley to "assist and cooperate" with Custer.

Captain Benteen's Testimony

Captain Benteen's testimony was, if anything, even more distorted than Major Reno's. During the Reno Court of

Inquiry, when he was not being evasive or manipulative, Benteen resorted to statements that were obviously dishonest. Some of his more outrageous statements were:

I supposed Custer able to take care of Himself.

I heard no vollies.

We were driven back from the Weir Peaks.

The position [Reno's in the wooded area], *did not threaten the village very much, though only six or seven hundred yards away.*

If I had joined Reno in the timber with the pack train, it could have made a particle of difference so far as Custer was concerned.

I was separated from Reno possibly fifteen miles when at the greatest distance.

I am convinced that when the order brought back by Martin reached me, General Custer and his whole command was dead.

The transparency of Captain Benteen's testimony becomes apparent when examined against the known facts and the testimony and narratives of nearly every other 7th Cavalry participant at the Battle of the Little Big Horn. However, in his collection of distortions and "cock and bull" stories, as one historian termed his testimony, Captain Benteen did tell the truth at least once at the Reno Court of Inquiry. Benteen said:

I was on as amicable terms with General Custer on the twenty-fifth of June as I ever was with him.

Of course he was, which was to say on June 25, 1876, Captain Benteen hated Custer just as much as he had every other day of his life.

Benteen and the Guidon

Attorney Gilbert then directed attention to an event which may or may not be of significance, depending on whether or not Custer and his command were alive or dead when it occurred:

Benteen placed the guidon of the 7th Cavalry. It was at a place where, as he afterward said, he was so far from Custer's battlefield that the point could not from there be seen.

But even if visible, it would have carried no message to those who had fought on the hills and valleys below because they had passed away from the region of human sense.

The guidon which Attorney Gilbert spoke of was placed by Captain Benteen on the Weir Peaks, that much, at least, of his statement is correct. With field glasses, however, those on Custer Hill could have seen the guidon and, "if visible," it definitely would have carried a message to those on the hill. Frederick P. Todd, author of *American Military Equipage 1851-1892*, said:

War Department general orders number 4, 18 January 1862, brought an entirely new type of guidon, a swallow-tailed stars and stripes. There should be little doubt that this style resulted from the need to more clearly identify separate groups of cavalry in combat.

A Dictionary of Soldiers' Talk, which lists in detail the definitions of various military terminology, makes the following statement concerning the cavalry guidon:

... used in mounted units to indicate direction and place of formation ...

It must be presumed that those on Custer Hill, if alive, would have been eagerly watching the back trail with field glasses for any sign of an advance of the other elements of the regiment. Captain Benteen and the guidon would have indicated to those on Custer Hill "place of formation," something that, one would imagine, would have been of interest to Custer and the officers with him.

Major Reno's Report

Attorney Gilbert, as he closed his summary for Major Reno's defense, mentioned Reno's report of the Battle of the Little Big Horn. As this report contained many statements which contradicted Reno's testimony at the Reno Court of Inquiry, and thus was potentially embarrassing, Gilbert's attempt to diffuse this issue is understandable:

Of the report made a few days after the battle and now submitted in evidence, I need say nothing to a Court familiar from long personal experience with the manner in which such reports are written.

They give a general statement of many matters of which the commanding officer cannot have a personal knowledge, and which may prove, under the minute examination of a court of inquiry, to rest on the recollection of others than himself, and for which he is not entirely responsible.

The 40th edition of *The Army Officer's Guide*, which has been continuously published since 1930, and is based upon continued United States Army traditions and regulations, says the following:

IMPORTANT CAUTION: An officer's signature on an official document means that he or she vouches for the accuracy of the facts stated, and that each recommendation represents his or her carefully considered, professional view.

A false official statement, whether oral or written, is a grave offense. Your word, or your signature, is your bond. Be very certain of the correctness of the official papers you sign.

The question should be asked again; which of Major Reno's statements were factual, those in his report, or those in his testimony at his Court of Inquiry? Obviously, both cannot be correct.

The Court's Findings

The official findings of the Reno Court of Inquiry are as follows:

The Court of Inquiry assembled by Recorder Lee's reply: Special Orders No. 255, dated Headquarters of the Army, A.G.O. Washington, November 25, 1878, reports in Comment: Obedience to that order the following facts involving the conduct of Major Marcus A. Reno, 7th Cavalry, in regard to the Battle of the Little Big Horn fought June 25th and 26th, 1876:

1st. On the morning of the 25th of June 1876, the 7th Cavalry, Lieutenant Colonel G.A. Custer commanding, operating against the hostile Indians in Montana Territory, near the Little Big Horn River, was divided into four battalions, two of which were commanded by Colonel Custer in person, with the exception of one company in charge of the pack train, one by Major Reno and one by Captain F.W. Benteen.

This division took place from about twelve (12) to fifteen (15) miles from the scene of the battle or battles afterwards fought.

The column under Captain Benteen received orders to move to the left for an indefinite distance (to the first

and second valleys) hunting Indians, with orders to charge any it might meet with.

The battalion under Major Reno received orders to draw out of the column, and doing so marched parallel and only a short distance from the column commanded by Colonel Custer.

2nd. About three or four miles from what afterwards was found to be the Little Big Horn River where the fighting took place, Major Reno received orders to move forward as rapidly as he thought prudent until coming up with the Indians who were reported fleeing, he would charge them and drive everything before him, and would receive the support of the column under Colonel Custer.

3rd. In obedience to the orders (given by Colonel Custer), Captain Benteen marched to the left (south) at an angle of about forty-five degrees, but meeting an impracticable country, was forced by it to march more to his right than the angle above indicated, and nearer approaching a parallel route to the trail followed by the rest of the command.

4th. Major Reno, in obedience to the orders given him, moved on at a fast trot on the main Indian trail until reaching the Little Big Horn River, which he forded, and halted for a few moments to reform his battalion.

After reforming, he marched the battalion forward towards the Indian village, downstream or in a northerly direction, two companies in line of battle and one in support, until about half way to the point where he finally halted, when he brought the company in reserve, forward to the line of battle, continuing the movement at a fast trot or gallop until after passing over a distance of about two miles, when he halted and dismounted to fight on foot, at a point of timber upon which the right flank of his battalion rested.

After fighting in this formation for less than half an hour, the Indians passing to his left rear, and appearing in his front, the skirmish line was withdrawn to the timber and the fight continued for a short time, half and hour or forty-five minutes in all, when the command, or nearly all of it, was mounted, formed and at a rapid gait was withdrawn to a hill on the opposite side of the river.

In this movement, one officer and about 16 soldiers and citizens were left in the woods besides one wounded man or more, two citizens and 13 soldiers rejoining the command afterwards.

In this retreat, Major Reno's battalion lost some 29 men, killed and wounded, and three officers, including Doctor DeWolf, killed.

In the meantime, Captain Benteen having carried out as far as was practicable the spirit of his orders, turned in the direction of the route taken by the remainder of the regiment and reaching the trail, followed it to near the crossing of the Little Big Horn, reaching there about the same time Reno on the hill.

Forty minutes or an hour later, the pack train which had been left behind on the trail, by the rapid movement of the command, and the delays incident to its march, joined the united command, which then consisted of seven companies, together with about thirty (30) or thirty-five (35) men belonging to the companies under Colonel Custer.

6th. After detaching Benteen's and Reno's columns, Colonel Custer moved with his immediate command on the trail, followed by Reno, to a point within about one mile of the river, where he diverged to the right (or northward), following the general direction of the river to a point about four miles below that afterwards taken by Major Reno, where he and his command were destroyed by the hostiles.

The last living witness of this march, Trumpeter Martin, left Colonel Custer's command when it was about two miles distant from the field where it afterwards met its fate.

There is nothing more in evidence as to this command, save that firing was heard proceeding from its direction, from about the time Reno retreated from the bottom up to the time the pack train was approaching the position on the hill.

All firing which indicated fighting was concluded before the final preparations in Major Reno's command for the movement which was afterwards attempted.

7th. After the distribution of ammunition and a proper provision for the wounded men, Major Reno's entire command moved down the river in the direction it was thought Custer's column had taken, and in which it was known General Terry's command was to be found.

This movement was carried sufficiently far to discover that its continuance would imperil the entire command, upon which it returned to the position formerly occupied, and made a successful resistance, 'till succor reached it.

The defense of the position on the hill was a heroic one against fearful odds.

The conduct of the officers throughout was excellent,

and while subordinates in some instances did more for the safety of the command by brilliant displays of courage than did Major Reno, there was nothing in his conduct which requires an aversion from this Court.

It is the conclusion of this Court, in view of all the facts in evidence, that no further proceedings are necessary in this case, and it expresses this opinion in compliance with the concluding clause of order convening the Court.

Jno. H. King,
Colonel 9th Infantry
President
J. M. Lee
1st Lieutenant and Adjutant 9th Infantry
Recorder.

Many historians and authors have agreed with at least one portion of the Reno Court of Inquiry's findings:

... while subordinates in some instances did more for the safety of the command brilliant displays of courage than did Major Reno....

Private Peter Thompson was a soldier with Custer's command the day of the Little Big Horn battle, who fell behind the main force and escaped the massacre. Joining with Renos' force, Thompson left perhaps the most critical opinion of Major Reno's behavior during the battle of the Little Big Horn. He said:

As I stood looking at him I could not help wondering if he knew what his duty was. Here he was with about four hundred men surrounded by hordes of savages. If ever soldiers needed a good example it was here. Did he show such an example?...

Did he show how a true soldier should act under difficulties? And die if needs be in the defense of his country? No! Instead of this he kept himself in a hole where there was no danger of being struck and no doubt would have pulled the hole in after him if he could [have].

Captain Tom Weir

CHAPTER 13

Major Reno's Accuser — Chicago Tribune Editorial — The Prediction of Army Officers — The Secret of the Reno Court of Inquiry — Lieutenant Jesse Lee's Letter — Captain French's Letter — Captain Weir — Was the Truth Told? — The Enlisted Men's Petition — Exhibits at the Reno Court of Inquiry — Exhibit Two — Testimony Concerning Exhibit Two — Why Was the Map Changed? — Master of Deceit

Many unanswered questions remain about the Reno Court of Inquiry of 1879, which, with the benefit of perspective, become evident. Many of these questions are not new. Major Reno's "accuser," Frederick Whittaker, ventured his opinion of the Reno Court of Inquiry in a public letter which appeared in various newspapers around the country not long after the Reno Court of Inquiry adjourned:

> *With the exception of the brief statement into which I was led by your accomplished reporter some two weeks ago, the people of Chicago may have observed that I have not hitherto attempted to comment on the progress of the evidence in the Reno Court of Inquiry, though that inquiry was called forth by my own letter to congress last spring.*
>
> *Owing to the precautions of Major Reno's counsel, and the orders under which the court was acting, I was barred out from my rightful position of accuser or prosecutor in the inquiry, on the narrowest technical grounds. I therefore had no opportunity to say one word in Custer's or my own behalf in court, and was obliged to remain a silent and powerless spectator of events in which I had so keen an interest.*
>
> *Now that the trial is over, and that Reno and the recorder have said their say, it becomes my duty, as the biographer of the late General Custer, to speak, if only for a moment, and put the position of Custer as well as my own in their proper light, to prevent future misunderstandings.*
>
> *I came to Chicago for two purposes – to vindicate Custer as a soldier and myself as a man of truth. The character of Reno was a mere incident in which I had no special interest.*
>
> *As far as Reno is concerned, if the army can endure him, after the double exposures of 1877 and 1879, I am sure I can, for I am not obliged to associate with him. Therefore, let him pass down to history as these trials show him.*
>
> *In the aspect of the case represented by me, however, the evidence adduced before this court shows all that I could desire. Before the date of this inquiry, Custer stood charged before the country with two military crimes – rashness and disobedience. Grant, Reno, Benteen and a host of others charged him with the first; General Terry and ex-President Grant with the last.*
>
> *This trial has established facts which prove Custer to have been, not rash, but prudent; not defeated by the enemy, but abandoned by the treachery or timidity of his subordinates. Hereafter, any man who accuses*

Custer of bringing on his own fate by rashness will write himself down a false defamer, who goes against the facts of history.

The charge of disobedience has yet to be met, and I promise the people of the United States it shall be met and refuted at no distant date, before Congress.

Author Whittaker's claim of "rightful position of accuser" at the Reno Court of Inquiry is debatable, considering he was a civilian in a military court. His attempt to strengthen his own case by attacking the character of Major Reno probably was not as successful as Whittaker intended either. However, his threat to take further action "before Congress" was obviously a statement which would cause some to take notice and, not long after the publication of Whittaker's letter, a reply was printed in several newspapers.

Major Reno's Accuser

To the Editor.

You have not failed, I trust, to observe two singular exhibitions of the workings of the mind of Mr. Whittaker, the accuser in the Reno case. He had made in his writings a public charge against Colonel Benteen, who commanded a battalion in the fight upon the Little Big Horn River, of disobedience to orders and of failure to support General Custer in proper manner, and of thereby assisting in the destruction of that officer and of his soldiers.

A charge so grave would rest, I thought, on reliable evidence, and be made only after long and dispassionate examination. But the reverse of the truth, and Mr. Whittaker is compelled, after talking with Martin the trumpeter, who carried the order to Colonel Benteen, to withdraw this charge, and to confess that it had been recklessly made against that gallant officer.

A slander so wide as this renders him who utters it unworthy to speak the thoughts and sentiment of honorable men. He will, no doubt, be dissatisfied with the result of the trial, and by agitation and the newspapers and appeals to Congress try to extend the sensation so long as it assists to advertise and sell his book.

Justice.

If Mr. Whittaker's letter could be termed defamatory towards Major Reno, then the letter by "Justice," whoever that person was, can be characterized as completely ignoring the proceedings of the Reno Court of Inquiry and instead focusing upon Whittaker himself. This "shoot the messenger" strategy is common enough, especially when the issue is an important one. However, "Justice" provided nothing of substance for Reno's defense.

Chicago Tribune Editorial

The two extreme points of view concerning the Reno Court of Inquiry were defined by Mr. Whittaker's letter and "Justice's" response. The *Chicago Tribune* then published an editorial which provided perhaps as much middle ground as possible:

The main facts came out about the same, while the details, as each witness presented his view of the case, constantly changed and, therefore, to a certain extent, the account of each witness was that of a new battle. In fact there have been furnished about as many different variations of the skirmish and battle of Little Big Horn as there were people telling the story. Not only where the variations novel within this limit, but they were full of action, fire, interest.

In fine, the investigation has been full of romance and excitement from beginning to end; and so much has this been the case that the public would not have regretted had there been more of it.

It is not often that the world has the opportunity to thus witness the analysis of great events by the mouths of actors, given under the solemnity of an oath and accompanied by all the rigors of a cross-examination.

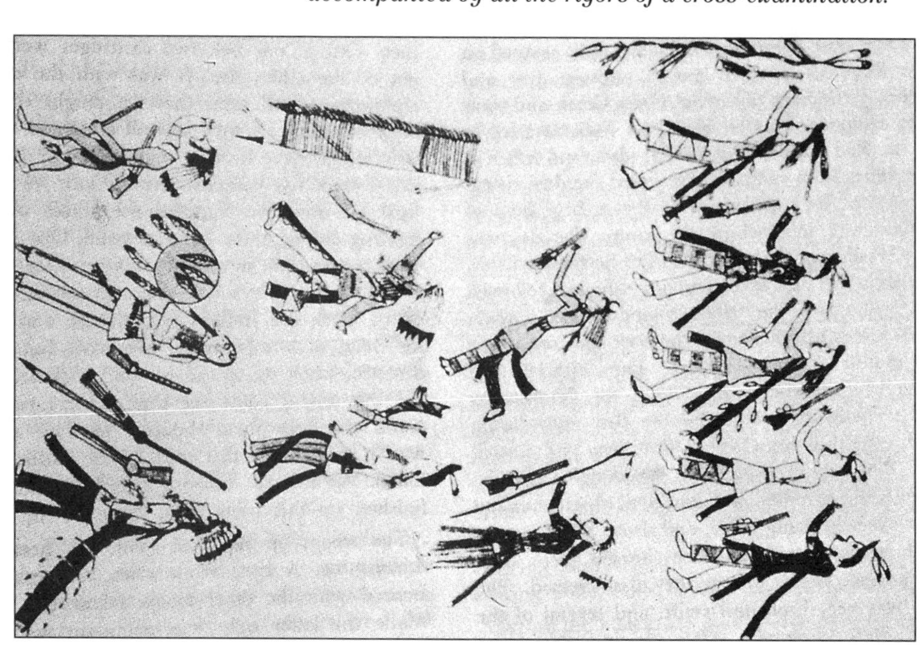

After all, beyond the enjoyment and excitement of the event, what good has been accomplished? Has anybody's judgment been affected by the testimony to the extent that such a one is now clear as to the guilt or innocence of the accused?

It hardly seems probable that any more has been done than to fortify preconceived opinions, and that those who believed Reno guilty before the trial began, as well as those who were assured of his innocence, are of the same opinion still, with the difference that the evidence has strengthened their already-formed conclusions. If there are any who had no conclusions on the matter, such people after having read the testimony will agree that a more difficult case, with reference to reaching a conclusion, has rarely been known.

If the commission can reach any decision from this testimony, it will be one surrounded with doubt. They may find that a preponderance of the evidence is on one side or the other; and yet about all this fact will admit of is that if the inquiry had gone a little further, more witnesses might have thrown the preponderance in an opposite direction.

The Prediction of Army Officers

Was the Reno Court of Inquiry of 1879 a fair and impartial court proceeding? Or was it, as Whittaker claimed, an event of which the primary purpose was to defame Custer?

Interestingly, on January 18, 1879, before the Reno Court of Inquiry convened, the *Army and Navy Journal* published an article entitled, *"The Prediction of Army Officers."* This article would seem to validate Whittaker's concern about the impartiality of the Reno Court of Inquiry:

The President of the court stated, however, that the inquiry would not be limited to the charges of Whittaker. "We shall" he said, "go outside of it. We intend to cover the whole ground."

The officers attached to General Sheridan's staff express no opinion regarding the charges of cowardice alleged against Major Reno. They believe, however, that the court will be able to elicit a vast amount of highly interesting testimony relating to the fight in which Custer and his band met with extermination.

Other officers of the Army, temporarily sojourning here, are more outspoken in their views of the case. Some of them do not scruple to say that the inquiry will result in tarnishing the luster of General Custer's name and renown as a warrior.

They are of opinion that it will be shown that Custer, by a hot-headed haste to achieve all the glory for himself, and by a virtual disobedience of orders, brought about the awful disaster which appalled the nation and the world.

This, they think will be one of the results of the inquiry; not that Custer's conduct is under investigation, but because in showing what Reno did or did not do to avert the calamity, it will also be shown in what degree Custer was alone responsible for his own lamented fate.

The testimony of Captain Benteen of the 7th Cavalry will, it is claimed in the Army circles, throw much light on the conduct, not only of Major Reno, but of General Custer as well. It is understood that Benteen and Custer were at feud for many years, but the Captain has the credit of being a fair-minded, honorable gentleman, and his friends say he will not allow his prejudices to warp his duties as a witness.

It should be noted that the "President of the court" stated, "we intend to cover the whole ground" and that it was also predicted by "other officers" that, among other accusations, "it would be shown" that Custer was guilty of "a virtual disobedience of orders."

Coincidentally, Captain Benteen is named in the article, apparently as a source for some of the information contained in it. Once again Benteen demonstrated his ability to skillfully arrive ahead of the issue at hand, in this instance the Reno Court of Inquiry. Fortunately, as the article stated, Captain Benteen would not allow "his prejudices to warp his duties as a witness," a statement which belongs in the inventory of other "Benteenisms."

The Secret of the Reno Court of Inquiry

On March 22, 1879, an article appeared in the *Army and Navy Journal* entitled "The Secret of the Reno Court of Inquiry":

The matter of the Court of Inquiry in the case of Major Reno of the 7th Cavalry, and the proceedings in that case, have been discussed very generally, and have been a subject of great interest to all officers of the Army.

There are few, if any, officers who have ever considered that the action of Mr. Frederick Whittaker, the biographer of General Custer, was fair or honest, but no officer of the Army has considered it necessary to come to the defense of Major Reno or Captain Benteen, for the reason that they could not do so without criticizing in an unfavorable manner the conduct of General Custer, who had paid the penalty of his rashness and disobedience of orders with his life.

General Terry, who was the commanding general of the Department, who was serving with the troops in the field, gave explicit and particular orders to Custer not to attack the Indians, but to inform him [General Terry]

if he discovered their whereabouts.

The success of the campaign depended entirely upon obedience to orders and upon Custer being able to attack the Indians from different directions at the same moment with the whole force of the command.

About this time, Colonel Weir of the 7th Cavalry was detailed on recruiting service and stationed in New York. Weir's only weakness was that of many other generous and whole-souled men too craving an appetite for exhilarating stimulants, and through it Whittaker found his opportunity.

As it had become pretty generally understood that Custer's mistake had been a fatal one for him in more senses than one, his "biographer" concluded to follow Josh Billings' advice as to the proper method of making a correction – by cussing somebody else for it. Weir died suddenly, and immediately after his demise there began to appear, from time to time, throughout the press of the entire country, insinuations against Reno and Benteen.

Hints soon became definite charges, and Custer was promoted from hero to martyr; even the subscription limitation on the circulation of the book was less rigorously enforced. Whittaker returned to the attack nobly and was again equal to the emergency.

Now, after Colonel Weir was dead, Whittaker professed to have an affidavit made by the dead officer, setting forth that Custer was overwhelmed and his command massacred because of the treachery of both Reno and Benteen.

On the meeting of the Court of Inquiry, Whittaker was asked to produce the affidavit. "But," says Mr. Price, "he declined." Two reasons effectively influenced its suppression: the first and merely nominal one was that Weir had never made the affidavit alleged; the second and material drawback was the presence of Captain Charles Braden, late of the 7th, now retired because of wounds received in the Yellowstone fight of 1873.

This gentleman was in Chicago to testify that he had been a guest at the same hotel in New York with Weir, some time before, and up to within a few days of the latter's death, and that Weir had frequently complained that Whittaker was constantly pestering him to sign a paper which stated that Reno failed to assist Custer when he could have done it, and was therefore responsible for the massacre.

He further expressed not only his intention of not doing it, but expressed his opinion of the self-sacrificing patriot who made the proposal in the strongest language and most emphatic eloquence of a trooper.

Those who followed the proceedings of the Court of Inquiry will recollect that during the long and patient examination, all of the officers who were examined gave it as their opinion that Reno did the very best thing that could have been done under the circumstances, and the court gave as its opinion that there was nothing in the conduct of Major Reno which called for the animadversion of the court.

But Mr. Whittaker again comes to the front, and in the Chicago papers of the 12th ultimo, he informs the public that, "As the biographer of the late General Custer, he deemed it his duty to promise the people of the United States that he would see that Congress righted the reputation of General Custer, and that at no late day."

The memory of Custer would not have been assailed, and his notorious incapacity would not have been spoken of if some overanxious relatives and friends, egged on by an interested writer, had not seen fit to endeavor to blast the good reputations of deserving men in order to make money out of a worthless book.

The brave men who went down to certain death with Custer knew to a man that they were the victims of an unholy ambition, and the widows and orphans made on that day of massacre would have shed their tears in silence and without murmuring. But these people who seek to "right the reputation of General Custer," will only succeed in making people think, as did General Sturgis, that if a monument must be erected to General Custer, it had better be in some spot where no human eye could ever gaze upon it.

Ebbitt.

How the issues concerning the Reno Court of Inquiry of

1879, and the Battle of the Little Big Horn, could evolve into a controversy over a monument, is interesting. The weakness of those attacking the position of Mr. Whittaker, however, becomes evident by the fact that the most irrelevant issues suddenly became important in diverting attention away from closer scrutiny of the actual Reno Court of Inquiry proceedings. Yet, over time, more facts would emerge concerning the Reno Court of Inquiry which would be unflattering to Major Reno, Captain Benteen, and the court proceeding itself.

Lieutenant Jesse Lee's Letter

Lieutenant Jesse Lee was the recorder at the Reno Court of Inquiry. Lee did perhaps as good a job as anyone could have, considering the handicaps, and yet, as he found out more about the actual facts concerning the Battle of the Little Big Horn over time, his perspectives did not so much as "change" from his closing statement at the court proceedings as they did "evolve."

After the publication of the memoirs of General Nelson Miles, Lieutenant Lee wrote Miles a letter concerning the Battle of the Little Big Horn, as described by Miles in his book:

> *Your chapter on Custer's last fight is a vindication I have long wished to see from the pen of one who writes "without fear of favor or affection"; one whose potent words of truth will carry conviction to millions who have wanted light in clean, straight-cut rays about that tragic event.*
>
> *I thank God that you have lived to spread before the world what I believe to be "the truth, the whole truth and nothing but the truth" about Custer.*
>
> *I was Recorder of the Reno Court of Inquiry, but the proceedings were never published in full. I talked with many Indians who were in that fight, and your chapter is almost identical with what I learned from a variety of sources.*

Apparently, Lieutenant Lee further contemplated the role that history had placed upon him and, several months after writing General Miles, Lee wrote to Mrs. Custer with his opinions on the issues:

> *I want to say to you in all frankness, that at one time I was in some degree influenced by the prejudiced opinions of those whose motives I did not then understand, and whose sources of information I then had no means of testing. But soon after, I was brought into close contact with thousands of Indians – the Sioux, Cheyennes and others; and in Jan. 1879, I was Recorder of the Reno Court of Inquiry: a year later, I visited the field of battle.*
>
> *Now, I tried to be honest and fairminded, and allow nothing but facts to make an impression on my mind. So it came about in the light of long and confidential talks with Indians under my charge; in the light of what was said to me by witnesses before they went on the stand, and in the light of much of that testimony on the stand; and finally in the light of my visit to the field, my judgment could no more escape the conclusion of facts than to deny that I am penning these lines.*
>
> *That conclusion I referred to in my letter to General Miles, and I am glad you consider it "generous and fair"– it is true! I do not believe any unprejudiced mind – any one whose heart is free from ... jealousy could with a knowledge of all the facts come to any other conclusion. When I got to the facts, it was then easy to understand how self-interest influenced opinions.*
>
> *How jealousy being unopposed could unmask its horrid front and loosen its tongue of calumny with none to answer, how the living could extol themselves for prudence and delay, and condemn the dead as rash and impetuous, how authority though inexperienced sought to evade responsibility through a loophole of escape. Had someone blundered? Then how easy to censure those who would not answer.*
>
> *It was both cruel and unjust for anyone to send that dispatch: "Orders were disobeyed, but the penalty paid." This dispatch reveals both weakness and incompetency. The sender, I believe, knew but little if anything about Indians, but he did know General Custer, and it verges on imbecility to suppose that anyone would expect those Indians to be held in position several days by one column waiting and making it convenient for another column to attack them.*
>
> *I was glad to see that General Miles had gotten at all the material facts, and of course there could be but one conclusion. I think Captain Philo Clark, in his life time, got the facts, and the conclusion was the same. Major Godfrey, when Captain in the 7th Cavalry, wrote a very fair article on this subject.*
>
> *There has been so much misrepresentation, so much from personal and interested motives that it would seem that the truth is hard to separate from the chaff ... I believe as an unprejudiced person, I have had better opportunities to get at the facts than almost any other person. These facts show beyond successful contradiction:*
>
> *1st. That General Custer was not disobeying General Terry's orders in attacking the Indians. Any other course under the circumstances would have been ridiculous and absurd.*
>
> *2nd. Major Reno, according to General Gibbon's testi-*

mony, left – abandoned a splendid position where he threatened the entire village, and thus enabled the entire force of Indians to concentrate on General Custer who was thus compelled to meet them with less than 2/5 of the effective force of his regiment.

3rd. Major Reno's disastrous retreat resulted in keeping out of the battle at a critical period fully 3/5 of the effective force, and in doing this, all chance for victory over the Indians was lost.

Captain French's Letter

One witness who did not appear at the Reno Court of Inquiry was Captain Thomas H. French. While his testimony would have been interesting, French was under court-martial and did not attend the court. He did, however, telegraph a letter which was then published in various newspapers:

Bismarck Dakota, Jan. 18. – Captain French of the 7th Cavalry, at Fort Lincoln, and a delayed witness before the Reno Court at Chicago, stated in an interview today that he did not see Reno from the evening of the 25th until noon of the 26th, when the Indians were weakening.

During the hardest portion of the fight, Reno was hid. French was walking about most of the time and claims that he could not find any one who did see Reno.

Captain Weir

Another witness who did not appear, and whose testimony could have been pivotal, was Captain Thomas Weir. Weir did not attend the Reno court for a very good reason: he was dead. Weir died suddenly on December 9, 1876, less than six months after the Battle of the Little Big Horn.

His obituary, which was printed in the *Army and Navy Journal*, was:

The Army will receive with surprise as well as with deep regret, the announcement of the death of Brevet Lieutenant Colonel Thomas B. Weir, Captain 7th Cavalry.

Colonel Weir was in the prime of life, 38 years of age, and no preliminary announcement of illness preceded the report of his death, which occurred suddenly in New York on Saturday, December 9, of congestion of the brain.

Colonel Weir was buried on Governor's Island with military honors on Wednesday, December 14.

Captain Weir's death was, to say the least, convenient. It removed the one person who, more than any other, could have been embarrassing to certain surviving officers of the 7th Cavalry. One author commented upon Weir's death in a later book and said:

Weir took suddenly ill in early December. He had begun a correspondence with Libbie Custer and had confided that there was something he could tell her in private that he could not set down on paper. His illness was never accurately diagnosed.

Thomas B. Weir died on 9 December 1876 of unknown causes, prompting rumors that he had been poisoned because of something he knew. His death has been attributed to "congestion of the brain" and "melancholia." He had gone to bed shortly before he died and refused to eat anything.

Weir may simply have died of a stroke; the notion that he was murdered because he was in on some dark secret is absolutely preposterous.

Interestingly, Captain Weir apparently believed there was a "dark secret" he was "in on" and before his death, he wrote Mrs. Custer:

I know if we were all of us alone in the parlor, at night, the curtains all down and everybody else asleep, one or the other of you would make me tell you everything I know.

Author Frederick Whittaker would later say he had an affidavit concerning the Battle of the Little Big Horn from a deceased 7th Cavalry officer, identified as Captain Weir. This affidavit, if it ever existed, has never surfaced.

Was the Truth Told?

There were a number of statements made after the Court of Inquiry of 1879 which seemed to question the sincerity of some of the witnesses, as well as the propriety of the conduct at the hearing of Major Reno and his counsel, Attorney Gilbert.

Lieutenant Godfrey was cautious, as usual, but he seemed to hint that pressure had been brought to bear on some of those testifying:

I never heard that there was a compact by officers as to testimony. I only know that I was importuned many times by Benteen, and by others, to call on Reno and visit in his room, drink his whiskey and smoke his cigars, etc.

I did know by circumstances that there was a lot of drinking going on in his room. I refrained from reading the proceedings of the Court, when I overheard someone express surprise at the testimony given by one witness, which was summarized by "he believes in Reno."

So, I did not visit Reno nor read the testimony given during the trial.

In an interview with Walter Camp, Fred Gerard, the interpreter, was less concerned about whom he offended and later directly accused Major Reno of attempting to influence those who were to testify before the Reno Court of Inquiry:

When I got to Chicago, Reno sent for me and treated me very hospitably and had me talk with his lawyer. This fellow tried to pick out of me what I was going to testify to, but I talked only in general terms.

After awhile, Reno came in and Gilbert said to him in an undertone: "This man is all right; he knows nothing that is damaging." After I got on the stand, I told some things that did not set very well with them, and Gilbert tried all manner of tricks, browbeating, etc., to get me to contradict myself, and at times our tilts at each other were rather bitter.

I understood from inside sources at the time that much that passed between us was not going to be permitted to go on record.

After I came off the stand, a commissioned officer of the 7th Cavalry with whom I was on very friendly terms, who was at the Little Big Horn, took me aside, grasped my hand, and said: "Gerard, I want to congratulate you for telling the truth so fearlessly and for maintaining your story unshaken. When I go on the stand, I will tell them a few things that I know." I replied by saying: "I am wondering whether you will or not." He said: "Well, just wait until you see."

Shortly after this, he and I were together when a porter came up with a note which he opened and later said: "An invitation to a champagne supper." I said: "Yes, and it will also be a blanket for you."

In due course, he was called as a witness, and I heard his testimony, and upon meeting him later, I said: "Well, I noticed that when they got you on the stand, you were not as well informed as you intended to be," and he replied: "Well, Gerard, they have got the whip over us; they have some things in the pigeonholes that could be used to make me feel rather uncomfortable, and I thought there was no use trying to stand against the whole gang by myself."

Gerard said the general understanding among all whom he talked with confidentially was that any officer who made himself obnoxious to the defense would incur the wrath of certain officers in pretty high authority in certain department headquarters farther west than Washington, and not as far west as St. Paul. There was much dining and wining all the time the trial was going on, and he knew the whole object was to compromise certain of the witnesses.

Before the trial began, he and Dr. Porter and certain of the officers were called into a room to talk over what information they could give on certain points. Dr. Porter admitted that he could testify thus and so in reference to certain pertinent questions, but said he hoped he would not be called upon to do so.

The trial had not proceeded far before it came to be known among the witnesses, including commissioned officers, some of whom were outspoken to me in confidence, that the way of the innocent and truthful could be made heard. It was amusing therefore to see how badly some of the memories had failed in the space of less than three years since the battle.

It was made the business of certain ones active for the defense to get hold of all the doubtful witnesses before they were called and entertain them well. On such occasions, they were cautiously sounded and discreetly primed.

Trumpeter John Martin also was interviewed by Walter Camp and said he believed that it had been desired he not tell all he knew at the Reno Court of Inquiry.

Shortly before the Reno Court of Inquiry convened, the scout George Herendeen had written to a newspaper and made an interesting claim:

I have read a good deal of late in the Herald *and other papers about the battle of the Little Big Horn, much of which is incorrect and calculated to mislead the public.*

If Herendeen was correct in his charge that information "calculated to mislead the public" was being published before the Reno Court of Inquiry, then it would seem the course the investigation was to take was being plotted before the first witness was called.

Captain Benteen wrote a letter in which he commented upon his testimony at the Reno Court of Inquiry, a letter which clears up any doubt as to the honesty of his testimony.

I heard not a criticism on the nature of my evidence in Reno and case.... Gilbert has written me since that it was wholly satisfactory to Army people ... they knew just what I thought long before the trial. I was closed mouth as I could be.

Captain Benteen also wrote:

Of course, I knew a great many things about the fight that isn't essential that the world should know.

Although it was magnanimous of Captain Benteen to admit to posterity that he demonstrated his usual perfidy at the Reno Court of Inquiry, that fact is also obvious to anyone who examines his testimony and compares it to the known facts. The simple fact is that Benteen did not tell the truth, and he later admitted as much.

The Enlisted Men's Petition

Soon after the Battle of the Little Big Horn, a petition was circulated among the surviving enlisted soldiers of the regiment. This petition was addressed to the president of the United States and requested the promotion of Major Reno and Captain Benteen to replace those killed at the battle.

Camp near Big Horn on Yellowstone River.
July 4, 1876
To his Excellency the President and
and the Honorable Representatives
of the United States

Gentlemen:

We, the enlisted men the survivors of the battle on the Heights of Little Big Horn River, on the 25th and 26th of June 1876, of the 7th Regiment of Cavalry who subscribe our names to this petition, most earnestly solicit the President and Representatives of our Country, that the vacancies among the Commissioned Officers of our Regiment, made by the slaughter of our brave, heroic, now lamented Lieutenant Colonel George A. Custer, and the other noble dead Commissioned Officers of our Regiment who fell close by him on the bloody field, daring the savage demons to the last, be filled by the Officers of the Regiment only.

That Major M.A. Reno, be our Lieutenant Colonel vice Custer, killed; Captain F. W. Benteen our Major vice Reno, promoted.

The other vacancies to be filled by officers of the Regiment by seniority.

Your petitioners know this to be contrary to the established rule of promotion, but prayerfully solicit a deviation from the usual rule in this case, as it will be conferring a bravely fought for and justly merited promotion on officers who by their bravery, coolness and decision on the 25th and 26th of June 1876, saved the lives of every man now living of the 7th Cavalry who participated in the battle, one of the most bloody on record and one that would have ended with the loss of life of every officer and enlisted man on the field only for the position taken by Major Reno, which we held with bitter tenacity against fearful odds to the last.

To support this assertion – had our position been taken 100 yards back from the brink of the heights overlooking the river, we would have been entirely cut off from water; and from those heights, the Indian demons would have swarmed in hundreds, picking off our men by detail, and before midday June 25th not an officer or enlisted man of our Regiment would have been left to tell of our dreadful fate, as we then would have been completely surrounded.

With prayerful hope that our petitions be granted, we have the honor to forward it through our Commanding Officer.

Very Respectfully,
(236 Signatures)

The enlisted soldiers' petition was described by one historian as:

... a distinguished mark of respect to their commandership and valor Major Reno and Captain Benteen, bestowed upon them by the survivors of the regiment, and constituting an outstanding landmark of the loyalty of men and officers, and of grateful and affectionate regard of the men of the regiment for all its surviving officers.

This type of laudatory response was exactly what the document was intended to inspire, and should have, had it truly been a spontaneous outpouring of gratitude by the enlisted soldiers of the regiment. The first indication that it was not came from a commentary by Lieutenant Godfrey years later:

The fact is that we were so stunned, overcome as it were, from the fatigue and strain of the several days before, during and after the battle, and its results, that we did not fully coordinate the events.

The men were grateful that we had escaped the disaster, and the petitions were put before them at the psychological time to gain their signatures. We know how such things can be set in motion.

There were several men of the 7th Cavalry at Soldiers

Home and in Washington in 1921 and 1922 who, when asked if they had signed the petition, denied ever having had such a thought, yet their signatures proved genuine.

Not one would admit that he had signed, until shown his signature.

In commenting upon the importance of the "psychological time" to have had the soldiers sign the petition, Lieutenant Godfrey was certainly correct. Godfrey fails to mention, however, the absolute authority the officers had over the enlisted men and the endless ways life for the common soldier could have been made miserable for those who defied that authority.

The petition listed 236 names and, as the survivors numbered almost 400, it is significant that a large number of the enlisted men did not sign the document. As the purpose of this petition was to place Major Reno and Captain Benteen in command of the regiment, it is certainly logical that a great effort would have been put into pressuring as many soldiers as possible into signing the petition by these two officers.

Since the soldiers Lieutenant Godfrey spoke to were unaware that they had signed the petition, then perhaps those who actually had taken the time to read the petition had refused to add their names. How many of the other signatories actually knew what they were signing is an open question.

Major Edward S. Luce was a former superintendent of the Custer Battlefield National Monument and, while acting in this role, Major Luce noted certain discrepancies on the enlisted men's petition. Major Luce then had this document examined by the F.B.I.

Besides those who had been coerced into signing, those who had the petition placed before them at the correct "psychological time," and those who had no idea of what they were actually signing, the F.B.I. discovered "79 probable forgeries." Soldiers who signed the payroll with an X had, besides taking part in a strenuous military campaign and fighting a terrific battle, also found the time to learn to write and had signed the petition with a full signature. Other enlisted men on detached service hundreds of miles away had, through some mysterious power, managed to also sign the petition.

The enlisted men's petition, this "outstanding landmark," was, in fact, a flagrant forgery. Besides receiving credibility by publication in the newspapers, which was undoubtedly one of the petition's purposes, it also prompted a reply from General Sherman:

The judicious and skillful conduct of Major Reno and Captain Benteen is appreciated, but the promotions caused by General Custer's death have been made by the President and confirmed by the Senate; therefore, this petition can not be granted.

When the Sioux campaign is over, I shall be most happy to recognize the valuable service of both officers and men by granting favors or recommending actual promotion.

Promotion on the field of battle was Napoleon's favorite method of stimulating his officers and soldiers to deeds of heroism, but it is impossible in our service because commissions can only be granted by the President on the advice and consent of the Senate, and except in original vacancies, promotion in a regiment is generally, if not always, made on the rule of seniority.

It has been speculated that the probable author of the petition was First Sergeant Joseph McCurry of Captain Benteen's H Company. This spontaneous eruption of deceit and forgery, presumably, did not originate with McCurry alone. Captain Benteen would have been behind it and, if true, he was again staying one step ahead of any potential advisories. The enlisted men's petition was intended to "prove" the "grateful and affectionate regard" the soldiers had for Reno and Benteen, a purpose this document did serve until Major Luce and the F.B.I. exposed it to history.

What the enlisted men's petition now proves is that Captain Benteen well knew that he had something to hide and he was willing to take criminal measures to disguise the truth very soon after the Battle of the Little Big Horn. The enlisted men's petition was also dated one day earlier than Major Reno's report and this is significant, for it demonstrates Benteen was active in formulating the "official" version of the Battle of Little Big Horn.

Exhibits at the Reno Court of Inquiry

There were eleven exhibits of evidence presented at the Reno Court of Inquiry of 1879. Exhibits nine, ten, and eleven pertained to the enlisted soldiers' petition which Major Luce and the F.B.I. determined to be a document containing many apparent forgeries.

Of the other exhibits presented at the Reno Court of Inquiry, exhibit one opened the proceeding. Exhibit three was a list of questions Frederick Whittaker requested of the court that he be allowed to ask Major Reno. Exhibit five was a message to General Terry from Major Reno, dated June 27, 1876. Exhibit six was a list of casualties. Exhibit seven was a sketch map of the dead on Custer Hill. Exhibit eight was a request by Major Reno to the court that he be allowed to testify. These exhibits cannot be characterized as evidence pertaining to Major Reno's conduct at the Battle of the Little Big Horn.

Exhibit two was Lieutenant Maguire's map of the battlefield. Exhibit four was Major Reno's report of the battle. Exhibits nine, ten and eleven pertained to the enlisted men's petition, as previously mentioned. These are the only exhibits that can be characterized as significant evidence relating to Major Reno's conduct at the Battle of the Little Big Horn.

Exhibit four, Major Reno's report, contains many dis-

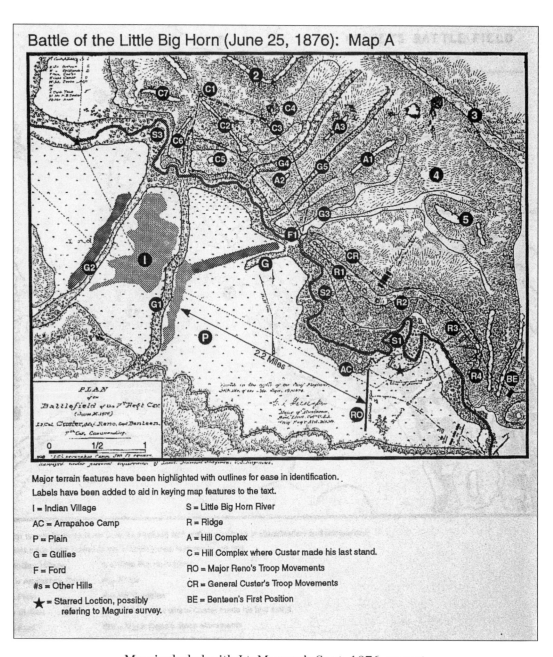

Battle of the Little Big Horn (June 25, 1876): Map A

2.2 Miles

0 1/2 1

Major terrain features have been highlighted with outlines for ease in identification.
Labels have been added to aid in keying map features to the text.

I = Indian Village	S = Little Big Horn River
AC = Arrapahoe Camp	R = Ridge
P = Plain	A = Hill Complex
G = Gullies	C = Hill Complex where Custer made his last stand.
F = Ford	RO = Major Reno's Troop Movements
#s = Other Hills	CR = General Custer's Troop Movements
★ = Starred Loction, possibly refering to Maguire survey.	BE = Benteen's First Position

Map included with Lt. Magure's Sept. 1876 report

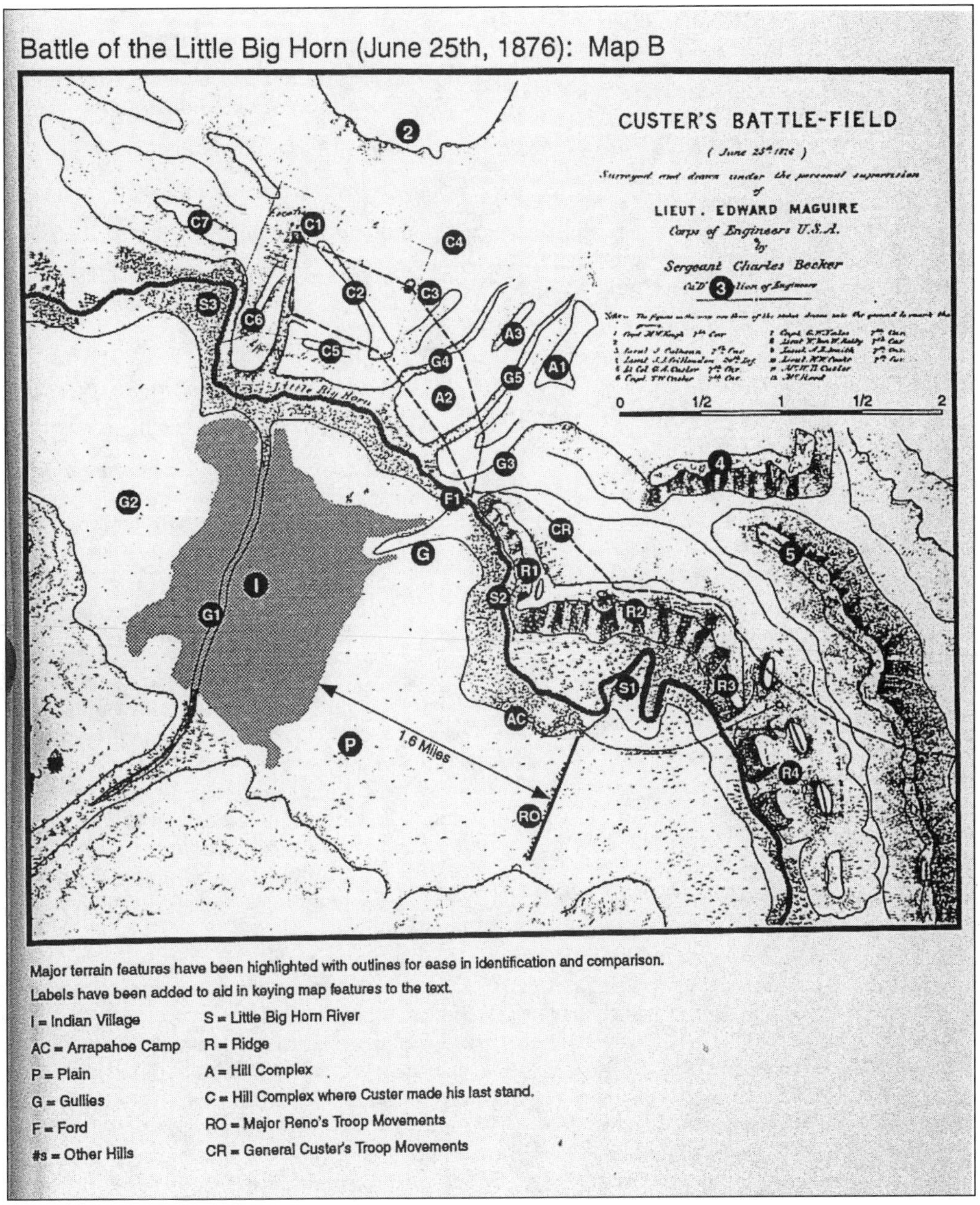

Battle of the Little Big Horn (June 25th, 1876): Map B

CUSTER'S BATTLE-FIELD

(June 25th 1876)

Surveyed and drawn under the personal supervision of

LIEUT. EDWARD MAGUIRE

Corps of Engineers U.S.A.

by

Sergeant Charles Becker

0 1/2 1 1/2 2

Major terrain features have been highlighted with outlines for ease in identification and comparison.
Labels have been added to aid in keying map features to the text.

I = Indian Village	S = Little Big Horn River
AC = Arrapahoe Camp	R = Ridge
P = Plain	A = Hill Complex
G = Gullies	C = Hill Complex where Custer made his last stand.
F = Ford	RO = Major Reno's Troop Movements
#s = Other Hills	CR = General Custer's Troop Movements

Map used at Reno Court of Inquiry, 1879

crepancies between it and Reno's testimony at the Court of Inquiry. The actual significance of exhibit four would seem to be its documentation of how Reno's version of the Battle of the Little Big Horn evolved between the date it was written, July 5, 1876, and Reno's testimony in 1879.

Exhibit Two

In describing a battle, any battle, perhaps no single detail could be more important than an accurate map. This is particularly true of the Battle of the Little Big Horn as there were no survivors from Custer's command to contest it.

Lieutenant McClernand would later write that he assisted in helping to prepare at least part of the map that was drawn on the spot by military officers before General Terry evacuated the battlefield. Lieutenant McClernand wrote:

I was not only among the first to visit the fatal field where Custer fell, but I also superintended the making of a considerable portion of the map thereof that will be found with the report of Lieutenant Maguire, Chief Engineer, Department of Dakota; printed with the report of the Chief of Engineers of the Army for 1876.

It is, perhaps, the best map that has been made of this field. I started the survey immediately upon the completion of our short march with Wallace and Hare to the foot of "Reno's Hill", and instructed my assistant, Sergeant Becker, as to the ground to be covered. He commenced the work at once and had covered about one-third of the territory concerned, when my superior, Lieutenant Maguire, said to General Terry that he thought the mapping of the battlefield should be under his own [Maguire's] *supervision.*

With the exception of one slight error the Maguire map is good.

Exhibit two at the Reno Court of Inquiry was offered into evidence and received as an identical copy of the map which Lieutenant Edward Maguire drew of the battlefield within a few days after he arrived there with General Terry's command on June 27, 1876. But it was clearly not the same map at all.

Lieutenant Maguire attached the map he prepared immediately after the battle to his report to the chief engineer of the Army, which he forwarded to Washington on September 9, 1876. That map was undated, but it was obviously prepared sometime between June 27 and September 9, 1876, and it was signed by a major of engineers, whose signature is illegible. The map that was submitted in evidence at the Reno Court of Inquiry shows on the legend that was "survey and drawn under the personal supervision of Lieutenant Edward Maguire by Sergeant Charles Becker, Company D, Battalion of Engineers."

Testimony Concerning Exhibit Two

As various participants at the Reno court testified, many of them took note that "exhibit two," the map, did not appear to them to be an accurate rendering of the battlefield.

Lieutenant Varnum testified:

... this map does not appear to me to be correct ... These bluffs on the map do not look right to me at all.

The scout George Herendeen said:

I don't like this map, I don't think it shows the country.

Lieutenant DeRudio:

In my opinion, this map is not correct as to the line of bluffs.

Lieutenant Godfrey:

The topography I do not think is correct.

The interpreter, Gerard, testified:

I think this map is wrong. My remembrance of the lay of the country and the course of the stream and where the skirmish line was, makes me think this map is wrong.

Lieutenant Wallace:

I would not know it to be the same piece of country.

While it might be argued that as untrained military officers the scout, Herendeen, and the interpreter, Gerard, perhaps, were unqualified to read the map accurately; the same cannot be said of the officers who testified. Several were West Point graduates, all were officers of some experience, and these soldiers would have been familiar and qualified to accurately read a map. Herendeen and Gerard both were frontiersmen of many years experience and, although probably self-taught, it is likely they had taken an interest in maps also.

Unfortunately, the court, with the exception of recorder Lee, ignored the many comments concerning the inaccuracies of exhibit two.

W. Kent King, in his book *Massacre,* identified a suspicious feature on the exhibit two map that did not appear on the map included with Lieutenant Maguire's report. This feature was a protruding ridge that does not appear on the modern geographical survey map either. What Mr. King noted in particular was a protruding ridge on the bluffs north and west of Major Reno's hilltop position. This ridge effectively blocks part of the view of the Little Big Horn Valley from Reno's final battlefield location. That portion of the valley is immediately across the Little Big Horn River from the point at which the trail Custer had taken along the bluffs came down to and crossed the river.

A cartography study compared these two maps in detail and in a 22-page report, dated April 1995, confirmed not only Mr. King's observation, but also noted numerous other discrepancies:

Those changes that appear on Map B that can be considered deliberate changes from Map A are:

1: The course of the river from Custer Ford (F1) to the meander (S2).

2: The shape of the ridge, and the addition of the spur (R1).

3: The shape and size of the Indian Village (1).

4. The distance of hill 2 from Custer Hill (C1-C2).

5: The placement of the legend, obscuring the major ridge (3).

6: The hills 4 and 5 that appear as distinct features and not as spurs of ridge 3.

7: The distance of Major Reno's skirmish line from the Indian Village.

8: The width of Major Reno's skirmish line.

9: The route General Custer took to Custer Ford (F1).

10: The final locations of Captain Yates' and Lieutenant Smith's commands (C6,C1).

The reason why these alterations were described as as "deliberate" was because the top half of both maps are extremely similar, indicating that:

It would seem highly probable that Map B was drafted with Map A as a visual guide ... the conclusion must be drawn that the changes were intentional. As [the second map] *and not* [the first map] *was used at the Reno Court of Inquiry, it may also be concluded that* [the second map] *was created to change the official view of the Battle of the Little Big Horn.*

Why Was the Map Changed?

Although the purpose of all of the changes to the Maguire map is not readily apparent, the purpose of some of them is.

The addition of the spur to the ridge line north of Major Reno's position had the obvious purpose of blocking the view from Reno's position toward the Indian village and any battle which occurred there. Any testimony at the Reno Court of Inquiry that said a battle could be seen down the valley becomes almost a moot point under defense cross-examination. How could a battle be seen through a geographical formation? It is true that this spur only serves its purpose partially, for part of the village is still visible on a direct line of sight from Reno's position. However, as this issue was never directly confronted at the Court of Inquiry, it can be speculated that this geographical formation served its purpose.

In making the distance between the Indian village and Major Reno's skirmish line in the valley much closer than the original map, the appearance was given that Reno was much more in the "thick of it" than he actually was. This would serve as additional justification for Reno's subsequent actions, including his retreat.

The prominent ridges and hills north and east of Major Reno's hill position, which were added to the Court of Inquiry map, gives the impression that Reno's hill position was much more corralled than it actually was geographically. The movement of the map legend to this area prohibits closer scrutiny of this area as well.

Some of the alterations are less clear in purpose although, perhaps, some of these changes were made merely to cause confusion. Certainly, this was the purpose in omitting on the map any line of movement indicating Captain Weir's advance to the Weir Peaks. This interesting event, according to both maps, simply did not occur.

If deliberate changes were made to the map used at the Reno Court of Inquiry, making significant alterations designed to distort the Battle of the Little Big Horn, then two conclusions must be drawn from this fact.

The first conclusion is that there was an intentional effort to manipulate and alter significant evidence pertaining to the Battle of the Little Big Horn.

The second conclusion is that the Reno Court of Inquiry was a proceeding affected by fraudulent evidence. Its conclusions were manipulated by Major Reno and his attorney and officers, including, apparently, those responsible for the "final" map and who assisted Reno and Gilbert in this conspiracy to obtain a sham outcome to the entire inquiry.

Master of Deceit

There was a cover-up of the facts after the Battle of the Little Big Horn. Although the manipulation of the facts involved many people, one person, over and over again, was intimately involved in these deliberate distortions.

With the arrival of General Terry on the battlefield, it was Captain Benteen who originated the farcical claim that Custer had "abandoned" the survivors.

Captain Benteen's distortions were quoted in General Terry's and Lieutenant Maguire's reports, and he probably was also instrumental in the formation of Major Reno's report.

Captain Benteen's own report was a calculated evasion of responsibility and he avoided any mention of his role at the battle after his arrival on Reno Hill. The subject of Captain Weir's advance was thus avoided entirely.

The enlisted soldiers' petition could not have been created without the knowledge and participation of Captain

Benteen and this fraudulent document probably originated under his direction, also.

In his published statements after the battle, Captain Benteen was manipulative and often flagrantly dishonest. It is difficult not to believe that in Major Reno's published accounts, if not created with Benteen's active participation, that Benteen was not lurking in the shadows behind Reno as he wrote them. At the Reno Court of Inquiry Captain Benteen's dishonesty is apparent and after these proceedings Benteen admitted as much.

In his last years Captain Benteen's letters to Private Goldin contained the slanderous rantings of a bitter and spiteful crackpot, as well as numerous and obvious dishonest statements.

Captain Benteen. Always Benteen. Calculated dishonesty, deliberate frauds, flagrant character assassinations, documented perjuries, published distortions. Always Benteen.

"Benteenism." A word that in the dictionary should be included in the definition of the word deceit.

Low Dog

CHAPTER 14

Custer's Retreat — Custer's Hill Position — Captain Weir's Advance — Was Custer Still Alive? — A Hard Fight — The Number of Indian Warriors Killed — Problem of Gunsmoke — Binoculars — The Guidon — Cowards Shot — Captain Benteen's Position — Custer's Decision — The Indians Attack — Custer Hill — Custer's Death

When Custer reached the ford across the Little Big Horn River where he was to cross and attack the Indian village, he was unopposed, as proven by the lack of dead horses or army casualties found there. Major Reno's attack on the village had, as the Indian participants admit, been a surprise. Custer's rapid advance across the bluffs to the east of the Little Big Horn Valley, and his subsequent attack on the eastern flank of the village, also had been a surprise.

From the Weir Peaks, Custer had seen Major Reno advancing in the valley and Captain Benteen coming up on the back trail. Custer's final plan, formed as he observed the battlefield from the Weir Peaks, was to cross the river and support Reno's attack in the valley. The attack then was to be as Custer had already ordered, supported by Benteen and the pack train hurrying forward. It is clear that Custer's intention was to bring over 250 soldiers and the pack train with the two battalions forward as quickly as possible to assist in exploiting the surprise attack.

When Custer formulated this final plan from the Weir Peaks he had no reason to suspect that his orders to Major Reno and Captain Benteen to advance and attack the Indian camp would not be carried out.

Custer did cross the Little Big Horn River and attack the Indian village to support Major Reno's attack, but Custer was forced to retreat because his attack was not supported by the other battalions of the regiment. That Custer was forced to retreat is not surprising. An unanswered riddle, however, is why Custer retreated to the north (to Custer Hill where the remains of his command were later found), instead of to the south, where the regiment was located.

Although Custer could not have known specifically what had happened to Major Reno, or why the regiment had not advanced to support him, he would have known the direction in which to find them. It would seem foolish to retreat away from the rest of the regiment and further disperse the regiment, especially since something had obviously gone wrong. Custer must have had a reason for retreating to the position he chose.

Custer's Retreat

Lieutenant Maguire's original map shows Custer's line of retreat to the final hill position to have been by two routes. One route follows the river northward before turning east to the hill, while the other is a more direct north-east route from the river ford where Custer crossed to the hill.

It would seem foolish, and very dangerous, to have divided the command on the retreat from the river ford when it is likely Custer had a multitude of Indian warriors following close behind. Custer's retreat would not have been like Major Reno's retreat, a disorganized route from the battlefield. It would have been orderly and there would have been a rear guard. Nevertheless, for Custer to divide his command for the retreat seems to be a strange decision.

One possibility that would explain the two paths to Custer Hill shown on the map, and also the choice of the final hill position, is that the two trails shown on the Maguire map were made at different times during the Battle of the Little Big Horn.

Custer had divided his command into two battalions. One battalion, under Captain Keogh, consisted of three companies: E, I, and L. The other, under Captain Yates, had two companies; C and F. In dividing his command into two battalions before the battle it is apparent Custer was foreseeing the possibility of using the two battalions as separate combat units.

Upon reaching the river ford there was no opposition waiting for Custer, as the evidence shows. Custer believed Major Reno would continue his attack in the valley and also that Captain Benteen and the pack train were on their way forward to reinforce them. It was characteristic at this point for Custer to have used the cavalryman's bluff and his own daring that had given him success in so many previous battles.

From the map evidence it would appear possible that at the river ford Captain Yates and his small battalion, about 80 soldiers, were sent further downstream to create a diversionary attack at a different point on the northeast flank of the village. This attack would have had the desired effect of further confusing the already surprised Indian camp, a key factor in achieving victory.

If this possibility is true, Custer's final attack plan was to have Captain Yates making another diversionary attack further downstream while Custer crossed the river ford and Major Reno created a main diversionary attack charging down the valley. Captain Benteen and the pack train were ordered to hurry forward to reinforce these initial attacks by Custer, Reno, and Yates.

It was the shock and panic of the surprise attack on the village from different directions that was Custer's goal, for the actual substance of the regiment was stretched dangerously thin. Custer's plan depended upon those in command positions following the orders that had been given them. If these orders were followed, the regiment would reunite in the village and hold off any attack by the Indian warriors while the village itself, or parts of it, were destroyed. Then the objective of the mission would have been achieved and the battle won by the 7th Cavalry.

Those in command positions did not follow their orders. After Major Reno's panicked retreat from the valley and his reinforcement by Captain Benteen and the pack train on Reno's Hill, the combined battalions of almost 400 soldiers listened to the gunfire and watched the battle in the valley, while hardly a single Indian warrior remained on their front.

How long Custer was in the village, or how desperate a battle was fought there, before Custer realized he had been abandoned and then retreated from the village, is a question that could be at least partly answered by archaeologists.

The initial advantage of surprise had been forfeited, but had Major Reno and Captain Benteen reorganized the regiment and advanced down the valley to support Custer it is possible, or even likely, that the foothold in the village could have been maintained, or even expanded. Custer's small force, now dispersed into two commands, however, could not hold their positions without support.

When Custer did withdraw from the village he had to go to Captain Yates' support or risk the destruction of that command. To have fallen back to the Weir Peaks would have left the Yates battalion of about 80 soldiers in a dangerous and exposed position miles downstream. When Custer retreated from the Indian village he could not abandon his men. He therefore retreated to the final hill position to support the Yates battalion and once there rallied the two battalions as one unit again.

Custer's Hill Position

Regrouping his force on and around the hill, Custer was now confronted with two choices. He could buckle down for a determined defense on the hill, or he could attempt a breakout to the Weir Peaks to rejoin the other elements of the regiment. A breakout could not have been made without risking serious casualties, for the Indian warriors were now fully alerted. By remaining on the hill, Custer's force was still a visible and immediate threat to the Indian village, this force could not be ignored, and from this position Custer could await the advance of the other three battalions of the regiment. Once these reinforcements advanced Custer could then decide what to do and how to do it.

As long as Custer's force was intact and in a relatively small area the chance of withstanding an assault by any number of Indian warriors was excellent. As is well recorded, the history of warfare with the American Indians in the West is full of precedents where a vastly outnumbered force held out against large numbers of Indian warriors. As a desperate last resort the horses of

the entire command could have been shot to form barricades, which would have made any attack against the hill position by the warriors extremely costly, with victory by them by no means certain. As far as actually winning a total victory against the Indian warriors and their village was concerned, Custer's position was now uncertain. He had counted heavily on surprise to balance the odds against a warrior force he knew outnumbered the 7th Cavalry, and that advantage had now been forfeited. Any victory would now be a hard fought one which would depend only upon the discipline and cohesion of the regiment acting together and with one purpose.

While on the hill, unsupported, Custer could only prudently await the advance of the other battalions of the regiment, as he had ordered. Custer would have known that when these battalions did advance, as he certainly expected they would, they could only come from the direction of the Weir Peaks. It would be expected that, knowing this, the attention of Custer and his men would have been riveted on the high ground to the south.

Captain Weir's Advance

At some undefined time (the testimony on this varies widely) some of the soldiers under Major Reno and Captain Benteen did advance, led by the courageous Captain Weir. This advance was unopposed and took place almost as easily as a parade field maneuver.

Major Reno and Captain Benteen later insisted that the Weir Peaks were a poor position for defense and they had been driven back to Reno's hill by Indian warriors. These claims are not supported by the facts. The Weir Peaks are an excellent defensive position and the statements of others who made the advance, along with the fact that exactly zero casualties were suffered by the combined battalions until they retreated, exposes the self-serving deceitfulness of these claims.

Of all the sensitive issues that would be raised concerning the Battle of Little Big Horn, Captain Weir's advance was to be one of the most worrisome to Major Reno and Captain Benteen. The evacuation ordered from the Weir Peaks could only have been justified if, at the time the advance was made, Custer's command had already been destroyed. If Custer's command had not been destroyed at the time the Weir Peaks were evacuated, then this evacuation resulted in the abandonment of Custer's still viable command.

Captain Benteen understood the issue perfectly. At the Reno Court of Inquiry Benteen testified:

From all the circumstances it is my judgement that this fight lasted from fifteen minutes to half an hour or an hour...

I am convinced that when the order brought by Martin reached me General Custer and his whole command were dead.

Considering Captain Benteen's propensity to deceive con-

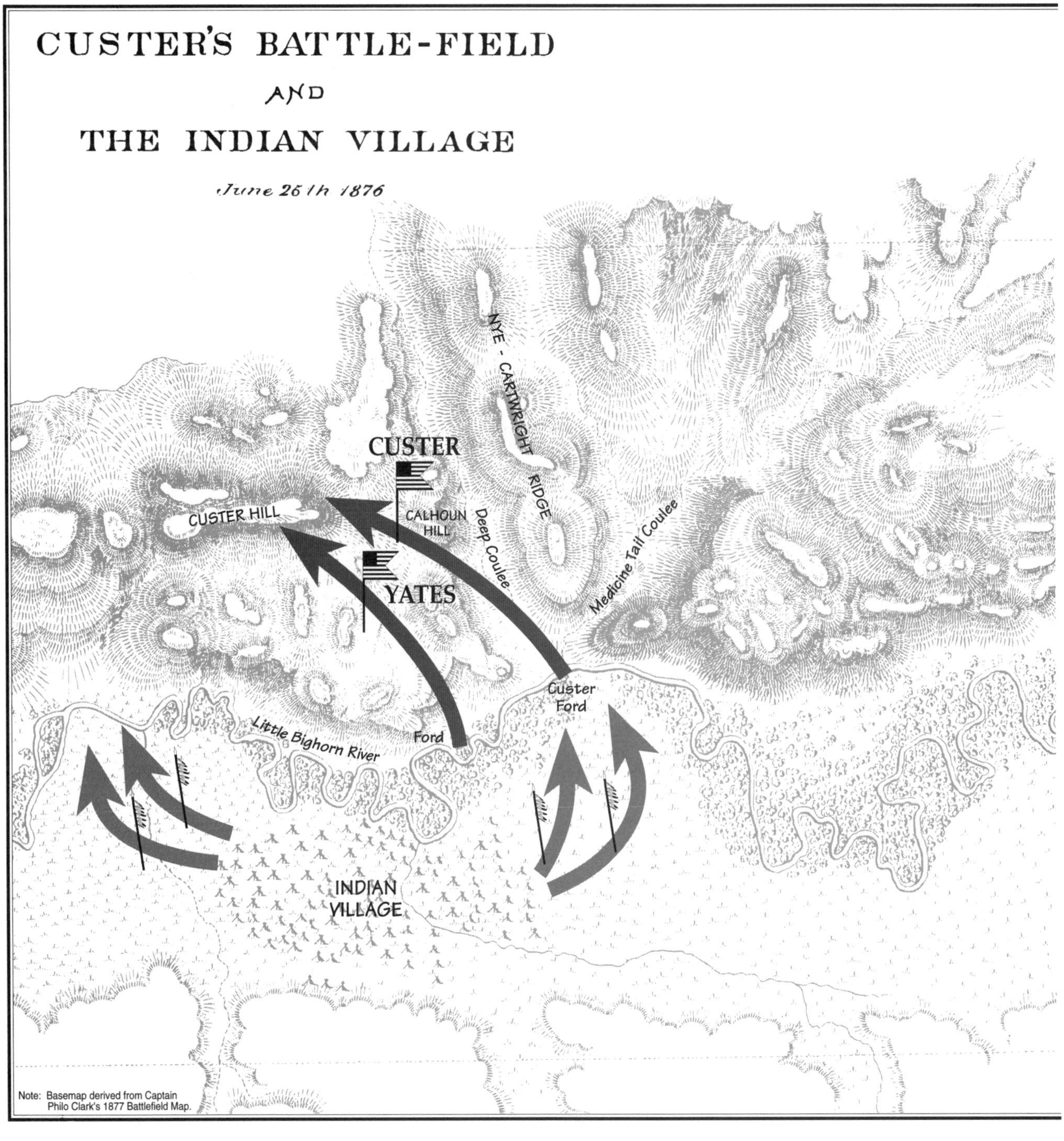

CUSTER'S BATTLE-FIELD

AND

THE INDIAN VILLAGE

June 26th 1876

NYE - CARTWRIGHT RIDGE

CUSTER

CUSTER HILL

CALHOUN HILL

Deep Coulee

Medicine Tail Coulee

YATES

Custer Ford

Ford

Little Bighorn River

INDIAN VILLAGE

Note: Basemap derived from Captain Philo Clark's 1877 Battlefield Map.

MAP FOUR:

BATTLE OF THE LITTLE BIGHORN

The pack train arrives at the Reno-Benteen bluff position. Gunfire is heard by members of the pack train. Custer continues to fight in the valley, but being unsupported, he is forced to retreat. Unable to withdraw to the rear and re-join the regiment without abandoning the Yates battalion further downstream, Custer retreats north and combines with Yates on the hill position now known as Custer Hill.

The Reno-Benteen-Pack Train force is not under attack, yet no advance is ordered.

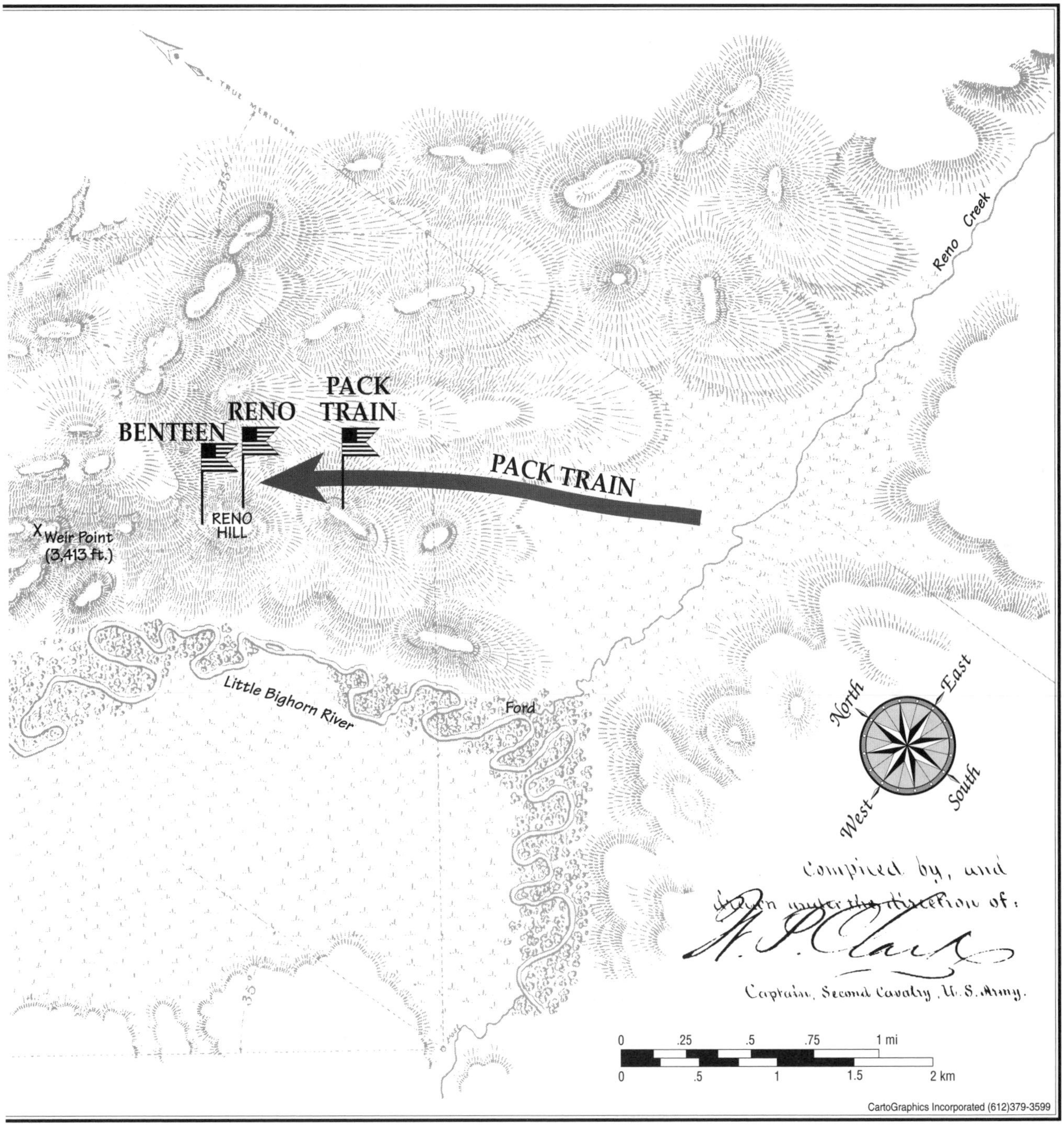

TRUE MERIDIAN

Reno Creek

PACK TRAIN

RENO

BENTEEN

PACK TRAIN

RENO HILL

X Weir Point (3,413 ft.)

Little Bighorn River

Ford

North

East

West

South

Compiled by, and ~~drawn under the direction~~ of:

W. P. Clark

Captain, Second Cavalry, U. S. Army.

0 .25 .5 .75 1 mi

0 .5 1 1.5 2 km

CartoGraphics Incorporated (612)379-3599

cerning nearly every aspect of the Battle of the Little Big Horn, his implication that Custer's command had been long destroyed by the time of Captain Weir's advance is, as with most of Benteen's statements, more than a little suspect.

In fact, the gunfire heard on Major Reno's hill position after Captain Benteen's arrival disproves Benteen's statement. Nearly every other person on this position heard the sound of gunfire and yet Reno and Benteen were to claim not to hear this gunfire.

At the Reno Court of Inquiry Captain Benteen made another astounding statement which revealed Benteen's desperation concerning Captain Weir's advance:

> *His* [Custer's] *battlefield is not visible from there* [the Weir Peaks], *I know that positively, though some officers think it was.*

Something might be remotely believable about Captain Benteen's statement had he not said "positively." Benteen's talents may have included telling the most pious and self-serving fabrications imaginable, but they did not also include the power to alter geography. Lieutenant Godfrey commented on his first view of the battlefield after the arrival of General Terry:

> *I can never forget the sight. The early morning was bright as we ascended to the top of the highest point [Weir Peaks] whence the whole field came into view, with the sun to our backs.*
>
> *"What are those?" exclaimed several as they looked at what appeared to be white boulders.*
>
> *Nervously, I took the field glasses and glanced at the objects, then, almost dropped them, and laconically said: "The dead!"*
>
> *Colonel Weir who was sitting near on his horse, exclaimed: "Oh, how white they look! How white!"*

The "highest point" Lieutenant Godfrey referred to was, of course, the Weir Peaks, and with the aid of field glasses the dead of Custer Hill were visible to those on the Weir Peaks. It is not necessary, however, to accept Godfrey's observance that Custer's final position is visible from the Weir Peaks. Even today individual marble headstones on the Custer battlefield can be seen from the Weir Peaks with the unaided eye and with a modest pair of binoculars the dress of individual figures on Custer Hill can be recognized. Benteen could not change this fact with a few mendacious words.

Was Custer Still Alive?

However, one important question still remains. When the Weir advance was made was Custer's command still alive? Those who made the advance to the Weir Peaks in the direction of Custer Hill made some interesting statements as to what they saw. Lieutenant Hare was interviewed by Walter Camp and Camp wrote the following:

> *While out in advance with Company D, the Indians were thick over on Custer ridge and were firing . . .*
>
> *... at that moment* [Hare] *thought Custer was fighting them.*

Private Edward Pigford also was interviewed by Mr. Camp and again Camp's notes reflect the belief by a participant that, while the soldiers were on the Weir Peaks, a battle was taking place on Custer Hill:

> *Company M went all the way to Edgerly* [Weir] *Peaks, from which could look down in direction of Custer ridge.*
>
> *... at first when looked toward Custer ridge the Indians were firing from a big circle, but it gradually closed until they seemed to converge into a large black mass on the side hill toward the river and all along the ridge.*

Lieutenant Godfrey also observed Custer's position from the Weir Peaks and later commented upon what he saw in his *Century* article:

> *Looking toward Custer field, on a hill two miles away, we saw a large assemblage....*
>
> *We heard occasional shots, most which seemed to be a great distance off, beyond the large groups on the hill.*

At the Reno Court of Inquiry, Lieutenant Godfrey was questioned as to what he saw from the Weir Peaks:

> *Q. At the same time you moved down to Captain Weir's position to the point known as Weir's Hill, did you look in the direction of the place of the massacre?*
>
> *A. Yes, sir.*
>
> *Q. Could you see it?*
>
> *A. I could see the general lay of the ground, but could not see any bodies or persons except Indians.*
>
> *Q. Could you see the point?*
>
> *A. I believe I could, my recollection is I could.*
>
> *Q. Was there anything in the way of fighting going on there at that time?*
>
> *A. No, sir, I don't think there was. I saw no evidences of fighting at that time.*

Sergeant Windolph was with the force on the Weir Peaks and he would later say:

> *Way off to the north you could see what looked to be groups of mounted Indians. There was plenty of firing going on.*

At the Reno Court of Inquiry Lieutenant Wallace testified as to what he saw on Custer Hill from the Weir Peaks:

I went to a point where I could see where General Custer's battle took place. Indians were all over the country but no firing was going on. There was no particular disturbance, all was quiet.

Lieutenant Varnum also testified as to what he saw while on the Weir Peaks at the Reno Court of Inquiry.

I went to the position of Captain Weir's company at the far point of the ridge downstream. At that time his men were firing at pretty long range, I should say 700 or 800 yards, at Indians here and there. At that time I could see all over the plain where towards where I afterwards knew the Custer battlefield had been, and it was just covered with Indians in all directions coming back toward us.

Walter Camp interviewed Lieutenant Edgerly who was with Captain Weir's D Company and Camp noted:

He went to a point ... Edgerly said that when he looked over toward Custer battlefield he saw Indians shooting as though objects on the ground and one part of the hill on Custer battlefield was black with Indians.

George Wylie was a trooper with the soldiers on the Weir Peaks and, when interviewed by Mr. Camp, made some very curious statements:

Soon after Benteen joined Reno on the hill, Captain Weir started to open up communication with Custer, and the troop marched out along bluff until came to a jumping off place from which could look down upon the hollow of Medicine Trail Coulee.

Men dismounted and put horses behind Edgerly [Weir] *Peaks and behind hill to east, and men formed line over this hill from east to west.*

Seeing many horsemen over on distant ridge with guidons flying, Weir said, "That is Custer over there," and mounted up ready to go over, when Sergeant Flannagan said "Here Captain, you had better take a look through the glasses: I think those are Indians."

Weir did so and changed his mind.

Wayne Michael Sarf, author of *The Little Big Horn Campaign*, is one of the many authorities who identified Captain Weir's advance, and the occupation of the Weir Peaks, as a sensitive subject among many of the surviving officers. Mr. Sarf said:

What could they see of Custer's battlefield? . . . Some of the officers apparently saw more than they would later admit. There is little doubt that Edgerly destroyed the portion of a letter to his wife dealing with the Weir Point episode....

A Hard Fight

From the reports of those who observed the Custer battlefield from the Weir Peaks, it is clear that Custer Hill could be seen from that position. And, as those on the Weir Peaks' position looked over to Custer's position, individual horsemen and even cavalry guidons could be seen. The fact that individual horseman and cavalry guidons could be seen from the Weir Peaks brings attention to another important issue.

The most furious and deadly battle ever to be fought in the American West was either about to take place, was taking place or had already taken place. What should, or could, those on the Weir Peaks have seen looking over to the Custer battlefield?

Captain Benteen testified at the Reno Court of Inquiry that the soldiers in Custer's command had died in a disorganized rout:

I went over the battlefield carefully with a view to determine in my own mind how the fight was fought.

I arrived at the conclusion then as I have now, that it was a rout, a panic, till the last man was killed: that there was no line formed.

There was no line on the battlefield: you can take a handful of corn and scatter it over the floor and make just such lines.

There were none ...

Captain Benteen's observations of the battlefield may have been "carefully" made, but he did not truthfully tell the court what he had seen, only what he wanted the court to believe. Others reported seeing something very different, including Captain Moylan:

> [They were] *killed in regular position of skirmishers. I counted 28 cartridge shells around one man and between intervals shells were scattered.*

Lieutenant Hare also did not agree with Captain Benteen's assessment of the battle on Custer Hill:

> *The evidence on the Custer field indicated very hard fighting.*

Lieutenant Godfrey testified at the Reno Court of Inquiry and said:

> *I found a good many cartridge shells ... carbine shells, caliber .45 ...*

Lieutenant Godfrey also testified at the Reno Court of Inquiry as to his observations on Custer Hill:

> *Q. In regard to the severity of the fighting on General Custer's battlefield, did you see any evidences that there was hard fighting there, or the contrary?*
>
> *A. I think there must have been very hard fighting, especially where General Custer fell.*
>
> *Q. You think there was a hard struggle?*
>
> *A. Undoubtedly there was a very hard struggle.*

Lieutenant Edgerly said during the Court of Inquiry:

> *I believe he* [Custer] *fought very desperately.*

Any question of the resistance of Custer's command was dispelled forever with the archeological examination of the battlefield. This examination proved that the soldiers of Custer's command fought in a combat formation and they fought desperately. The victory by the Indian warriors over Custer's command was not quite as easy as some have chosen to believe.

The Number of Indian Warriors Killed

One of the most ludicrous myths of the Battle of the Little Big Horn is the contention that the Indian warriors suffered only a very few casualties, perhaps thirty or forty killed. This often repeated "fact" defies elementary logic and is based upon the statements of a few of the Indian warrior participants. In spite of the often repeated warnings of meticulous historians and those who lived during the era, these statements have often been taken at face value.

War for the American Indian was a mystical event and the dead were regarded with fear. Many tribes refused even to speak of the dead. War was also a personal endeavor for the individual and a male's status in the tribe was largely determined by his powers as a warrior. The Indian warrior participants spoke of the Battle of the Little Big Horn as they understood it as individual warriors and the figure of thirty or forty dead could have been only the number a warrior actually saw killed, or perhaps only the number killed from a specific tribe. The figure could also have been given as a deliberate attempt to mislead.

Custer noted that the Indian warriors always attempted to remove their dead from the battlefield:

> *The Indians invariably endeavored to conceal their exact losses.*

There were other Indian sources which told a different story of losses suffered at the Battle of the Little Big Horn by the Indians. Red Horse, a Sioux warrior who participated in the battle, mentioned large Indian losses:

> *The soldiers killed 136 and wounded 160 Sioux.*

In an interview shortly after the battle a warrior by the name of Little Buck Elk told Major Thomas Mitchell at Fort Peck, Montana, that the Indian losses were being deliberately hidden:

> *He says they have tried to keep the number lost by them from being known but there is no use lying about it, that they lost over 100 killed in the fight.*

An account of the Indian reports which came into Standing Rock Agency after the Battle of the Little Big Horn was given by Colonel Burke in an official communication:

> *An Indian who came in from the hostiles says there were nine bands, in more numbers than he could count, engaged with Custer and they lost more men than he did. The Uncpapas alone lost 160 killed . . .*

George Herendeen who, as an experienced frontier scout should have been able to render an intelligent opinion on certain aspects of the Battle of the Little Big Horn, said:

> *The Indians must have lost as many killed and wounded as the* [soldiers] *did.*

The casualties suffered by the Indian warriors during Major Reno's fight in the valley could not have been significant. During the fight on the skirmish line most reports say the Indian warriors were cautious and kept out of the range of the soldiers' weapons, and during the panicked retreat from the valley Reno's men were in no condition to inflict serious losses upon the Indian warriors.

No reports exist of any Indian warriors killed during Captain Weir's advance or the retreat from the Weir Peaks. During the siege on Reno's Hill afterwards a few warriors were shot, however, they were not in exposed positions as the soldiers were and their losses could not have been significant.

Most of the Indian warriors killed at the Battle of the Little Big Horn must have fallen in the two fights with Custer. First in the battle for the Indian village, and then on Custer Hill. Most, probably, would have fallen in the furious battle on Custer Hill.

Problem of Gunsmoke

In a battle in which about 210 soldiers died with Custer, and a similar number of Indians probably died, it would be a fair guess that the amount of gunfire during the battle had to have been terrific.

Author Joseph Rosa wrote a number of books which studied and detailed the gunfighters of the American West including "Wild Bill" Hickok. His studies naturally included the weapons of that era and Mr. Rosa personally fired many of these weapons and he made an interesting observation. In speaking of the accuracy of the pistol in relation to the effect of the gunsmoke it generated, Mr. Rosa noted:

> *Even though careful attention was paid to the sights and to the loading and oiling of the weapons, a further problem remained.*
>
> *Black powder creates a great deal of smoke.*
>
> *Writers who credited trick shots with the ability to hit repeatedly hats, tin cans, or other targets tossed into*

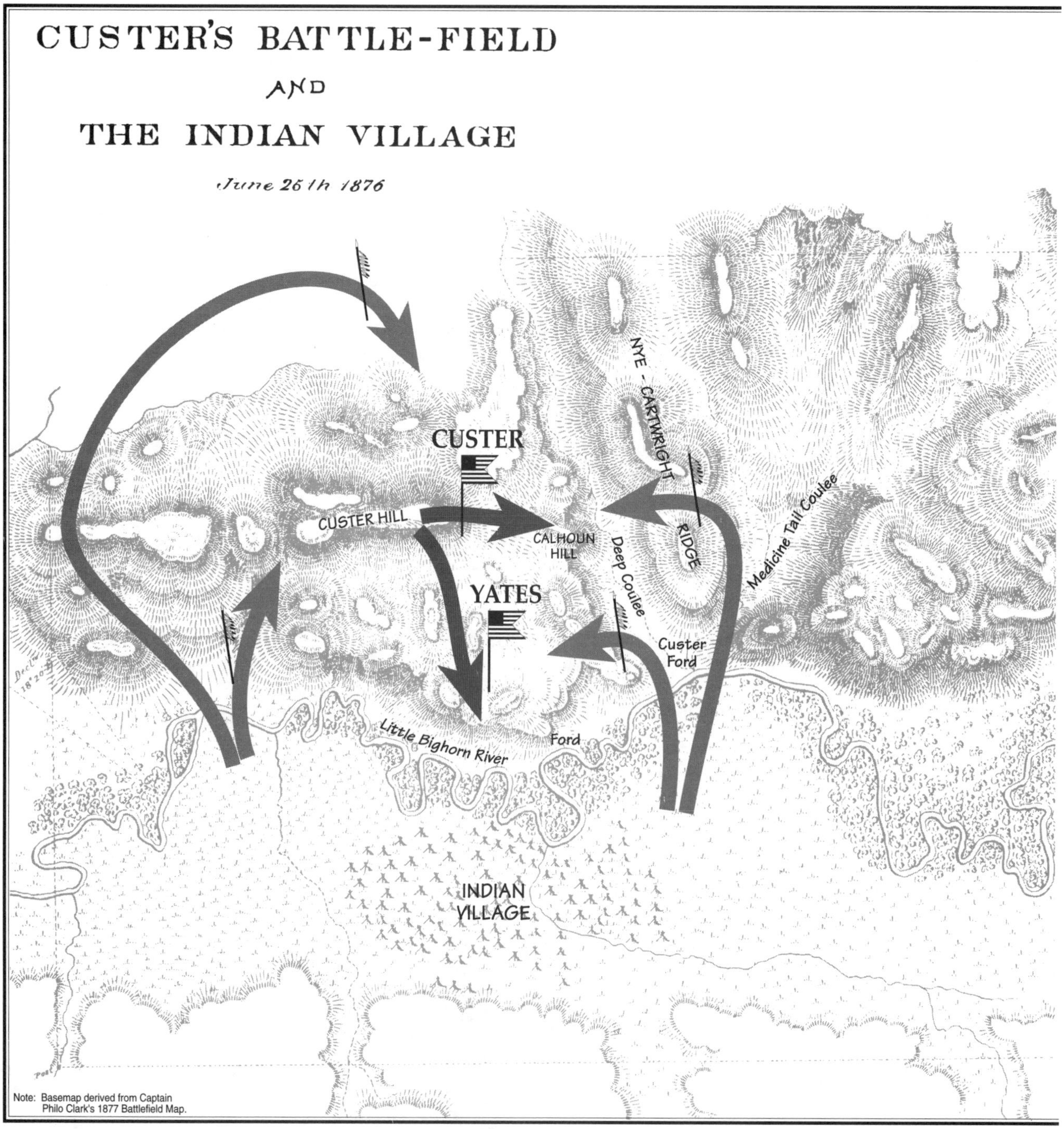

CUSTER'S BATTLE-FIELD

AND

THE INDIAN VILLAGE

June 25th 1876

CUSTER

CUSTER HILL

CALHOUN HILL

YATES

NYE - CARTWRIGHT

RIDGE

Deep Coulee

Medicine Tail Coulee

Custer Ford

Ford

Little Bighorn River

INDIAN VILLAGE

Note: Basemap derived from Captain Philo Clark's 1877 Battlefield Map.

MAP FIVE:

BATTLE OF THE LITTLE BIGHORN

Disgusted with the inactivity of Reno and Benteen, Captain Weir advances toward the cluster of hilltops now known as the "Weir Peaks." Captain Benteen follows with several more companies and this force now occupies the Weir Peaks unopposed.

The Pack Train, and perhaps even Reno, never reach the peaks. Captain Benteen uses a cavalry guidon to 'signal' Custer, then orders a retreat from the position. One soldier is wounded during the entire movement, and he is left behind.

The reinforcements are seen on Custer Hill and Custer orders Calhoun's and Keogh's companies to advance to the south to open up a corridor from the Weir Peaks. Smith's and Tom Custer's com-

TRUE MERIDIAN
BENTEEN
WEIR
RENO
X Weir Point
(3,413 ft.)
RENO
HILL
Reno Creek
Little Bighorn River
Ford
North
East
South
West
Compiled by, and drawn under the direction of:
W. P. Clark
Captain, Second Cavalry, U. S. Army.
0 .25 .5 .75 1 mi
0 .5 1 1.5 2 km
CartoGraphics Incorporated (612)379-3599

panies are sent to the south/southwest towards the river to open a corridor for an advance in that direction once the regiment is re-united on Custer Hill. F Company remains on Custer Hill in reserve.

Indian war parties are stationed around the fringe of the battlefield. The Weir advance/Benteen retreat and Custer's offensive maneuver are unopposed, demonstrating how wary the Indian warriors are at that point.

the air, rarely considered the effect of the smoke.

When attempting some of the shots (with varying degrees of success), I have quickly found that the target is obscured unless there is a strong breeze to blow away the smoke.

When this problem of gunsmoke on the Custer battle field was presented to Mr. Sam Fadala, long time blackpowder editor of *Guns* magazine, he commented upon blackpowder and how it might obscure one's vision:

Partly cloudy and little wind would allow perhaps a condition conducive to holding smoke on the air. Therefore, it would be no surprise to see the battlefield enshrouded in smoke.

Black powder, remember, is a term we use today. In the past, it was simply "gunpowder." After all, there was no smokeless propellant to compare with. Naturally, black powder did emit smoke ...

It is my belief that the battlefield would have looked like a grassfire had raged over the prairie.

The smoke would appear somewhat blue in the distance, more than white. It would also hang heavy on the air. A soldier or Indian would find it almost difficult to breathe at times due to lack of wind and what could have been a humid situation.

Mingled with dust, the smoke would have helped to create a rather eerie look, I dare say.

I have tested my own black powder rifles, only one person shooting – me – and in a short time found myself almost engulfed in smoke ...

... if indeed there was almost no breeze and a bit of humidity on the air, the battleground would have resembled the aftermath of a huge fire with smoke billowing up out of the ground.

All of the firearms at the Battle of the Little Big Horn used black powder. And there was not a "strong breeze" to carry away the smoke on the day of the battle. Lieutenant Wallace took note of the weather that day:

It was a cloudy day, not much wind.

Lieutenant Varnum also corroborated Lieutenant Wallace's observation of the weather:

I remember no wind on the 25th, but it was a little cloudy.

How many shots were fired during that terrific battle on Custer Hill? Thousands of participants fought and, adding to the confusion of battle, gunsmoke would quickly have become a hindrance to accurate firing. For every bullet that struck a target there had to be many that did not.

Thousands upon thousands of shots were fired during the destruction of Custer's command and, to add to the gunsmoke, there would have been a considerable amount of dust raised by the circling Indian ponies and the cavalry mounts turned loose and stampeding off the battlefield. Most of the horses of Custer's command were not found on Custer hill and many Indian accounts say they had been let go by the soldiers during the battle.

The gunsmoke, as well as the dust raised by the cavalry horses and any Indian ponies used to charge various points in Custer's position, would have created a tremendous veil over the battlefield. In fact, this is what many of the Indian participants say happened.

Through an interpreter Sitting Bull said:

The tumult of smoke of the battle was so great that combatants were often obscured entirely, and the fighting therefore promiscuous.

Run's the Enemy, a Sioux Warrior, said:

The smoke rolled up like a mountain over our heads.

Two Moon said:

The smoke was like a great cloud and everywhere the Sioux went the dust rose like smoke.

When interviewed by Walter Camp, a warrior named Turtle Rib said:

There was a big dust and the Indians were running all around.... in the smoke and dust [the Indians] *hit their own men.*

There are also accounts by the Indian participants of the firing of their weapons at the soldiers bodies, after the soldiers had already been killed, in celebration of their victory. This firing in celebration may have continued for quite some time. Had the soldiers on the Weir Peaks been viewing Custer Hill during or after the destruction of Custer and his command, they would have seen the one thing none of them reported to have seen, a battlefield completely obscured by smoke and dust. There could not have been a "great assemblage" seen, no individual cavalry guidons, nor any individual horsemen.

Those on the Weir Peaks would have made no mistake had they been viewing the Custer battlefield during the battle or after the soldiers had been destroyed. The smoke and dust would have hung over Custer Hill "like a mountain." When the soldiers on the Weir Peaks looked over at Custer Hill the evidence indicates that Custer and his men were still alive.

Binoculars

To those who traveled and lived in the west during that era, the horse and the firearm were most important. Also of tremendous value were the field glasses and telescopes then in use. With them an enemy or wildlife could be spot-

ted at a distance and this could make the difference between survival and death. In his book *My Life on the Plains*, Custer mentioned the use of his field glasses on many occasions and actually made many more references to them than he did his weapons.

In an interview on record in the *North Dakota Historical Records*, Sitting Bull said of those on Custer Hill:

> *As they stood waiting to be killed they were seen to look far away to the hills in all directions and we knew they were looking for the hidden soldiers in the hollows of the hills to come and help them.*

Of course they did, and these soldiers would have been looking "far away" with field glasses.

In the accounts of the Battle of the Little Big Horn field glasses are mentioned many times and the importance of this handy item can not be overemphasized. On the day of the battle Custer had borrowed Lieutenant DeRudio's field glasses because they were said to be the best in the regiment.

On the Weir Peaks the soldiers gathered there, including Captain Benteen with his "trusty binoculars," could observe the horses and guidons on Custer Hill with their view unobstructed by smoke and dust. A reasonable conclusion that on Custer Hill the officers there, watching the Weir Peaks for the anticipated advance, observed the gathering of soldiers on the Weir Peaks. With the aid of field glasses each group of officers could certainly see the other group clearly.

The Guidon

For those on Custer Hill the appearance of the soldiers on the Weir Peaks signaled the much awaited advance of the regiment. If there was any doubt by those on Custer Hill that the regiment was indeed advancing, Captain Benteen thoughtfully dispelled it:

> *We then showed our full force on the hills with guidons flying, that Custer might see us.*

Captain Benteen also spoke of an incident with the guidon which, while much overlooked in significance, was possibly of extreme, if not decisive, importance. Captain Benteen also said:

> *I planted a guidon there as a guide to our position to Custer.*

Captain Benteen mentioned this incident on other occasions. However, by 1890 when he had written a narrative of the battle he was, apparently, having second thoughts about raising this interesting point and he omitted the guidon episode entirely.

At the Reno Court of Inquiry, Captain Benteen was questioned about the guidon incident:

> *Q. What was the purpose of placing the guidon on that high point.*
>
> *A. To present an object to attract the attention of General Custer.*

Major Reno was also questioned about the guidon incident at his Court of Inquiry:

> *Q. Do you remember about a guidon being placed at a point termed Captain Weir's hill?*
>
> *A. It was done ... at the suggestion of Captain Benteen.*

The question must be asked: to the soldiers on Custer Hill, surrounded by thousands of Indian warriors, exactly how important would the "planted guidon" or "full force on the hills with guidons flying," have been to them? Did these soldiers interpret the guidons meaning to be precisely what Captain Benteen later claimed: "as a guide to our [Benteen's] position?"

Custer, himself, had written of two similar incidents involving the cavalry guidon he had personally experienced while in hostile Indian country. In one incident, Custer had chased a buffalo for miles and accidently shot his horse when the desperate quarry lunged sideways at him. Many miles from his command, and uncertain of the direction of the column, Custer set out in a hopeful direction and after traveling several miles spotted a column of dust. Hiding with his dogs in a nearby ravine, Custer described his thoughts as he watched the approaching dust cloud through his field glasses:

> *... far ahead in the distance I saw a column of dust rising.*
>
> *A hasty examination soon convinced me that the dust was produced by one of three causes; white men, Indians, or buffaloes. Two to one in my favor at any rate.*
>
> *Selecting a ravine where I could crawl away undiscovered should the approaching body prove to be Indians, I called my dogs to my side and concealed myself as well as I could to await developments. The object of my anxious solicitude was still several miles distant. Whatever it was, it was approaching in my direction, as was plainly discernible from the increasing columns of dust.*
>
> *Fortunately I had my field-glass slung over my shoulder, and if Indians I could discover them before they could possibly discover me. Soon I was able to see the heads of mounted men running in irregular order. This discovery shut out the probability of their being buffaloes, and simplified the question to white men or Indians.*

CUSTER'S BATTLE-FIELD

AND

THE INDIAN VILLAGE

June 26th 1876

NYE - CARTWRIGHT RIDGE

CUSTER

CUSTER HILL

CALHOUN HILL

Deep Coulee

Medicine Tail Coulee

YATES

Custer Ford

Ford

Little Bighorn River

INDIAN VILLAGE

Note: Basemap derived from Captain Philo Clark's 1877 Battlefield Map.

MAP SIX:

BATTLE OF THE LITTLE BIGHORN

The disbursement of Custer's command, simultaneous with Benteen's withdrawal, presents the Indian warriors with an unbelievable opportunity. They quickly react and probably within minutes Custer's command is under attack from all directions.

Calhoun's command is overrun and destroyed, and then Keogh's. The soldiers stationed toward the river are also attacked and soon destroyed.

TRUE MERIDIAN

Reno Creek

BENTEEN

WEIR

RENO

X Weir Point
(3,413 ft.)

RENO
HILL

Little Bighorn River

Ford

North

East

West

South

Compiled by, and
drawn under the direction of:
W. P. Clark
Captain, Second Cavalry, U. S. Army.

0 .25 .5 .75 1 mi

0 .5 1 1.5 2 km

CartoGraphics Incorporated (612)379-3599

One of our officers tied a handkerchief to a stick and commenced waving it from side to side as a signal. It was soon answered the same way … the army code of signals was spelling out for us the information we wanted.

"Cowards" Shot

To the soldiers on Custer Hill the appearance of the reinforcements lined across the Weir Peaks would have been a welcome sight and would not have been overlooked. This was the advance of the regiment they had been watching and waiting for. Then, after showing his force with "guidons flying," Captain Benteen ordered the abandonment of the Weir Peaks.

At this point the Weir Peaks were not under attack, nor had a single casualty been suffered by Benteen's command. The position itself was a fortress nearly immune to assault and as long as the Weir Peaks were held the threat alone of the soldiers positioned there was enough to make the Indian warriors wary of any attack against Custer's command. There was no military reason for Benteen to order the abandonment of the Weir Peaks.

It would appear possible that military logic had absolutely nothing to do with Captain Benteen's decision to abandon the Weir Peaks. Benteen had a choice to make, a simple choice, and this was either the survival of Custer and his command or that of himself. Benteen chose himself.

In discussing the Battle of the Little Big Horn, not long after the event, a reader wrote to a newspaper and made an interesting observation:

Now Mr. Editor, cowardice in the face of the enemy is, under the laws of war, punishable by death.

This harsh military maxim is a universal law historically practiced to some extent by nearly every military establishment in the world. Disobedience of orders is also included as an offense meriting, for some, the death penalty.

The reason for this unpleasant penalty is that, under combat conditions, cowardice and disobedience of orders will not only lose battles, but also will get soldiers killed, sometimes a lot of them. Under universally accepted military law Major Reno's panicked retreat from the valley was both cowardly and in disobedience of orders.

Inevitable death, as barbaric as it seems, has historically been an effective stimulus for soldiers to fight bravely, or at least not to run away, as well as to obey orders. When fighting against the enemy there is always a chance for survival, but the firing squad does not err.

Panic is contagious and can quickly cause the disintegration of a military unit. Troops in combat simply cannot

Never during the war did I scan an enemy's battery or approaching column with half the anxious care with which I watched the party then approaching me.

For a long time nothing satisfactory could be determined, until my eye caught sight of an object which, high above the heads of the approaching riders, told me in unmistakable terms that friends were approaching.

It was the cavalry guidon, and never was the sight of stars and stripes more welcome.

During a battle Custer had with the hostile Sioux during the summer of 1873, he and a detachment of the 7th cavalry were cut off from the regiment for a brief time. Again the cavalry guidon played a significant role in Custer's identifying the approach of cavalrymen:

Looking far to the right and over the hills already described, we could see an immense column of dust rising and rapidly approaching … All eyes were turned to the bluffs in the distance, and there was to be seen, coming almost with the speed of the wind, four separate squadrons of Uncle Sam's best cavalry, with banners flying, horses manes and tails floating on the breeze and comrades spurring forward in generous emulation as to which squadron should land its colors first in the fight. It was a grand and welcome sight …

Concerning the guidon, could it have actually been used to exchange signals beyond the accepted "guide to our position" that Benteen admitted he used it for on the Weir Peaks? Interestingly, Colonel John Gibbon, in his *American Catholic Quarterly Review* article of 1877, commented upon the improvised use of the Army code of signals under field conditions:

afford to be infected by panic resulting from cowardice. For this reason many, perhaps most, of the instances of battlefield cowardice and disobedience of orders never reach the court-martial phase. They are handled directly and immediately by the fellow soldiers of the soldier who has panicked, and sometimes that soldier does not survive the experience.

Major Reno's flight from the valley is a classic example where, within a few minutes of panicked confusion, he reduced his battalion from an effective combat force to a panic stricken mob. Among Major Reno's men that day the harsh laws of military discipline were plainly in effect and the battle itself records several clear examples of this.

Private William Morris later mentioned an incident concerning Major Reno's fight in the valley which illustrates this fact:

Reno gave the command, "retreat to your horses, men."

Some started for the timber but Captain French countermanded the order immediately.

"Steady men! I will shoot the first man that turns his back to the enemy. Fall back slowly and keep up your fire."

The scout, George Herendeen, told of an incident in the wooded area after Major Reno had fled the valley and had left him and a number of other soldiers behind:

I told them I could get out alone and if they would do what I told them, I could get them out also.

The wounded sergeant then spoke up and said:

"They will do what you want, for I will compel them to obey. I will shoot the first man who runs or disobeys orders."

Captain French apparently regretted later that he had not taken more decisive action during Major Reno's panicked retreat from the valley and he wrote a friend concerning this:

... although the idea flashed my mind ... I did not dare to resort to murder, the later I now believe would have been justified.

Escaping battlefield justice, Major Reno and Captain Benteen still had another worry, this one being *"Article 57"* of the *"Revised Army Regulations"* of March 1, 1873.

"Article 57"

"Any officer or soldier who shall misbehave before the enemy, run away ... shall suffer death, or such punishment as shall be awarded by a court-martial."

Major Reno's conduct, certainly, falls under *"Article 57"* and Benteen's conduct would have been closely scrutinized. Custer's death, and the political climate of the day, prevented the military legal proceedings which very well may have "awarded" Reno and Benteen an unpleasant end to their military careers.

Captain Benteen's Position

On the Weir Peaks observing Custer Hill, Captain Benteen's position was similar, if not identical, to that of the soldier in the rifle pit of whom Lieutenant Godfrey had spoken of in his article. Benteen failed to follow his orders to advance and would suffer the consequences, if Custer were to live.

Major Reno's position was, if anything, worse than Captain Benteen's. Reno was second in command of the regiment and his panicked retreat form the valley had been a disgrace. He too had then failed to advance. This was the reason Reno could not muster the courage to advance even as far as Benteen had. Neither Reno or Benteen could escape the facts of military law.

By the time of Captain Weir's advance, had Custer lived, Major Reno and Captain Benteen, at the very least, were finished as soldiers. Custer did not live to press the issue but, had he, there can be little question but that Reno and Benteen would have been lucky to see the sun set that ill-fated day, saved only for a court martial and an inevitable guilty verdict. Captain Weir would have been a star witness.

Looking across the ravines and hills to Custer Hill, the thought of what Custer would do to him did not just flash

through Captain Benteen's mind. It undoubtedly raged there like a firestorm. Benteen knew the consequences of his actions and he knew Custer and the officers with him. It was with that thought in mind that Benteen gave Custer a final farewell with the cavalry guidon and then evacuated the Weir Peaks, leaving Custer and his command to fend for themselves, with hopefully unsuccessful results. Benteen chose his own life over that of Custer and more than 200 soldiers. Through his actions, Benteen sealed the doom of Custer and these soldiers.

Custer's Decision

Using field glasses and observing the soldiers on the Weir Peaks with "guidons flying," and seeing Captain Benteen signal it as their "position," Custer could again take action which, as usual for him, would be aggressive. Believing Captain Benteen and the soldiers on the Weir Peaks about to advance, or perhaps even exchanging signals ordering them to do so, Custer deployed his men to facilitate that movement.

He sent Lieutenant Calhoun with L Company down the ridge leading south towards the Weir Peaks, and behind Calhoun was Captain Keogh with I Company. These two companies would open a corridor for the advance from the Weir Peaks. These two companies probably advanced at a fast trot, or even a gallop. Keogh's company only advanced part way before they halted, perhaps to prevent any flanking movement or attack on the rear of Calhoun's company.

At the same time Lieutenant Calhoun an Captain Keogh were sent along the south ridge to link up with the expected advance from the Weir Peaks, Custer sent a second force west, down the sloping ridges and twisting ravines toward the Little Big Horn River. This force would prepare the aggressive advance that Custer now planned, and it consisted of C and E Companies. F Company apparently held in reserve near the command post on Custer Hill.

Captain Benteen drew a map shortly after the battle. At the foot of the bluffs, in the direction C and E Companies were sent, his map shows a river ford. The fact that there were several other river fords downstream from Reno's hill position was mentioned at the Reno Court of Inquiry. Sergeant Davern commented on "several lower fords," one of them which Benteen shows on his map.

What was Custer's intention in sending C and E Companies in this direction? These soldiers were found in skirmish position after the battle.

Cavalry Tactics and Regulations of the United States Army, regulation 295:

> *The objects of skirmishers are to cover movements and evolutions, to gain time, to watch the movements of the enemy, to keep (the enemy) approaching so close to the main body as to annoy the line of march and to weaken and harass (the enemy) by their fire, to prepare the way for the charge...*

It may be these two companies were in position to open a corridor to the river. Once the regiment had reformed on Custer Hill, the combined force could then advance down this corridor to the river, cross it, and again attack the village. The fact that two companies were able to advance this far as skirmishers demonstrates that, at this stage of the battle, the Indian warriors were still very wary of the soldiers.

Near the time Lieutenant Calhoun's company reached its furthest advance, or shortly thereafter, Captain Benteen had evacuated the Weir Peaks position. How much of Custer's maneuver, which was clearly offensive in nature, Benteen saw before he committed his act of treachery, can only be guessed. Benteen may have witnessed the entire deployment or he may have only seen the beginning of it. One thing is certain, the evacuation of the Weir Peaks left Custer out on a limb, so to speak, and gave the Indian warriors an unbelievable opportunity.

By evacuating the Weir Peaks Captain Benteen had determined the fate of Custer and the soldiers with him. The Indian warriors would no longer face a threat from the seven companies under Major Reno and Benteen and could now turn their full force on the now dispersed companies under Custer.

The Indians Attack

From the archeological study done on the battlefield, it would appear that a main thrust toward Custer Hill began with the destruction of Lieutenant Calhoun's position and from there followed the ridge through Captain Keogh's position. This was determined by following the trail of shell casing, from the same weapons, to Custer Hill. On and around a small hilltop Calhoun and his soldiers fought desperately until they were annihilated.

The situation Custer was now confronted with is very similar to the "crossing the T" in the now outdated battles of Naval surface ships. In "crossing the T," a column of naval ships advancing in a single line is confronted with an enemy force also moving in a single line but advancing at a right angle to the first. Only the guns of the first ship in the first column can be brought to bear on the enemy line while all of the ships guns in the second column can be fired at the leading ship, quickly sinking it and, then continuing the maneuver, the line fires at each succeeding ship one by one. This battle scenario took place on May 27, 1905, when the Japanese fleet crossed the Russian "T" and sank almost the entire Russian fleet, winning that war for the Japanese.

The force which Custer had sent to open a corridor to Weir Peaks was facing the wrong direction to bring to bear the full weight of their guns against the assault by the Indian warriors. To compound the already unfavorable position of the soldiers was the fact the Indian warriors vastly outnumbered them and were also armed with repeating rifles, able to fire very rapidly during the attack

CUSTER'S BATTLE-FIELD
AND
THE INDIAN VILLAGE
June 25th 1876

CUSTER
CUSTER HILL
CALHOUN HILL
NYE - CARTWRIGHT RIDGE
Deep Coulee
Medicine Tail Coulee
Custer Ford
Ford
Little Bighorn River
INDIAN VILLAGE

Note: Basemap derived from Captain Philo Clark's 1877 Battlefield Map.

MAP SEVEN:

BATTLE OF THE LITTLE BIG HORN

On the summit of Custer Hill, horses are shot as barricades and a last stand is made. These soldiers may have held out until near sundown but the fight is hopeless and they are ultimately wiped out also.

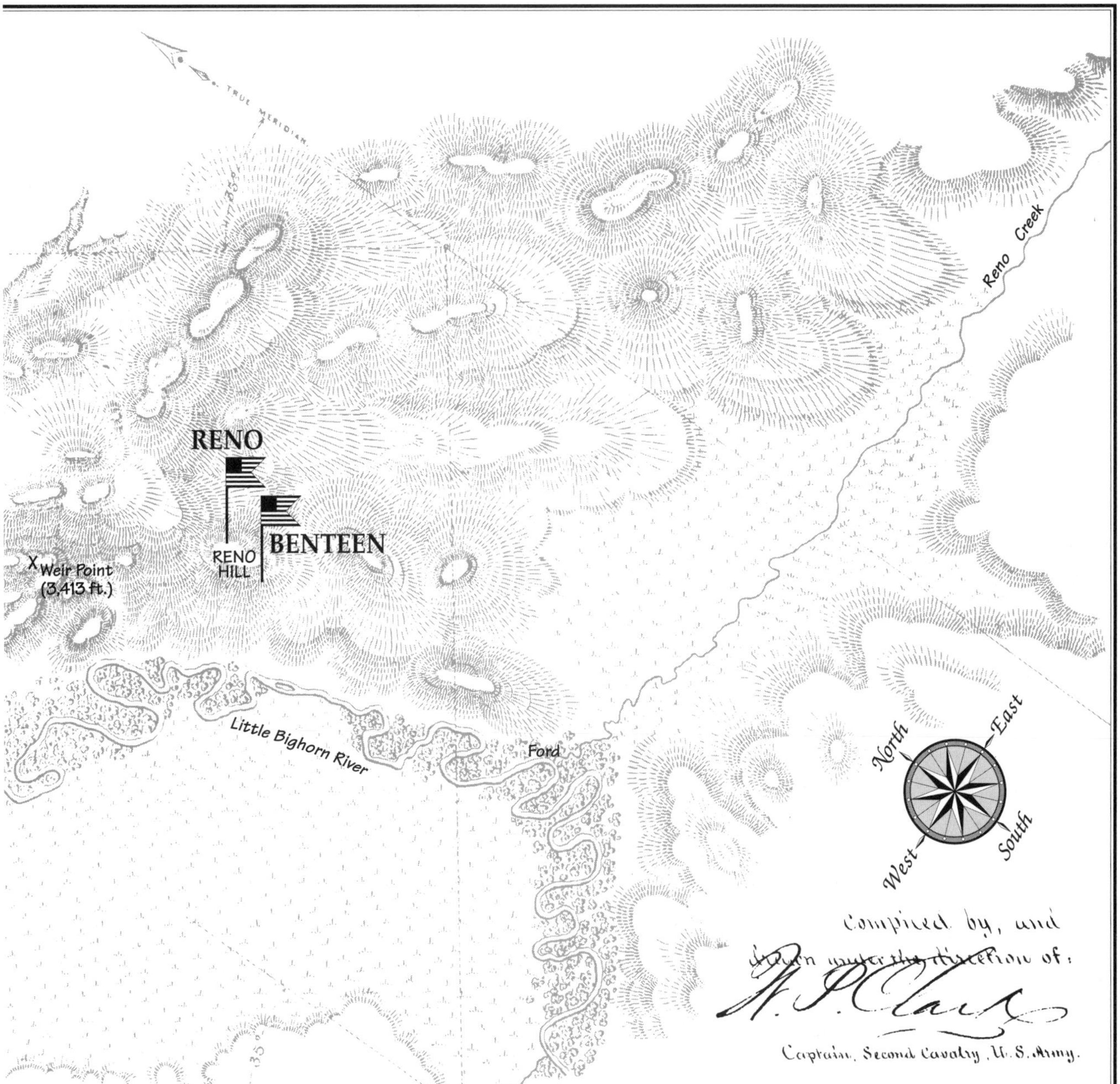

TRUE MERIDIAN

RENO

RENO HILL

BENTEEN

X Weir Point (3,413 ft.)

Reno Creek

Little Bighorn River

Ford

North

East

South

West

Compiled by, and drawn under the direction of:

W. P. Clark

Captain, Second Cavalry, U. S. Army.

0 .25 .5 .75 1 mi

0 .5 1 1.5 2 km

CartoGraphics Incorporated (612)379-3599

on the soldiers positions. The army had not armed its soldiers with repeating rifles for the reason that, under the stress of combat, a soldier has a tendency to fire as rapidly as possible and can quickly uses up all the ammunition that can be carried by an individual.

In most situations the Springfield single shot carbine was a superior weapon to most of the rifles carried by the Indian warriors. The Springfield Carbine had a longer range, was more accurate, and had a heavier bullet than most of the weapons carried by the Indian warriors. On open ground, such as the situation Major Reno had been confronted with on his skirmish line in the valley, the Springfield carbine was probably a better weapon. However, had Lieutenant Calhoun's command been armed with repeating rifles, and had they been able to fire rapidly and in vollies, they may have been able to halt the advance by the Indian warriors, Calhoun might have been able to continue his retreat to Custer Hill picking up Keogh on the way. As it was, Calhoun was at every disadvantage both out-numbered and out-gunned.

Probably numbering at least 2,500, and perhaps considerably more, the Indian warriors outnumbered Custer's force, now abandoned by Captain Benteen and Major Reno to fight alone, probably at least 10 to 1, perhaps much more. Regimental-sized war parties were roaming around the fringes of the battlefield before Custer had deployed his command and, undoubtedly, many of them had stationed themselves at advantageous locations.

At the same time Lieutenant Calhoun's company was attacked, or not long after, pandemonium broke out all over the battle field as the Indian warriors seized the opportunity that had been handed to them by Captain Benteen.

C and E Companies quickly found themselves under attack from the north. These dispersed skirmishers were, if possible, in worse shape than Lieutenant Calhoun's men and as Calhoun's position disintegrated C and E Companies also found themselves under attack from the south. F Company apparently had been held in reserve on or around Custer Hill, but they were too few to have a significant influence anywhere on the battlefield. The Indian participants of the fight say this part of the battle did not last long and it was probably only minutes after the attack began before everywhere the thin skirmish lines of soldiers were shattered.

Custer Hill

On Custer Hill, a number of horses were shot for barricades and from behind them a last stand was made. Custer was alive and fighting at this point, according to Lieutenant Garland of the 6th Infantry who was with General Terry's command and examined the battlefield. Lieutenant Garland said:

We found seventeen cartridge shells by his side, where he had kept them off until the last moment.

Captain Keogh was the second ranking officer with Custer and, had Custer been killed or wounded early in the battle, Keogh would have been at the command post on the hill. Instead, Keogh was found with his company.

General Custer, his brother Tom, Lieutenant Cooke, Captain Yates, most of the other officers, and many of the enlisted men, were expert shots and among them had fought hundreds of skirmishes and battles. The final minutes of desperate combat must have been as furious a battle as any ever fought.

The Indian participants would later say that many of the soldiers killed themselves. The archeological examination of the battle would indeed find army bullets vertically impacted into the ground where final death pacts between the soldiers were carried out. Death was one fate, death by slow torture another, and no soldier wanted to be taken alive. From the evidence it would seem that many of the soldiers shot a wounded companion to spare that soldier capture and torture.

Unfortunately, in the smoke and confusion of battle, other soldiers became isolated and, once wounded, fell under the power of the warriors while still alive. Although they probably did not remain alive long, death would not have been pleasant and these unfortunate soldiers would have been cut up alive on the spot. Some authorities believe this, in fact, may have been the fate of many of the soldiers and this fact hidden to protect the surviving family members.

There are other account by those who examined the battle field which say as many as thirty soldiers were missing from the dead. There were rumors that at least a few of these soldiers were taken alive and tortured to death in the village.

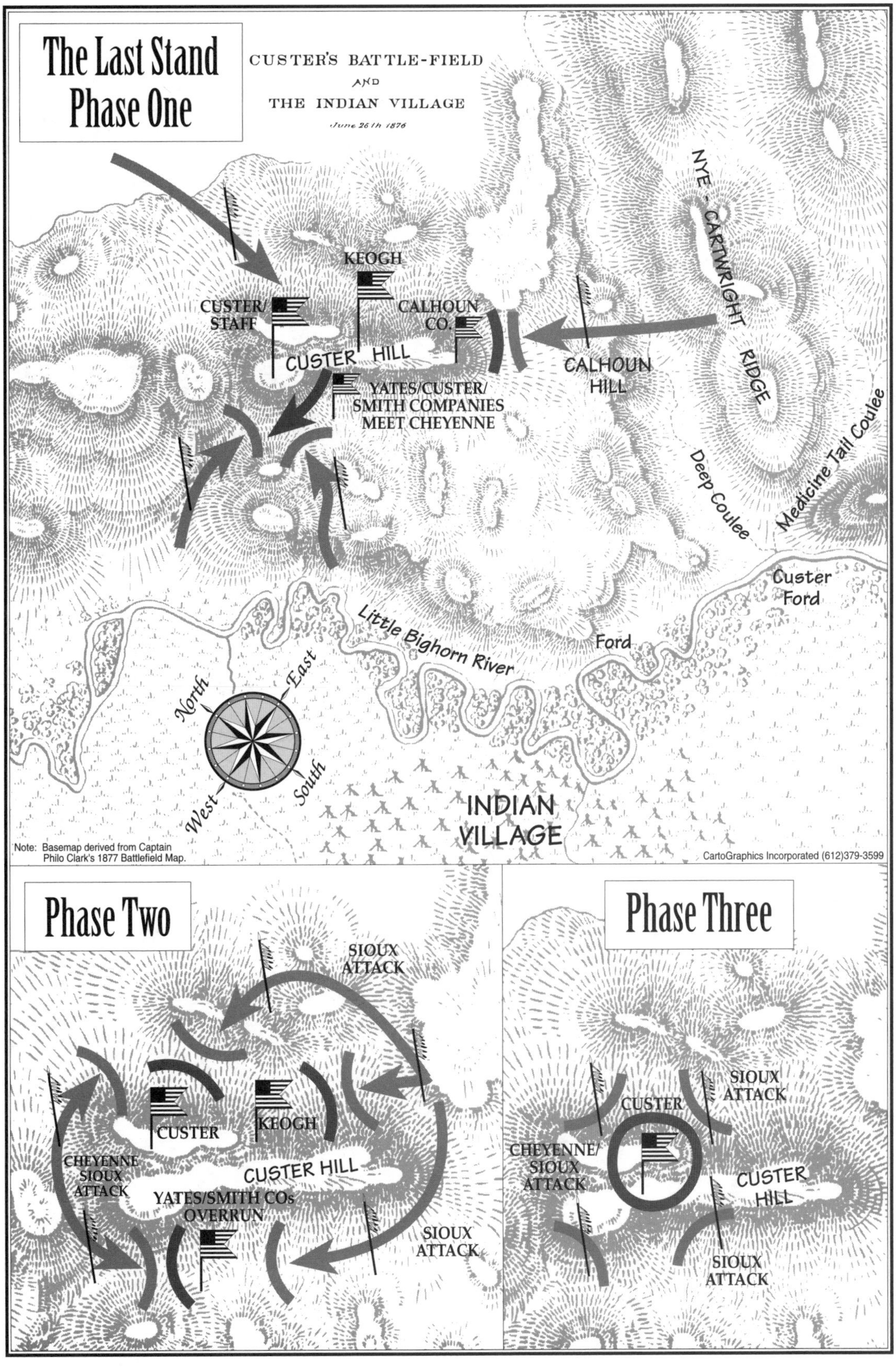

The Last Stand Phase One

CUSTER'S BATTLE-FIELD
AND
THE INDIAN VILLAGE
June 26th 1876

KEOGH
CUSTER/ STAFF
CALHOUN CO.
CUSTER HILL
YATES/CUSTER/ SMITH COMPANIES MEET CHEYENNE
CALHOUN HILL
NYE - CARTWRIGHT RIDGE
Deep Coulee
Medicine Tail Coulee
Custer Ford
Ford
Little Bighorn River
North
East
South
West
INDIAN VILLAGE

Note: Basemap derived from Captain Philo Clark's 1877 Battlefield Map.

CartoGraphics Incorporated (612)379-3599

Phase Two

SIOUX ATTACK
CUSTER
KEOGH
CHEYENNE SIOUX ATTACK
CUSTER HILL
YATES/SMITH COs OVERRUN
SIOUX ATTACK

Phase Three

SIOUX ATTACK
CUSTER
CHEYENNE/ SIOUX ATTACK
CUSTER HILL
SIOUX ATTACK

Custer's Death

Of the soldiers who fought to death in that terrible battle, the Indian warriors were to speak of one who seemed to impress many of them. The Sioux warrior Red Horse said:

Among [the soldiers] *was an officer who rode a horse with four white feet.*

The Indians have fought a great many tribes of people, and very brave ones too, but they all say this man was the bravest man they had ever fought. I don't know whether this man was General Custer or not; some say he was.

I saw this man in the fight several times, but I did not see his body...he alone saved his command a number of times by turning his horse in the rear of the retreat.

Two Moon also spoke of the last moments of the battle and of the conspicuousness of one soldier:

Soldiers drop and horses fall on them. Soldiers in line drop, but one man rides up and down the line - all the time shouting. He rode a sorrel horse with white face and white forelegs. I don't know who he was. He was a brave man.

This soldier could have been any one of several officers with Custer who would have courageously fought until the end. However, in death Custer was recognized by the Indian warriors, and was spared the mutilation most of his command suffered. Low Dog of the Sioux commented on sparing Custer's body from mutilation:

The wise men and chiefs of our nation gave out to people not to mutilate the dead white chief, for he was a brave warrior and died a brave man, and his remains should be respected.....

No white man or Indian ever fought as bravely as Custer and his men.

Sitting Bull eventually was interviewed about the battle, and he paid special tribute to Custer:

It was said that up there where the last fight took place, where the last stand was made, the Long Hair stood like a sheaf of corn with all the ears fallen around him.

Not wounded? (Sitting Bull was asked.)

No.

How many stood by him?

A few.

When did he fall?

He killed a man when he fell. He laughed.

You mean he cried out?

No. He laughed, he had fired his last shot.

Of General Custer, Sitting Bull, ironically, would give higher respect than most historians have.

Perhaps Custer's greatest enemy in life, and certainly the most successful in fighting against him, Sitting Bull paid a very simple tribute to his fallen adversary. He said:

He was a great Chief.

EPILOGUE: ONE SURVIVOR?

Crow Scout Curley

"About 9 a.m., June 27, a Crow scout from Custer's command reached the boat . . ."

Grant Marsh, Captain of the Far West, later gave information to the Bismark Tribune and said:

> *". . . on the morning of June 27, Curley, a crow scout, came out of the timber near the boat and was recognized as one who was with Custer; he proves to be the last survivor.*

Curley could not make his gestures understood, but given a pencil, he drew a sketch of the battlefield. Making a few dots, he conveyed by signs that they represented white men; these he surrounded by dots to represent Indians. Curley said . . . "White men all dead, me get two ponies."

There was one known "only survivor" of the Battle of the Little Bighorn. This was Captain Keogh's horse, Commanche. Commanche was found near the river, badly wounded, and was given medical treatment and then transported on the steamship *Far West* with the wounded of the 7th Cavalry back to Fort Lincoln. Thereafter, Commanche was to enjoy celebrity status in the United States Army and was to attend many special events and parades until the horse's death many years after the epic battle he had survived.

There also may have been one other "only survivor," a human. The 17 year old Crow scout, Curley, is believed to have witnessed the destruction of Custer's command and somehow escaped. It is known for certain that Curley did not end up on Reno's hill position with the other Crow scouts who had been with Custer. Instead, on the morning of June 27,Curley arrived at the mouth of the Little Big Horn River where the steamship Far West was anchored.

Captain Steven Baker was on board the Far West when Curley arrived, and in a dispatch of June 29, said:

Throughout his life, Curley was to give many conflicting accounts of how he escaped death with Custer's command. Some of these accounts were probably garbled through poor translation, as Curley spoke almost no English at the time of the battle. Other accounts may have been embellished by those who interviewed him. A superstitious fear of the event and the dead also could have influenced what Curley said about the battle.

This young Crow scout had also experienced an event which, in trauma and significance, would have dwarfed any other experience of his life. Confusion is a natural occurrence in any traumatic event and this would have been the same for Curley.

Yet, the question remains; could Curley have actually witnessed and then escaped Custer's last battle? One statement made, if correct, would seem to indicate he did.

Since the Crow scouts joined Major Reno on his hill position without Curley, at some point he obviously must have separated from them. These scouts would later say they had been left behind by Custer near the Weir Peaks. Fear that these scouts might be mistaken for hostile Indians and killed was the reason given for leaving these scouts behind. Yet, if Curley was not with them, where had he gone?

It would seem unlikely that Curley, or anyone else, would have wandered away from the battlefield alone while in the proximity of thousands of Sioux warriors. If he did not

remain at Weir Peaks with the other scouts, common sense would seem to indicate that he would have remained with Custer's command. He also would have remained near the only other scout who stayed with Custer who was the only other person in that command that was known to speak the Crow language. This person was Mitch Boyer.

In the many accounts left of Custer's adventures in the American West, it was pointed out again and again that Custer not only placed a great deal of confidence in the scouts, but while on campaign he was almost always near them. There would have been no role for Mitch Boyer at the Battle of the Little Big Horn except to remain near Custer to advise him. Curley, then, would have been near both Boyer and Custer throughout most of the battle.

When he arrived at the steamship on June 27, Curley indicated that Custer's command had been surrounded and wiped out. The problem of gun smoke on the battlefield would seem to rule out that Curley was at a distance from the battle. He would also have had to escape the attention of the Sioux warriors and their allies while observing the course of the battle. Curley's description of the battle would seem to indicate that he was on the inside looking out, not on the outside looking in.

Mitch Boyer was not found with Custer and those on the hilltop with him. He was found near the river and this may also be the escape route taken by Curley. A possibility exists, but can never be proven, that Custer, seeing his command being destroyed, and knowing those remaining were doomed, ordered Mitch Boyer and Curley to escape, perhaps with a last message, and these two headed for the river where they hoped to hide in the brush to later escape. It would seem unlikely that Boyer would have left Custer for any other reason and it would also seem likely that Curley would have remained near Boyer, at least until he was killed.

In his accounts of the battle, Curley would often say he did nothing "wonderful" and, unlike many of the other survivors of the battle, seemed to never embellish his stories with heroics of himself. Yet, two events would seem to indicate that Curley may have been a young man of unusual courage. When he arrived at the steamboat, Curley had with him two Sioux ponies, demonstrating that, even while escaping the massacre of Custer and his command, he had the presence of mind to steal something from the enemies of the Crow.

The second event occurred when, after the Crow scouts became discouraged after the outcome of the battle and returned to their homes, Curley remained behind and did not leave until he received permission from General Terry to do so. It would seem that if anyone had a reason to head to the hills and not look back, Curley did. Yet, he did not, and his personal courage should not preclude this young Indian scout from being considered the only survivor of Custer's last stand.

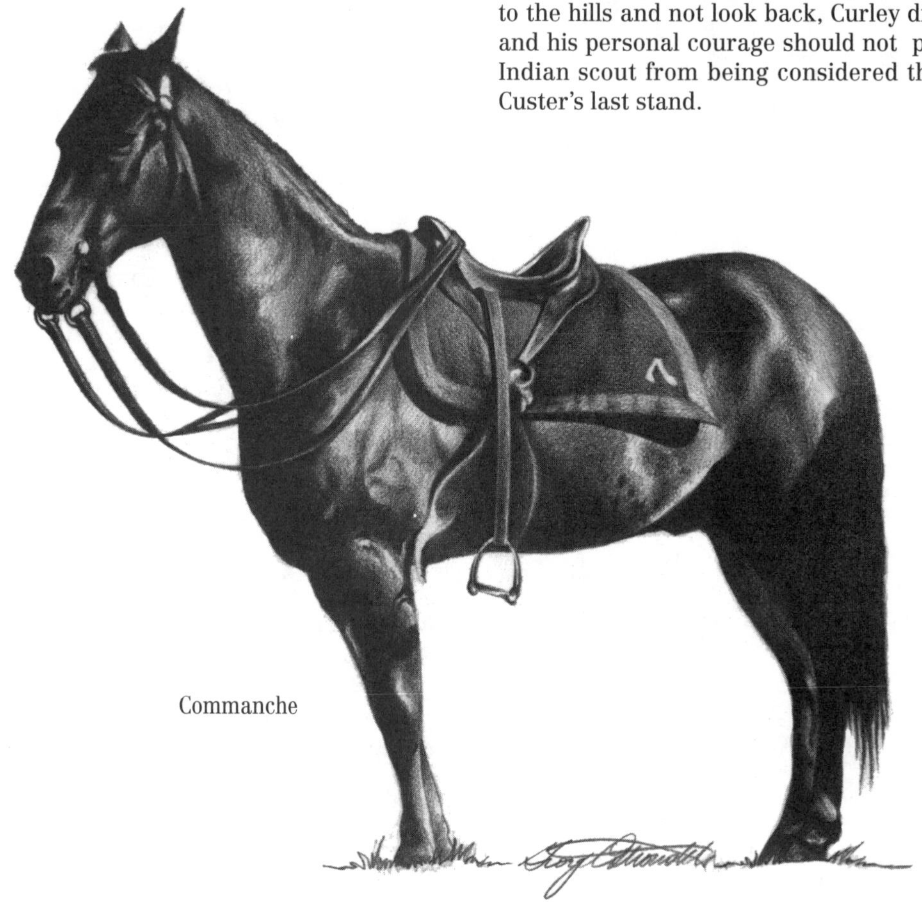

Commanche

RECOMMENDED READING.

Battle of the Little Big Horn

One of the best books on the battle is *The Little Bighorn Campaign, March-September 1876* by Wayne Michael Sarf, published by Combined Books, Inc. of Conshohocken, PA.

A book of primary documentation with many interviews and narratives by participants is *The Custer Myth* written and compiled by Colonel W.A. Graham, published by University of Nebraska Press, of Lincoln, NE.

A complete and unabridged transcript on the Reno Court of Inquiry of 1879 is *Reno Court of Inquiry - Proceedings of a Court of Inquiry in the case of Major Marcus A. Reno* compiled and edited by Ronald H. Nichols, published by Custer Battlefield Historical and Museum Association.

Another publication containing transcripts of the Walter Camp interviews with participants of the Battle of the Little Big Horn is *Custer in '76* which includes Walter Camp's notes on the Custer Fight as edited by Kenneth Hammer, published by University of Oklahoma Press, Norman and London.

Perhaps the most insightful information available on Captain Benteen is *The Benteen-Goldin Letters on Custer and His Last Battle* edited by John M. Carroll, Illustrated by Lorence Bjorklund, published by University of Nebraska Press, Lincoln and London.

A good overall picture of the Seventh Cavalry comes to us in *Custer's 7th Cavalry: from Fort Riley to the Little Big Horn* by E. Lisle Reedstrom, published in 1992 by Sterling Publishing Company, Inc. of New York, NY.

A good source book of primary accounts of the battle and the Seventh Cavalry is *The Custer Reader* edited by Paul Andrew Hutton, published in 1992 by the University of Nebraska Press.

Another good source of material comes from the *St. Paul Pioneer Press* year 1876. In 1876, St. Paul, Minnesota was the last major city before entering the American frontier and also the home duty station of the 7th Cavalry. Many articles on the Battle of the Little Big Horn, Custer, and the American West were published within this newspaper. They are available on micro-film, check your local library.

Little Big Horn Associates Newsletter - ongoing research into the Battle of the Little Big Horn and related information published ten times a year and also two "research review" booklets. For more information, contact: Tom O'Neil, Editor, 105 Bartlett Place, Brookland, NY 11229

Custer

Considered one of the best biographies on Custer is Custer - *The Life of General George Armstrong Custer* by Jay Monaghan, published by the University of Nebraska Press, Lincoln and London.

The original biography of Custer published six months after his death is *A Complete Life of General George A. Custer* by Frederick Whittaker, published by University of Nebraska Press, Lincoln and London.

Custer's own story of his adventures in the American West can be found in *My Life on the Plains or, Personal Experiences with Indians* by General George Armstrong Custer with an introduction by Edgar I. Stewart, published by University of Oklahoma Press, Norman.

Custer Victorious by Gregory J. W. Urwin, published by Associated University Presses, Inc. in 1983 details Custer's Civil War career.

A short account of Custer during the Civil War by a solder who served with him is *Historical Sketch of General Custer* by James H. Kidd, published by The Monroe County Library System, Monroe, Michigan.

U.S. Frontier Army

One of the best overviews on the U.S. Frontier Army is *Frontier Regulars The Untied States Army and the Indian 1866-1891* by Robert M. Utley, published by University of Nebraska Press, Lincoln and London.

A dose of frontier soldiering: the memoirs of corporal E.A. Bode, frontier regular infantry, 1877-1882 edited by Thomas T. Smith, published by University of Nebraska Press, details what it was like to be a frontier soldier by a person who was.

The United States Army and Navy Journal of the year 1876 provides a lot of in depth information on the frontier army as well as other era military issues.

Indian Wars

Perhaps the best book on the entire history of the Indian Wars which is well researched, written, and illustrated is the *Chronicle of the Indian Wars* by Alan Axelrod, published by Pretince Hall General Reference.

Part autobiography of General Nelson Miles and part history and insights into the Indian Wars of the Frontier West

is *Personal Recollections and Observations of General Nelson A. Miles* originally published in 1896; 1992 by the University of Nebraska Press.

Reporter John Finerty's account of the Crook Campaign of 1876 with commentary on the Battle of the Little Big Horn is *War-Path and Bivouac The Big Horn and Yellowstone Expedition* by John F. Finerty, edited by Milo Milton Quaiffe, published by University of Nebraska Press, Lincoln and London.

First published in the 19th Century, *A Century of Dishonor* by H.H., published by Corner House Publishers of WIlliamstown, MA, documents frauds and abuses which were committed against the American Indian.

A frontier soldiers view of the Plains Indian is depicted in *Our Wild Indians: Thirty-Three Years' Personal Experience among the Red Men of the Great West* by Colonel Richard Irving Dodge, published by Archer House, Inc. 1959.

Art of the Frontier West

An interesting book of American Frontier West art is *The Lure of the Great West* by Frank Getlein, published by Country Beautiful Corporation.

Artists and Illustrators of the Old West 1850-1900 by Robert Taft, published by Princeton University Press, Princeton, NJ, lists information on artists and art of the American Frontier West.

A full color, quality monthly publication with excellent art work and articles is *Wild West* published by Cowles History Group, 741 Miller Drive SE, Leesburg, VA, 22075.

Organizations

Custer/Little Bighorn Advocate, Box 792, Malibu, CA, 90265-0792

Custer Battlefield Historical and Museum Association, Box 902, Hardin, MT, 59034

Custer Battlefield Preservation Committee, Box 7, Hardin, MT, 59034

Custer Memorial Association, Box 111, New Rumley, OH, 43984

Frontier Army of the Dakota, RR 1, Box 44, Surrey, ND, 58785

Little Bighorn Associates, Box 640286, El Paso, TX, 79904-0286

Westerners International, 17 NE 63rd Street, Oklahoma City, OK, 73111

Order of the Indian Wars, Box 7401, Little Rock, AR, 72216-0401

National Indian Wars Association, 1707 Bates Court, Thousand Oaks, CA, 91362.

APPENDIX

A. Appeal to Army Board of Correction of Military Record by Ed Zimmerman, Esq., Military and Veterans National Law Center

B. F.B.I. examination of the Enlisted Soldiers Petition

C. Acoustical study of Professor Terry Flowers of The College of St. Catherine, St. Paul, Minnesota

D. Cartographic Study of the Little Big Horn maps by Cartographics Incorporated

APPENDIX A

Appeal to Army Board of Correction of Military Record by Ed Zimmerman, Esq., Military and Veterans National Law Center

Military and Veterans National Law Center
Pentagon Office Park Tower
4940 Viking Drive, Suite 505
Edina, MN 55435
(612) 925-2500 & (612) 831-7100

August 4, 1995

Mr. Robert Nightengale
One Appletree Square
Bloomington, MN 55420

Dear Mr. Nightengale:

You have asked me to provide an analysis of the legal process by which the official record of the Battle of the Little Big Horn might be revised to reflect the true facts that are coming to light as you continue your research into the events of the battle and its aftermath.

You have provided me with copies of sound studies and map studies and other research which provide evidence that the official conclusions about the battle which were reached by the Army in a Court of Inquiry in 1879 are highly inaccurate. I have reviewed these studies and the official record of the Court and I agree with your analysis.

The evidence I have reviewed includes studies of sound propagation characteristics of the .45-70 (or "Trapdoor") breech-loading rifle issued to the Frontier Army in the 1870s and used by the men of the 7th Cavalry. These studies apply computer modelling and analysis to determine the distances at which volley firing of these weapons could be heard. There is testimony in the official record that many soldiers on Reno Hill (including Major Reno himself, according to his statement in his official report) heard volleys from Custer's forces. The conclusion of the sound studies is that these volleys could not have originated from the hill known as "Last Stand Hill" where Custer's forces died, since that hill is over four miles away from Reno Hill. The conclusion that must be drawn is that these volleys originated from some closer source and were therefore fired much earlier in the battle before Custer's forces got to Last Stand Hill. This indicates they were probably heard at a time when it would still have been possible to send forces to Custer's relief.

I also understand that the "70" in the designation of this weapon refers to the maximum amount of black powder used in the cartridge and that, in actuality, a .45-55 load was the standard cartridge the Army issued the cavalry at that time. Therefore, I assume that the use of a .45-70 load in the sound study tests would actually have generated a much louder sound of gunfire than the loads Custer's troops were likely to have carried, (unless, of course, they all hand-loaded their cartridges.) Based on this understanding, the sound studies appear to be conservative and should be accepted as reliable evidence, even though they are based on computer modelling of the range of sound pressure levels of single shots. I understand it is your intention to arrange further testing of volley firing at appropriate locations on the battlefield, and the evidence obtained from these tests should provide further support for the conclusion that Reno had time to come to Custer's aid.

I have also reviewed various maps you have found in your research and cartographer's studies concerning these maps. These studies conclude that the map submitted in evidence at the Reno Court of Inquiry was extremely inaccurate in placing a large cliff formation between the line of sight and sound from Reno Hill to the area of the ford across the Little Big Horn River where you believe Custer crossed to fight the Indians in their own encampment. The selection of this map to offer in evidence may be viewed as evidence of an effort to cover up the testimony of several soldiers on Reno Hill that fighting could be observed in the Indian camp shortly after they retreated to Reno Hill. Again, the significance of this testimony is that there would have been ample time to send forces to support Custer and prevent the massacre.

I have also reviewed an FBI Report concerning an analysis of the Enlisted Men's Petition which was submitted in evidence in support of Major Reno. It is clear from this study that a large number of the signatures on that petition were forgeries. For example, many were from men who were illiterate and signed their payroll with an "X." The petition was drawn up shortly after the battle to ask the War Department to give command of the 7th to Major Reno, and its relevance to the issues before the Court of Inquiry is questionable. However, it is certainly possible that this fraudulent show of support for Reno could have influenced the officers on the Board, and this petition is further evidence of a concerted effort to cover up the true facts surrounding the battle.

I have also accompanied you in a tour of the battlefield and we have used optical equipment with magnifications comparable to the field glasses used by cavalry officers in 1876 to assess view lines on the battlefield. These observations demonstrate the following:

1) From Reno Hill Reno and his men could see the area immediately west of the ford of the Little Big Horn at the foot of Medicine Tail Coulee and the area of the Indian encampment to the west.

2) The Weir Peaks to the north of Reno Hill block all view of Last Stand Hill and are some barrier in the direct line of sound transmission from Last Stand Hill to Reno Hill.

3) From Custer's line of advance toward the Weir Peaks, at the point where testimony indicates Custer was last seen by Reno's men when they were down in the river valley, there is a clear view of the area where Reno's men would have been

fighting and much of the area through which they retreated to Reno Hill.

4) From the base of the Weir Peaks, near the point where the farthest advance is indicated of the troops Weir took forward, there is a clear line of sight to the top and eastern approaches to Last Stand Hill and the top of Deep Coulee below Calhoun's Hill. However, the ford and bottom of Deep Coulee and Medicine Tail Coulee are not visible from that point.

5) From the top of the Weir Peaks there is a clear view of most of the battlefield.

It is my understanding you are arranging to have these observations documented by qualified cartographers. This evidence should support the conclusion that Major Reno and Captain Benteen and the men under their command on Reno Hill and at the Weir Peaks had an opportunity to view Custer's movements or the activity of battle around Custer's forces.

I have also reviewed the record of the Reno Court of Inquiry, and I find a number of instances of testimony which conflicts with testimony or official reports in key matters. There is strong evidence that the findings of the Reno Court of Inquiry were wrong and were not supported by the evidence given or by other evidence readily available to the Court.

My conclusion is that the evidence presented at the Reno Court of Inquiry and the larger historical record shows that Major Reno and Captain Benteen abandoned Custer. There is also ample evidence that Custer conducted his movements according to accepted military doctrine and in complete accord with the broad orders and full discretion given him by General Terry. Had Major Reno sustained his attack or come to the aid of Custer after his retreat, the Battle of the Little Big Horn might have had a very different outcome. The findings of the Court that Major Reno was not at fault are unjustified.

You have also inquired whether it is possible to correct the military record so that the official history will record the truth about the battle.

There is a remedy, even today, for the erroneous findings of the Reno Court of Inquiry. Title 10 of the United States Code provides in Section 1552 that the Secretary of a military department may correct any military record of that Department when necessary to remove an injustice. Under the authority of this statute, the Secretary of the Army has established the Army Board for the Correction of Military Records. The Board operates under Army Regulation 15-185, which provides, in Section II, paragraph 4 of that regulation:

The function of the Board is to consider all applications properly before it for the purpose of determining the existence of an error or injustice.

Although there is a time limitation of 3 years after discovery of an error or injustice to file a petition to the Board, the Board itself has complete discretion to waive this time limitation "if it finds it would be in the best interest of justice to do so." The Board has waived this time limitation many, many times to prevent injustice. Whether the Board would be willing to waive this time limitation to hear a petition to revise the official findings concerning the Battle of the Little Big Horn is likely to depend on the Board's view of the equities and merits of such a petition.

Concerning the equities of hearing such a petition, there is much to be said. The Reno Board of Inquiry had an opportunity to serve the American people by clarifying and correcting misconceptions about the last great battle on the American frontier. The evidence was before the court, and the Court chose to ignore it or skirt around it. This was an injustice, not just to General Custer and his family, but to the American people as well -- the sort of injustice the Army Board for the Correction of Military Records was established to correct.

The findings of the Court of Inquiry were evasive, ambiguous, and biased and were, in major respects, completely inconsistent with the bulk of the evidence presented to the panel. In fact, the Court only made one direct finding as to the conduct of Major Reno -- that nothing in his conduct "requires the animadversion from this Court" -- and no findings at all as to the conduct of Custer. But the message the Court of Inquiry gave to history was that Lieutenant Colonel (Brevet Major General) George Armstrong Custer acted rashly and in violation of his orders and led his men to death unnecessarily.

The motives behind the unjustified findings of the Reno Court of Inquiry appear to be mostly political. It seems unlikely the Army was as much concerned with Reno as it was with Custer. Note that the time to bring charges against Reno had probably expired. In fact, at the time the Court convened, Reno was actually serving a one-year suspension from rank and duty as the result of a court-martial conviction for drunken and disorderly behavior. (He was later dishonorably dismissed from service after a court-martial for a second incident that combined drunkenness with voyeurism.)

It is more logical to believe that the real motive behind the Reno Court of Inquiry was, in fact, the need of officials in power to deal once and for all with the troublesome ghost of General George Armstrong Custer.

Accepting that concern as the motivation behind the Court of Inquiry raises more troublesome questions. Why, two and a half years, after Custer's death did Congress and the Army care to inquire about the battle? Why was the Court charged to investigate the conduct of Major Reno when the time for bringing court-martial charges against him for cowardice had passed? Why wasn't the Court of Inquiry charged to investigate the conduct of others in the battle, such as Custer? Why was false and misleading evidence introduced to show that the line of sight and sound to the river crossing was blocked by high hills? Why was perjured testimony given that Custer's whereabouts was unknown?

And beyond that, why did Reno and Benteen not come to Custer's aid? Why was Captain Weir ordered back from the high ground overlooking the river crossing and Last Stand Hill? Why did Reno retreat from the South end of the Indian encampment in the first place?

And still beyond that, why was Custer given such broad and vague orders by General Terry? Why did General Terry, immediately after the battle, claim that Custer had violated those orders? Why was Custer permitted to rejoin his regiment in the first place? Why were threatened court-martial charges against him following his testimony before Congress never brought? And why did President Ulysses Grant refuse to see General Custer before he left Washington?

In the Court proceedings, of course, Custer had no advocate to raise such questions, and this allowed Reno's lawyer to orchestrate the proceedings carefully to preserve the honor and career of his client. The Court Recorder, Lieutenant Lee, did try zealously to bring out the true facts of the battle, but he was frustrated at every turn by the skillful maneuvering of Reno's lawyer, who entertained key witnesses in his Palmer House suite. After the hearing results were published, Lieutenant Lee wrote a long letter of apology to Custer's widow, expressing his frustration and deep personal regret that he was not able to achieve a just result.

Unfortunately, Reno's ability to manipulate the evidence has affected our view of a national hero for over a century. More unfortunate still is the fact that this outcome has literally buried our knowledge of the important things that Custer had to say. Today a few historians and Custer buffs know about his testimony before Congress about the greed and corruption of the Grant administration and how it stole the promised food and shelter of the Indian people and drove them from the reservations. Few know he believed that the horrors and butchery on both sides of the Indian Wars of the American prairies were largely unnecessary. Few know that Custer saw the Indian warrior as an honorable foe whose people deserved respect and fair and humane treatment.

It is, of course, difficult to answer all the questions that could be raised about Custer and his "Last Stand" 120 years after the battle. But it isn't necessary to question whether Custer was set up or shut up to deal with the simpler issues concerning his conduct of his last battle which still cloud his name today. Many, if not most Americans believe today that Custer was rash, that he was seeking glory, that he violated his orders, and that he got his men killed. The evidence you have presented for my review shows that such assumptions are unjustified. To present this evidence to the Army, I have prepared a draft petition to the Army Board for the Correction of Military Records.

The enclosed petition requests the Secretary of the Army to revise the findings of the Reno Court of Inquiry to show that Custer was not rash, that he followed accepted cavalry doctrine and tactics in making a flank attack, that he acted in full compliance with his orders, and that he was abandoned by his subordinates, Major Reno and Captain Benteen.

The passage of 120 years has not diminished the need to set the official record straight about the Battle of the Little Big Horn. The battle is one of the most significant events in American history, and it deserves better treatment. The legend of General George Armstrong Custer and the Battle of the Little Big Horn has been the subject of hundreds of books, thousands of articles, dozens of movies and documentaries, and scores of paintings and other works of art. The Battlefield is now a National Monument visited by hundreds of thousands of Americans every year. Societies have formed to study the battle, and one of them, the Little Big Horn Associates, has published a monthly newsletter for over two decades. More has been written about this single battle, and more controversy has been generated about its particulars, than about almost any other subject in American history. Yet, so long as the debate continues, the findings of the Reno Court of Inquiry still remain the official position of the United States Government.

In time, we often can learn more about historical events through research into sources not available at the time of the event, analysis available through modern technology, and re-examination of the historical record. The evidence available today about the Battle of the Little Big Horn shows that the findings of the Reno Court of Inquiry were a lie, based upon a cover-up. That is an injustice to all Americans, then and now, which the following petition seeks to correct.

It remains, of course, to determine how this petition should properly be brought before the Army Board for Correction. As you know, George Armstrong Custer left no direct lineal descendants. In fact, most of the male members of his family died with him. His wife Elizabeth survived him by many years and authored three books. The descendants of the Custer family today come from the line of Custer's brother Nevin.

While the honor of the memory of Major General George Armstrong Custer is at stake for the surviving members of his brother's family, it is also a matter of legitimate concern for all the American people. It is, after all, their official record of their Army which was distorted by false evidence and perjured testimony at the Reno Court of Inquiry. The historical view of Custer as rash, glory-seeking, and rebellious has obscured the fact that, as a military leader and author, he was openly and boldly critical of Federal policies and practices that afflicted and suppressed the American Indian peoples.

The First Amendment to the Constitution guarantees every American the right to petition the government for a redress of grievances. In the case of Custer, any American should have the right to petition the Army to correct the false findings in the official record of the battle.

Very truly yours,

Edward A. Zimmerman

APPLICATION FOR CORRECTION OF MILITARY RECORD UNDER THE PROVISIONS OF TITLE 10, U.S. CODE, SECTION 1552
(Please read instructions on reverse side BEFORE completing application.)

Form Approved OMB No. 0704-0003 Expires Dec 31, 1988

PRIVACY ACT STATEMENT

AUTHORITY: Title 10, U.S. Code 1552, Executive Order 9397, November 22, 1943.

PRINCIPAL PURPOSE: To apply for correction of a military record.

ROUTINE USES: To docket a case. Reviewed by board members to determine relief sought. To determine qualification to apply to board. To compare facts present with evidence in the record.

DISCLOSURE: Voluntary. If information is not furnished, applicant may not secure benefits from the Board.

1. APPLICANT DATA

a. BRANCH OF SERVICE *(X one)*

[X] (1) ARMY [ ] (2) NAVY [ ] (3) AIR FORCE [ ] (4) MARINE CORPS [ ] (5) COAST GUARD

b. NAME *(Last, First, Middle Initial) (Please print)*	c. PRESENT PAYGRADE	d. SERVICE NUMBER *(If applicable)*	e. SOCIAL SECURITY NUMBER
CUSTER, George Armstrong	N/A	N/A	N/A

2. TYPE OF DISCHARGE *(If by court-martial, state type of court.)*	3. PRESENT STATUS, IF ANY, WITH RESPECT TO THE ARMED SERVICES *(Active duty, Retired, Reserve, etc.)*	4. DATE OF DISCHARGE OR RELEASE FROM ACTIVE DUTY
N/A	N/A	N/A

5. ORGANIZATION AT TIME OF ALLEGED ERROR IN RECORD
Seventh Cavalry
United States Army

6. I DESIRE TO APPEAR BEFORE THE BOARD IN WASHINGTON, D.C. *(No expense to the Government) (X one)*
[X] a. YES [ ] b. NO

7. COUNSEL *(If any)*

a. NAME *(Last, First, Middle Initial)*	b. ADDRESS *(Street, City, State and Zip Code)*
ZIMMERMAN, Edward A.	4940 Viking Drive, Suite 505 Edina, Minnesota 55435

8. I REQUEST THE FOLLOWING CORRECTION OF ERROR OR INJUSTICE: I seek correction of the record of the Court of Inquiry convened by Special Order No. 255 dated November, 1878, as set forth in the attached Statement of Requested Relief.

9. I BELIEVE THE RECORD TO BE IN ERROR OR UNJUST IN THE FOLLOWING PARTICULARS:
I believe the record and findings of the aforesaid "Reno Court of Inquiry" to be in error as set forth in the attached Statement of Requested Relief.

10. IN SUPPORT OF THIS APPLICATION I SUBMIT AS EVIDENCE THE FOLLOWING: *(If Veterans Administration records are pertinent to your case, give Regional Office location and Claim Number.)*
See attached Statement of Supporting Evidence.

11. ALLEGED ERROR OR INJUSTICE DATA

a. DATE OF DISCOVERY October, 1994, to June, 1996, and continuing

b. IF MORE THAN THREE YEARS SINCE THE ALLEGED ERROR OR INJUSTICE WAS DISCOVERED, STATE WHY THE BOARD SHOULD FIND IT IN THE INTEREST OF JUSTICE TO CONSIDER THIS APPLICATION. Not applicable. See attached Statement of Reasons for Waiver of Three-Year Period.

12. APPLICANT MUST SIGN IN ITEM 16. IF THE RECORD IN QUESTION IS THAT OF A DECEASED OR INCOMPETENT PERSON, LEGAL PROOF OF DEATH OR INCOMPETENCY MUST ACCOMPANY APPLICATION. IF APPLICATION IS SIGNED BY OTHER THAN APPLICANT, INDICATE RELATIONSHIP OR STATUS BY MARKING APPROPRIATE BOX.

[ ] a. SPOUSE [ ] b. WIDOW [ ] c. WIDOWER [ ] d. NEXT OF KIN [X] e. LEGAL REP [ ] f. OTHER *(Specify)*

13. I MAKE THE FOREGOING STATEMENTS, AS PART OF MY CLAIM, WITH FULL KNOWLEDGE OF THE PENALTIES INVOLVED FOR WILLFULLY MAKING A FALSE STATEMENT OR CLAIM. *(U.S. Code, Title 18, Sec. 287, 1001, provides a penalty of not more than $10,000 fine or not more than 5 years imprisonment or both.)*

14. COMPLETE CURRENT ADDRESS, INCLUDING ZIP CODE *(Applicant should forward notification of all changes of address.)*

DOCUMENT NUMBER *(Do not write in this space.)*

15. DATE SIGNED	16. SIGNATURE *(Applicant must sign here.)*

DD Form 149, FEB 86 *Previous editions are obsolete.*

STATEMENT OF REQUESTED RELIEF

8. *I REQUEST THE FOLLOWING CORRECTION OF ERROR OR INJUSTICE:*

1. The Board is requested to find that Major Marcus Reno was ordered to attack the Indian encampment from the South for the purpose of creating and maintaining a diversionary action that would enable Lieutenant Colonel George Custer to attack the encampment at the center and drive through, with the objective of dividing the Indian forces and forcing a dispersal.

2. The Board is requested to find that Major Reno did not carry out his orders and did not apply standard cavalry tactics in the conduct of his attack and subsequent retreat which could have enabled him to succeed in maintaining his position or in remaining in contact with the enemy and thus continuing the diversionary engagement.

3. The Board is requested to find that Lieutenant Colonel Custer would have been able, from his position on the ridgeline, to observe the position on the opposite side of the Little Big Horn River in the valley below through which the forces under Major Reno retreated.

4. The Board is requested to find that Bloody Knife, who was reported by Sergeant Kanipe to have been with Lieutenant Colonel Custer after the division of forces, subsequently made contact with Major Reno during his retreat from the south end of the Indian encampment, but was then struck in the head by a bullet and died in such a sudden, violent, and horrible manner that Major Reno became greatly demoralized and remained in an incapacitated condition, unable to maintain effective control of the forces under his command.

5. The Board is requested to find that, after the retreat to the position now known as Reno Hill, Major Reno and Captain Frederick Benteen and many of the troops under their command became aware that Lieutenant Colonel Custer was attacking into the center of the Indian encampment at a point within reach of their forces.

6. The Board is requested to find that, after learning of this attack, Captain Weir led an element of forces north to the highest point in the area now known as the Weir Peaks.

7. The Board is requested to find that Captain Fredrick Benteen then brought the majority of the effective forces on Reno Hill up to the Weir Peaks and ascended the western point with a banner and binoculars and that men with him reported seeing men on horseback on Last Stand Hill.

8. The Board is requested to find that Captain Weir, who died before he could testify, and then Captain Benteen, after he joined Captain Weir on the Weir Peaks, would have been able to observe Lieutenant Colonel Custer, either during Custer's retreat from the

Indian encampment or during his deployment on Last Stand Hill, depending upon the time of their respective arrivals on the Weir Peaks.

9. The Board is requested to find that Lieutenant Colonel Custer was able to see men on the Weir Peaks from his position on Last Stand Hill and that he ordered his men to extend south along the ridgeline running from Last Stand Hill toward the Weir Peaks in the belief that the men on the Weir Peaks were there to support him and would attack to the north.

10. The Board is requested to find that, seeing Lieutenant Colonel Custer on Last Stand Hill, Captain Benteen, the ranking officer in charge at the scene, did not go his aid and retreated with all his men back to Reno Hill.

11. The Board is requested to find that, in the subsequent investigation held by the Court of Inquiry, Major Reno, Captain Benteen, and those supporting them presented false testimony and altered documentary evidence in support of their claims that they were not aware of the location of Lieutenant Colonel Custer's forces and were unable to come to his aid.

12. The Board is requested to find that, in the conduct of the Battle of the Little Big Horn Lieutenant Colonel George Armstrong Custer followed accepted military doctrine and applied sound tactics and did not violate his orders.

STATEMENT OF SUPPORTING EVIDENCE

10. IN SUPPORT OF THIS APPLICATION I SUBMIT AS EVIDENCE THE FOLLOWING:

1) Report of sound studies conducted by Professor Terry Flowers
2) Report of sound studies conducted by Dr. Rick Van Doeren
3) Report of cartographer's study, "Observations on the Battle Maps of the Little Big Horn," by Philip Schwartzberg, March, 1995
4) Report of cartographer's study by Cartographics, Inc., May, 1996
5) Various maps prepared by Army authorities and the United States Geological Survey concerning the battlefield area
6) Report of examination of the Enlisted Men's Petition (Exhibits numbers 9, 10, and 11 at the Reno Court of Inquiry) by the Federal Bureau of Investigation, 1954
7) Record of Proceedings of the Reno Court of Inquiry in the Case of Major Marcus A. Reno, compiled and edited by Ronald H. Nichols, Custer Battlefield Historical & Museum Association, Inc., Crow Agency, Montana
8) Letters, reports, and news articles contemporaneous with the time of the battle and of the Reno Court of Inquiry
9) Correspondence of Captain Frederick Benteen
10) Correspondence of Theodore Golden
11) Official Report of the battle submitted by Major Marcus Reno made shortly after the Battle of the Little Big Horn
12) Letter and report of Lieutenant Edward McGuire to General Terry prepared shortly after the battle and subsequent maps
13) The Cavalry Manual in effect in 1876
14) The orders given Lieutenant Colonel Custer by General Terry
15) Pictures, video tapes, maps and models of the Little Big Horn Battlefield showing lines of sight and distances involved

ELEMENTS OF PROOF

> Sound studies and an analysis of the battlefield terrain show Lieutenant Colonel Custer's men fired from the area running from the river crossing into the center of the Indian encampment after Reno's men were assembled on Reno hill, about 2 miles away.

> Testimony at the Court of Inquiry supports the thesis that Lieutenant Colonel Custer's men fired in volley formation and had penetrated toward the center of the Indian encampment at the time that Major Reno's element had retreated to Reno Hill and Captain Benteen's element had come north to join them.

> Map studies show the map submitted with the original Engineer's Report was altered substantially before presentation as Exhibit 2 at the Court of Inquiry, and that these alterations present a false picture of the terrain and the battle, appear to be deliberate, and were supportive of Major Reno's position at the Court.

> FBI examination of the enlisted men's petition in support of Major Reno shows a probability that numerous signatures were forged and supports the thesis that there was intense command pressure to submit perjured testimony and altered evidence in support of Major Reno's position at the Court of Inquiry.

> Testimony as to the observations of the men under Captain Benteen who advanced to the Weir Points and visual sightings at the battlefield using equipment with magnifications comparable to field binoculars used by Lieutenant Colonel Custer and the officers leading his forces show that much of Captain Benteen's testimony about his observations was false and support findings that Lieutenant Colonel Custer saw men on the Weir Points and deployed toward them and was abandoned.

> Inconsistencies between the testimony of Captain Benteen and others who were with him and admissions by Captain Benteen in subsequent correspondence with Private Golden show further evidence that Captain Benteen's testimony at the Court of Inquiry was perjured.

> Testimony and knowledge of the characteristics of the powder in use at the battle show that, when Captain Benteen abandoned the Weir Points, the attack on Lieutenant Colonel Custer had not begun.

> Inconsistencies in the reports and testimony of Major Marcus Reno and the testimony of the men in his element show that he committed perjury in several key respects in his testimony at the Court of Inquiry.

> The Cavalry Manual in effect in 1876 shows that Major Reno did not follow accepted tactics in any respect throughout the entire battle and that his retreat was cowardly, unnecessary, and in violation of his orders and that Lieutenant Colonel Custer did follow accepted tactics in the movement and deployment of the

forces under his direct control and in the orders he gave to his subordinate element commanders.

> The written orders given Lieutenant Colonel Custer by General Terry prior to the beginning of the campaign gave him broad discretion, and his actions at each stage of the way up to his death on Last Stand Hill were completely consistent with those orders and accepted Army doctrine for the Cavalry in the attack. There is no support in those orders or Lieutenant Colonel Custer's actions for the later charge by General Terry and others made after the battle that Custer acted rashly and in violation of his orders.

CONCLUSION>> The actions of Lieutenant Colonel George Armstrong Custer from the time he ordered his forces to move to contact with the Indian force until the time he chose to extend his remaining forces along the ridgeline of Last Stand Hill toward the forces on the Weir Points were consistent with continuing the attack to break and disperse the Indian forces.

EAZ:jrs/MA117BCR.PTN

APPENDIX B

F.B.I. examination of the Enlisted Soldiers Petition

United States Department of the Interior

NATIONAL PARK SERVICE
Little Bighorn Battlefield National Monument
Post Office Box 39
Crow Agency, Montana 59022-0039

IN REPLY REFER TO:
K14 (LIBI)

April 5, 1995

Robert Nightengale
Blue Book Publications
1 Apple Tree Square
Minneapolis, MN 55425

Dear Mr. Nightengale:

Herewith enclosed are the copies of the documents relating to the FBI examination of the Reno petition. The results of the examination were inconclusive, yet the limited handwriting samples available to them suggested that many, if not most, of the signatures were forgeries. There was some evidence to suggest that First Sergeant Joseph McCurry wrote the names, but this could not be determined with certainty because of the paucity of samples of his handwriting.

I hope this information will be of value to your research.

Sincerely,

Douglas C. McChristian

Douglas C. McChristian
Chief Historian

Enclosures

Cust r Battlefield National Monument
Crow Agency, Montana,

September 29, 1954

Mr. Hillory A. Tolson,
Assistant Director
National Park Service
Washington 25, D.C.

My dear Mr. Tolson:

Just about the time I started this letter I received your letter of the 23rd. Many thanks for your interest and getting things rolling concerning our water and electric systems. Region Two Office are taking immediate steps to correct the two matters.

About four years ago, November 1950, you very kindly assisted me in trying to "ferret out" a mystery of 78 years. I was not able to supply all of the material that the FBI would have liked to have had so that they could make a complete report. However, during the last eighteen months, I have been able to get this information from the GAO, and as we would legally say, can now produce the "irrefutable evidence." Four years ago I was only able to produce the signatures on a Petition. There were no actual signatures by which the petition signatures could be compared with. Now I have them.

On the report you secured for me, i.e., Report of the F.B.I. Laboratory, File No. 95-38320, Lab. No. D-123677 DG, dated Nov. 20, 1950, and forwarded to me under letter W3423 CUST dated December 7, 1950, this FBI report stated: " . . . Characteristics in common were noted in the "John A. Bailey" and the "John McCabe" signatures . . ." Further on in this report they stated that they were unable to make complete comparisons as they did not have other signatures of the petitioners with which to compare them. Therefore, they could not give us an out and out statement that some of these signatures were forgeries.

Now I have secured from the GAO the muster and pay rolls of the 12 companies of the 7th U. S. Cavalry, the Staff and Band, from which comparisons can be made with the Petition.

There are quite a number of apparent "forgeries" and irregularities that show up on comparing the signatures on the Petition with the signatures on the Muster and Pay Rolls. One irregularity that can easily be seen are those of the troopers who were unable to write their own names. The name would be written in the signature column with the notation "His Mark X" and then would be initialed by the troop commander. On the Petition these names were written by some one, but not verified.

For many years it has been known by the military as well as by historians, that there was "something rotten in Denmark." They could not seem to lay their finger on it. Many historians have written me during the years that I have been here, as to why we (NPS) are covering up this deception. It is also referred to by historians as being a "nefarious scheme" on the part of Major Reno and Captain Benteen to gain quick promotion in lineal rank. Both those officers were junior in rank in their respective grades. There has been rumors in the regiment for many years that both Reno and Benteen used pressure tactics to get the men to sign such a petition. The other officers refused to sign the petition, but, in Troop H, more than other troops was the pressure used. Presumably by Captain Benteen. By looking at Troop H petition you will see more signatures than from the other 11 troops. I have heard it stated in the regiment that 1st Sergeant Joseph McCurry was the "pressure agent."

It is also understood that word got through to General Sherman about this petition before it arrived in that city, and that the proper promotions were made before the petition arrived in Washington. You can see by one of the enclosed photostats that this was done in General Sherman's letter.

What I would greatly appreciate, would be a report on which names were forged on the petition; who wrote the petition, and was it possibly 1st Sergeant McCurry who did majority of the written in names.

Now to another matter. This is in regard to the heroic statue that Mr. Eugene McAuliffe of Omaha, Nebraska, is trying to have erected at this area. Colonel William A (Wild Bill) Harris, who commanded the regiment in Korea, and is now at the Army War College, Carlisle Barracks, Pa., and Dr. Lawrence A. Frost, Curator of the Custer Museum at

Monroe, Michigan, who are two of the four members of a committee of the 7th U. S. Cavalry Association who are investigating whether the Association should sponsor this statue are definitely against it and on the side of the NPS. Perhaps Colonel Harris will call on you or Director Wirth sometime this month to get your views.

It so happens that Evelyn and I are going on leave to her home in Iowa, and I am going to take a trip down to Topeka, Kansas, and see Colonel Brice C.W. Custer. You remember meeting and having lunch with Colonel Custer when we were all in Washington for the purpose of taking General Lee's flag of surrender to Appomattox. Colonel Custer has just returned from Korea, and is stationed now in Topeka, Kansas. I am sure that he would not be in favor of this heroic statue if he knew that the NPS did not desire it.

As things stand now, Mr. McAuliffe is rather disheartened that about everyone is against such a huge statue, and I believe that with proper action, he will give up his pet idea.

I am mailing all these photostats in a large tube and will enclose a carbon copy of this letter with the material.

Assuring you that I deeply appreciate your great interest in this area and Custer history, I remain

Sincerely

E. S. Luce
Superintendent.

14 double page (28)
photostats of 7th Cav.
Muster & Pay Rolls
13 Pages of Petition

In reply refer to:
H2215-T

October 12, 1954

J. Edgar Hoover, Director
Federal Bureau of Investigation
Department of Justice
Justice Building
Washington 25, D. C.

My dear Mr. Hoover:

On October 31, 1950, we sent tp you, in compliance with the request of Superintendent Edward S. Luce, Custer Battlefield National Monument, Crow Agency, Montana, some photostats of the Reno-Benteen promotion petition filed by members of the 7th Cavalry, U.S.A., after the Battle of the Little Big Horn in Montana in 1876, with the request that the Federal Bureau of Investigation determine, if possible, whether some of the signatures on the petition were written by the same person. On November 13, 1950, some additional information was sent to you relating to these photostats. Copies of the two letters mentioned are attached. The F.B.I. Laboratory report of November 20, 1950, was sent to Superintendent Luce.

We have received a letter of September 29, 1954, from Superintendent Luce, and that part of it relating further to the above-mentioned matter is quoted below:

> "About four years ago, November 1950, you very kindly assisted me in trying to 'ferret out' a mystery of 78 years. I was not able to supply all of the material that the FBI would have liked to have had so that they could make a complete report. However, during the last eighteen months, I have been able to get this information from the GAO, and as we would legally say, can now produce the 'irrefutable evidence.' Four years ago I was only able to produce the signatures on a Petition. There were no actual signatures by which the petition signatures could be compared with. Now I have them.
>
> "On the report you secured for me, i.e., Report of the F.B.I. Laboratory, File No. 95-38320, Lab. No. D-123677 DG, dated Nov. 20, 1950, and forwarded to me under letter W3423 CUST dated December 7, 1950, this FBI report stated: ' . . . Characteristics in common were noted in the 'John A. Bailey' and the 'John McCabe' signatures . . .' Further on in this

report they stated that they were unable to make complete comparisons as they did not have other signatures of the petitioners with which to compare them. Therefore, they could not give us an out and out statement that some of these signatures were forgeries.

"Now I have secured from the GAO the muster and pay rolls of the 12 companies of the 7th U. S. Cavalry, the Staff and Band, from which comparisons can be made with the Petition.

"There are quite a number of apparent 'forgeries' and irregularities that show up on comparing the signatures on the Petition with the signatures on the Muster and Pay Rolls. One irregularity that can easily be seen are those of the troopers who were unable to write their own names. The name would be written in the signature column with the notation 'His Mark X' and then would be initialed by the troop commander. On the Petition these names were written by some one, but not verified.

"For many years it has been known by the military as well as by historians, that there was 'something rotten in Denmark.' They could not seem to lay their finger on it. Many historians have written me during the years that I have been here, as to why we (NPS) are covering up this deception. It is also referred to by historians as being a 'nefarious scheme' on the part of Major Reno and Captain Benteen to gain quick promotion in lineal rank. Both those officers were junior in rank in their respective grades. There has been rumors in the regiment for many years that both Reno and Benteen used pressure tactics to get the men to sign such a petition. The other officers refused to sign the petition, but, in Troop H, more than other troops was the pressure used. Presumably by Captain Benteen. By looking at Troop H petition you will see more signatures than from the other 11 troops. I have heard it stated in the regiment that 1st Sergeant Joseph McCurry was the 'pressure agent.'

"It is also understood that word got through to General Sherman about this petition before it arrived in that city, and that the proper promotions were made before the petition arrived in Washington. You can see by one of the enclosed photostats that this was done in General Sherman's letter.

"What I would greatly appreciate, would be a report on which names were forged on the petition; who wrote the petition, and was it possibly 1st Sergeant McCurry who did majority of the written in names."

It will be greatly appreciated if you will kindly have these documents examined in your Laboratory with a view to determining which names were forged on the petition; who wrote the petition; and whether First Sergeant McCurry wrote in a majority of the names.

No other laboratory examinations of the photostats referred to above have been, or will be, made by any other agency.

Sincerely,

(SGD) HILLORY A. TOLSON
Hillory A. Tolson
Assistant Director

Enclosures 4

Copy to: Supt. Luce, Custer Battlefield

In reply refer to:
H2215-T

UNITED STATES
DEPARTMENT OF THE INTERIOR
NATIONAL PARK SERVICE
WASHINGTON 25, D. C.

November 5, 1954

Memorandum

To: Superintendent, Custer Battlefield

From: Acting Director Tolson

Subject: Handwriting Comparison for Custer Battlefield

Referring to your letter of September 29 and to my letter of October 12 to Director J. Edgar Hoover of the Federal Bureau of Investigation, in which we requested that the F.B.I. laboratory determine, if possible, which names on the petition sent in by you were forged; who wrote the petition; whether First Sgt. McCurry wrote any majority of the names, there is attached a copy of the F.B.I. report (F.B.I. File No. 95-38320 and Laboratory No. D-192503 DG) covering the examination made by the F.B.I. laboratory of the documents in question, which are being returned to you under separate cover.

Hillory A. Tolson
Acting Director

Enclosure

REPORT
of the

FEDERAL BUREAU OF INVESTIGATION
WASHINGTON D. C.

To: National Park Service
U. S. Department of the Interior
Washington 25, D. C.

November 2, 1954

Attention: Mr. Hillory A. Tolson
Assistant Director

Re: HANDWRITING COMPARISON FOR CUSTER BATTLEFIELD NATIONAL MONUMENT
DEPARTMENT OF THE INTERIOR
WASHINGTON, D. C.

J. Edgar Hoover
John Edgar Hoover, Director

YOUR FILE NO. H2215-T
FBI FILE NO. 95-38320
LAB. NO. D-192503 DG

Examination requested by: Addressee

Reference: Letter 10/12/54

Examination requested: Document

Specimens:

Resubmission of Qc1.

Kc1 Photostat of a letter dated August 10, 1876, in the known handwriting of E. D. TOWNSEND.
Kc2 Photostat of a Muster Roll of the Field, Staff and Band of the 7th Calvary showing known signatures of members of this unit.
Kc3 Photostat of a Muster Roll of a Detachment of the 7th Calvary showing known signatures of members of this unit.

Photostats of Muster Rolls of 12 companies of the 7th Calvary bearing known signatures of members of each company as follows:

Kc4 Company A
Kc5 Company B
Kc6 Company C
Kc7 Company D
Kc8 Company E
Kc9 Company F
Kc10 Company G
Kc11 Company H
Kc12 Company I
Kc13 Company K
Kc14 Company L
Kc15 Company M

Continued next page

Result of examination:

The signatures on the petition previously submitted and designated as Qcl have been compared with the respective signatures on specimens Kcl through Kcl5 but because of the limited amount of comparable known handwriting and the fact that the original specimens are not available a definite conclusion could not be reached regarding these questioned signatures. However, variations were noted in the signatures listed below and the corresponding known signatures which suggest the probability that the signatures on the petition are forgeries.

Henry Fehler	(Company A)
John T. Easley	(Company A)
David McVeigh	(Company A)
John Bringes	(Company A)
Stanislos Roy	(Company A)
Louis Baumgartner	(Company A)
John W. Franklin	(Company A)
Emil O. Jonsan	(Company A)
William D. Nugent	(Company A)
John M. Gilbert	(Company A)
Anton Siebelder	(Company A)
Samuel Johnson	(Company A)
Neil Bancroft	(Company A)
John Crump	(Company B)
Michael Crowe	(Company B)
John O'Neill	(Company B)
James Pym	(Company B)
Ansgarious Boren	(Company B)
Patrick Crowley	(Company B)
Hiram W. Sager	(Company B)
John Sweeny	(Company F)
Martin Mullin	(Company C)
Frank Burwald	(Company E)
Fredrick Schutte	(Company F)
Charles Bank	(Company L)
Thomas McLaughlin	(Company H)
Mathew Maroney	(Company H)
George Geiger	(Company H)
William Ramell	(Company H)
Edward Diamond	(Company H)
Henry Haack	(Company H)
William C. Williams	(Company H)

Continued next page

Timothy Haley	(Company H)
James Kelly	(Company H)
William O'Ryan	(Company H)
John Hunt	(Company H)
Charles Windolph	(Company H)
James McNamara	(Company H)
Aloyse L. Walter	(Company H)
C. H. Welch	(Company D)
Charles H. Houghtaling	(Company D)
William Gibbs	(Company K)
John Foley	(Company K)
W. W. Lasley	(Company K)
William Whittlon	(Company K)
George B. Penwell	(Company K)
Charles Chesterwood	(Company K)
Henry W. Raichel	(Company K)
John Rafter	(Company K)
Joseph Brown	(Company K)
Thomas A. Gordon	(Company K)
Michael Murphy	(Company K)
Christian Schlafer	(Company K)
Alonzo Jennys	(Company K)
John Schwerer	(Company K)
John Donahue	(Company K)
George Heid	(Company M)
Jean B. D. Gallenne	(Company M)
Charles Weidman	(Company M)
Morris Cain	(Company M)
Frank Stratton	(Company M)
Edward Pigford	(Company M)
Hugh N. Moore	(Company M)
Walter S. Sterland	(Company M)
Frank Sniffin	(Company M)
Levi Thornberry	(Company M)
Charles Kavanuagh	(Company M)
Bernard Golden	(Company M)
Daniel Mahoney	(Company M)
Andrew Fredrick	(Company K)
Christian Boissen	(Company K)
Cornelius Bresnahan	(Company K)
John Shauer	(Company K)
Charles Burkhardt	(Company K)
Wilson McConnell	(Company K)

Continued next page

Thomas Murphy	(Company K)
Martin McCue	(Company K)
August Siefart	(Company K)
John R. Steintker	(Company K)

It could not definitely be determined whether or not JOSEPH McCURRY prepared any of the above-listed signatures because of the limited amount of comparable known handwriting of McCURRY available.

There are listed below the names of the individuals whose names appeared on the petition but who signed their payroll marked with a witnessed "x":

James E. Moore	(Company B)
William Trumble	(Company B)
Henry Stoppel	(Company F)
J. Mahoney	(Company C)
William Etzler	(Company L)
Daniel Neelan	(Company H)
J. Adams	(Company H)
George W. Dewey	(Company H)
Thomas Lawhorn	(Company H)
Fredrick Deetline	(Company D)
William Hardden	(Company D)
James Hurd	(Company D)
James Seavers	(Company M)
Harrison Davis	(Company M)
George Weaver	(Company M)
William Rye	(Company M)
John Whisten	(Company M)

No known signatures could be located in the known specimens for comparison with the following signatures:

William Reese	(Company E)
William Channell	(Company H)
Edler Neis	(Company H)
Charles Fisher	(Company H)
M. J. Lacy	(Company H)
James Miles	(Company M)
Rollins Thorpe	(Company M)
William Williams	(Company M)

Continued next page

There is insufficient comparable known handwriting of any individual available in the known specimens to determine whether or not any of these individuals wrote the petition designated as Qc1.

The evidence submitted is being returned under separate cover. No photographs have been made.

APPENDIX C

Acoustical study of Professor Terry Flowers of The College of St. Catherine, St. Paul, Minnesota

Acknowledgments

This project was made possible with the help of many individuals, some who provided thoughtful insights into the design of the experiment and the interdisciplinary nature of the study and others who made actual contributions in making it happen. Ms. Laura Miller, a student at the College of St. Catherine, provided assistance in the design of the mathematical model and in data acquisition while Charles Flower, a student at the University of St. Thomas, performed most of the actual firings of the weapons used in the experiment. John Bremer owned the land where the firings were accomplished while Frank Vukmonich served as photographer. Tony Willeke of Hastings, MN and Vern Berning of St. Michael, MN provided the 1873 Springfield firearms. To these and all others who provided suggestions and support thanks is due.

Sound Analysis of Rifles Used at Custer's Last Stand

Introduction:

There are many different interpretations of the Little Big Horn Campaign of 1876, punctuated by the event known as Custer's Last Stand. Diverse historians paint different pictures of the events leading up to that disaster, some judging Custer's actions, some characterizing him as heroic, others portraying him as foolish. Some blamed the other columns of men under the commands of Major Reno and Captain Benteen for the tragedy.

This study is not intended to reflect positively or negatively on General Custer and his men, nor to judge their actions or intentions. Neither does it directly implicate anyone else. Instead, it is designed to answer questions about the sequence of events of June 25, 1995.

Statement of the Problem

A Court of Inquiry, assembled at the Palmer House Hotel in Chicago in January of 1879, was convened to inquire into the conduct of Major Marcus A. Reno at the battle of the Little Big Horn River. After extensive testimony the court found that "... there was nothing in his conduct which requires animadversion from this Court." (Hunt, page 181) But in that investigation several statements appear in conflict with each other. Witnesses heard shots and volleys of shots from the position secured by Major Reno, known as **Reno Hill.** (See selected statements following.) Some historians discount the shots. Others indicate that any shots came from the final Custer Battlefield. The question as to the origin of those shots needs to be answered to understand the events of that fateful day. To gain a better insight into the course of action of General Custer's column the following statements from the Reno Court are considered. These are select statements which point to the possibility that General Custer may have actually crossed the Little Big Horn River and attacked the Indian village. The reader should consult the full report for more details.

Day Four: (Lt. Wallace)

Q. During the time that Major Reno was there and before Captain Weir moved out, what kind of firing did you hear in the direction which Custer was afterward found?
A. Well in that direction I didn't hear any. I heard some firing to the left.

Day Five: (Lt. Wallace)

Q. You testified that firing was heard to your left?
A. Yes sir.

Q. From what direction did that sound come with reference to where you found General Custer's body?
A. It was nearer and on the opposite side of the stream from where his body was found. I heard not over a dozen shots and they were not in quick succession.

Day Nine: (Lt. Varnum)

Q. ... describe the firing, its character and duration, and to what command it pertained and all you saw or heard with reference to it.
A. About the time or probably a few minutes after Captain Benteen came up, I heard firing from away down the stream and spoke of it to Lieutenant Wallace. I don't recollect any except that one time.

Q. Describe your manner of speaking of it.
A. I had borrowed a rifle of Lieutenant Wallace and had fired a couple of shots at long range and as I handed the rifle back to him I heard the firing and said, "Jesus Christ, Wallace, hear that! And that!" Those were my words.

Q. Describe that firing.
A. It was not like a volley firing but a heavy fire, a sort of crash, crash. I heard it only for a few minutes.

Q. State whether that fire impressed you with anything in regard to General Custer.
A. I though he was having a warm time down there, a very hot fire, evidently.

Q. You described certain firing that you heard in that direction. How did that impress you?
A. Well, that he had got to the other end of the village and struck this force of Indians that we had been fighting and that he was having a siege of it too.

Day Twelve: (Capt. Moylan)

Q. Did you hear any firing in the direction of General Custer's battlefield after you reached the top of the hill?
A. Yes.

Q. Describe the sound of the firing.
A. It was evidently volley firing, but very faint.

Day Fourteen: (Lt. Hare)

A. ... and in addition to that I heard firing down there.

Q. Describe the firing; when it was, where you were when you heard it, and how long it lasted, and all you know about it.
A. It was just after Captain Benteen came up with his command. My attention was called to it by Captain Godfrey. He asked if I heard that volley. I said yes, I heard two distinct volleys, that was just before I started for the pack train.

Day Fifteen: (Lt. DeRudio)

Q. Go on and state if you heard any firing after Major Reno's command got to the river. If so, in what direction and how long did the firing last?
A. The firing started soon after Major Reno got to the top of the hill, at least a few minutes after. I could hear immense volleys on the other side of the village. It was down the river and the fire lasted probably an hour and a half and then died off at a distance with small shots, and pretty soon the fire entirely died away. Before it died away entirely the same Indians who left Major Reno soon after he left the timber, came right back again and part of them went on the bluff, and part of them went across the plain and to the south of Major Reno's position on the bluff.

Q. Did it seem to grow much more distant?
A. Yes, sir. The first volley was very plain, then it got farther on and then it died out.

Q. Did it seem to go very much farher away?
A. No, not much. I could hear the volleys and tell they were going away.

Q. Was there a decrease in the volume of sound as to indicate a very great change of position?
A. The firing was steady for a long time, and in volleys, and after that it was scattering and lasted but a short time.

Q. How soon after Major Reno left the timber did the heavy firing commence?
A. Almost simultaneously. Major Reno was about at the top of the hill when that firing started.

Day Sixteen: (Sgt. Davern)

Q. Did you hear any firing after you got on the hill?
A. The firing had ceased, only there were some scattering shots by the Indians on the left.

Q. Did you hear any firing from any other direction, from downstream, anywhere?
A. Shortly after I got on the hill I did.

Q. Describe that firing.
A. It was in volleys.

Q. Where did it seem to come from?
A. From downstream.

Q. How did you happen to hear it? Did you go out to any point, or were you there with others?
A. On the hill where the others were.

Q. Was the firing plain or faint?
A. It was not very distinct, but a person could distinguish it was firing.

Q. You could tell it was volleys?
A. Yes, sir.

(Sgt. Culbertson)

Q. State if you heard from the direction in which General Custer's battlefield was ascertained to be, if so, when was it as compared with the time Captain Benteen's column came up? Describe that firing and what was said about it.
A. It was when Lieutenant Varnum called me to ask for some water. He was sitting at the edge of a bank. While sitting there talking to Lieutenant Edgerly we could hear the firing. At first it was a couple of volleys, very heavy, afterwards it was lighter and appeared to be more distant. Lieutenant Varnum made the remark that General Custer was hotly engaged or was giving it to the Indians hot, or words to that effect, and in a few minutes after, Major Reno came up, and we went to the river, and I did not hear it anymore. If there had been any firing after that the hills would have broke the sound.

Day Nineteen: (Lt. Edgerly)

Q. State whether upon joining Major Reno's command, or soon after, you heard any firing. If so, in what direction, and to what command did that firing pertain? Describe it fully.
A. Shortly after I got on the hill, almost immediately I heard firing and remarked it, heavy firing by volleys down the creek. Captain Weir came to me and said General Custer was engaged and we ought to go down. I said I thought so too. He went away, walking up and down rather anxiously. I heard the fire plainly. The first sergeant came up then and I saw a large cloud of dust and thought there must be a charge, and said, "There must be General Custer. I guess he is getting away with them." He said, "Yes sir, and I think we ought to go there." I did not answer him.

Day Twenty: (B.F. Churchhill, packer citizen)

Q. Describe the sound of it, whether in volleys or not.
A. I remember hearing what I took to be volleys and spoke of it to some of the men. I heard 4 or 5 volleys.

Q. Where did it appear to come from and at what distance?
A. It came from down the river and I thought at the time that it was 2 1/2 or 3 miles away from the sound. It was not a very plain report of guns.

Q. From which end of the village did the firing apparently come?
A. It appeared to come from the lower end of the village.

The above information is helpful to the person interested in answering certain questions about the shots and volleys of shots. It is important to realize that volleys of shots indicate a fighting formation used by Custer's men. This study will examine the nature of the sounds of shots and volleys of shots, and using classical physics consider whether they originated from the Indian campground or from the actual Custer battlefield where he and his men were found. A model applying both divergence and absorption is used to estimate the sound levels at varying distances. Finally, the real question is not what the sound levels were, but whether or not they could be heard by the human ear. Thus, physiological and psychological conditions are regarded attentively.

Design of the Experiment:

To answer the basic question as to whether gun shots and volleys of them could be heard from **Reno Hill**, the simplest arrangement would be to visit the Battlefield and place observers on **Reno Hill** while shooters fired volleys of shots from the final battlefield site and from the campground. Because political conditions prevent actually performing the real test, an experiment was devised to answer the question. Using firearms similar to those used by Custer's men and ammuntion similar to the actual cartridges, test shots were fired and sound levels measured at varying distances. These values were entered into a mathematical model based on classical divergence and absorption. Estimates of sound levels were compared with the human ability to hear those levels at varying distances.

45-70 Government Rifles and Ammunition:

History may well question whether Custer's men were outgunned by repeating weapons and may debate whether a Gatling Gun would have made a difference. Some say it made no difference because typical Indian fighting was not at close-quarters, but at distances of perhaps 100 yards, and in volleys. (See for example, Sarf, page 117.) At this time it is a moot point. His men were equipped with the 45 Calibre Springfield 1873 Allin-style "trapdoor" Carbine. The carbine rather than the long rifle was suitable for the cavalry merely because of the shorter barrel and lighter weight. The 45 Calibre Government cartridge was the standard military issue. According to Doug Wickland of the NRA Museum (private communication) the ammunition used a Benet inside primed case. Sarf (page 116) reports that these casings were made of copper-alloy, rather than the highly polished brass used in modern cartridges. Such cases readily corroded (that green or blueish-green rust-like deposit from leather belt loops) and dirty cases sometimes stuck in the chambers of the weapons. It is said that some broken knife blades were found at the site indicating extraction troubles.

The carbines typically shot 55 grains of black powder rather than 70 grains as used in the rifle. (Black powder was then called gun powder. There was no other kind.) This information is not merely a matter of interest, but necessary to understand possible sound levels and those considered in this report. According to the NRA Museum the cartridges most likely fired 55 grains of FFg black powder (type of granulation), pushing a 500 grain lead bullet at 1100 fps muzzle velocity. Sam Fadala of **Guns** (Magazine) reports (private communication) that this was probably Fg granulation. Specialty black powder loads were developed by **Joe's Custom Reloading** of Campbell Hall, NY. These used 70 grains FFg black powder in Winchester brass cases with Federal # 210 large rifle primers and a 385 grain lead bullet. These do not necessarily exactly duplicate the load used by Custer's men. But, since our test load is the 70 grain powder charge, it is reasonable to assume that the actual sounds made in 1876 were no louder than those of our test ammunition (and more than likely of lower intensity.) For comparison, a 20 gauge short barreled shotgun shooting a 7/8 oz lead slug (7/8 oz is approximately 385 grains) was fired. It should be noted that in the experimental firings two weapons were used, a 1873 Springfield Carbine and a 1873 Springfield Rifle. Neither experienced any cartridge malfunctions and sounds were not significantly different.

Experimental Apparatus:

To measure the sound levels of the rifles typical college laboratory equipment was used. Two devices were used to measure the sounds:

1. Sound Meter, Model 840005 by Sper Scientific measuring dB levels.

2. A microphone connected by a ULI (Universal Laboratory Interface) to a laptop PC, recording sound pressure levels. This equipment was manufactured by Vernier Corporation of Portland, Oregon.

Both values were used to acquire a sense of the nature of the sound and how it diminishes with distance. The rifles were fired at distances of 10, 20 and 30 metres with values measured at each distance. This way the sound was in effect calibrated against itself to determine the level at the source. Ms. Laura Miller (College of St. Catherine student) assisted in data acquisition and Mr. Charles Flower (University of St. Thomas student) performed the actual firings. These firings were conducted near Hastings, Minnesota on the John Bremer farm April 8 and 17, 1995. The following data was acquired:

Sample Test Curves:

20 Gauge, 7/8 Ounce Lead Slug

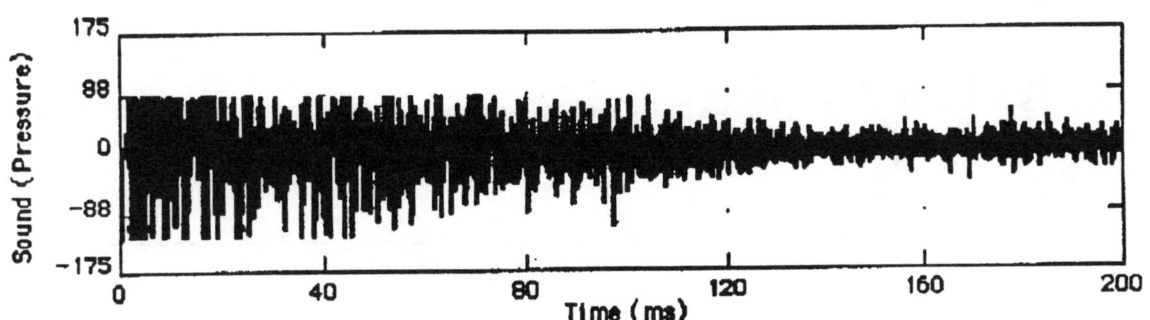

Figure 1. 20 Gauge, 7/8 ounce slug, Sound Pressure Levels

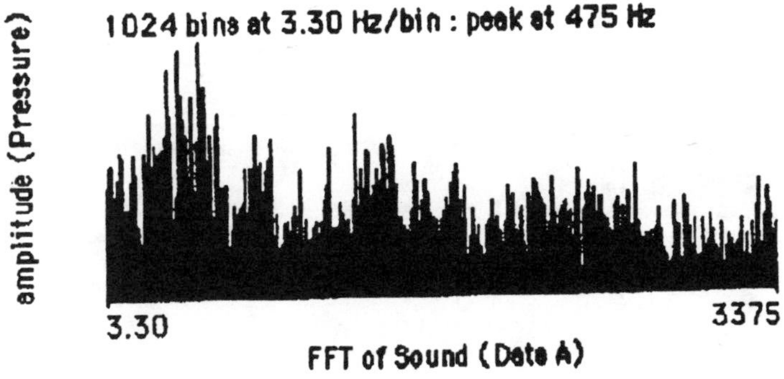

Figure 2. FFT of 20 Gauge, 7/8 ounce slug

The 20 gauge slug makes a sound that lasts typically 125 milliseconds before diminshing to a level .1 of the initial value. i.e., the sound lasts about one eighth of a second. (see Figure 1) A fast fourier transform (FFT) shows that while the sound peaks at 475 Hz, significant levels are produced at higher frequencies as well

Sample Test Curves:

45-70

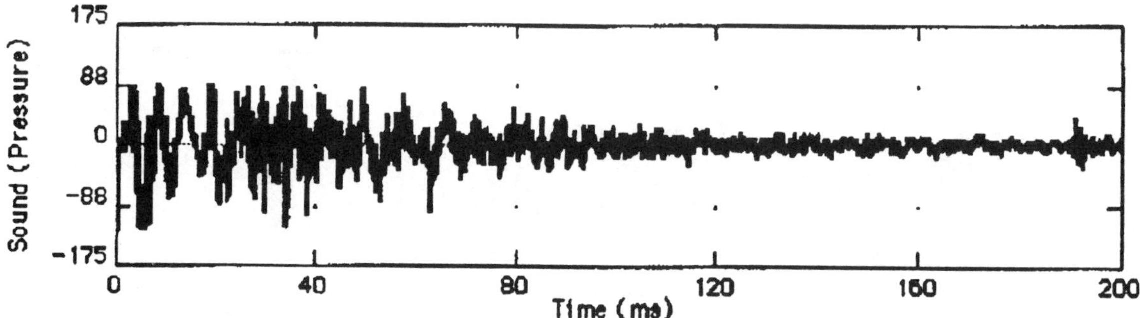

Figure 3. 45-70, Sound Pressure Levels

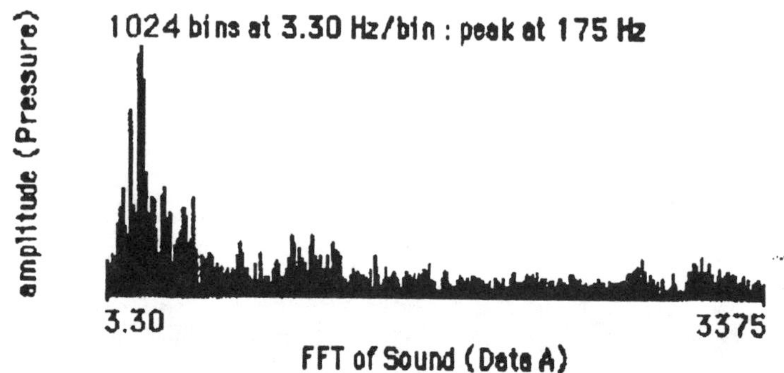

Figure 4. FFT of 45-70

The duration of the sound levels is somewhat shorter, 95 ms (about 1/10th second), than the modern, smokeless powder shotgun. Decibel levels (see Tables following) indicated the modern firearm made somewhat higher initial sounds as well. To the human ear (sometimes the most sensitive of instruments) it sounded less intense. One observer (land owner, John Bremer) remarked that "... the sound from the 45-70 sure falls off fast." But remarkable is the FFT curve, indicating that most of the sound is at a rather low frequency. This accounts for the "BOOM" sound rather than a "BANG!" This fact is significant in hearing sound levels because the sensitivity of the human ear is frequency dependent.

One rightly notes that the sound levels vary up and down and an integral of the curve would properly yield zero. Consequently, an **rms** value (root mean square) was calculated for each firing. The rms value effectively gives an average value to compute the sound intensity over the entire duration of the sound. These values can then be used to make effective comparisons between actual sound levels. Sounds were recorded with firings away from and to the side of the microphone. To answer the question about the possible sources of the sounds, the higher values were used to give the "best chance" scenario. It was found that more than angle, the atmospheric conditions, i.e., wind and humidity, had the greatest impact on the experiment. These variables are considered with the model.

There was no opportunity to fire volleys of shots with only two weapons. Professor H.J. Sneck, Visiting Professor at the United States Military Academy at West Point was contacted (private communication) about volleys. He indicated that maybe the movie **Gettysburg** had more realistic volley firing than other possible sources. The movie, **Gettysburg** was rented at a local video store and played on a home theater system using Klipsch surround sound speakers (including powered sub-woofer) to reproduce the sounds of volleys of shots. The volley formation used in the Civil War is the same kind of formation used against the Indians in the Little Big Horn Campaign. Custer earned his star with distinguished conduct during the Civil War. The weapons at Gettysburg were different, they were muzzle loaders. And certainly the intensity of the volleys were electronically set so as not destroy electronic equipment or adversely affect viewers. The sounds were recorded and analyzed just as the above 45-70 firings were, but not for intensity. Rather we wanted to "see" what a volley looked like, especially the duration. Firings at Cemetary Ridge and Little Round Top were considered. It was noted that the volley sounds were also "blended" with music and excited cries of infantrymen which made analysis somewhat more difficult. Still, the duration was noted to be approximately 1.2 seconds and the FFT was consistent in that it showed again, a low frequency "BOOM" effect suggesting that indeed it was the volley itself that was recorded. (see Figure 5.)

To consider the intensity of the volley so one could estimate the sound levels heard at Reno Hill, the integrated rms level over the duration of one shot was multiplied by 40 (an estimate of how many might fire in a volley) and divided by the duration of a volley.

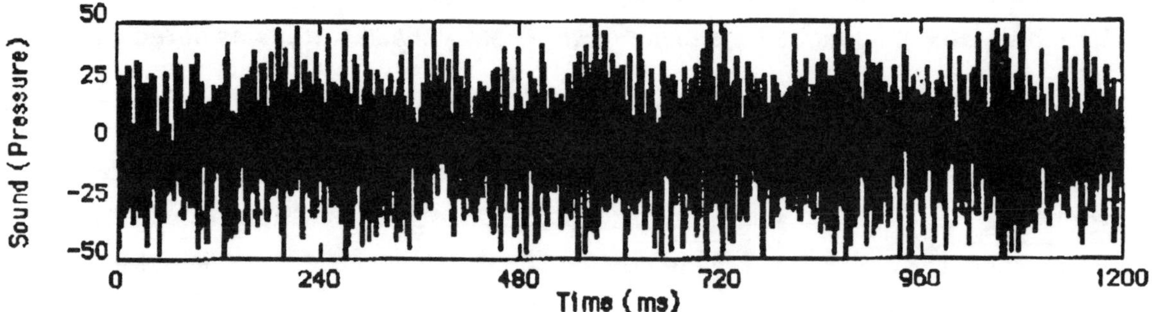

Figure 5. Volley of Shots, Gettysburg

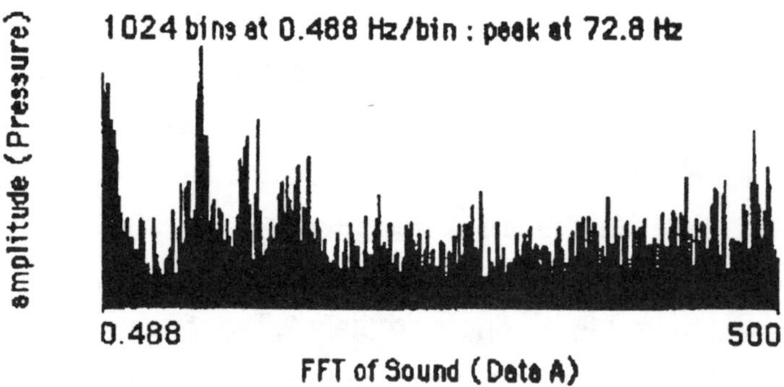

Figure 6. FFT of Volley

	Fired away from microphone	Fired 90° to microphone
April 8	dB levels	dB levels
45-70(10m)	82.5	87.3
45-70(20m)	68	72
45-70(50m)	-na-	63

Table 1. Average dB levels for 45-70 rifle. (Averages of multiple firings)

	Fired away from microphone		Fired 90° to microphone	
17 April	RMS Pressure	dB level	RMS Pressure	dB level
20 ga	47.3	100	-na-	108
45-70 (10m)	49.0	94	59.3	100
45-70 (20m)	33.9	92	45.1	96
45-70 (30m)	26.9	86	28.8	90

Table 2. Average data values for rms pressure and dB levels. (Averages of multiple firings)

On April 17, 1995 the weather conditions were calm wind and 50° F temperature. The wind turbine on the roof of my house was not turning. The reader will note that during this time the dB levels are higher than those measured on the first date, April 8. On April 8 a mild wind, 10 mph, was blowing. This immediately dissipated the white smoke accompanying the shots and the sounds were considerably of lesser intensity than those on the calm day. The temperatures were the same on both days. Due to a computer malfunction pressure levels were lost for the first day of firings. Information from The Freeman Journal (Capt Henry B Freeman with Gibbon's Montana column) tells us (page 57) that the atmospheric conditions were "very hot" and that it "rained all night" on June 25th, suggesting the humidity may have been high as well. The **Reno Court of Inquiry** (pages 39, 165, 456) confirms that the sky conditions were "partly cloudy" and there was "little or no wind." These factors are considered in the mathematical model. For safety reasons, firings were not directed at the microphone equipment. Peterson and Gross (page 111) indicates that for low frequencies the microphone is essentially omnidirectional. The values acquired in the Minnesota test firings at the John Bremer farm undoubtedly show different rates for which the sounds diminish than those that would result at the actual battle site. That was assumed to be true. But actual firings do give us a sense of what the original sound was like at the source. That will allow us to answer the fundamental question as to whether they could be heard or not atop Reno Hill. From this information we consider the nature of sound propagation and a rigorous analysis of its ability to be heard at various distances.

The Nature of Sound and Sound Levels

We consider the source of sound to be the shots and volleys of shots and the standard atmosphere to be the medium through which it is transmitted as a longitudinal wave. The intensity of a sound, energy per sec per unit area, is defined as:

$$I = p^2 / \rho c$$

where p is the rms (root-mean-square) pressure, ρ is the density of the medium (dependent upon temperature, humidity and altitude), and c is the velocity of sound in the medium. For a spherically propagating wave the intensity at distance r can be written:

$$I(r) = p(r)^2 / \rho c = W / 4\pi r^2$$

where W is the power of the wave. One can readily see that the power, or energy per sec, of the wave is related directly to the square of the pressure. It is the pressure that is sensed by the human ear or measured with electronic equipment.

Because sound waves vary positively and negatively with respect to the steady state level of the medium the average value is rightfully zero. Thus each value is squared (so that all values are positive), averaged and then the square root is taken. The **rms** value is the **effective** sound pressure. This value is calculated for the individual shots and volleys of shots.

The human ear can respond to sound pressures that vary over an extraordinarily wide range of values. Because this range is so great the logarithmic decibel scale is used to describe sound levels. This allows us to measure how sound levels change. It makes it possible to fire the 45-70 rifles and essentially calibrate the sounds against their own levels. The important consideration is how the sound changes. We define the difference in decibels between two sound pressures to be:

$$\Delta L = 10 \log_{10} P_2 / P_1$$

or

$$\Delta L = 10 \log_{10} P_2 - 10 \log_{10} P_1$$

where P_1 and P_2 are power values (related to pressure squared.) Then we can write (other factors being constant such as atmospheric conditions and speed of the wave)

$$dB = 10 \log_{10} (I_2 / I_1)$$

$$dB = 10 \log_{10} p_2^2/p_1^2$$

$$dB = 10 \log_{10} (p_2 / p_1)^2$$

$$dB = 20 \log_{10} (p_2 / p_1)$$

The p_1 and p_2 values are rms pressures. The significant observation is that one needs only the change in pressure, not an absolute measure. Thus as the sound pressures change drastically, small, manageable numbers are produced. Zero decibels, or dB, is the threshold of hearing while 120 dB is the sound of a jet aircraft at takeoff. 140 dB is considered to be the threshold of pain.

For adding two sounds (a volley is considered the addition of multiple gunshots at roughly the same time) the effect is straightforward. If one considers the integrated average impulse per area of the rms values of one shot multiplied by the total number of shots we get:

40 (shots) X 59.3 (rms press) X .095 (sec) / 1.2 (sec) = 187.8 rms value

Thus the effect of a volley of shots is not 40 times the intensity but rather this impulse is spread over a larger time and the net effect is an impulse roughly three times as large:

187.8 / 59.3 = 3.166

Using the logarithmic scale, $\log_{10} 3.166 = .5$ This value is multiplied by 20 to get the decibel difference, or 10. i.e., the decibel level is increased by 10 dB for the volley compared to a single shot. The insightful reader will note that if the volley time is even longer (than the above 1.2 sec.,) the net effect will result in a lower rms pressure and even less than a 10 dB increase. From personal experiences at big bore rifle matches this is reasonable. The sound is somewhat louder, but definitely not forty or fifty times more intense. For the model consideration, then it is assumed the volley dB level will be 110 dB and the single shot level at 100 dB at 10m. These values are considered conservative. The NRA museum suggests that the actual dB level of the 45-55 gunshot from the carbine was 62 dB at 10 feet.

The Effect of the Terrain

Sound waves dissipate energy as they travel outwards from the source. They interact with their environment in the usual fashion that waves do. i.e., they reflect, refract, diffract, diverge, and attenuate energy due to absorption. It is difficult to exactly consider the effects of reflection, refraction, and diffraction. At the battlefield the changes in elevation are slight. Even though the retreat of Reno's forces from the valley of the Indian campground to Reno's Hill seemed to be extremely steep at the time, the total change in elevation is merely a few hundred feet. Reno described " ... this incline was the steepest that I have ever seen either horse or mule ascend." (Frazier, pg 166) Between **Reno's Hill** and the **Last Stand Hill** is **Weir Point**, about 150 feet elevation difference. This hill stands in the line of site. One can note this on the contour maps, pages 20 and 21. An obstacle such as **Weir Point** can affect the propagation of the sound. But the effect is not clear. Sound waves bend and go around corners. This effect is called **diffraction**. Because of diffraction sounds can indeed be heard around a hill, but most likely at a diminished volume. The points of interference where they may alternately be strong and weak are not well defined. For the purpose of this study we recognize that diffraction does occur and that it might make the sound less likely to be heard, but we do not calculate its effect because of the many variables affecting the situation. One would have to have more precise knowledge of the sound distribution patterns and the origin. One will note in the following paragraphs that if the sounds came from **Last Stand Hill**, they would most likely not be heard at this distance anyway.

As sound waves travel outward they diverge radially and decrease inversely with the square of the distance. Thus as the distance is doubled, the intensity decreases by a factor of 4, as it is tripled it decreased by a factor of 9 and so on. One simple rule that sound scientists use is that sound typically decreases about 6 dB for every doubling of distance. (White, pg 43) Again, the logarithmic nature of the dB scale shows that the changes occur slowly. From 10m to 20m, 20m to 40m, and so on would require 9 doublings to 5120m, or account for a sound drop of 54 dB due to divergence alone.

$$I(r_1) / I(r_2) = R_2^2/R_1^2$$

The difference in sound level, then, due to divergence is written as:

$$\Delta L_{div} = 10 \log_{10} I(r_1)/I(r_2)$$

$$\Delta L_{div} = 10 \log_{10} R_2^2/R_1^2$$

$$\Delta L_{div} = 20 \log_{10} R_2/R_1$$

But divergence is not the only factor in diminishing energy. Energy is also absorbed by the atmosphere. Over large distances the atmosphere may be inhomogenous. Over the short distances of several miles and small elevation changes it is reasonable to assume a relatively homogeneous medium in which the sound travels and is attenuated. The decrease is complex and dependent upon frequency of sound and air density which itself depends on temperature, altitude, and humidity. It is an exponential decrease, written as

$$P = P_0 e^{-\alpha r}$$

White (page 62) indicates that a typical value for such absorption is 10 dB per 1000 ft. This is not insignificant, and even more consequential than divergence! The effect of wind is also significant, but we neglect it for our model since the stated conditions of June 25, 1876 were "little or no wind." (**Reno Court of Inquiry**, pages 39, 165.) White (page 68) indicates that a low velocity wind could result in excess attenuation of 1 to 2 dB per 100 m. For our model we select a very conservative absorption coefficient of $\alpha = .001\ m^{-1}$. We neglect the effect of wind while noting that even a low wind could reduce sound levels significantly.

A model using iteration applied to both divergence and absorption was developed using the **EXCEL** Spreadsheet. Results follow:

Dist.	Relative Press.	dB	Single Shot Net dB	Volley of Shots
10	.09900		100.00	110.00
20	.04901	6.107	93.89	103.89
30	.03235	3.609	90.28	100.28
100	.00905	11.066	79.22	89.22
200	.00409	6.889	72.33	82.33
300	.00247	4.390	67.94	77.94
400	.00168	3.367	64.57	74.57
500	.00121	2.807	61.76	71.76
600	.00091	2.452	59.31	69.31
700	.00071	2.208	57.10	67.10
800	.00056	2.028	55.08	65.08
900	.00045	1.892	53.18	63.18
1000	.00037	1.784	51.40	61.40
1100	.00030	1.696	49.70	59.70
1200	.00025	1.624	48.08	58.08
1300	.00021	1.564	46.52	56.52
1400	.00018	1.512	45.00	55.00
1500	.00015	1.468	43.54	53.54
1600	.00013	1.429	42.11	52.11
1700	.00011	1.395	40.71	50.71
1800	.00009	1.365	39.35	49.35
1900	.00008	1.338	38.01	48.01
2000	.00007	1.314	36.69	46.69
2100	.00006	1.292	35.40	45.40
2200	.00005	1.273	34.13	44.13
2300	.00004	1.255	32.87	42.87
2400	.00004	1.238	31.64	41.64
2500	.00003	1.223	30.41	40.41
2600	.00003	1.209	29.20	39.20
2700	.00002	1.196	28.01	38.01
2800	.00002	1.184	26.82	36.82
2900	.00002	1.173	25.65	35.65
3000	.00002	1.163	24.49	34.49
3100	.00001	1.153	23.33	33.33
3200	.00001	1.144	22.19	32.19
3300	.00001	1.136	21.05	31.05
3400	.00001	1.128	19.93	29.93
3500	.00001	1.120	18.80	28.80
3600	.00001	1.113	17.69	27.69
3700	.00001	1.107	16.59	26.59

3800	.00001	1.100	15.48	25.48
3900	.00001	1.094	14.39	24.39
4000	.00000	1.088	13.30	23.30
4100	.00000	1.083	12.22	22.22
4200	.00000	1.078	11.14	21.14
4300	.00000	1.073	10.07	20.07
4400	.00000	1.068	9.00	19.00
4500	.00000	1.064	7.94	17.94
4600	.00000	1.059	6.88	16.88
4700	.00000	1.055	5.82	15.82
4800	.00000	1.051	4.77	14.77
4900	.00000	1.048	3.72	13.72
5000	.00000	1.044	2.68	12.68
5100	.00000	1.041	1.64	11.64
5200	.00000	1.037	0.60	10.60
5300	.00000	1.034	-0.43	9.57
5400	.00000	1.031	-1.46	8.54
5500	.00000	1.028	-2.49	7.51
5600	.00000	1.025	-3.52	6.48
5700	.00000	1.022	-4.54	5.46
5800	.00000	1.020	-5.56	4.44
5900	.00000	1.017	-6.58	3.42
6000	.00000	1.015	-7.59	2.41
6100	.00000	1.012	-8.60	1.40
6200	.00000	1.010	-9.61	0.39
6300	.00000	1.008	-10.62	-0.62
6400	.00000	1.005	-11.63	-1.63
6500	.00000	1.003	-12.63	-2.63
6600	.00000	1.001	-13.63	-3.63
6700	.00000	0.999	-14.63	-4.63
6800	.00000	0.997	-15.63	-5.63
6900	.00000	0.995	-16.62	-6.62
7000	.00000	0.994	-17.62	-7.62

Hearing the Sounds:

Sources of the sounds (shots and volleys of shots) were considered to have originated from **Last Stand Hill and Miniconjou Ford.** Measurements made using a U.S. Department of the Interior Geological Survey Map indicate that the distance from **Last Stand Hill to Reno Hill** is approximately 7000 metres while from **Miniconjou Ford to Reno Hill** is approximately 4300 metres. Using the model described above a **Sound Contour Map** was developed for each source. See Figures 7 and 8 respectively.

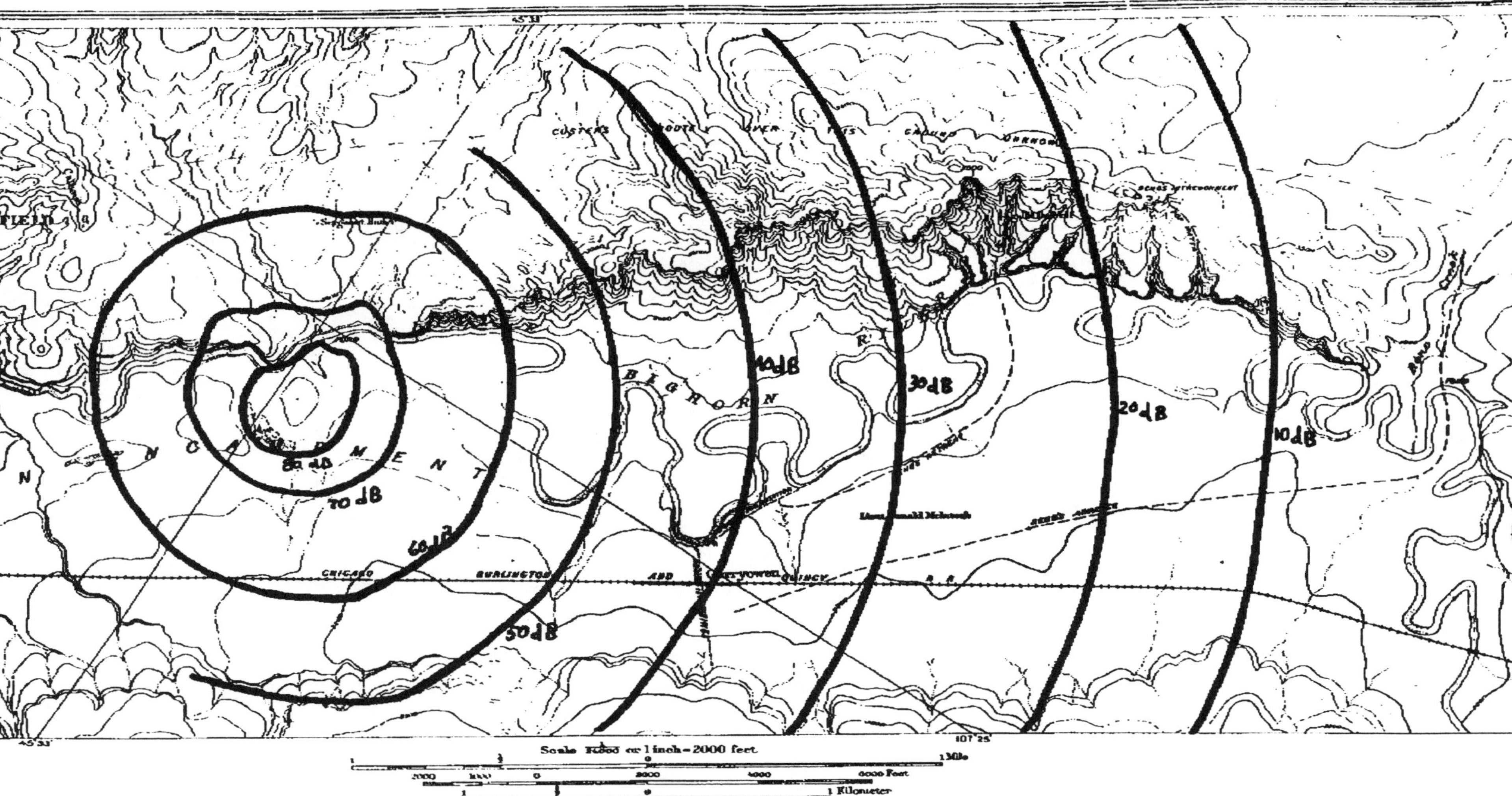

Figure 7. Sound Contours originating from the valley of the campground

UNITED STATES
DEPARTMENT OF THE INTERIOR
GEOLOGICAL SURVEY

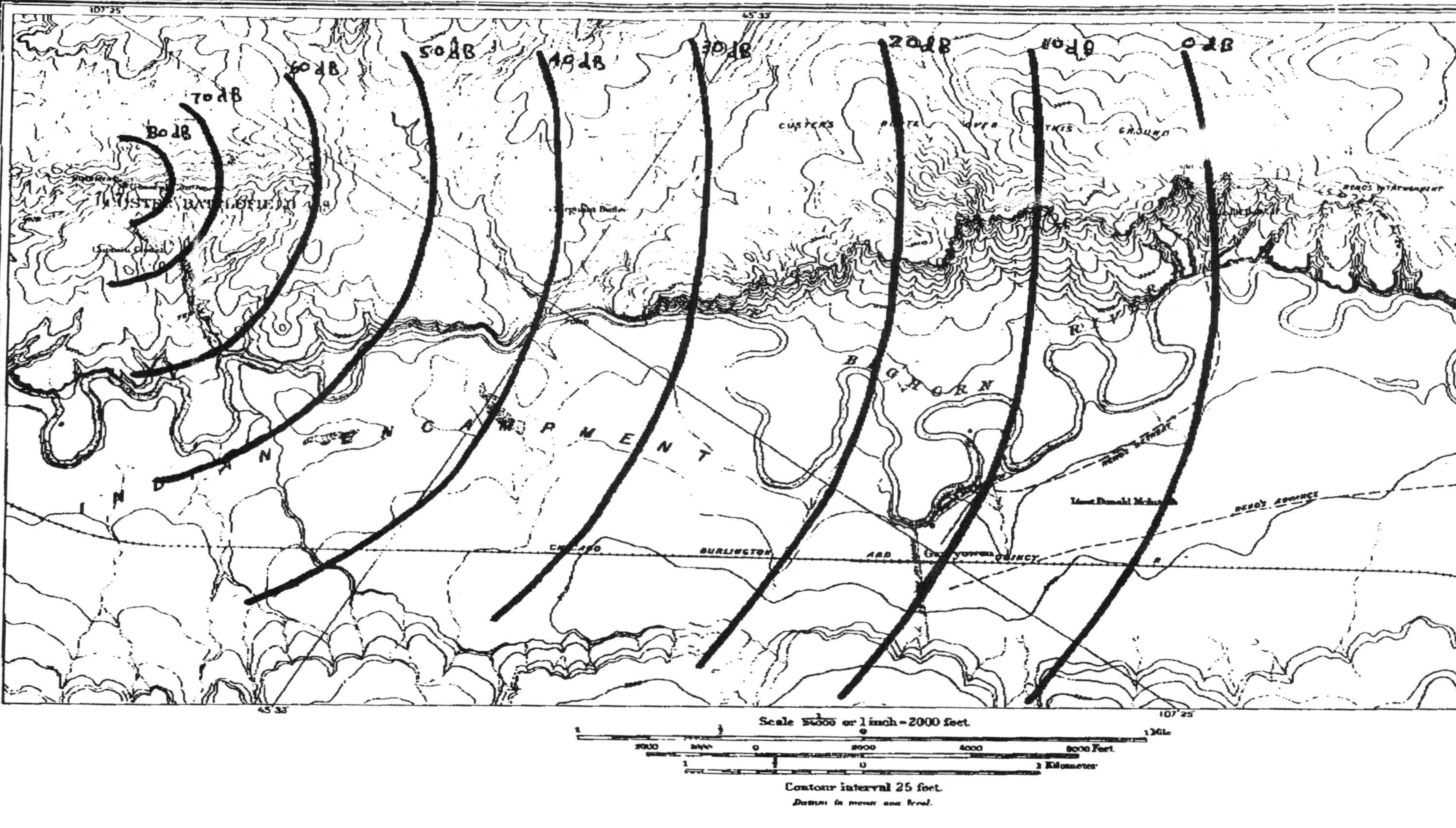

Figure 8. Sound Contours ordginating from Last Stand Hill

Sound countours are drawn in by hand, displaying rough dB levels 80, 70, 60, down to 20 and 10 dB of the sounds of the volleys of shots. There may be as much as a 10% uncertainty in these values. Coletta (page 402) shows us what the human ear is capable of hearing. Earlier we showed the FFT of the 45-70 sounds with most of the sound level at or below 200 Hz. Note on the diagram below that the human ear is not as sensitive at 200 Hz as it is at 3000 to 4000 Hz. In other words, a sound of that frequency would need to be nearly 20 dB to be heard. In fact, only 1% of the population can hear a sound at that intensity. The average person may require the sound to be more on the order of 30 dB to be heard clearly! This severely limits the distance at which blackpowder shots can be heard.

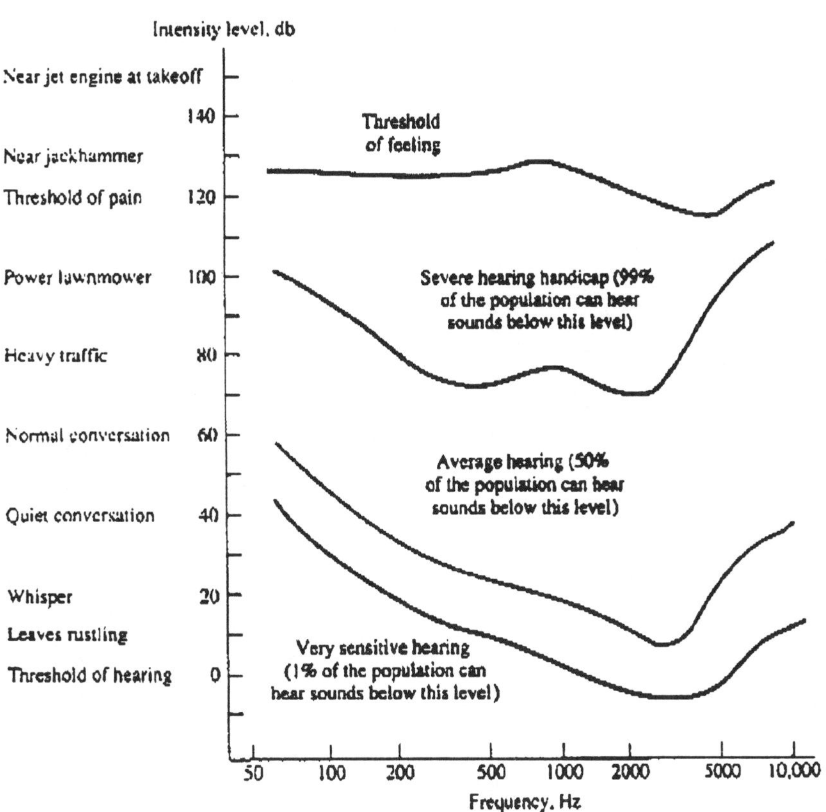

Figure 9. Audibility Curves. (Coletta, page 402)

Effect of Masking or What about the Background Noise?

The **Court of Inquiry** statements about when the sounds were heard indicate the shots were fired immediately or shortly after Major Reno's men reached the point of entrenchment on **Reno Hill**. It is extremely difficult to estimate what the level of background noise was at this time. Men had just been shot or shot at. Horses had just reached a difficult climb to that point. Heavy breathing and snorting by the horses, men clamoring for water, help, or whatever, would lead a reasonable thinking person to consider that the background noise would certainly exceed that of quiet conversational levels, 25 - 30 dB. In other words this level of sound would "mask" the sounds of shots. White (page 122) and Peterson and Gross (pages 36, 37) indicate that background noise increases the threshold of hearing. The sounds of shots or volleys of shots would effectively have to exceed this level by several dB to be audible. The above values are conservative.

It is not clear if those who heard the sounds were in the midst of the others where this effect would have been most pronounced. But additional considerations must be made. One is the temproary decrease in hearing ability after being exposed to loud noises. White (page 466) explains TTS or Temporary Threshold Shift as the shift in audible hearing level due to exposure to loud noises. This depends on the level of the noise, the duration of exposure and individual factors. He points out that an 80-120 dB may produce a threshold shift of 5 dB for a sound with frequency > 1000 Hz. These men just came from a brief battle. Additionally, the effect of fatigue and excitement also impact negatively on the ability to hear sounds. No two people are exactly the same. No two people hear sounds the same way. If they all had instrumentation with computers we could all agree on the qualitative and quantitative values of certain sounds.

Conclusions

Considering the above information as to the kind of sound a black powder, 45 Calibre rifle makes, we recognize that the power of the sound is essentially carried at the lower frequencies. The threshold of hearing at these frequencies is at best nearly 20 dB and higher for the average person. Using the initial intensities from multiple test firings, the dB level for a single shot was estimated at 100 dB and 110 for a volley. Using these values and a conservative atmospheric attenuation coefficient (α = .001), the mathematical model with both divergence ($1 / r^2$) and absorption ($e^{-\alpha r}$) suggest that the sounds of volleys decrease to 20 dB level at approximately 4300m and to 0 dB by 6300m. Thus volleys at **Reno Hill** could only marginally be heard from the campground site and most likely not heard at all from the final **Last Stand Hill**. Perhaps Custer and his men were even closer, down in the valley of the campground.

An additional set of firings (not by this group) was conducted in November 1994 near Northfield, Minnesota using the same kinds of weapons and ammunition. St. Paul Pioneer Press journalist Larry Millett reported that downwind the sounds could be heard well at 1 mile, barely at 1.5 miles and were entirely inaudible at 2.2 miles. Upwind they were very faint at 1.7 miles. This does not exactly duplicate the conditions of the actual battlefield of 1876 but the results are consistent with the predictions of the model shown above.

There is a caveat. The best test of the question is to perform actual firings on site. Sound waves can interfere constructively in strange ways. It may be that the actual battlefield acts like a natural amphitheatre which could effectively amplify sounds at certain locations. These factors could not be considered in the model. The conclusions are those using reasonable data in a reasonable manner.

BIBLIOGRAPHY

Coletta, Vincent A., Physics, Mosby-Year Book, St. Louis, MO, 1995.

Custer, Elizabeth B., Following the Guidon, Harper & Brothers, New York, 1890.

Fadala, Sam, Private Communication, Casper, Wyoming, June

Fougera, Katherine Gibson, With Custer's Cavalry, The Caxton Printers, Ltd, Caldwell, ID, 1940.

Gettysburg (video movie), Turner Home Entertainment, Cat No 6139

Hunt, Frazier and Robert, I Fought with Custer, The Story of Sergeant Windolph, Charles Scribner's Sons, New York, 1953.

Peterson, Arnold and Gross, Ervin, Handbook of NOISE MEASUREMENT, General Radio Company, Concord, MA, 1972.

Sarf, Wayne Michael, The Little Bighorn Campaign, Combined Books, Conshohocken, PA, 1993.

Schneider, George A., The Freeman Journal, Presidio Press, San Rafael, CA, 1977.

Sneck, H.J., USMA, West Point, NY, Private telephone, April 1995.

Stewart, Edgar I., Custer's Luck, University of Oklahoma Press, Norman OK, 1955.

White, Frederick A., Our Acoustic Environment, John Wiley & Sons, New York, 1975.

Wickland, Doug, NRA Museum, Private telephone, April 1995.

APPENDIX D

Cartographic Study of the Little Big Horn maps by CartoGraphics Incorporated

1313 Fifth Street SE, Suite 136
Minneapolis, MN 55414

Phone (612) 379-3599
Fax (612) 379-3875

A Cartographic Analysis of Selected Custer Battlefield Maps

Of the many and varied representations of the battlefield upon which George Armstrong Custer was vanquished, this report focuses on two extant maps in particular. These two maps (hereafter referred to simply as Map A and Map B, respectively) are entitled *PLAN of the Battlefield of the 7th Regt. Cav. (June 25th, 1876)* and *CUSTER'S BATTLE-FIELD (June 25th 1876).* Both maps bear the name of a Lieut. Edward Maguire who personally supervised the survey of the battlefield. According to a notation near the lower middle portion of Map A, it was "Traced in the Office of the Chief Engineer, Mil. Div. of the Mo. Sept. 19, 1876." The exact origin of Map B is less certain, but it is known to be the map submitted as "Exhibit No. 2" at the Reno Court of Inquiry, which convened January 13, 1879.

Both maps appear to have been carefully constructed, though somewhat different methods were utilized to portray the physical relief of the Little Bighorn River valley where the battle took place. Map A has the look of a more mechanically rendered map, relying exclusively upon hachuring to show the topography, while Map B is more sketchy in appearance, with mostly hand-drawn relief shading and much less hachuring. Although the two maps are in general agreement regarding the principal physiographic features, there are some significant discrepancies. For instance, the position of the Little Bighorn River and the shapes and number of its meanders do not correlate well between the two maps as indicated by Figure 1 and and Figure 2, shown on following pages. Also, a second gully, running through the Indian Village, as indicated on Map A, does not appear at all on Map B (see Fig. 2).

There are a number of inconsistencies between the maps in their delineation of the bluffs along the north side of the river. The baseline of the bluffs as depicted on Map A extends much farther toward the riverbanks, whereas Map B shows a much broader floodplain with the base of the bluffs set back more. The shape and alignment of the bluffline itself also differs greatly from Map A to Map B. The bluffline on Map A runs generally northwest to southeast in a fairly straight fashion before curving eastward around the hairpin meanders. Map B has the bluffline in a more northerly orientation, then angling eastward toward the hairpin meanders, thus creating a protrusion midway along the bluffline which does not appear on Map A.

Another topographical discrepancy may be seen at the right side of Map B (indicated by a row of X's on Fig. 2) where some rather pronounced bluffs are shown, for which no counterpart exists at the same location on Map A.

A number of other features shown on both maps differ significantly. Specifically, Maps A and B both indicate Reno's "skirmish line" extending southward from the same point near the river, just at the edge of a wooded area. However, the skirmish line on Map B diverges from the one shown on Map A, by approximately 23° in the direction of the Indian Village. Also, the length of the skirmish line on Map B is almost 20% greater than the line on Map A (0.8 miles versus .66 miles). The portrayal of the Indian Village also differs tremendously between the two maps, as to both its shape and extent. On Map A, the village covers more ground, and has a very high concentration of tepees strewn along the gullies running through that area. Moreover, a linear grouping of tepees extends eastward to the river from about the midpoint of the eastern gully. There is no such formation of tepees indicated on Map B.

Finally, Map A displays various notations not shown on Map B, such as positions of Custer's forces before the battle. Other markings on Map A, but not to be found on Map B, are some dashed lines, apparently related to the battlefield survey, and locations marked by stars along with the dates June 27, and June 28.

Several historical maps of the Custer Battlefield (including the two that were used in this study) are reproduced on the pages following. The original documents are in the map collection of the National Archives of the United States.

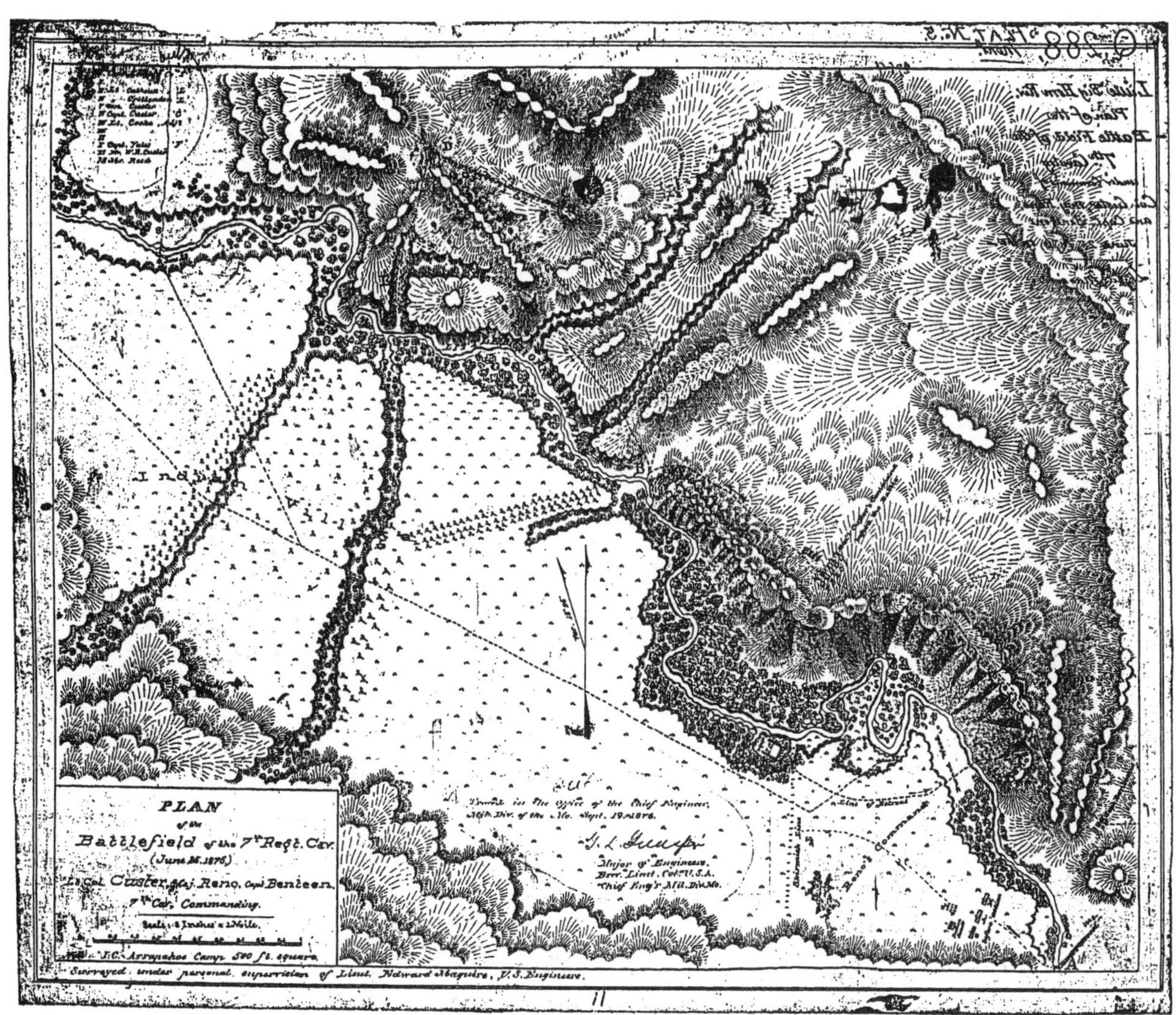
PLAN
of the
Battlefield of the 7th Regt. Cav.
(June 25. 1876)
Lt. Col. Custer, Maj. Reno, Capt. Benteen,
7th Cav. Commanding.
Scale: 3 Inches = 1 Mile.
J.C. Arrapahoe Camp 500 ft. square
Surveyed under personal supervision of Lieut. Edward Maguire, U.S. Engineers.
Traced in the Office of the Chief Engineer, Mil. Div. of the Mo. Sept. 19, 1876.
Major of Engineers,
Brev. Lieut. Col. U.S.A.
Chief Eng'r Mil. Div. Mo.

MAP A

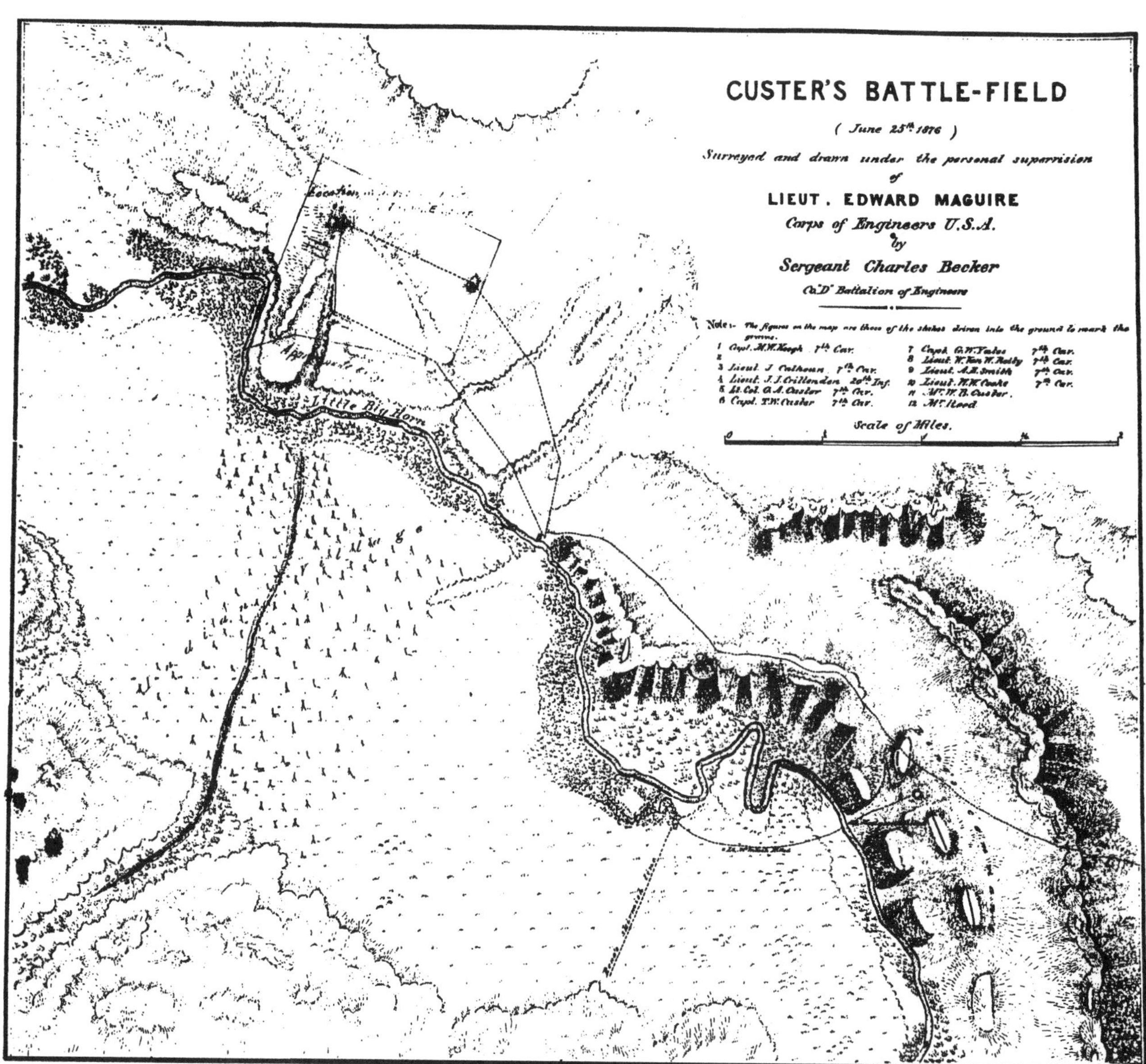

CUSTER'S BATTLE-FIELD
(June 25th 1876)
Surveyed and drawn under the personal supervision
of
LIEUT. EDWARD MAGUIRE
Corps of Engineers U.S.A.
by
Sergeant Charles Becker
Co. "D" Battalion of Engineers
Note:- The figures on the map are those of the stakes driven into the ground to mark the graves.
1 Capt. M.W. Keogh 7th Cav.
2
3 Lieut. J. Calhoun 7th Cav.
4 Lieut. J.J. Crittenden 20th Inf.
5 Lt. Col. G.A. Custer 7th Cav.
6 Capt. T.W. Custer 7th Cav.
7 Capt. G.W. Yates 7th Cav.
8 Lieut. W. Van W. Reily 7th Cav.
9 Lieut. A.E. Smith 7th Cav.
10 Lieut. W.W. Cooke 7th Cav.
12 Mr. Reed
Scale of Miles.
0
2
Little Big Horn

MAP B

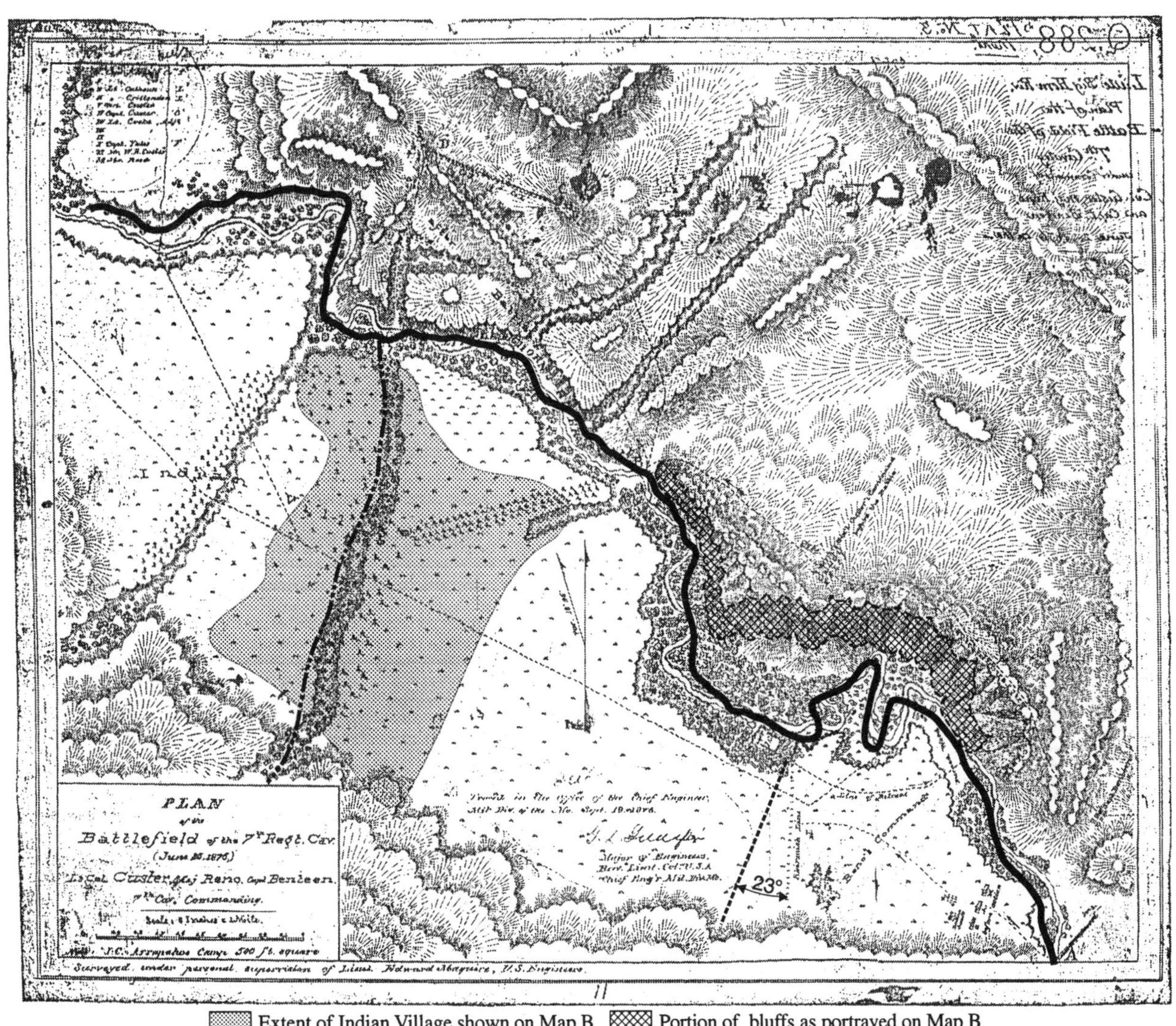

Figure 1. Grayed version of Map A with principal features of Map B superimposed

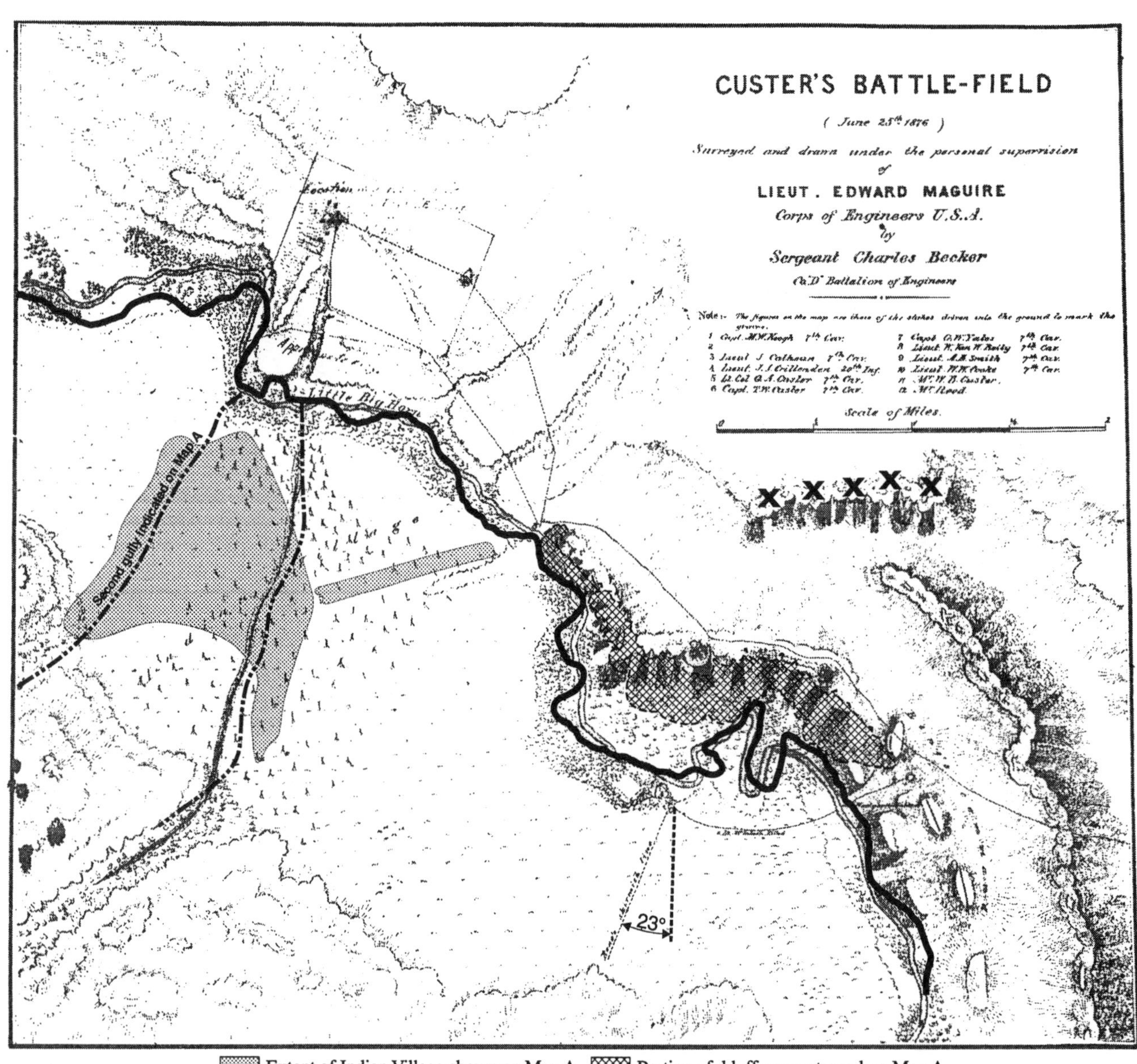

Extent of Indian Village shown on Map A — Portion of bluffs as portrayed on Map A

Figure 2. Grayed version of Map B with principal features of Map A superimposed